Couple Observational Coding Systems

Couple Observational Coding Systems

Edited by

Patricia K. Kerig
Donald H. Baucom

University of North Carolina at Chapel Hill

Routledge
Taylor & Francis Group
NEW YORK AND LONDON

Camera ready copy for this book provided by the editors

First published 2004 by Lawrence Erlbaum Associates, Inc., Publishers

This edition published 2013 by Routledge
711 Third Avenue, New York, NY 10017
27 Church Road, Hove, East Sussex BN3 2FA

Routledge is an imprint of the Taylor & Francis Group, an informa business

Lawrence Erlbaum Associates, Inc.
10 Industrial Avenue
Mahwah, New Jersey 07430-2262

Cover design by Kathryn Houghtaling Lacey

Library of Congress Cataloging-in-Publication Data

Couple observational coding systems / edited by Patricia K. Kerig, Donald Baucom.

p. cm.

Includes bibliographical references and indexes.
ISBN 0-8058-4357-4 (cloth : alk. paper)
1. Married people—Research—Methodology. 2. Couples—Research—Methodology. 3. Observation (Psychology)—Methodology. I. Kerig, Patricia. II. Baucom, Donald H.

HQ728.0679 2004
306.872'072—dc22 2003058305
CIP

10 9 8 7 6 5 4 3 2 1

To Marge and Fil Argenbright—
For a love that inspires us and ours.

—PKK

With great respect and appreciation to Bob Weiss,
Kurt Hahlweg, and John Gottman—
You gave us codes that we might see and hear.

—DHB

Contents

Contributors

Brian Baucom, *Center for Marital and Family Studies, University of Denver*

Donald H. Baucom, *Department of Psychology, University of North Carolina at Chapel Hill*

Thomas N. Bradbury, *Department of Psychology, University of California, Los Angeles*

Andrew Christensen, *Couples Therapy Project, Department of Psychology, University of California, Los Angeles*

James V. Cordova, *Department of Psychology, Clark University*

Carolyn E. Cutrona, *Department of Psychology, Iowa State University*

Amy Decker-Haas, *Prevention Coding Lab, Marital Interaction Lab, Arizona State University, Tempe*

Marina Dorian, *Department of Psychology, University of Illinois at Urbana–Champaign*

Janice L. Driver, *Department of Psychology, University of Washington*

Frank J. Floyd, *Department of Psychology, Georgia State University*

Katy Gilbert, *Center for Marital and Family Studies, University of Denver*

Tondeleyo Gonzales, *Center for Marital and Family Studies, University of Denver*

John M. Gottman, *Department of Psychology, University of Washington*

Shannon M. Greene, *Department of Human Ecology, University of Texas-Austin*

William A. Griffin, *Department of Family Resources and Human Development, Arizona State University*

Kurt Hahlweg, *TU Braunschweig, Institut fuer Psychologie*

Keith W. Harris, *Department of Psychiatry, University of California at San Francisco*

Scott Hartman, *Department of Psychology, University of Denver*

Richard E. Heyman, *Department of Psychology, State University of New York at Stony Brook*

Sandra L. Jensen, *Department of Psychosocial Oncology, Division of Psychology, Roswell Park Cancer Institute*

Danielle Julian, *Department of Psychology, University of Quebec at Montreal*

Patricia K. Kerig, *Department of Psychology, University of North Carolina at Chapel Hill*

Galena H. Kline, *Department of Psychology, University of Denver*

Krista K. Krebs, *Hastings Regional Center*

Jennifer Langhinrichsen-Rohling, *Department of Psychology, University of South Alabama*

Kristin M. Lindahl, *Department of Psychology, University of Miami, Coral Gables*

Neena M. Malik, *Department of Psychology, University of Miami, Coral Gables*

Howard J. Markman, *Department of Psychology, University of Denver*

Kathleen McGrath, *Philadelphia Veteran's Administration Medical Center, University of Pennsylvania Health System*

Lauri A. Pasch, *Department of Psychiatry, University of California at San Francisco*

Jennifer Langhinrichsen-Rohling, *University of Southern Alabama*

Catherine H. Rogers, *Department of Psychology, Georgia State University*

Steven L. Sayers, *Philadelphia Veteran's Administration Medical Center, University of Pennsylvania Health System*

Marc S. Schulz, *Department of Psychology, Bryn Mawr College*

Mia Sevier, *Couples Therapy Project, Department of Psychology, University of California, Los Angeles*

Alyson F. Shapiro, *Department of Psychology, University of Washington*

Lorelei Simpson, *Couples Therapy Project, Department of Psychology, University of California, Los Angeles*

Julie A. Suhr, *Department of Psychology, Ohio University*

Kieran T. Sullivan, *Department of Psychology, University of California, Los Angeles*

Laura J. Sullivan, *Department of Psychology, University of North Carolina at Chapel Hill*

Amber A. Tabares, *Psychology Department, University of Washington*

Dina Vivian, *Department of Psychology, State University of New York at Stony Brook*

Robert J. Waldinger, *Close Relationships Project, Judge Baker Children's Center, Department of Psychiatry, Harvard Medical School*

Robert L. Weiss, *Department of Psychology, University of Oregon*

Preface

This volume serves as a companion to Kerig and Lindahl's (2001) earlier text, *Family Observational Coding Systems*. In this volume, we have moved from the triad to the dyad and provide a showcase for significant developments in the coding of intimate couple interactions. Just as with the family field, couple investigators are often faced with the complex and time-consuming task of creating a coding system that will allow them to capture their constructs of interest, with evidence for reliability and validity limited by the plethora of measures that are newly minted or "home-grown." We hope that this book will contribute to the broadening and deepening of the field by disseminating information both about the coding systems that have been developed as well as the conceptual and methodological issues involved in couple observational research.

The primary readership for this book is expected to be researchers interested in the study of couple interactions. However, we anticipate that this work also will be of interest to clinicians who work with couples. A number of the contributors to this volume are clinical psychologists, including the editors. Our training in coding couple interactions has benefited our clinical work by making our observations of couple relationships more astute and by refining our understanding of the implications of these interactional dynamics for individual and marital health.

The first three chapters present overviews of conceptual and methodological issues in the study of couple processes. The remaining chapters describe contributions to the field by sixteen teams of researchers. Each chapter provides information about the conceptual underpinnings and structure of the coding system developed by the author(s) as well as evidence for its psychometric properties. To ease the process of comparing across systems, every chapter uniformly addresses a number of key issues, including the theoretical foundations of the measure, the strategic conceptual and methodological choices made in its development, the properties and content of the measure, the task and setting for which the system is appropriate, the processes of coding and training coders, evidence for reliability and validity, limitations to generalizability, clinical applications, and the variety of studies with which the instrument has been used.

Due to our interest in making this volume timely, diverse, and representative of the field, a range of contributions was solicited. Some of these represent the most well-established and widely used measures with a significant history of research behind them. Others represent the most recent developments by leading scholars in the field or the contributions of relatively young investigators who are on the crest of the next wave of couple research. Although the field is growing and changing even as this volume goes to press, it is our hope that this collection will remain pertinent and contemporary for some time to come.

The editors would like to experss their appreciation to Bill Webber of Lawrence Erlbaum Associates, Inc., and his wife, Nancy M. Proyect, who provided us the best of all dimensions of relationship addressed in this volume: astute problem-solving skills, good communication, warm affect, intelligent information processing, and social support. Finally, we thank each of the contributors for their hard work, their patience, and the pleasure of their collegiality.

I

Conceptual and Methodological Issues

1

Coding Couples' Interactions: Introduction and Overview

Donald H. Baucom and Patricia K. Kerig
University of North Carolina–Chapel Hill

People have been observing couples interact since the dawn of time: "Did you see the way he ignored her at the party?"... "Wasn't that elderly couple sweet? I hope we're that affectionate with each other when we get older."... "I wonder if their marriage is in trouble. No matter what one says, the other disagrees."... "They're going to have a hard time coping with the medical problems, but if anyone can do it, they can. They are so supportive of each other." Over the past several decades, couple researchers have joined the brigade of "people watchers," focusing on the interactions that occur in these most important intimate relationships.

This emphasis on couple interactions is based not only on our inherent interest in watching people. Instead, the focus on dyadic interactions derives from a broader behavioral commitment to the direct observation of human behavior. If we are going to understand intimate relationships, then we need to observe directly how partners behave toward each other. And as scientists, we must derive systematic ways to rate, describe, and categorize these ongoing flows of complex interaction. Direct observation is not necessarily a superior source of data about couples; the relative utility of various sources of data must be established empirically. How couples respond to questionnaires or their physiological reactions during interactions can be valuable sources of information about relationship functioning. Couple interaction data is one potentially valuable source of couple information, and we believe that the findings described in this volume strongly support what we all might assume: How individuals interact with their partners tells us a great deal about them as individuals and as a unit.

The challenge for couple researchers committed to developing an interaction coding system is to take an ongoing stream of dyadic behaviors and devise a way to parse it into meaningful units that can be reliably coded, yet capture important aspects of this very rich interaction. We have been fortunate to obtain contributions from the majority of couple interaction researchers who have helped to shape the field since the 1970s. At present, there is no single source for researchers and clinicians to read to gain an understanding of the different ways to evaluate couples as they interact; hopefully this volume will help to fill that void.

ORGANIZATION AND CONTENT OF THE CHAPTERS

Before focusing on specific coding systems, it is important to understand the state of the field of couple interaction research: the issues it confronts, the successes and limitations of the field to date, methodological issues that must be understood in evaluating couple coding systems, and a variety of strategies that can be employed to analyze the data that are derived from the coding systems. Weiss and Heyman provide the reader with a frank and thoughtful perspective on the current state of the field. Although describing themselves tongue-in-cheek as the village idiots of the couple coding village, we believe the reader will recognize the wise sages who challenge us not to rest on our laurels and to integrate our impressive technologies with theories of relationship functioning that will guide future research. Anyone who has delved into coding couples' interactions likely has experienced the following: "This stuff is complicated. I have this huge amount of detailed data on couples, but I'm not quite certain what to do with it." There is a great deal of complicated methodological and statistical information to understand to make good use of interactional data. Floyd and Rogers do an excellent job of explaining in understandable language the variety of methodological issues to consider in creating, evaluating, and employing a couple coding system. Whereas the vast majority of this volume is about the coding systems themselves, once "raw data" from interactions are boiled down into codes or ratings, an investigator must know how to analyze the data. There are a variety of strategies for such purposes, ranging from statements about the frequencies with which couple phenomena occur during the interaction to complex analyses that take sequences of behaviors and contingencies among behaviors into account. Sayers and McGrath provide a clear and thoughtful discussion of these data analytic strategies, along with essential references for more detailed discussions of technical, statistical issues for couple interaction researchers.

The second section of this volume is devoted to the coding systems themselves, with a separate chapter describing each of the 16 measures. To assist the reader in comparing various coding systems, each chapter employs the same subdivisions.

First, the authors introduce the coding system with a brief summary description and then discuss the theoretical foundations guiding the research. Next, the authors describe the development of the coding system and the strategic decisions that they made along the way. Following this, the authors present details of the coding system, including the task and setting for which the coding system is appropriate, the dimensions and categories that are coded, and the coding process, including how coders are trained and what training materials are available. The authors then provide information about the psychometric properties of the measure, including reliability and validity as well as limitations to, or evidence of, the generalizability of the coding system across different tasks and samples. We also asked the authors to discuss ways in which their coding systems might be used clinically. Finally, the authors give an overview of the range of studies that have been conducted using the coding system.

Dimensions of Coding Systems

Deciding on the sequence of chapters for the coding systems was complicated, reflecting the multifaceted nature of coding systems themselves. As Floyd, Baucom, Godfrey, and Palmer (1998) pointed out in their review of issues to consider in creating an observational coding system, any couple observational coding system involves a large number of decisions by the investigator creating the coding system. These decisions shape the coding system and what information can be obtained from it. For example, the constructor must decide what aspects of couple interaction are important to him or her (e.g., specific behaviors such as interruptions, patterns of interaction such as mutually avoiding addressing areas of concern, supporting each other during difficult personal times, etc.). Second, the coding system must be applied to some interaction, and the constructor, researcher, or clinician must once decide on the type of interaction or instructions for interaction, if instructions are provided to the couple. Thus, couples might be asked merely to talk to each other, to try to resolve some relationship problem, to support each other as individuals, to share feelings openly with each other, or interact with each other as naturally as possible in a laboratory apartment over a number of hours. After deciding on the aspects of a couple's interaction to code and the instructions or "task" presented to the couple, the constructor must decide whether to create a coding system that looks at the interaction in an extremely detailed, microanalytic manner (e.g., coding every few seconds) or in a more global, macroanalytic manner (e.g., rate the entire interaction on some dimension). In addition, someone has to rate or evaluate the couple's interaction. In most of the coding systems described in this volume, outside trained raters are employed—an outsider's perspective; however, at times the partners themselves are asked to rate their behaviors and interactions—an insider's perspective. Clearly, insiders' versus outsiders' perspectives provide potentially different information about the interaction. As a result of the many decisions made during the development of a coding system, any coding system exists in multidimensional space, just as couples' interactions themselves are multidimensional. As a result, grouping the wide variety of coding systems described in this volume into broad categories is somewhat arbitrary because two coding systems might be quite similar in that they are both microanalytic, yet they might be very different in the content of what they are assessing in a detailed manner. In this volume, we have grouped the coding systems into broad categories based on the specific domains, or dimensions that they assess.

Problem Solving and Communication

We begin with a set of coding systems that were developed primarily to assess a broad range of couple behaviors that occur while partners are problem solving or discussing conflictual issues. Historically, this is where couple observational coding systems began within a social learning perspective. In the 1960s and 1970s, couples' communication was almost synonymous with problem solving or conflict resolution. Behavioral couple therapy (then called behavioral marital therapy) and couple observational research developed "interactively," with basic observational research shaping treatment, and treatment findings setting the way for additional basic research on couple interactions. At present, there are over 20 controlled treatment outcome investigations of behavioral (or cognitive–behavioral) couple therapy (Baucom, Hahlweg, & Kuschel, in press). Almost all of these treatment studies included communication training, which fundamentally meant strategies for resolving problems or conflict. Three major microanalytic coding systems evolved to assess couples' abilities to problem solve: the Marital Interaction Coding System (MICS; Hops, Wills, Patterson, & Weiss, 1972), the Couple Interaction Coding System (CISS; Gottman, 1979), and the Kategoriensystem für Partnerschaftliche Interaktion (KPI; Hahlweg, Reisner, et al., 1984). In this volume, Hahlweg provides a description of the KPI, along with an impressive set of validational studies which demonstrate that coding systems initially developed for a specific purpose often have much broader applicability.

These microanalytic coding systems have the virtue of providing detailed information about couples' interactions and have resulted in many valuable findings. On some occasions, however, investigators do not need or want this level of detail, and the time and labor required for microanalytic coding is considerable. As a result, a new generation of less detailed coding systems that focus on partners' communications during problem solving or conflict resolution conversations has been developed. Even among these less detailed coding systems, the level of specificity varies considerably. As an example of a coding system that retains an intermediate level of detail, Heyman describes the Rapid Marital Interaction Coding System (RMICS), the successor to the MICS. The RMICS provides codes for a number of positive, negative, and neutral behaviors, and raters provide a code each time that the speaker changes. The MICSEASE described by Griffin, Greene, and Decker–Haas also was inspired by the MICS and includes the opportunity for the partners to code their own affect experienced during the interaction employing a video recall procedure. Kline and colleagues describe a more macroanalytic coding system, the Interaction Dimensions Coding System (IDCS). The IDCS employed basic research findings from investigations using microanalytic coding systems such as the MICS and CISS to provide a global rating system in which coders provide ratings on a number of dimensions (e.g., withdrawal) after viewing the entire interaction. Whereas the IDCS moves toward an increasingly macroanalytic approach by providing overall ratings based on the entire interaction, Floyd took a different macroanalytic approach in the development of the Communication Skills Test (CST). Noting that in many investigations, detailed behavioral codes have been grouped into broader positive and negative ratings, Floyd created a system in which coders rate each person's talk turn from very positive to very negative, rather than coding specific categories of positive and negative communication.

The aforementioned coding systems were developed to assess a broad range of types of communication during couples' interactions. In recent years, more specific aspects of couples' interaction have been investigated and corresponding coding systems have been developed. For example, Sevier, Simpson, and Christensen describe the Couples Interaction Rating System (CIRS), which focuses on one specific area of communication that has received a great deal of theoretical and empirical attention: demand–withdraw patterns. This pattern has been studied extensively by Christensen and his colleagues, focusing on the tendency for one partner to criticize and demand change while the other withdraws in a variety of ways. Several investigations have demonstrated that this pattern is related to lower levels of relationship satisfaction. In turn, Malik and Lindahl present the System for Coding Interactions in Dyads (SCID), which was designed to focus on maladaptive dynamics of power and control within couple relationships, including such behaviors as verbal aggression, coerciveness, and control. In addition, it assesses aspects of communication that may be related to domestic violence and other indicators of relationship power dynamics such as negative escalation and conflict management style.

Affect and Intimacy

One of the best known couple coding systems is the Specific Affect Coding System (SPAFF), which assesses emotion at a nonverbal level. The SPAFF was designed to teach coders about cues that reflect specific affects, while using coders' judgments as socially competent cultural judges to code specific affects that are recognizable from a cultural instead of a physical features perspective. This differentiation among different affective states is important, given that Gottman and his colleagues have demonstrated that various emotions have differential predictability regarding the long-term adjustment of marriages. In this volume, Shapiro, Gottman, and Driver describe the most recent version of the SPAFF.

Recognizing that negative interaction is unavoidable, Tabares, Driver, and Gottman describe the Repair Attempts Observational Coding System, which assesses the de-escalation of negative affect during marital conflict. Repair attempts are behaviors that are aimed at preventing or reducing negativity during conflict. Tabares et al. describe 17 different repair attempt codes that they have gleaned from intensive study of couples' interactions. In addition, they describe 11 responses to these repair attempts from the other individual. Not only is this a valuable coding system, but it provides great insight for both researchers and clinicians about how partners attempt to halt and alter negative interaction cycles.

Early coding systems focused primarily on negative interactions and negative emotions. In more recent years, there has been increasing awareness that communication between partners is not only about problems, conflict, and negative interaction. To the contrary, the ways in which couples communicate during more positive interactions also is important for understanding relationships. In response to this awareness, in recent years observational coding systems have been created to assess these more positive conversations and interactive processes. An important aspect of positive interactions is the extent to which partners attempt to engage each other in some connected fashion. In a recently developed coding system, Driver and Gottman describe the Turning Toward Versus Turning Away Coding System (Turning System) which assesses one individual's attempt to interact with or gain attention from the other partner, and the partner's response to this bid to interact. At times, partners attempt to engage in more intimate ways, and Dorian and Cordova describe the first validated coding system to assess the degree to which partners engage in intimate conversations (the Intimacy Coding System). Although the notion of intimacy is often described as a "fuzzy construct" (Prager, 1995), Cordova elucidates the specific behaviors of both partners during an intimate interaction, assessing the degree to which the discloser engages in vulnerable statements to the other person and the degree to which the responder either reinforces or suppresses these disclosures.

Other than the MICSEASE described earlier, all of the previous coding systems rely on external observers in the form of trained raters. However, when partners interact, they not only are behaving externally, but they also are having their own internal subjective experiences of the interaction. This internal experience is inaccessible to the outside rater. Therefore, the partners themselves can provide valuable insight into their own interactions. Schulz and Waldinger describe a strategy for obtaining individuals' ratings of their own and their partners' emotional experience during an interaction. They employ a video recall technique in which participants review a videotape of their couple interactions and are then asked what they were feeling and what they believe their partners were feeling during the interactions. They provide useful detail about how this general methodology can be employed in a variety of interpersonal interactions.

Social Support

Most of the coding systems described thus far focus on relationship issues conversations about the couple or issues of concern to both of them as a couple. However, partners also having meaningful conversations with each other when the focus of the conversation is on one partner. Social support focuses on the ways that one individual attempts to be helpful or supportive to the other partner when the latter partner is experiencing personal distress that is not focused on the relationship (e.g., work-related or health concerns). The chapters by Suhr, Cutrona, Krebs, and Jensen and Pasch, Harris, Sullivan, and Bradbury describe the two major coding systems for assessing social support. Findings from investigations focusing on social support confirm that couple researchers must attend to these positive ways that partners interact, in addition to they ways that they confront conflict or problems.

The Individual as Part of a Couple

Almost all of the aforementioned coding systems have a dyadic focus on the process of communication, with an emphasis on interaction patterns or specific forms of positive and negative communication. In addition, some coding systems have focused on specific aspects of the individual that are elucidated during dyadic interactions. For example, Sullivan and Baucom describe the Relationship Schema Coding System (RSCS), which assesses the behavioral manifestation of a certain form of information processing, the degree and quality with which an individual thinks in relationship terms. They propose that the ability to think in terms of interpersonal interactions and the mutually reciprocal impacts that partners have on each other is an essential skill for long-term, successful relationships. The RSCS provides separate assessments of the quantity and quality of each individual's relationship schematic processing; among other findings, their results demonstrate that wide discrepancies between the two partners' abilities to process in relationship terms are indicative of relationship distress.

Vivian, Langhinrichsen–Rohling, and Heyman also focused on the individual in their development of the Thematic Coding of Dyadic Interactions (TCDI). Strikingly, almost none of the aforementioned coding systems assess the specific content that is being discussed during the interaction. Instead, various forms of communication such as criticizing or denying responsibility serve as the codes. However, there is no code regarding the content or topic that is being discussed when criticism occurs, for example. In the TCDI, the coder assesses seven interpersonal content themes that reflect core individual needs displayed by each partner. These involve different aspects of emotional attachment and interpersonal power, including such issues as needs for love, commitment, equality, and autonomy. A large number of investigations from a variety of methodological perspectives demonstrate that there are core relationship-oriented and individually-oriented needs that are important in intimate relationships (Epstein & Baucom, 2002). Thus, the TCDI helps to clarify the content of these needs demonstrated during interaction, along with assessing several process themes, such as resisting change and invalidating.

CONCLUSION

As the contents of this volume attest, the methods for observing and understanding couples' interactions have greatly diversified over the past decades. Early coding systems, which are still of great value, were microanalytic and attempted to provide a comprehensive assessment of couples' interactions, primarily during discussions of problem areas or conflictual interactions. Over time, more macroanalytic coding systems with the same overall focus were developed. Subsequently, coding systems to assess specific aspects of negative interaction came into being. More recently, investigators have become concerned that there has been a disproportionate amount of emphasis on negative aspects of couples' interactions, with a relative paucity of attention to more positive, constructive components of interaction. As a result, there has been an increasing emphasis on assessing positive aspects of couples' interactions. Furthermore, investigators have come to recognize that there are both individual and dyadic aspects of healthy and maladaptive relationships. Consequently, coding systems have been developed which focus on the individual within a dyadic context. Finally, investigators recognize that outsiders and insiders might have quite different and equally valid information to provide about a couple's interaction, thus leading to methodologies such as video recall techniques. And, as these coding systems have evolved, researchers have become more aware of the methodological issues to take into account in developing these coding systems, along with increasingly sophisticated statistical techniques for analyzing the data. As should be apparent, the field of observational coding and couples' interactions is alive and progressing. We are delighted to give the reader an opportunity to explore the myriad faces of couple interaction coding systems as described in this volume.

2

Couples Observational Research: An Impertinent, Critical Overview

Robert L. Weiss
University of Oregon

Richard E. Heyman
State University of New York at Stony Brook

Every village has its idiot, railing that the good townspeople have lost their way, shouting out impertinent questions, and asking why the emperor has no clothes. The Couples, Observational Research (OR) coding village has two self-identified idiots, and you're looking at 'em (or reading their words, to be precise). So, before reading the rest of this volume about the myriad tools that couples observation researchers have painstakingly developed, gather 'round our soap box and hear us out. Do read the other chapters, but while doing so, keep in mind what the village idiots have to say.

RANT 1: WOE UNTO THOSE WHO HAVE FORGOTTEN WHY THEY MOVED TO OBSERVATIONAL RESEARCH

If you are reading this volume, you are either a Couples, OR resident or you are thinking of moving to OR. Why? "I've always lived in OR" is not a good enough excuse; neither is, "My mentor (or funding agency) made me move here." Furthermore, why did you move to a particular neighborhood (i.e., MICS Pines, CISS Plains, Social Support Estates)? What are you trying to accomplish in OR?

The Couples, OR founders knew why they were homesteading here. They held two bedrock beliefs: (a) reinforcement contingencies shape and maintain human behavior, and (b) people are unable to report their behavior and behavioral sequences accurately. So, if you are going to understand why people behave as they do and what clinicians can do about it, you have to watch. "Why?" and "what to do?" also happen to be the purposes of all behavioral science undertakings (i.e., predication and influence or control; e.g., Skinner, 1953).

What to watch? The iterative scientific cycle of observation shown in Fig. 2.1 offers some guidance. First, one must have an overarching theory (e.g., behaviorism) and specific research questions in mind (e.g., Do distressed couples' conflict behaviors differ from those of nondistressed couples? If so, why and what can be done about it?). Without a theory, there are simply far too many things that one could see to bring any of them into sharp focus. Second, one can use this theory to define the important things to observe (i.e., create or choose a coding system) and conduct the observations. Third, one must analyze and understand implications of the observational findings. Finally, this process must cycle back to theory, leading to refinements and expansions.

The problem with an iterative loop like Fig. 2.1 is defining where to start. Even if you have a theory of the processes under which behavior is shaped, which behaviors should one watch? The behavioral founders in OR decided that families, not

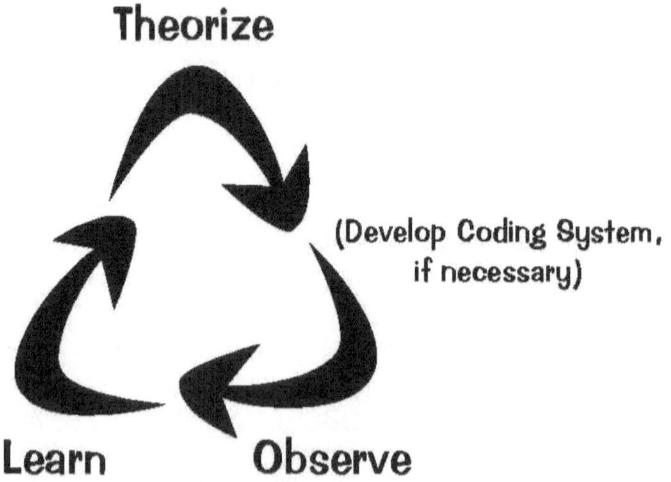

FIG. 2.1. The Scientific Observation Cycle.

brainstorming academics, should provide the raw inputs for this decision. So, as described in more detail in another chapter in this volume (Heyman), they went into families' homes and wrote down the behaviors that they saw, as they witnessed them. This early descriptive system evolved into the Marital Interaction Coding System (MICS).

The golden years of OR ensued during the 1970s. So little was known about couple and family functioning that many seminal works were published during this period about methodology (e.g., Reid, 1978), intervention (e.g., Jacobson & Margolin, 1979; Weiss, Hops, & Patterson, 1973), statistics (e.g., Sackett, 1979), and research and theory (e.g., Gottman, 1979; Patterson, 1982).

Since that time, the Couples, OR field has not progressed at the same pace. We have several theories about why this happened: (a) researchers, having identified behaviors on which distressed and nondistressed couples differ, let their clinical efforts blind them to the fact that describing differences was the beginning, not the end, of determining why distressed couples become distressed (e.g., observed "communication" differences were framed as "communication skills deficits," which could be rectified by "communication skills training" borrowed from humanistic and eclectic approaches—case closed); (b) descriptive research expanded into a plethora of content areas (e.g., health, physical abuse) but did not iterate back to the theory phase of the cycle; (c) many explanatory theories were proffered but not tested sufficiently; (d) researchers let the coding system determine what could and could not be studied, rather than letting their theoretical questions guide their use (or creation) of coding systems; and (e) functional analysis of contingencies requires an idiographic rather than nomothetic approach and longitudinal data, increasing the level of difficulty of OR research.

Whatever the reason, the uncomfortable truth is that Couples, OR's infrastructure is strong on description (including discriminating between distressed and nondistressed couples) and replete with descriptive tools but is weaker on explanation. In contrast, the neighboring village of Families, OR—founded on the same principles by many of the same founders as our own fair burg—was coerced into upgrading its infrastructure:

> In the 1980s ... a group of ... site vist[ors] from our funding agency asked, "Where are your theories?" and "Where are your models?" Our answer was that we were behaviorists and that our strategy was to obtain data first and then develop a theory if one were justified. Their response was terse and to the point: ... "If you want to collect data at all, you must first show us a model." (Patterson, Reid, & Dishion, 1992, p. 1)

The progress made in Families, OR can serve as a model for Couples, OR. That is, we have theories, we have observational tools, we have a large body of descriptive literature, and we have an energetic and creative community. What we are lacking are sophisticated tests of our theories. Looking at Families, OR, one sees the use of multitrait, multimethod, multireporter structural equation and growth curve models (e.g., Bank & Patterson, 1992; Conger, Patterson, & Ge, 1995;

Dishion, Li, Spracklen, Brown, & Haas, 1998; Eddy, Dishion, & Stoolmiller, 1998; Patterson, 1982, 1993; Patterson et al., 1992). As summarized in a recent edited volume (Reid, Patterson, & Snyder, 2002), Families, OR has demonstrated empirically how children develop into antisocial adults (i.e., basic training in coercion at a young age via parental ineffectiveness, reaction of the social environment via school failure and peer or adult rejection, adolescent association with deviant peers and refinement of antisocial skills, adult adjustment problems and antisocial behavior). The approach found in the Patterson et al. (1992) and Reid et al. (2002) volumes, which describes a 10-stage method of model building (including construct validation) and the results of the empirical tests of the model, can serve as a blueprint for the evolution of the couples field.

RANT 2: YOU SAY POTATO, I SAY PA-TAH-TOE; LET'S CALL THE WHOLE THING CONVERGENT VALIDITY

There are three types of OR residents: those who create their own coding systems, those who faithfully use existing coding systems, and those who create constructs by mixing and matching elements of an existing coding system. Coding is simply a tool used to accomplish a larger goal (prediction and influence), and thus all three types of residents can do good or ill through use or misuse of the tool. The first group has a high capability to contribute to breakthroughs, but they also can get so absorbed into their own existing systems that they do not maximally contribute to theoretical and methodological progress (Kuhn, 1970). The second group, users of existing coding systems, can add to the psychometric database regarding particular coding systems or codes (Heyman, 2001) and can use existing tools to test their theories (as long as the existing tools are a good fit to their constructs). The third group appears to be searching for ways to measure constructs of interest that are not currently found in a coding system (which indicates positive theoretical foment). However, in this approach, creativity can exceed scientific rigor when investigators attempt to create constructs from elements that are imperfect fits (Heyman, 2001).

Thus, for all three groups, the usefulness of their OR efforts is heavily dependent on the questions of "What to code?" and "What codes?" (also known as the nitty-gritty of psychometrics, such as code construction and observational situation operationalizations). Fortunately, there are tremendous resources available to guide interested readers on the basics of behavioral assessment (Haynes & O'Brien, 2000), observational research (e.g., Bakeman & Gottman, 1997; Heyman & Slep, in press), content validity (e.g., Haynes, Richard, & Kubany, 1995), and issues to consider in developing observational coding systems (Floyd, Baucom, Godfrey, & Palmer, 1998).

First, we focus on the important issue of creating codes. In Table 2.1, we present the coding categories and constructs used by the five most widely used coding sys-

TABLE 2.1

Macro Categories and Microcodes From Four Systems Used in Couples Observation Studies

Macrocategory	*Microcode*
Acceptance	acceptance
Affection and caring	affection and caring
Agree	agree
Anger	anger, contempt, hostile withdrawal
Anxiety	anxiety
Avoidance	avoidance, deny responsibility, disengagement, discussion, not tracking, off-topic, no response, withdraws
Belligerence	belligerence
Conflict engagement	criticize, disagree
Congeniality	humor, smile and laugh
Contempt	contempt
Criticism	criticism
Defensiveness	defensiveness
Demand	blames, discussion, pressures for change
Demand–withdraw	w anger, w defensiveness, w domineering, h stonewalling, h anger
Depressive affect	depressive affect
Disagreement	disagreement
Disgust	disgust
Domineering	domineering
Emotional aggression	belligerence, contempt and disgust
Engagement	criticize, disagree
Excitement and joy	excitement and joy
Facilitative	accept responsibility, agree, approve, assent, attention, comply, humor, mind read positive, paraphrase and reflect, positive physical touch, question, smile and laugh
Fear	fear
High negative affect	belligerence, contempt, defensiveness
Humor	comply, humor, smile and laugh
Interest and curiosity	interest and curiosity
Interrupt	interrupt
Irritated affect	irritated affect
Justification	justification
Metacommunication	metacommunication

TABLE 2.1 (cont.)

Macrocategory	*Microcode*
Negative	anger, belligerence, command, complain, contempt, criticism, defensiveness, deny responsibility, disagreement, disgust, disapprove, domineering, dominates discussion, dysphoric affect, excuse, expresses critical feelings, fear/tension, interrupt, justification, mind read negative, negative affect, negative problem description, negative solution, negative listening, noncomply, no response, not tracking, problem description (negative), put down, sadness, self-disclosure (negative), stonewalling, turnoff, whining withdrawal
Negative listening	negative listening
Negative nonverbal	no response, not tracking, turnoff
Negative self-disclosure	negative self-disclosure
Negative social reinforcement	complain, criticize, deny responsibility, disagree, excuse, interrupt, no response, not tracking, put down, turnoff
Negative solution	negative solution
Negative–demand	negative affect, pressures for change
Neutral	inaudible/irrelevant utterances, metacommunication, neutral, neutral affect, neutral withdrawal, normative, positive or neutral listening, problem description
Nonconstructive	Command, criticize, excuse, interrupt, mind read negative, noncomply, put down, turnoff
Nonhostile negative	defensive withdrawal, fear, sadness, whine
Positive	accept responsibility, acceptance, affection, agree, approve, assent, attention, caring, communicates clearly, comply, compromise, humor, interest, joy, joy/excitement, listener backchannels, negative solution, negotiates, neutral, paraphrase/reflect, positive affect, positive physical touch, positive or neutral listening, positive solution, request for change, self-disclosure, smile/laugh, validation
Positive or neutral listening	positive or neutral listening
Positive social reinforcement	agree, approve, assent, humor, positive physical touch, smile and laugh
Positive solution	positive solution
Problem description	negative solution, problem description (internal), problem description (external), question, solution past

TABLE 2.1 (cont.)

Macrocategory	*Microcode*
Problem solving	accept responsibility, command, compromise, negative solution, paraphrase/reflection, positive solution, problem description (external), problem description (internal), question
Problem-focused	complain, compromise, disagree, disapprove, negative solution, positive solution, problem description (external), problem description (internal)
Rest	rest
Sadness	sadness, whining
Self-disclosure	self-disclosure
Smile and laugh	smile and laugh
Stonewalling	stonewalling
Tension and fear	tension and fear
Validation	accept responsibility, agree, approve, assent, mind read positive
Whining	whining
Withdraw	avoidance, discussion, no response, not tracking, turnoff, unintelligible talk withdrawal

Note. Categories and codes from studies using the MICS, CISS, CRS, KPI, and SPAFF. A full table listing the exact categories and codes used in over 100 observational studies can be found at http://www.psych1.psy.sunysb.edu/marital or by emailing either author.

tems. Autogenesis is evident: coding approaches have heavily influenced one another, and investigators have either taken over or relabeled codes or constructs from one system to another. This approach has not caused anyone to take legal action, but it has two unfortunate end products. First, it has lent a false sense of validity to our efforts; seemingly independent coding systems might produce convergent results, but it might be more an indicator of replication of coding systems rather than validity as applied to couples' relationships. Second, coding system inbreeding may be why the intellectual growth in Couples, OR has been less than optimal at times: borrowing descriptors from each other does not truly push our understanding further. This volume, with its bounty of coding systems, indicates that this need not be the case. To paraphrase Shakespeare, the fault, dear colleagues, is not in our systems, but in ourselves, that we are theoretical underlings.

RANT 3: CONSTRUCTING CONSTRUCTS IS SERIOUS BUSINESS

Returning to Fig. 2.1, the OR cycle provides potential for theoretical and applied advancements. Descriptive codes can lead to construct building, which, through accumulated literature, can lead to improved theory, which may lead to an evolution in coding, and the cycle continues. Given that this bottom-up approach (i.e., "obtain data first and then develop a theory if one were justified," Patterson et al., 1992, p. 1) is the predominant one in Couples, OR, we focus on it, rather than top-down (i.e., create codes to operationalize preexisting theory) approaches, which have been less common but are quite defensible.

One of the first considerations is whether one is measuring the phenomenon of interest directly (a sample) or indirectly (i.e., through indicators, or signs, of a latent construct). This distinction between sign and sample applies equally today as it did decades ago (e.g., Weiss, 1968). The behavioral tradition brought to the table a methodology based on the relative purity of sampling behaviors either singly or as members of response classes. The sample of behavior indicates what individuals are capable of doing (maximal), or at least how they typically behave in specific settings. Samples per se do not qualify as constructs. Behavior as sign starts an inferential cascade in that the observed behavior serves as a proxy for still other (latent) constructs. Behavior viewed as something other than itself provides a window to something beyond itself. The concept of latent variables is familiar within various modeling strategies (e.g., structural equation modeling, latent growth curve modeling). With the advent of structural equation modeling, the distinction between signs and samples became somewhat blurred. As noted earlier, a careful approach to construct building has already been laid at our feet. Researchers should turn to Reid et al. (2002), Patterson et al. (1992), or Bank and Patterson (1992) for guides on how to build constructs through modeling.

Couples, OR, as evidenced by the various approaches described in this volume, has been much less about samples of discrete behaviors displayed by the participants than it has been about the constructs implied by the code definitions as listed in Table 2.1. The codebook in each instance instructs the observer regarding what to observe using the various decision rules. And there's the rub! How do these codes see the light of day? Who decides what the codes should be? Table 2.1 lists, in one place, the many different constructs and their defining codes that we have gleaned from the Heyman (2001) review. Table 2.1 is the lexical map of behaviors selected for observation from studies using various problem-solving (conflict related) tasks. For the most part, these codes and their constructs are based more on a priori assumptions rather than their strong conceptual relevance.

As implied earlier, there are plenty of clinical theories that have guided the clinical couples area for decades but are as yet poorly tested (e.g., dysfunction is a result of reinforcement; distressed couples are unhappy because they are deficient in skills). Behavioral observation as a methodology has been confused with theory. A tautology developed: couples are unhappy because of the coded behavioral differences. That is, because distressed couples demonstrated certain behaviors more or less than nondistressed couples, it was assumed that the high or low rate of these behaviors was the cause of distress. As has been noted time and again, correlation does not imply causation. Communication patterns might cause relationship distress, but distress might result from many other factors, which result in the deterioration of communication, as well.

On the flip side, functional marriage is not well understood. A behavior analytic approach to marriage, one that would systematically define the skills required for maintaining a mutually satisfying, stable relationship, has not been well articulated. The behavior analytic approach (e.g., Goldfried & D'Zurilla, 1969) is the method of choice for establishing content validity. One would, for example, first establish what satisfied couples deem important in how the partners handle conflict (or otherwise accommodate each other). The next step would determine whether they actually demonstrate these behaviors as they interact in various settings. Codes would subsequently be defined that reflect the behaviors identified; the codes then would be more directly tied to what needs to be assessed. This approach would ensure the relevance of the behaviors introduced by the coding system.

RANT 4: WE ARE NOT ABOVE GORING OUR OWN OX

In a very real sense, with the benefit of hindsight, this tendency toward construct stagnation has been largely true in the development of our own systems, the MICS (MICS; Weiss & Summers, 1983) and its next generation offspring, the Rapid MICS (RMICS; see Heyman, this volume). As the first and most widely used coding system (Heyman, 2001), the MICS exemplifies both the gains that descriptive systems made and all the pitfalls that we have already noted.

A number of archetypal problems with the MICS and RMICS are worth considering in light of our previous concerns. MICS codes were often grouped into categories based strictly on a priori grounds, thus obscuring the contribution of single codes. This approach is sensible, in that there are not 30 to 40 separate constructs in the MICS, and the reliability of single codes is not adequate. However, almost no investigators have employed the same combination schemes, making it difficult to make inferences about construct validity (Heyman, 2001), let alone use the growing MICS knowledge to iterate through Fig. 2.1.

The most common MICS categories, positive–negative–neutral, reflected broad notions of affect and behavior, which, although discriminative in many instances, really were not cost effective; too much labor was involved for making judgments about relationship distress that was more readily accessed through self-report measures (e.g., the Dyadic Adjustment Scale, DAS; Spanier, 1976). A subsequent factor analysis of more than 1,000 interactions coded with the MICS (Heyman, Eddy, Weiss, & Vivian, 1995) generated factors that gave some empirical guidance as to what, through the eyes of the MICS, were the classes of behaviors that described what individuals did in the conflict discussion tasks. As described in detail in a subsequent chapter in this volume, the RMICS was created as a way to measure these behavioral classes, saving time and increasing reliability and validity over the MICS.

Nevertheless, a more psychometrically sound, next-generation descriptive system is still a descriptive system. Although the RMICS could be used to test core elements of behavioral theory, it has not been used in this way thus far. Furthermore, most of the interesting elements of behavioral theory (e.g., how reinforcement shapes the anger intensity trajectories of couples during conflicts, and how these trajectories cause distress and violence-propensity) cannot be tested with a categorical system that intertwines content and affect. Both within and outside the MICS tradition, iteration through Fig. 2.1 is necessary, but has been scant.

RANT NUMBER 5: WHAT'S THE SOUND OF ONE PARTNER CLAPPING?

A problem with factor analysis of microcodes to create classes is that such behaviors simply look at the covariance of microcode frequencies, effectively ignoring the intent of a dyadic observational coding approach. Unless the raw codes themselves describe interactions (i.e., the temporal joining of individuals' behaviors, something no mainstream coding system does), we learn which individual behaviors are likely to coalesce based simply on frequencies of occurrence, not on function (Gottman, 1979) or dyadic patterning.

The process becomes more complex when investigators combine codes into code conglomerates, which in turn suggest higher level constructs. Germane to this discussion of the origin of constructs is how codes are used in data analytic formats that go beyond single or base rate frequency counts. The applications of sequential analytic tools attempted to capture functionality in interactions. No longer was it a matter of how often a single behavior was observed (e.g., criticism) but rather the frequency of a behavioral unit: do occurrences of behavior X predict contingent occurrences of behavior Y? Higher order empirical relations can be defined in this way using conditional analytic methods. A sequential pattern (e.g., conditional probability) thus introduces a new behaviorally relevant construct into the lexicon for describing interactions.

Constructs may become more sign-like as data analytic strategies become increasingly sophisticated, that is, as we move further and further from the actual behavior. The descriptions based on such techniques are potentially of greater theoretical interest than the information provided by raw frequency counts.[1] However, a danger lurks here as well: The potential utility of defining constructs based on data analytic schemes does not in itself bestow any higher order of validity on the coding scheme than that bestowed by a priori code definitions. The interaction patterns that various sequential analytic methods can disclose must still be vali-

[1] Certain codes in Table 2.1 are of interest in their own right because their prevalence can have clinical significance (e.g., criticism).

dated or demonstrated to be of utility for understanding relationships (i.e., that engaging in such patterns has implications for marital adjustment).

Alternatively, one might define codes in terms of interactional units, as is often done in rating schemes, where molar or category-behaviors are recorded. Part of the difficulty with this approach is that natural language does not provide the wealth of descriptors for interactions that it does for individual trait descriptors. What might couples researchers and clinicians come up with if, based on their experiences, they were challenged to write a codebook of interactional unit codes? For example, Julien, Bégin, and Chartrand (1993) coined the term, *synchrony*, or *meshing velocity*, in their gear model of interaction. Would it be possible to reliably microcode how well a couple "fits together" as their interaction unfolds over time? This approach leads us increasingly into the realm of interpretation in coding rather than observation of discrete behaviors. Thus, the coding system developer can define more molar patterns either by aggregating smaller discrete behaviors coded separately or coding a more molar, complex set of behaviors as a single unit. For example, the code developer could cumulatively create the construct of "support" by adding, as it were, discrete microbehaviors, or start with the macrounit "support," which is comprised of macroevents that lead one to the impression that "support" has occurred.

The research strategy depicted in Fig. 2.1 is especially germane to our emphasis on the importance of discovering dyadic (interactional unit) codes. We will need to use theory as a guide to which dyadic codes are initially important and then set out to test whether in fact they are empirically respectable.

CONCLUSION: RANTS 1 THROUGH 5

To summarize this section, one must carefully examine the constructs reflected in any given behavioral observation approach. The codes themselves, like Trojan horses, can potentially obscure one's thinking by creating the illusion that one has measured a process that has more theoretical significance than is actually the case: The researcher is using a coding system that is very detailed, coded reliably, and everyone else uses it, so the researcher assumes it must provide meaningful findings. If codes are taken as samples of behaviors, it is the behaviors themselves that are of interest. However, in many instances the codes are meant as proxies for some other process (i.e., as signs), so the genealogy of the construct being indexed bears careful scrutiny. Constructs can arise out of usage dictated by everyday experience ("forgiveness," "acceptance," "trust," "hostility," etc.), whereas other constructs become familiar and take on a life of their own based on the methodology or technology that attempts to operationalize them ("escalation," "power," "reciprocity," etc.). Our suggestion is to be vigilant and clarify the conceptual importance of the particular code relative to the construct one is using; it is not enough to say, "I want an observational measure of couples' interaction."

RANT 6: WHY DON'T WE HEAR MUCH ABOUT "GENERAL IZABILITY?"

The ultimate utility of behavioral coding lies in its ability to generalize to relationship dynamics that go beyond the immediate observation that has been coded. Almost always we are interested in more than how the couple interacts during a 10-min conversation in the laboratory when they have been primed to have a particular type of conversation. So, "General Izability" is a high ranking official in our fair village, or at least she should be. We would hope that she would be at the forefront of all of our minds as we ask, "What would 'General Izability' say? Would she allow us to reach this conclusion based on the information that we have?" When considering whether a given episode of interaction behaviors is representative of the domain of interest (and here the domain can be narrowly or broadly defined), the investigator needs to be aware of the various constraints imposed by the interaction task. One major factor is the nature of the conversation that the couple is asked to have: Are the partners being asked to engage in a support interaction, or are they being asked to resolve a major, long-term problem in their relationship? Likewise, are they being asked to engage in typical behavior (e.g., "Respond as you typically would") or optimal or maximal behavior (e.g., "While your partner describes her personal concern, your job is to be as supportive as possible"). In essence, behaviors occur in a context, not a vacuum. Because the codes we obtain usually do not explicitly note this context, it is easy to interpret the codes in an absolute manner, ignoring that the codes resulted from behavior in a given context. Whether partners display similar behaviors in other contexts (either in other settings at home or with different instructions in a research setting) is an important issue centered around generalizability and situational specificity (see Heyman, 2001, for recommendations about designing the sampling context).

SOAP BOX PHILOSOPHIZING: CONSIDERATION OF NONLINEAR APPROACHES

At present, almost all of our data analytic strategies for couples observational data have assumed that the best way to understand dyadic interaction is in a straightforward, linear fashion. A given behavior might occur early in a conversation, and the same behavior might occur later in the same conversation; these identical behaviors can then be summed. A challenging alternative might be to assume that the behaviors of interest are part of complex systems and are not linear (i.e., although topographically similar, the same behaviors function differently as the interaction progresses). What if coded elements are not additive (i.e., unfold linearly as assumed in sequential analyses) but rather follow properties of complex adaptive systems (Eidleson, 1997; Lewis, Lamey, & Douglas, 1999)? Chief among the defining properties of dynamic systems (DS) is that change can occur not only nonlinearly but catastrophically; a small input can disrupt an ongoing process in a major (disproportionate), nonlinear way.

Although Gottman and associates have published two studies involving couples interaction that embody many of the concepts of DS (Cook et al., 1995; Gottman, Swanson, & Murray, 1999), couple researchers have not generally taken advantage of such approaches. Interestingly, DS methodology has been applied in a number of developmental psychology studies involving parent–child interaction. This approach is understandable given the centrality of change in this intellectual pursuit and the awareness that developmental change is not always linear in nature (cf. Dumas, Lemay, & Dauwalder, 2001; Granic & Hollenstein, 2003; Lewis, Lamey, & Douglas, 1999).

Granic and Hollenstein (2003) reviewed many DS strategies and provide a primer on DS concepts that initially sound quite foreign to the uninitiated. It is only possible here to outline some of the more immediate analytic possibilities that DS thinking holds for behavioral observation data collection. "DS theory is a *meta-theoretical framework* that encompasses a set of abstract principles that have been applied in different disciplines (e.g., physics, chemistry, biology, psychology) and to various phenomena (e.g., lasers, ant colonies, brain dynamics) at vastly different scales of analysis (from cells to economic trends)" (Granic & Hollenstein, 2003, p. 644). DS methodology falls into two categories: graphical representation of temporal changes from state to state (i.e., "state space" grid analysis and their variants used in the developmental studies cited earlier) and mathematical modeling of nonlinear parameters that reflect system changes (Cook et al., 1995; Gottman et al., 1999).

Central to both approaches are systems theory concepts embodying the temporal organization of interrelated elements, such that lower level or simpler (system) components self-organize into more complex organizations over time. (This concept is in contrast to more familiar notions that systems will tend to dissipate toward lesser structure.) These processes are nonlinear, and, as noted earlier, small perturbations can produce major transition changes. Of particular interest is the notion of attractors. The behavioral repertoire is seen as a topographical landscape of states (recurring patterns). Although there are seemingly limitless possibilities for transitions to occur between and among states, certain transition patterns seem to be drawn repeatedly to specific locations in the state space landscaped grid, hence the term *attractors*. It is as if patterns of interaction are drawn to these attractor areas of state space.

We can illustrate a state space grid (cf. Lewis et al., 1999) using a marital interaction coded with four codes (e.g., positive, negative, withdrawal, problem solve) that define a 4 × 4 matrix, with Husband and Wife as row and columns respectively. In each unit of real time (e.g., every second, every minute), a dot is placed in a cell to record the state of the interaction at that time (e.g., H positive, W withdrawal). Starting with the first cell in the time sequence, the dots are connected sequentially by straight lines, thus creating a graphic temporal representation of the sequence and of how often and for how long each cell is "visited." Studies have used the amount of time spent in a cell or the number of different cells visited to describe various processes and to test a variety of hypotheses about interaction (e.g., Granic et al., in press).

Dumas et al. (2001) described a conceptually similar procedure for plotting phase transitions using Karnaugh maps. These are configurations of variables in N–dimensional space where the intersects of rows and columns define cells which represent unique combinations of up to four binary ("on" or "off") coded events. Thus, if two of four variables were allotted to each spouse, a given cell would represent a pattern that coded the pattern of these four variables in their "on" (occurred) or "off" (did not occur) state. As with the state space grid analysis (Granic et al., in press), time and frequency in any cell can be analyzed and complexity measures can be computed to determine whether one participant unit (either a dyad or group of couples or families) shows more or less diversity (nonstereotypy) in its interaction patterns.

These procedures present some important advantages over lag sequential analyses. They provide rich temporal information, and they have the ability to depict relatively complex patterns. They also make possible comparisons of system complexity and the role of attractors. These graphical approaches could be readily applied to behavioral coding of marital interactions, and we recommend that investigators consider such data analytic strategies. In doing so, it is important not to simply jump on the village bandwagon of the popular analytic strategy of the moment. Instead, investigators must clarify whether they believe that the particular elements of interaction that they are investigating are linear in nature or nonlinear in nature and select the appropriate strategy.

As an example of how nonlinear models have been applied in the couples' arena, consider the dynamic mathematical modeling approach presented in Gottman et al. (1999). Their goal was to demonstrate that a specific pattern of interaction dynamics would be predictive of marital stability or satisfaction based on data from a newlywed sample. Using nonlinear difference equations, they estimated parameters having an influence function; that is, whether a spouse's behavior at time T changes (influences) the other person's behavior at T+1. Using the Specific Aspect Coding System (SPAFF) codes as measures of affect, they developed a process to account for changes in affect over and beyond the first person's steady (uninfluenced) state. Emotional inertia can be quantified (e.g., W not having an effect on H's affect at T+1). This approach led to defining thresholds for negativity and positivity. Thus, at what point does one person's negative behavior perturb a steady affective state and thereby influence where the other person moves in phase space? (Phase space is a map of H and W's scores as coordinates with each person's affect score plotted for each time block.) The result plots a trajectory of moving interaction points that can show stable states (those to which a person returns to when perturbed) and unstable states. Of more general interest in this complex system of analysis is the way it can show specifically how and where couples get stuck in certain transition patterns. Making interventions at these unique intersections and testing the outcome in each instance is one way to assess the adequacy of the model.

In summary, DS approaches illuminate basic processes within interactions by making time a central focus of the description. They also force the researcher to make explicit which variables are theoretically important. The graphical techniques can provide a useful qualitative understanding of transitions drawn to attractors. The mathematical approaches require estimating parameters in difference equations, but here, too, trajectories of change may be useful for predicting clinical outcomes.

CODA

How could something so seemingly simple—looking at how couples interact—become so complicated? Hopefully by serving as the village idiots, we have made the complex simple and the simple deserving of more careful thought. Our intended message is simple: Do not confuse a hammer with architecture. Coding systems are merely tools geared to help us understand specific aspects of couples' relationships. What needs to remain in focus are the behaviors that make a difference in couples' lives, which means that we need to be more explicit about what actually are these behaviors. By giving careful attention to the behaviors that are important in a given interaction, observational coding systems can be extremely valuable tools for the relationship architect. The chapters that follow in the current volume demonstrate that such advancement is possible in the couples' area. The authors of these chapters, who have created these coding systems, have employed a variety of strategies to operationalize specific behaviors of interest in couple interactions. These new approaches, along with continuing development in data analytic strategies, demonstrate that Couples, OR has a bright future; even the village idiots can see that.

ACKNOWLEDGMENTS

Thanks to Danielle Black for creating the complete coding construct table from which Table 2.1 was derived. Thanks also to the University of Oregon CADS (Complex Adaptive Dynamical Systems) group for their encouragement for the leap into the unknown.

Richard Heyman's preparation of this chapter was supported by the National Institute of Mental Health (Grant R01MH57779) and National Center for Injury Prevention and Control, Centers for Disease Control and Prevention (Grant R49CCR218554–01).

3

Methodological Guidelines for Conducting Observations of Couples

Frank J. Floyd and Catherine H. Rogers
Georgia State University

Investigators who conduct observations of couples confront exceptional methodological challenges. These challenges stem in part from the fact that observations of couples' behaviors are treated as both "signs" and "samples" of relevant processes under investigation. They are signs because investigators usually want to understand broader constructs or domains in couples' relationships than merely the specific behaviors observed, processes such as dyadic problem solving, power dynamics, or social support mechanisms. Observations are conducted to either predict to other situations or to evaluate these broader domains of dyadic relationships. As psychometric instruments, therefore, couples observational measures must meet the same psychometric standards for reliability and validity as other instruments that assess psychological constructs and processes. At the same time, these observations are also treated as actual samples of the domain of interest, actual instances of dyadic behavior. As samples, concerns about the representativeness and comprehensiveness of the content become paramount. A related concern is the need to obtain unbiased assessments from the observers. Thus, investigators must be alert to situational factors that can influence both the behavior of the couples being observed and the perceptions of the observers.

The methodological challenges of couples observation also stem from the lack of easy portability for most measures of couples' interactions. We refer to portability as the use of the measure by different investigators; that is, the generalizability of the measure across investigators. With most paper-and-pencil measures, we assume that once the measure has been shown to be reliable and valid for an assessment purpose, the questionnaire can be used widely by most investigators, in most settings, and for most purposes that reasonably approximate the original context. However, this assumption of portability is more tenuous with observational coding systems. Each new application must demonstrate that the procedures elicit meaningful samples of couples' behaviors, that the coders are reliable, and that the coding criteria are being applied in a manner that is consistent with the manual and the theory that guided its development.

The purpose of this chapter is to help investigators adopt couples interaction coding systems by describing practical guidelines for enhancing and evaluating the reliability and validity of new applications. We first describe procedures for assessing observer agreement and measurement reliability, then review several statistics commonly used to evaluate agreement and reliability. Afterward, we present some guidelines for enhancing the validity of observational assessments, with emphasis on insuring adequate content sampling.

RELIABILITY AND OBSERVER AGREEMENT

Two Purposes for Evaluating Observer Agreement

There are two major purposes for evaluating agreement between observational coders. The first is to monitor the coders as they conduct their observations of the couples' interactions to ensure that they are using the coding system accurately. The second is to demonstrate that the measurement of the variables used in the study is dependable, that variance in the coded data can be attributed to individual differences among the couples rather than idiosyncrasies among the coders in how they used the coding system. These two purposes are complementary. If training is successful and coder agreement remains high during the course of the data collection, then the measurement should be dependable, and the bulk of the variance in the data should be attributable to couple differences on the factors under investigation. However, in theory, monitoring observer agreement differs from the assessment of measurement reliability because we are not concerned with estimating true-score variance, but rather we want to know how often raters agree when they make their evaluations. In contrast, reliability of the measure in the classical sense of true-score variance is the central concern when using observational data to make inferences about constructs. Accordingly, the two purposes call for both different procedures to examine agreement and different statistics to calculate agreement.

Monitoring Coder Agreement. When training new coders, the investigator evaluates how training is progressing, whether the coders are learning to use the coding system in a way that matches the guidelines in the coding manual, and when the coders have reached a satisfactory level of agreement with criterion codes so that they can begin to evaluate actual data. For this purpose, observer agreement is usually calculated for every interaction session evaluated by a coder. After training is completed, the investigator continues to monitor agreement among the observers to detect observer drift so that corrective training can be conducted. Commonly, investigators monitor coder agreement on 20% to 25% of sessions evaluated by trained coders.

For the purpose of monitoring coders, observer agreement should be assessed for whatever unit of behavior the coders record. For example, if the coders record content codes for specific events, then agreement should be assessed for the specific content codes. If the coders make ratings at fixed time intervals, agreement should be assessed for the individual ratings made at each time interval. In both cases, each categorical code and each rating is considered an observation, and agreement is assessed to determine the number of observations for which the two coders agree and the number for which they disagree.

Agreement is usually evaluated for each observational session, such as a 10-minute-long problem-solving discussion by a couple. The level of agreement across all codes given in the session is a useful index of overall coder agreement. However, it may also be helpful to calculate agreement statistics for individual codes to determine if specific types of behaviors are being coded inconsistently, so that additional training can focus on those behaviors in particular. During training, and later when monitoring coders, if agreement is assessed on a point-by point basis, it is not usually necessary to correct for the possibility of chance agreement due to the base rates of different codes. As discussed later, corrections for chance agreement are highly influenced by the range of behaviors used by an individual couple. Because some couples display a limited range of behaviors, chance-corrected indices computed on individual couples can produce erroneous, overly negative evaluations of the accuracy of the coders' performance, which can confuse and discourage the coders.

Verifying the Reliability (Dependability) of Measures. When reporting observer agreement statistics to verify that variables in the study are assessed dependably, it is important that the statistic address the reliability of the variables actually used in the study. In most cases, these variables are aggregates of individual codes. The unit of agreement should match the unit of analysis in the study (Margolin et al., 1998). Thus, observer agreement statistics used to monitor coders that address agreement on individual codes are not usually the most appropriate statistics to report in the presentation of the findings. Instead, if one uses aggregate codes, one should use agreement statistics based on aggregate analyses rather than individual item analyses. The investigator must show that rates, relative frequencies, lag-sequential dependencies, mean ratings, or whatever measures are used in the data analysis, are sufficiently free of error variance to be trusted as dependable scores.

In most cases, the reliability statistic for reporting purposes should be based on coded data from all couples who were evaluated by two or more coders. Currently, it is common practice for investigators to calculate coder agreement statistics, such as percent agreement or kappa, for each observation session, then report the mean and ranges of these values in the presentation of the findings. However, with the exception of single case designs, we are often interested in reliably detecting variability in behaviors across couples rather than variability within couples. An average of the coders' agreements within each couple may not accurately reflect their agreement about differences among couples. For the purposes of between-couple comparisons, information about coder agreement on aggregate scores across couples provides a reliability statistic that more directly addresses the concerns of the study.

Reliability Statistics

In addition to the purpose of the evaluation, the choice of a reliability statistic is largely dependent on the type of data to be analyzed and the degree of stringency desired. A discussion of several of the most commonly used agreement statistics follows.

Percent Agreement. Percent agreement is easily understood and therefore a common choice for a reliability statistic with categorical data. Additionally, it is easy to compute. There are several different types of percent agreement statistics commonly calculated. The most basic form is a *frequency ratio*, which assesses agreement for the total frequencies of each type of coded behavior. This frequency ratio is calculated by first tallying the number of occurrences of the behavior recorded by each coder. The formula for the frequency ratio is as follows:

$$\text{Frequency ratio} = (\text{smaller tally}/\text{larger tally}) \times 100.$$

Thus, if coder A recorded 9 occurrences of a behavior and coder B recorded 11 occurrences of that behavior, the frequency ratio is 82%. A weakness of this statistic is that the resulting value does not tell whether the raters agreed on the same occurrences, and thus it may not be useful for the purposes of monitoring agreement during coder training. It is probably most appropriate for reporting purposes when total frequency of one type of behavior is the unit of analysis.

Another form of percent agreement is *exact agreement*, or *point-by-point agreement*. This statistic is an improvement over measures of total frequency agreement because it reveals the extent to which exact instances of behavior were agreed upon. The formula is as follows:

Point-by-point agreement = $(A_{freq} / (A_{freq} + D_{freq})) \times 100$,

where A = agreement and D = disagreement. For example, with event data in which there are multiple categories of coded behaviors, A_{freq} is the number of instances in which the two observers recorded exactly the same behavioral codes, and D_{freq} is the number of instances in which the two observers either disagreed on the code for an event, or one observer recorded a code for an event that the other coder failed to detect. With interval data in which the coders report the number of times an event occurs in each interval, A_{freq} is the number of intervals in which the two observers recorded exactly the same number of occurrences, and D_{freq} is the number of intervals in which the two observers did not record the same number of occurrences. Bakeman and Gottman (1997) argued that there is no standard by which to judge adequate levels of percent agreement because the interpretation of agreement is influenced by many factors, including the base rates for the behaviors. Nevertheless, for training purposes, it is useful to know that coders can agree on 80% to 90% of their coding decisions. However, for reporting purposes, percent agreement statistics should be supplemented with other indices that take into account base rates and chance agreement (Haynes & O'Brien, 2000).

With behaviors that occur at either very high or very low base rates, the overall percent agreement may be strongly influenced by chance agreements between the coders. Also, under these circumstances, kappa, which is described later, tends to give an overly pessimistic estimate of observer agreement because of the large correction for chance. In these cases, it is useful to calculate both *occurrence agreement* and *nonoccurrence agreement* separately:

Occurrence agreement = $(A_{occ}/ (A_{occ}+D_{occ})) \times 100$,

where A_{occ} is the total number of intervals in which both coders recorded a behavior as present, and D_{occ} is the total number of intervals in which only one coder recorded the behavior;

Nonoccurrence agreement = $(A_{non}/(A_{non}+D_{non})) \times 100$,

where A_{non} is the total number of intervals in which neither coder recorded the behavior, and D_{non} is the total number of intervals in which one coder did not record the behavior, but the other coder did record the behavior. Occurrence agreement is most sensitive for detecting coder disagreement about low-base-rate behaviors, and nonoccurrence agreement is most sensitive for detecting coder disagreement about high-base-rate behaviors.

Kappa. For the purpose of reporting findings, it has become common practice to correct for chance agreement between coders when using a percent agreement statistic. Kappa is often the statistic of choice for this purpose. Kappa adjusts for chance agreements by taking into account the base rates for each behavior, and thus the likelihood that observers would agree simply by coding randomly, but in accordance with the base rates. The possibility of random agreement would seem to be most problematic when there are relatively few codes overall or when there is a small subgroup of codes with relatively high base rates and the coders use these high-rate codes as "best guesses" when they are uncertain. Nevertheless, even when data do not match these conditions, editorial standards usually require that investigators report chance-corrected agreement.

Kappa is usually calculated to represent agreement between two coders in assigning a set of observed behaviors to any of a variety of categorical codes (as opposed to evaluating agreement about the frequency of occurrence of a single type of behavior). The data are tallied in a *confusion matrix*, which is a symmetrical matrix with all possible codes for coder A listed in the rows and all codes for coder B listed in the same order in the columns. Each behavior evaluated by the coders is tallied according to the code it received from coder A and coder B. Thus, the tallies in the diagonal of the matrix represent instances in which both coders assigned the same code to the same behavior, and tallies in other locations represent instances in which the coders disagreed in their evaluations. The observed proportion of agreements (P_o) is the proportion of the total tallies (i.e., total number of behaviors coded) that fall on the diagonal. For each code, the proportion of agreements between the coders expected by chance is the cross product of the base rates for that code for the two coders (i.e., the cross product of the proportion of total behaviors assigned to that code by each observer). Thus, if coder A assigned 50% of the behaviors to a particular code and coder B assigned 25% of the behaviors to that code, the probability that they would assign the same behavior to that code is .125 (i.e., .50 x .25 = .125). The sum of these probabilities for all codes is the total probability of agreements expected by chance (P_c).

Kappa may be calculated on a point-by-point basis or for aggregate scores. The general formula for kappa is as follows:

$$\text{Kappa} = (P_o - P_c) / (1 - P_c),$$

where P_o is the observed proportion of agreements, and P_c is the probability of chance agreements, as defined earlier. A *point-by-point kappa* can be computed from the type of confusion matrix described earlier when data are collected so that we can pair individual codes given to each behavior by each coder, and both coders code the same number of behaviors. If the coders are allowed to assign a code at any point that they detect a relevant behavior, there are usually unequal code frequencies across coders because of instances in which one coder assigns a code and the second coder fails to detect that a relevant behavior occurred. In this case, point-by-point kappa can be calculated using a modified confusion matrix with an additional row and column inserted for "no code." Instances in which only one coder assigns a code are tallied in the row or column, and the values of P_o and P_c are calculated using these additional data points. Jacob, Tennenbaum, and Krahn (1987) described a method for computing an *aggregate kappa* from aggregate scores only, when coders record only total frequencies for each of the codes. In this case, the confusion matrix also includes a "no code" category. For each code, the smaller frequency given by either of the two coders is entered in the diagonal, so that these are treated as agreements, and the remainder is entered in the "no code" category and treated as disagreements. For example, if coder A reported a total of 17 instances of one code and coder B reported 20 instances of the same code, the value 17 would be entered into the diagonal position for that code, and the value 3 would be entered into the "no code" row under the column for that code, and thus treated as three disagreements. The calculation of kappa proceeds using the same methods as with point-by-point data.

There is no set standard for a desirable value for kappa, although lower limits of acceptability usually fall in the range of .60 to .70 (e.g., Bakeman & Gottman, 1997). Note that when the actual base rates for different behaviors are uneven, such that a few behaviors occur much more commonly than others, it is difficult to obtain high values for kappa. This situation is most problematic when kappa is calculated on data from an individual couple. For example, if a particular couple is highly consistent during the discussion and displays a limited range of behavior, such as being consistently neutral or consistently negative in their behaviors, the base rate for the consistent behavior is very high for the couple, and thus the correction for chance is great. In this case, even if the coders agree on all but a few coded behaviors, the few disagreements have a large impact on reducing kappa because of the large correction for chance agreement. In essence, kappa penalizes the coders because of the high base rates for the limited range of behaviors exhibited by the couple. If the investigator accepts kappa as a meaningful statistic here, the investigator essentially assumes that any agreements between the coders on the high-rate behaviors can be attributed to chance rather than the coders' accurate use of the coding system. Clearly, such an assumption is overly conservative.

To counteract potential problems with kappa when high-base-rate codes occur for an individual couple, Bakeman and Gottman (1997) suggested using samplewise estimates of expected agreement derived from the base rates of the entire data set in these instances. An alternative strategy would be to calculate kappa from the pooled data on all interactions that were subjected to reliability checks. Kappa based on pooled data are probably better estimates of the dependability of the data for the entire sample. Additionally, when categories can be arranged in an ordinal fashion, or when certain types of disagreement are considered more problematic than others (e.g., disagreement across general categories as opposed to within a category), it might be useful to compute a *weighted kappa*, which assigns weights based on the degree of disagreement (e.g., for ordinally arranged codes, distance from each other in the confusion matrix). Guidelines for weighted kappa are given in Bakeman and Gottman (1997).

Product-Moment Correlation. When dealing with interval-scaled data, the product-moment correlation can be used to describe the amount of covariance shared by the scores from two coders. Interval-scaled data are most commonly found when codes are aggregated for the purposes of data analysis, such as when frequencies or relative frequencies are calculated from categorical codes, or when measures of sequential dependency are calculated for individual couples, such as lag-sequential *z* scores or the *phi* coefficients. Rating scale measures are also usually treated as interval-scaled data unless the investigator specifically examines the points on the scale as categorical codes. In most cases, the correlation is computed from total scores on one variable across a number of couples. For example, the correlation coefficient might be used to assess the similarity of scores for the relative frequency of positive behaviors, as calculated from two sets of codes assigned by independent coders. Each spouse or each couple would obtain one relative frequency score from each coder, and the correlation would be calculated using data from all participants who were coded by two coders. Thus, if an investigator uses multiple variables in a study of couples' interactions, such as relative frequency scores for multiple types of behaviors, correlations should be computed to assess the reliability of the scores for each variable. Occasionally, correlation coefficients are used to assess reliability within individual participants, such as when a sequence of interval-scaled ratings is obtained for each couple. For example, if each speech turn is rated for the positiveness of the behavior displayed, the correlation between sets of ratings produced by two coders would indicate shared coder variance in the ratings given to that one couple.

The formula for a product-moment coefficient is as follows:

$$r = \Sigma(d_x)(d_y) / N\sigma_x\sigma_y,$$

where d_x and d_y are the deviations of each score from its mean, N is the total number of observations made, and σ_x and σ_y are the standard deviations of each score. This coefficient is widely recognizable to diverse audiences and gives a standardized distribution (Jacob et al., 1987). There are several weaknesses to using this approach. For instance, the statistic does not discriminate on an item level and thereby does not indicate which items were agreed on and which were not. Additionally, the statistic is not sensitive to the mean activity level of the two raters, so that a high correlation coefficient might be obtained even when the raters' mean levels of ratings are very different (Poling, Methot, & LeSage, 1995).

Intraclass Correlations. The intraclass correlation is a form of reliability statistic derived from generalizability theory. Intraclass correlations determine the amount of variance in scores that can be attributed to variation among couples as opposed to coders. Similar to the product-moment correlation, this form of reliability statistic is a good choice for interval-scaled data. It is also most advantageous when data are collected from more than two coders because there is no need to calculate individual correlations for all possible pairs of coders. However, a good deal of data are required for intraclass correlations so that a sufficient range of different behaviors among different couples is recorded to maximize between-couple variance. The intraclass correlation is actually calculated using analysis of variance procedures. These procedures are too lengthy to describe in this summary and are given in Shrout and Fleiss (1979).

Rater Agreement Index. Burry–Stock, Shaw, Laurie, and Chissom (1996) introduced Rater Agreement Indexes (RAIs) as a method for calculating rater agreement for interval-scaled ratings. The index judges the closeness of the raters' scores in reference to the possible range of the scores. The basic formula is as follows:

$$RAI = 1 - (|R_1 - R_2| / (I - 1)),$$

where R_1 and R_2 are the ratings given by the two raters, and I is the number of interval points on the rating continuum. The index ranges from 0 to 1, with scores approaching 1 indicating higher levels of rater agreement. RAIs can be calculated for individual ratings of individual couples by two coders. There are different variations of equations allowing for the consideration of various numbers of raters, subjects, and behaviors observed.

Reliability of Sequential Data

There appears to be disagreement within the field as to how best handle the reliability of sequential data. Margolin et al. (1998) suggested that sequential data should be evaluated by point-by-point agreement between coders on the individual codes used in the sequential analysis. However, several researchers advise against using individual codes when dealing with sequential data (Wampold & Holloway, 1983). For example, Bakeman and Gottman (1997) demonstrated that the value of point-by-point agreement may be sharply deflated if one coder inserts extra codes from time to time, even when the agreement about the sequential pattern of codes is high. The controversy probably stems from differences in the nature of studies that address sequential dependencies. For exploratory studies in which the purpose is to identify sequential dependencies between pairs of coded behaviors, the unit of analysis is individual behaviors; therefore, it is wise to demonstrate that individual behaviors are coded accurately. However, when indices of sequential dependency, such as the lag-sequential *z* score, *phi* coefficient, or Yule's *Q* statistics, are used as dependent measures in studies of individual differences between couples on these indices, it would be most appropriate to use product-moment or intraclass correlation to show that these indices are indeed reliably assessed. These indices are continuous scales, rather than categorical variables, and thus, are suitable for correlational analysis.

Procedures and Software to Detect and Calculate Observer Agreement

At first glance, it would seem to be a straightforward task to compare two coding records to count instances of agreement and disagreement between the coders. However, in practice, the task can be quite difficult. This is particularly so with the type of event-level coding used in most couples observational coding systems, where the coders record codes when they detect that a relevant event is occurring. The resulting data record is a list of events in the order they were noted, usually with the actor (husband or wife) also noted. If the coders are using the coding system in a consistent, accurate manner, the records from independent coders can be expected to line up reasonably closely. However, difficulties occur when the coders detect and code different events, so that either or both of the records contain additional codes that do not match the other record. When coder agreement is very high and such additional events are rare, the remaining pairs of codes may be easy to align. However, in other cases, sections of the coder records become misaligned in a way that makes it impossible to match pairs of codes. Even when the pairs are matched, it is unclear whether disagreements reflect instances in which the coders detected the same action but labeled it differently, which would be one coding disagreement, or instances in which each coder attended to a different action, and thus produced a different code, which would be counted as two coding disagreements.

For this reason, it is usually necessary to keep a record of the time at which each code was recorded. With videotaped interactions, a stopwatch device can be inserted into the video image so that the coder can copy the time from the screen and record this time along with the code. Note that the day/date/time stamp that comes with most videorecorders gives the time only in hours and minutes, which is not sufficiently precise for most coding purposes. Alternatively, most electronic data entry devices or software programs record the time when each code is entered. Codes for different records can then be paired by setting a time window during which matching codes must be detected to be counted as an agreement. The size of the time window depends on the nature of the behaviors observed. In our experience with coding either individual events or speech turns, we find that a 5 sec window works well.

At the initial stages of training new coders, it is advisable to evaluate each coder in reference to a standard set of codes produced by a highly experienced coder or by the investigator. When untrained coders are compared with each other, it is impossible to know which coder is using the coding criteria improperly, or whether both are inaccurate. With a criterion set of codes, the investigator tallies agreements and disagreements by examining each criterion code and determining whether the coder produced a matching code within the preset time window. Additionally, any additional codes produced by the coder that are not included in the criterion record should also be counted as disagreements.

There are commercially and publicly available software systems designed to tally agreements and disagreements, then compute observer agreement statistics.

In our experience, these systems tend to have idiosyncratic characteristics that warrant a few caveats about their use. For example, the reliability program included with the Observer observational software (Noldus, 1991) compares both coders with each other rather than treating one coder as the criterion. The program accurately tallies agreements when the two coders produce the same code within the preset time window, but it produces an inflated number of disagreements because every code by both of the coders that does not have an exact match is counted as a disagreement. Thus, if the two coders detect the same behavior at the same point in time, but assign different codes to that behavior, the Observer system counts this as two disagreements, one for the lack of match for coder A's code, and a second for the lack of match for coder B's code. In contrast, the reliability program included in Bakeman and Quera's (1995) Generalized Sequential Querier (GSEQ) system treats the first set of codes entered as the criterion set, and judges whether each criterion code has a match in the second set, which is produced by the new coder. Again, exact matches are accurately detected. However, because the system only searches for matches from the codes in the criterion set, any overcoding by the new coder, in which the coder erroneously notes additional events not included in the criterion set, are simply ignored. Thus, whereas the Observer system can grossly underestimate coder agreement by counting too many codes as disagreements, the GSEQ system can overestimate agreement somewhat if a new coder tends to insert additional codes. If overcoding is suspected to be a problem, an alternative approach with the GSEQ system is to reverse the order of entry of the criterion codes and the new coder's codes so that the system searches for matches to the new coder's codes within the criterion set of codes. In this case, instances in which the coder inserted additional codes would have no match, and thus would be counted as disagreements.

Another notable characteristic of the GSEQ system is that, with timed data, it treats timed events as if they are ongoing actions that terminate when the next event is coded, and then calculates agreement–disagreement for each unit of time in the observation. If the coding software records time in tenths of seconds, GSEQ would use 600 time units for each minute of observation. If observations are actually discrete events, the program tends to inflate the estimate of reliability. Roger Bakeman, the author of the program, has an alternative version that counts each event as one unit, but still uses the time to track agreements. This alternative version is probably most appropriate for the types of timed events used in studies of marital interaction.

VALIDITY

Just as reliability and coder agreement can be affected by circumstances within a given investigation, validity can also be affected by these situational factors. A review by Heyman (2001) summarized information on construct validation for most longstanding couples coding systems. Construct validation encompasses all other forms of validity (e.g., concurrent, predictive, and discriminative validity) that collectively reveal the extent to which each coding system measures what it purports to measure. The accumulation of this psychometric evidence across multiple investigations by multiple users builds confidence that the coding system can be successfully adopted for use in a new study addressing the same domain. However, each new use of the system must address the question of whether it is a valid application of the measure. In the case of analogue measures such as couples observational systems, the critical issue is one of content sampling in the new assessment situation.

The most often asked question of any observational marital researcher is as follows: "To what extent do the behaviors displayed in the analogue setting resemble the couple's usual ways of interacting together?" To this question we might add the following: "Even if the behaviors that are elicited do not occur regularly in the natural setting, do they accurately reflect actions that might be demonstrated if the circumstances are right?" Fundamentally, these are questions about the content validity of the observation. They concern whether the observation elicits behaviors that are relevant to the issue under study, representative of the couple's behavioral repertoire, and typical for the partners.

The relevancy of the behavior sample involves the extent to which the behaviors elicited and measured in the observation are salient to the construct under investigation. Relevancy can be addressed at the level of the coding system and at the level of the specific sample of behavior obtained from a given couple. Regarding coding systems, Haynes (2001) noted that, in general, few analogue observational systems follow recommended guidelines for insuring the content validity of the measure, including the use of multiple sources for the selection of coding content, and the acquisition of input from a variety of experts, including researchers, clinicians, and couple members themselves. For marital observations, the failure to provide a clearly specified theoretical foundation for many coding systems further obscures content relevancy (Heyman, 2001). Thus, in selecting a coding system for use, each new investigator should evaluate the content of the system for its relevancy to the construct of interest in a particular study, and not assume that because the system has been widely used it necessarily measures relevant content. Regarding the relevancy of specific samples of behavior, the concern is whether each couple who completes the procedures produces a segment of interaction that reflects the processes under study. For example, a couple might be instructed to problem solve about an important source of animosity to evaluate their conflict resolution skills, but they quickly change the topic to a more benign issue, or use the time to discuss their mutual frustration with the research procedures. Is this activity a relevant sample of problem-solving behavior in the form of avoidance, or merely a failed attempt to implement the procedures, which should be discarded from further analysis? The investigator should have a plan for dealing with circumstances such as this, should implement the plan consistently, and should explicitly note these circumstances in the presentation and interpretation of the findings.

Whereas relevancy concerns specific behavioral codes, the representativeness of observation concerns whether the procedures on the whole assess the full repertoire of behaviors that relate to the process being investigated. That is, is there sufficient breadth of content sampling; are all relevant behaviors included? Although many couples coding systems claim to "exhaustively" code couples' behaviors, the comprehensiveness of the coding system is restricted to the conditions under which the couples are observed. Clearly, no system can be expected to sample all possible ways that partners relate together. It has become traditional in this field to sample only 10 to 15 min of interaction, and the existing evidence suggests that this is sufficient for evaluating global positive and negative ways of relating (Weiss & Heyman, 1997). However, as we begin to ask more specific questions about interaction processes, and as we further develop our theories about various domains of functioning, existing procedures lose their validity for addressing this new framework (Haynes, 2001). For example, a notable emerging issue concerns the assessment of culturally-relevant behaviors that are not incorporated in most couples coding systems. Black, Asian, or Hispanic couples, older couples, gay and lesbian couples, and so forth, may all have unique ways of relating that are not captured by most existing coding systems.

Finally, a related aspect of representativeness concerns the typicality of the behavior observed. Observations are reactive; they elicit self-consciousness in the least, and in some cases, frank attempts to dissimulate. Under these circumstances, observations of couples appear to be remarkably robust, at least for detecting the types of negative behaviors that discriminate distressed from happy couples (Weiss & Heyman, 1997). Evidence suggests that in problem solving, couples' behaviors are less negative in research labs than at home (Gottman, 1979). Heyman (2001) proposed that this finding implies that lab-based observations of negativity in distressed couples may be less sensitive than home-based measures. It is also possible that typical behaviors, which are a feature of performance, are not necessarily the best index of ability. It may be more important to know what couples are able to do, given the opportunity, than what they typically do day-to-day. For example, Foster, Caplan, and Howe (1997) demonstrated that, during a lab-based social support task, spouses who were judged by their partners to be behaving less supportively than they typically do obtained the highest correlations between their behaviors and criterion measures. Thus, the fact that behaviors are not typical does not mean that they are invalid for any assessment purpose. If fact, Haynes (2001) suggested that because analogue observations are subject to situational influences, they may be relatively inaccurate for estimating actual rates of behaviors in natural settings, but highly sensitive for detecting functional relationships within a specific context.

Haynes (2001) described the "conditional nature of validity" as applied to analogue observational measures. One implication is that validity may differ for different couples at different points in time. Some procedures may tap recent-onset symptoms, whereas others may tap more long-standing abilities. For example, in the heat of overwhelming negative affect that accompanies severe marital distress, observations of a couple may accurately tap their overwhelming negative affect, but not the skills or abilities that the couple has when negative affect is under control. In this case, the observation is measuring an aspect of performance as influenced by poor negative affect regulation, but not problem-solving abilities, per se. This situation may account in part for the fact that most studies of couples' communication behaviors have successfully identified the negativity that characterizes severely distressed couples, but have been unable to identify the positive features that characterize loving couples. Jacobson and Christensen (1996) suggested that these negative behaviors may result from the negative affect and mutual hostility associated with marital distress rather than being causes of distress. To obtain valid measures of the communication behaviors that precede, and possibly cause, marital unhappiness, research may need to assess communication before the negative affectivity associated with distress has fully set in. Alternatively, perhaps we need longer assessment periods and more varied situations to evaluate the range of possible behaviors for couples who are experiencing significant distress.

Heyman (2001) outlined recommendations for reducing measurement and inferential errors in couples observational research. His recommendation for enhancing content validity is to attend closely to the way the task is structured for couples. He suggested that error can be reduced by using standardized instructions for couples, narrowing the topic of discussion to focus the couple on a specific rather than a broad issue (e.g., a specific disagreement rather than a broad concern such as "communication"), and attending to the relevancy of the issue for both partners. The latter point relates to findings showing that patterns of communication during a problem discussion differ depending on which partner selects the complaint under discussion (Christensen & Heavey, 1990). Although there is no direct empirical evidence to support the need for standardized instructions and narrow topics of discussion, each investigator should consider how failure to do so in a given study might bias the data obtained or increase error variance.

CONCLUSION

Observational measures of couples' interactions developed by behavioral and cognitive–behavioral researchers are among the most sophisticated, carefully designed, and highly researched observational instruments in the field of clinical psychology. There is every reason to expect that, if done with care, these instruments can be broadly adopted in research and clinical settings. In addition to attending to the guidelines reviewed in this chapter, we encourage new users to contact the originators and other users of coding systems to verify that the new application matches with previous uses of the measure. Only through calibrating our measures consistently across studies can we hope to advance our empirical knowledge about couples interaction processes.

ACKNOWLEDGEMENTS

Preparation of this chapter was funded by grants R01 HD24205 and R01 HD35988 from the National Institute of Child Health and Human Development, NIH. The chapter was prepared when Frank Floyd was a Visiting Professor at the University of Hawaii at Manoa.

4

Data Analytic Strategies for Couple Observational Coding Systems

Steven L. Sayers and Kathleen McGrath
Department of Psychiatry
University of Pennsylvania

It is easy to be disheartened by the task of conducting an observational study. The development of a coding system is often long and arduous, training reliable coders can be an uphill journey, and data entry can be wearisome. The feeling of intimidation perhaps becomes most acute when faced with the data analysis task. The investigator typically faces questions such as these: Do I need to conduct sequential analyses? What is the correct method? Do I have enough data? Our hope is that this chapter will give the reader a solid start in answering these questions. Furthermore, we hope to point readers toward excellent resources that will help them complete their investigations.

Time is obviously a key element in understanding interactional behavior between participants in an intimate relationship. In observational coding and data analysis, the use of time is sometimes explicit (i.e., code X starts at 1 min 32 sec and ends at 1 min 38 sec) and sometimes implicit (i.e., codes occur in this sequence: X Y A B C). The relevance of time is further illustrated by the fact that we make careful plans to observe couples for long enough to obtain stable estimates of the proportion of time that spouses spend criticizing, providing support to one another, or other important behaviors. We also may be interested in sequences of behaviors and key turning points in a discussion. Our hope is that this chapter focuses couples researchers on the various ways of handling time in the data analysis of observational data.

The approach of this chapter is to start with questions that couples researchers have of their observational data, and then proceed to the methods that address these questions. Not all issues or methods can be addressed in this single chapter, and many are covered in other chapters in this volume. Reliability procedures and analyses, for example, are covered in the chapter by Floyd and Rogers (this volume). Also, we review time-series analysis of couples' data relatively briefly, and the reader is encouraged to consult the broad literature within and outside the social sciences for details about using these methods. Finally, there is an existing body of literature that addresses past and present controversies in analysis of observational data, and many of these issues are addressed in chapters 2 and 3 in the current volume and thus are not addressed here.

The methods in this chapter are based on work that is not necessarily new and it is not restricted to couples' interaction. Early examples include Sackett's (1979) work with primates, Bakeman's work in child development (Bakeman & Adamson, 1984; Bakeman & Brownlee, 1980), and Gottman's (1979) work in marital interaction. This chapter emphasizes methods useful for couples, wherein the codes used apply equally to each person in the dyad, and distinctions are made between the specific members of the dyad (i.e., husband vs. wife). For ease of presentation, we refer to "husband" and "wife" in this chapter, although the applications here will apply equally to unmarried dyads such as engaged couples.

PRELIMINARY ISSUES IN ANALYZING OBSERVATIONAL DATA

Types of Questions Researchers Ask Using Observational Data

Types of research questions can be separated into three basic analytic methods for simplicity: (a) questions associated with base rates (or proportions), (b) questions about two-event (or greater) sequences, and (c) questions with explicit time information, including very detailed timed events and time-series. Table 4.1 presents examples of common research questions and the recommended data analytic strategies, although not all possible questions are represented. Note that often there is more than one method to address a research question. Also, the questions addressed in Table 4.1 do not imply that finding a temporal relation between a marital behavior of one type and a specific type of response by the partner demonstrates a causal connection (see Yoder & Feuer, 2000). In many cases, however, the goal is to identify sequences that may be part of larger chains of marital behaviors.

TABLE 4.1

Research Questions and Recommended Data Analytic Approaches

	Data Analytic Approaches				
Prototypical Research Questions	*Mean Differences in Proportions, Durations, or Rates of Behavior (i.e., ANOVA)*	*Yule's Q Index Correlated with Variable of Interest*	*Yule's Q Index Used to Assess Differences in Two Groups of Couples (i.e., ANOVA)*	*Log-Linear Modeling*	*Time-Series Analysis*
Do discordant spouses (or husbands-wives) criticize more than nondiscordant spouses?	X			X	
Is H → W negative reciprocity associated with wives' self-reported marital satisfaction?		X			
Is a W → H demand/withdraw pattern stronger in clinic couples compared to nonclinic couples?			X	X	
Are spouses more likely to respond with greater empathy when a negative topic about the spouse is identified with high skill, compared to statements delivered with low skill (events are "cross-classified;" see text)?				X	
Do husbands and wives differ in the predictability of their negative responses to their spouse's previous negative affect or negative verbal behavior?				X	X
Does the overall level of withdrawal exhibited by one spouse increase after the partner issues a verbal threat?					X
Are spouses who are negative listeners when hearing complaints likely to reciprocate complaints?				X	

Methods of Data Recording, Data Types, and Data Representations

Understanding data analysis for observational data requires some familiarity with the forms in which data become available for analysis. To do so, we describe the Sequential Data Interchange Standard (SDIS; Bakeman & Quera, 1995a), which is a relatively new specification developed to provide a common notational system for behavioral data. Four SDIS data types cover the majority of the types of forms analyzed: event sequential data, state sequential data, interval sequential data, and timed event sequential data. We describe SDIS here to provide a framework for discussing the ways that investigators conducting sequential analysis have represented their data. Note that the notation described here was designed to be read by a computer program also called SDIS, and analyzed by the analytic program described by Bakeman and Quera (1995a), called the Generalized Sequential Querier (GSEQ). There are other software tools available for reading, storing and analyzing data, but they are usually highly specialized for individual laboratories (e.g., Yoder & Tapp, 1990) or specific coding systems (e.g., Marital Interaction Coding System-IV, MICS-IV, Weiss, 1992; Rapid Marital Interaction Coding System, RMICS, Heyman, this volume).

Using SDIS, *event sequential data* are essentially a list of codes, without explicit reference to time. Using a very simplified example, we can describe a system consisting of five codes: C = Complaint, P = Problem Solving, S = Support, I = Invalidation, and O = Other. We can code for the identity of the speaker who exhibited the behavior (i.e., h = husband, w = Wife). An interaction could be represented by the following sequence of codes: Ph Cw Ch Ph Pw Sw Oh Pw Ih Cw Ow Ph … and so forth. *State sequential data* have the added information of duration, as well as sequential position. One way SDIS can be used to notate this type of data is to record the code name and the onset of each occurrence. The state sequential data type is useful when the investigator wants efficient time-based estimates of certain types of behavior (e.g., to state that the spouses engage in problem-talk for 30% of the time) and the behaviors of interest are relatively nonoverlapping and describe the interaction fairly completely. *Interval sequential data* are perhaps one of the most common types of data, and consists of predetermined time intervals wherein the coder indicates whether a behavior did or did not occur. Various investigators have designed their coding systems to utilize this data type in different ways: some allow the coder to assign multiple behaviors per interval and some do not; some coding systems specify that behavior is tallied only once, if the behavior spans over more than one interval. The *timed event sequential data* type carries the richest amount of information in that codes can co-occur, and are recorded along with their onset and offset times. This form of data also has provisions for recording dual streams, and may be useful when analyzing data from husband–wife dyads.

Transformations and Other Considerations in Data Types

It is possible to transform data between one SDIS data type and another. Furthermore, some coding situations combine several data types in the recording stage and for certain purposes utilize another data type for certain analyses. For example, behaviors coded sequentially in 15-sec intervals could be entered into electronic form as interval sequential data, event sequential, or even state sequential (given that some minimal onset time data were included), depending on the level of precision and the type of analysis desired. An investigator may transform data that are represented in interval sequences into event sequential data, if he or she can argue that only the sequence of events, and not the duration, is of interest to the particular research question.

Commonly, couples researchers want to represent behavioral sequences in dual streams of behavior, one for each partner, particularly when the phenomena of interest involve simultaneous or overlapping behaviors from each spouse. For example, the following sequence of events may occur: while the wife proposes a solution to a problem, the husband begins to roll his eyes, but the wife continues anyway. There are several questions the investigator might ask in this situation: (a) Are husbands' eye rolls more likely after wives' solutions? (b) Do husbands' eye rolls tend to terminate constructive behaviors such as solutions, agreement, and so forth? (c) Are couples who tend to show these patterns more likely to be seeking treatment? Each of the sequential data types—event, state, timed, and interval—can be represented in dual streams of behavior (or more) and capture these types of data. Some specific data types might handle some questions better than others; for example, the second question listed earlier (Do husbands' eye rolls tend to terminate constructive behaviors such as solutions, agreements, and so forth?), might require timed event sequential level data because of the need to consider information about the termination, or offset, of the wives' constructive behavior in the data.

Behavior in couples' interaction samples are sometimes simultaneously coded in several ways: by use of discrete behaviors, by rating scale (e.g., affective intensity), or by another qualifier of specific type of events (e.g., a successful vs. unsuccessful interruption). This has been described as the coding of *cross-classified* events (Bakeman & Gottman, 1997). Using cross-classified events can help answer questions about several characteristics of a particular behavior of interest. Walsh, Baucom, Tyler, and Sayers (1993) illustrated this approach in a study examining the verbal responses of 56 discordant couples in a task focusing on sharing feelings about changes spouses desired in themselves and in the partner. Walsh et al. (1993) were interested in whether several elements of these expressions may lead to negative or unempathic responses by the partner, including the skill of the expression, the focus of the expression (i.e., the self, partner, or the relationship), and the valence of the emotion or thought being expressed. Thus, each statement was coded using three types of ratings. The investigators found that skill was not an important element that predicted the negativity of the subsequent response, but that the focus of the statement (i.e., on the partner or the relationship), as well as the valence of the statement, was sequentially associated with a negative response. Cross-classifying the speakers' statements using multiple schemes made it possible to examine the separate contribution of each element of the statement to the response.

MAJOR TYPES OF OBSERVATIONAL DATA ANALYSIS STRATEGIES

Rates, Probabilities, and Durations

The analysis of base rates and similar types of indices focuses on the question of "how much" of a certain type of behavior is exhibited in a sample interaction. As shown in Table 4.1, a typical question addressed using base rate data might be, "Do discordant spouses (husbands or wives) criticize more than do nondiscordant spouses?" This type of question, however, can be operationalized using an index of total frequencies, rates per time period (e.g., per minute), probabilities, or average durations or lengths of utterance of the behaviors. After selection of one of these indices, the usual procedure is then to use another data analytic method such as analysis of variance (Wickens, 1993) or correlation- or multiple regression-based method to answer specific research questions.

Frequencies of coded data are simply counts of specific kinds of codes that occurred during the sample of interaction coded. Frequencies are usually converted to rates per unit of time to compare data collected from different individuals and dyads over variable lengths of interaction durations. If the data being analyzed are of the event sequential type, the investigator can then divide by the total duration of the interaction, assuming this information is available. Often the most useful unit with which to express this index is rate per minute. If the data are of the interval sequential type, it is possible to provide an approximation of rate by dividing the total number of occurrences by the number of intervals for the time unit desired. For example, if the data are recorded and analyzed in 15-sec intervals, then dividing the number of intervals with a specific behavior by the total number of full or partial minutes would provide an approximate rate per minute. This assumes, of course, that coding rules for the system prevented the recording of single occurrences of specific behaviors more than once if the behavior extended beyond a single interval. Event-based rates can also be obtained from timed event sequential data by counting the number of onsets of a specific behavior as the numerator of the rate computation, although timed event sequential data can be used to obtain more refined indices as described later.

In addition to rates, probabilities are also used to describe observational data. Probabilities can be either event-based or time-based. Thus with event sequential data type, dividing the number of events coded a particular way by the total number of events coded yields the event-based proportion or probability. Thus, event- based probabilities show the proportion of all events that were coded for a particular type of event. Alternately, multiplying the proportion by 100 yields the percentage for a particular type of event. When using event-based probabilities, the rules for the coding system must define a set of mutually exclusive and exhaustive codes and coding rules. Under this condition, every event corresponds to only one code and every event is coded. This ensures that within each interaction, the sum of the spouse's individual codes will equal and not exceed the total number of coded events.

Time-based probabilities and percentages for specific behaviors can be derived if time information for the coded behavioral data is available, such as when using state sequential, timed event sequential, and interval sequential data. Dividing the amount of time coded a particular way by the total observation time yields a time-based probability for that behavior. As in the case discussed earlier, multiplying the quotient by 100 yields the percentage of time coded a particular way. Time information can either be measured through the onset and offset times of events, or approximated through coding intervals. Time-based probabilities are approximated when using intervals because one must make the implicit assumption that the behavior occurred for the entire interval. Accordingly, this assumption is most appropriate when the typical length of utterance is approximately the same duration as the chosen time interval. Contrasting with data that yields event-based probabilities, codes need not be mutually exclusive and exhaustive when using time-based probabilities. The advantage of time-based probabilities and percentages is that the overall amount of time spouses spend exhibiting a specific type of behavior is captured best for situations in which the number of events and their duration vary widely across spouses.

In addition to rates and probabilities, the mean durations of behaviors can also be used to describe observational data when time information has been recorded during the coding process. Dividing the amount of time coded for a particular type of event or state by the number of times that particular event or state was coded yields the mean duration. Mean durations might convey useful information where the number of critical comments, for example, do not differ across couples, but their length does. Like rates and probabilites, mean durations may also be used as a score for traditional analysis of variance or in correlation- or regression-based analyses.

Rates, probabilities, and mean event durations convey similar and related information; reporting all three indices would be redundant, as the value for any one of these can be deduced by the values for the other two. Investigators can consider the strengths and limitations mentioned earlier in considering which one or two indices to utilize.

Sequential Analyses

Transitions. Traditional sequential analysis, often known as lag-sequential analysis, deals with a fundamental question: Given that behavior A just occurred, does behavior B occur more often than expected? This is essentially a question about the strength of the sequential pattern of behavior A followed by B, assessed across a sample of discussion behavior between spouses. Investigators have used the question of sequential pattern in various ways. One of the most common has been to examine whether spouses reciprocate negative behavior.

Using our simplified 5-code system described earlier (C = Complaint, P = Problem Solving, S = Support, I = Invalidation, O = Other), we illustrate how we might determine whether reciprocation of negative behavior is occurring. Again, we code for the identity of the speaker using “h” or “w.” In this example, spouses' codes are assigned on the basis of homogeneous content, and a spouse may receive two or more codes in a row with no code exhibited by the same person repeating itself. If we can suppose that this discussion continues for about 200 coded behaviors, we can imagine that there are a number of times that the husband responds to the wife's Complaint with Complaint (i.e., Cw → Ch). Specific sequences have often been referred to as transitions of one behavior to another, and the frequency of such occurrences is known as the transitional frequency (Bakeman & Gottman, 1997). How do we tally the number of transitions of a specific type? Imagine a moving window of two-behavior sequences, as depicted later. We count each type of sequence bracketed as indicated and then move the window one behavior over. Thus, every behavior (except the initial spouse statement) is the second behavior of the two-behavior sequence, and then it becomes the first behavior as the window moves over.

Spouse:	H	W	H	H	W	W	H	W	H	W	W	H		Sequence
Code:	Ph	Cw	Ch	Ph	Ph	Sw	Oh	Pw	Ih	Cw	Ow	Ph	...	Tallied
First tally:	└	┘												Ph→Cw
Second tally:		└	┘											Cw→Ch
Third tally:			└	┘										Ch→Ph

The first element of our sequence Cw →Ch of interest is called the given behavior, and the second the target behavior (also referred to as the antecedent and consequent behaviors, respectively). When the focus here is on the given behavior followed immediately by the target, with no intervening events, it has classically been called an analysis of lag-1 events (Sackett, 1979). Note that there are always (N–1) 2 behavior sequences in a list of N coded behaviors, because the last behavior has no behavior to follow it.

The transitional frequency itself does not immediately tell us, however, whether the target behavior occurs more often than expected when following the given behavior. Constructing a 2 × 2 transition table, or contingency table, for a particular couple, as shown in Fig. 4.1, helps us discuss this issue more clearly. For this example, let us assume that all of the spouses' verbal behaviors in their videotaped discussion has been coded using the scheme described earlier—the mutually

Given Codes	Target Codes: Ch	Target Codes: ~Ch	
Cw	a 30	b 20	50
~Cw	c 40	d 109	149
	70	129	199

FIG. 4.1. Complaint-wife (Cw), Wife's non-Complaint & all of husband's codes (~Cw), Complaint-husband (Ch), husband's non-Complaint & all of wife's codes (~Ch)

exclusive and exhaustive assumption. The first row in Fig. 4.1 represents the tallies of the wife's behavior coded as Complaint, and the second row is the wife's behaviors coded in categories that are not Complaint and the tally of all the husband's behaviors (i.e., labeled ~Cw). Similarly, the columns represent the frequency of Complaint behavior of the husband, or alternatively, all other behaviors on the part of the wife or husband. Following statistical precedent, we have labeled the cells *a*, *b*, *c*, and *d*. Cell a holds the frequency of the transition frequency of interest. For the data in Fig. 4.1, this frequency is 30. How do we know if this transition occurs more often than expected, signifying a sequential connection between wife's Complaint behavior and the husband's Complaint response? There have been several approaches to examining this question.

One way we can describe the sequential connection in a particular transition is the transitional probability. The transitional probability has traditionally been called the conditional probability, because the probability of a target behavior is calculated conditional on the prior occurrence of the given behavior. The sum of the cells a and b is the total number of times the wife's behavior was coded Complaint, and can be seen as the opportunity for the husband's response behavior to be coded as Complaint, following his wife's Complaint. Thus, in 30 cases (cell *a*), the husband responded with behavior coded as Complaint. The formula, and the value for the transitional probability of our sequence, is the following: $a / (a + b) = 30 / (30 + 20) = .60$. This has some descriptive use because it expresses the probability of the husband responding in a particular way given the opportunity. Its use is limited, however, by the fact that it does not express the degree to which the transition is expected. Stated in another way, the transitional probability for the Complaint-w→Complaint-h transition can be affected solely by the probability of husband's Complaint, in that the more numerous the husband's Complaint behaviors are, the higher the frequency in cell *a* is likely to be (and cell *c*, which we are ignoring for now). There is a similar effect with the overall probability of the wife's Complaint behavior, which also affects the probability of the Complaint-w→ Complaint-h transition.

Yule's Q: An Index Based on the Odds Ratio. The most useful indices that directly address our question of the expected occurrence of transitions are all based on the odds ratio, which is usually estimated as follows, using the notation from Fig. 4.1: $(a/b) / (c/d)$. Multiplying numerator and denominator by d/c yields the following computational formula: ad / bc. The odds ratio is in broad use in a variety of fields, such as in clinical epidemiological to express the increased risk of a particular outcome when a specific condition or circumstance is true (i.e., increased risk of cancer with [vs. without] exposure to a putative carcinogen). For the current context, we focus on Yule's *Q*, a derivative of the odds ratio. It is computationally related to the odds ratio and log odds, and has the advantage of being more readily interpreted by investigators. Yule's *Q* is easily computed in the following manner:

$$\text{Yule's } Q = \frac{ad - bc}{ad + bc}.$$

Similar to the Pearson correlation coefficient, Yule's *Q* has a mean of zero and varies from −1 to +1, indicating the strength and direction of the sequential association between the two behaviors. Stated another way, negative values indicate that the target behavior occurred less often than expected given the antecedent behavior and positive values indicate that the target occurs more often given the antecedent behavior. A value of zero indicates no sequential relation between the two behaviors, or that the target behavior occurs neither more nor less often than expected given the antecedent behavior. Note that if cells *a* or *d*, and *b* or *c*, are zero, Yule's *Q* cannot be computed. Using the transition table in Fig. 4.1, Yule's $Q = .607$.

How do we use Yule's *Q* to answer questions about sequential association? The index can be calculated for each couple's data, and used in tests of differences between groups labeled maritally distressed versus nondistressed, or used in correlation- or regression-based methods. For example, Sayers, Baucom, Sher, Weiss, and Heyman (1991) used Yule's *Q* to examine evidence that maritally discordant spouses treated with behavioral marital therapy (BMT) learned to engage their partners constructively by responding to nonconstructive behavior (e.g., criticize, put-down) by being problem-focused (e.g., disagree, positive solution). Sayers et al. (1991) also tested whether changes in the strength of this sequential pattern were associated with increases in marital satisfaction. Videotaped samples of problem-solving discussions for 60 treatment or wait-list control couples were coded using the MICS-IV. One of the sequences of interest included the transition of nonconstructive to problem-focused problem-solving behavior—each of the types of behavior consisted of several MICS-IV codes and constructed on an a priori basis. Scores for each of the couples were used in a MANOVA of two such functional wife → husband sequences, finding that husbands were less likely to respond to their wives' nonconstructive behavior with problem-focused behavior after therapy than before (Yule's Q pretherapy $M = -.35$, post-therapy $M = -.64$). Although it was not surprising that husbands responded to wives' nonconstructive behavior less than expected with problem-focused behavior before treatment, it was a surprise to see this index decline even more after treatment. To examine this further, Sayers et al. (1991) used the Yule's Q index for nonconstructive-W→ problem-focused-H transition in an analysis of residualized change in marital satisfaction over the course of treatment. Indeed, this sequence was positively associated with improvements in wives' marital satisfaction, pretreatment to posttreatment, which suggested that the nonconstructive-W→problem-focused-H transition was functional. The finding that the index may show an overall decline as a function of treatment led the investigators to speculate about the potential negative implications of BMT as an intervention.

A consideration of the value of Yule's Q under a variety of scenarios shows both the strengths and the weaknesses of our sequential data analysis methods, particularly under low frequency conditions. In general, the frequency of both the given and target behaviors affect the value of the index of sequential connection. It is also important to keep in mind that cells with a frequency of zero create extreme values on Yule's Q (see Bakeman, McArthur, and Quera, 1996, for an illustration of this). This result is more likely when there are relatively fewer behaviors coded.

Other Indices of Sequential Connection and Their Evaluation. Early sequential analysis methods focused to a great extent on indices based on the conditional probability, such as the z score. Sackett (1979) advocated the use of the z score, using the normal approximation for the binomial test, although Allison and Liker (1982) later recommended a modified formula. The bottom line, however, is that the z score has a fundamental limitation for our use in sequential analysis, as the z score increases as the number of total tallies of events increases. When z scores are computed within each couple, it reflects both the number of total tallies, as well as the strength of the sequential association of interest. The z score, therefore, is not comparable across couples when used in this way.

Two other indices of sequential association that are similar to Yule's Q bear mention. Transformed kappa (Wampold, 1989) and phi (Bakeman, McArthur, & Quera; 1996; Cohen & Cohen, 1983) also have been promoted as indices of sequential association, and range from -1 to $+1$, with zero indicating no association. Like Yule's Q, they are not affected by the total number of tallies and are computationally very similar to it. However, under identical conditions (i.e., the same set of transition tables), phi results in less extreme values than Yule's *Q*. On the other hand, transformed kappa yields somewhat different rank orders from Yule's *Q* and phi. Transformed kappa has another undesirable quality—in contrast to Yule's *Q* and phi, it is negatively biased, it has a mode greater than zero, and it has a negative skew. Also, in situations in which the target behavior is twice as numerous in one group than another, phi might yield group differences whereas Yule's *Q* and transformed kappa may not (see Bakeman et al., 1996, pp. 450–451, for a full discussion of how this may occur; see also Yoder & Feuer, 2000). In the final analysis, either Yule's *Q* or phi appears to be the best choice as an index of sequential connection.

Log-Linear Methods of Data Analysis. There are more complex questions that often interest couples researchers, such as whether there is a stronger association of husband to wife Complaint → Complaint sequences compared to wife to husband sequences. From another perspective, this analysis permits us to extend analysis of the two-way (2 × 2) transition tables as depicted in Fig. 4.1, to a three-way question. In this three-way table, the third factor is the identity (husband vs. wife) of the spouse emitting the target behavior in the sequence: 2 (given C, ~C) × 2 (target C, ~C) × 2 (target behavior, husband vs. wife). The benefits of using the log-linear approach to this type of question include the following: (a) the methods have been very well developed, (b) the methods are commonly available in major statistical packages, and (c) the methods do not carry the distributional assumptions implied when using traditional analysis of variance or multiple regression or correlation methods.

We describe the logic and approach of the analysis using our question posed earlier regarding Complaint→Complaint sequences although leaving many of the details to other sources (See Bakeman, Adamson, & Strisik, 1989; Bakeman & Quera, 1995b; Bakeman & Robinson, 1994). The log-linear approach is based on the idea of testing the predicted cell tallies in the n-way table against the observed data using a chi-square test. At the most general level is the null model, which generates equal values for every cell based on the total number of tallies. A test of this model against the observed data likely generates a significant, but uninteresting, chi-square value. Next, entered are the terms for the "main effects" of given behavior, target behavior, and direction of the transition based on which spouse produced the target behavior. Thus, another chi-square value is generated based on the main effects model from the differences between predicted and observed values in the cells of the table. One then proceeds to the higher-order terms (two- and three-way interactions) that address more interesting questions. The primary question of interest lies in whether the incremental chi-square test associated with the three-way interaction is significant. If so, this indicates that there is a difference in Complaint sequences based on whether one is referring to the husband → wife or the wife → husband sequence. A comparison of odds ratios or Yule's *Q* associated with subtables (husband → wife or wife → husband) would reveal the nature of the difference.

It is useful to understand that the 2 × 2 transition table is a collapsed version of a 10 × 10 table that includes the husband's five codes and wife's five codes. It is possible to collapse this larger table into various 2 × 2 tables focusing on specific transitions of interest, each with a specific behavior from one spouse as the given behavior, and a specific response behavior from the partner as the target behavior. It is important to review this circumstance to examine two different computational models used when conducting sequential analysis using a log-linear approach. The way that the data stream for our example is constructed, and the way that our coding system rules are defined, each code cannot be followed by itself. In other words, there is no circumstance that allows the sequence, Cw → Cw. This produces what is called *structural zeros* such that a zero tally is required for some of the cells. In a 10 × 10 table of all the transitions of a husband's and wife's codes, the structural zeros would be on the diagonal. This situation necessitates some alternations in the computation of some indices of sequential association, accomplished easily by the data analysis programs developed by Bakeman and Quera (1995a). We describe later other data analysis situations that do not result in structural zeros.

In one type of log-linear analysis called a logit model, the response (or "dependent") variable is segregated from the predictors (or "independent") variables, which may aid in interpretation when a specific response is of interest. For example, as described earlier, Walsh et al. (1993) were interested in the predictors of negative spouse responses during an interaction task. Log-linear models are particularly useful in the analysis of these cross-classified events, which were discussed earlier.

An analysis of sequences longer than two events can be examined using log-linear analyses, although data demands rise exponentially. Fortunately, Bakeman and Quera (1995b) have described a set of procedures for reducing data demands by first testing for more complex effects, describing the effects, or then collapsing across multiway tables if the effects are not significant. There are other methods for examining longer sequences of behavior (e.g., Hooley & Hahlweg, 1989; Revenstorf, Hooley, & Hahlweg, 1989), although they carry with them several liabilities as well, including the practice of aggregating data across couples (discussed later), and the reliance on indices such as the conditional probability.

Time-Series Analyses. The use of time-series analysis allows us to test a number of other notions we might have about couples' interactions. Traditional time-series analysis uses many data points of relatively continuously or discretely collected data across time. In the present context, the data used are often some index of the degree of negativity present in the interaction at any given point of time. It is possible to use indices that represent other theoretically important dimensions, as well, such as the degree of "demand" (i.e., requesting or pressing for change in the marriage) and a second dimension that reflects the degree of withdrawal from the discussion. Time-series analysis can also be used with continuous affect ratings from an electronic dial, made by a spouse who is watching a videotape of the couple's problem-solving discussion (Gottman & Levenson, 1992).

What questions about couples' interactions can be best answered using time series analysis? It is important first to note that time series methods may be used in several ways for different goals. One useful goal might be to examine the effect of certain powerful but low-frequency events on the series of data, called *interrupted time-series analysis* or *impact analysis* (Yaffee, 2000). For example, an investigator may wish to examine whether a verbal threat from one partner at one point in the interaction leads to substantially greater withdrawal from interaction in the other partner. Fig. 4.2 illustrates an example of this effect using hypothetical data. The interrupted time-series analysis examines the differences in mean level before the threat, to the mean level after the event. These mean levels are symbolized using the horizontal lines across the series as it varies across the graph. A mean level change in a series is only one of several types of changes that may occur due to the effect of some event. Gottman (1981) described other types of changes after the event for which one might test—a change in direction of the series, a change in variability, decaying changes, accelerated changes, and so forth.

Another use of time-series analysis in the context of couples' interaction data is to develop a model that reflects the communication processes that underlie the data, and then determine whether it reflects marital dysfunction. For example, an

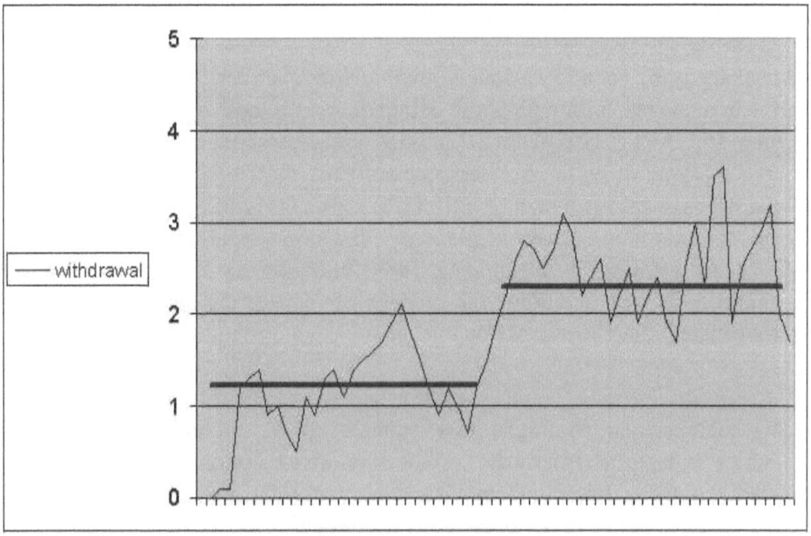

FIG. 4.2. A hypothetical graph of withdrawal levels for an interrupted time-series analysis.

investigator may hypothesize that the affect of one spouse in a communication task may be "driving" the affect of the other; as one spouse becomes more negative, then the partner's communications become more negative. This is tested by comparing the cross-correlations of two data streams for, say a husband's value at time t to predict the wife's value at time t+1, and the wife's values at time t used to predict the husband's values at t+1. If there is an asymmetry in predictability, with the husband's values predicting the wife's values at the next time point more closely than the wife's data predicting the husband's values (at the next time point), then this is an illustration of interactional dominance (Gottman, 1979). Note also that the use of the term *dominance* in this context is highly specific and is used in a different sense than in the literature examining marital equality (c.f. Gray-Little, Baucom, & Hamby, 1996).

Those readers interested in pursuing time-series analyses might consult several sources. Yaffee (2000) provided a good introductory but technical volume on time-series; the benefit of this book is that it provides data analysis code for two widely available statistical packages, the Statistical Analysis System (SAS; SAS Institute Inc., 1992), and the Statistical Package for the Social Sciences (SPSS; SPSS, Inc., 2003). The Yaffee (2000) volume, however, did not extensively address cross-correlation in time-series when there are two series, one for the husband and one for the wife. Gottman (1981) provided a highly useful and relevant introduction to the use of time-series in the context of couples' interactions, and also provided a set of computer programs tailored to this content area (Williams & Gottman, 1981).

Gottman and colleagues have developed a mathematical and theoretical model of marital interaction that illustrates the potential usefulness of times-series models. Their model (Gottman, Swanson, & Murray, 1999) entails the prediction of values from several parameters of a times-series that represented coding of spouses' expressions of positive and negative affect. These parameters include those that represents the spouses' individual steady state levels of negativity, uninfluenced by the other spouse, and parameters that reflect spouses' steady state levels of negativity, influenced by the other spouse. Also estimated by the model is the threshold at which one spouse's values of negativity at time t+1 are predicted by the other spouse's values of negativity at time t. Threshold, in this context, refers to the level of time t negativity required in one spouse to be predictive of time t+1 in the other spouse. Gottman et al. (1999) reported, for example, that the level of both husbands' and wives' uninfluenced steady state parameters in the interactions of newlywed couples predicted the risk of divorce at 3 to 6 years. In addition, newlywed couples that eventually divorced had a negativity threshold that was more negative compared to those that did not divorce (i.e., their husbands had to be much more negative before getting a response from their partners). The details of conducting these analyses are beyond the scope of this chapter; however, consult Cook et al. (1995) for a description of this approach.

OTHER IMPORTANT CONSIDERATIONS FOR SEQUENTIAL DATA ANALYSIS

How Much Data Should One Have for Data Analysis?

There have been few attempts to provide systematic guidelines about the question of whether one has enough data for proceeding with the analysis of observational data. Following Waters (1978), Heyman, Chaudhry, et al. (2001) described the problem of how much data are needed for reliable estimates of base rates of specific behaviors in relation to one's observed level of reliability. Because longer behavioral samples and more numerous observations of each code can lead to higher reliability indices for a given code in a given coding system, then the task becomes to conduct reliability analyses and work backward to the length of interaction one would want to have collected for a target reliability figure. Using the RMICS, which records data on an interval basis, Heyman, Chaudhry, et al. (2001) described the use of the Spearman–Brown correlation for obtaining split-half reliability of a measure using odd and even time intervals as one would use odd and even items on a self-report measure. Using the reliability for the full observational sample calculated using this split-half approach, then one can calculate a "multiplier" which specifies how many times longer the length of the behavior needs to be for the desired reliability level. In their illustration with the RMICS, Heyman, Chaudhry, et al. (2001) showed that with the obtained and desired reliability figures of .6 and .9, respectively, then an investigator would need to increase a 10-min interaction by six times to reach the desired reliability of .9. Thus, with an observed reliability of .6, the investigator would have to obtain 60-min videotape samples to have adequate samples for data analysis. Heyman, Chaudhry, et al. (2001) reported (split-half) interval-based reliabilities for the base rates of RMICS behaviors that were primarily greater than .90 for 15-min behavioral samples, although reliabilities for low-frequency codes tended to go much lower or could not be estimated.

It should be noted, however, that split-half reliability estimates for the base rates of a set of codes are not the same as the reliability estimates among a set of coders, which are usually of more concern for investigators. Moreover, there is no adjustment in the approach described earlier for degrees of unreliability of different coders, which should surely attenuate the ability of investigators to detect replicable findings for behavioral sample of a given length of time.

The problems of unreliability on estimates of sequential coding can be severe. Gardner (1995) illustrated a problem inherent in the familiar Cohen's kappa statistic used to estimate reliability of judgments about base rates to begin with—kappa is affected not only by the accuracy of coders but also on the base rates of the behaviors that are coded. Furthermore, divergent base rates between given and target codes in an index of sequential connection affect the estimates of the reliability of that index. Extending Gardner's work, Bakeman, Quera, McArthur, and Robinson

(1997) showed, using a statistical simulation, that even a Yule's *Q* value that indicates a strong underlying sequential connection (i.e., .90) can degrade quickly, under certain circumstances. Specifically, they showed that the worst conditions for estimating Yule's *Q* include situations in which the number of codes in the system are relatively few, and the disparity in the underlying base rates between behaviors in the sequential index is very wide. On the positive side, Bakeman et al. (1997) also showed that under these unfavorable conditions, Yule's *Q* tends to be attenuated, but the index does not reverse direction (i.e., wherein Yule's *Q* would become negative when the true association is positive).

There are several guidelines that investigators can follow for judging whether they have adequate amounts of data for sequential analysis. Bakeman (2000) described a relatively arbitrary rule of the thumb approach—one should not calculate an index of sequential connection if the marginal sums of the rows and columns of the transition table do not equal at least 5. Another set of criteria is based on guidelines used when one makes an inference from the table, such as when determining the significance of chi-square from a contingency table (Wickens, 1989). First, expected frequencies for each of the cells in 2 x 2 tables should be greater than 2 or 3, although the expected values for larger tables may be closer to 1 in 20% of the cells. Second, the total number of tallies should be at least 4 to 5 times the number of cells. Bakeman and Gottman (1997) noted that one should not simply exceed these minimums, but attempt to exceed them by as wide a margin as possible.

To Aggregate or Not to Aggregate?

Thus far, we have discussed sequential indices calculated on the data from individual couples. We have recommended that these indices are submitted to a standard method of analysis to detect group differences (Wickens, 1993) or examined for their association with indices of couple- or individual-level differences (i.e., marital satisfaction, level of femininity). Other investigators have aggregated, or pooled, couples' data primarily as a way to increase the number of data points analyzed when examining sequence lengths greater than two events (e.g., Hooley & Hahlweg, 1989; Revenstorf, Hahlweg, Schindler, & Vogel, 1984). The usual objection to aggregating arises from the inability to understand how individual differences present among the "units"(i.e., couples) being analyzed may affect the findings (Bakeman & Gottman, 1997). In some cases, the couples that contribute many data points might have an unrepresentative impact on the findings simply because more distinct turns in speech occurred for those couples. In the context of couple interactions, it is probably safe to assume substantial between-couple variability on key variables. At the very least, if broad differences in proportions or sequences of interest among couples thought to be similar are apparent (i.e., distressed couples in a study show widely different levels of negativity), an investigator might well avoid aggregation for sequential data analysis.

Methods of Constructing Transition Tables: Data Representations Revisited

There are many paths from the point of data collection to the transition table. As described earlier, data collected using one data type, say interval sequential data, may be transformed into another type for reasons specific to the question at hand. Some of the decisions made by coding system developers that affect the type of questions one asks, or can ask, deserve some discussion.

Consider the sequence of codes presented in our earlier example in the section "Sequential Analyses." The behaviors in that interaction sequence were assembled assuming that no code follows itself, resulting in structural zeros in the full 10 x 10 transition table as described earlier in the section on log-linear methods. Another feature of this sequence is that a behavior of one spouse can immediately follow another behavior by that same spouse. However, it is not possible to examine the behavior of the spouse who does not "have the floor," because no "listener" behavior is represented. Imagine that the investigator has constructed a coding system in which there is listener behavior with three valences—Listener Positive (LP), Listener Negative (or "minus," LM), and Listener Neutral (LN)—is also coded, and spouses' behaviors are recorded in dual streams, as follows:

Speaker:	H	W	H	H	W	W	H	W	H	W	W	H	
H codes:	Ph	LMh	Ch	Ph	LPh	Lh	Oh	LNh	Ih	LNh	LNh	Ph	...
W codes:	LNw	Cw	LMw	LPw	Pw	Sw	LPw	Pw	LMw	Cw	Ow	LPw	...

Each pair of simultaneous speaker–listener codes forms a unit (such as the "Dyadic Behavior Units" or DBUs, formed with the MICS-IV system; Weiss, 1992). It is possible to test more complex hypotheses about the sequential association of spouses' simultaneous behaviors and one partner's subsequent response. For example, an investigator might be interested in testing whether negative listeners of negative behavior turn into negative speakers (see Table 4.1). One might want to examine the sequential association between the wife's Complaint behavior, while the husband listens with negative nonverbal behavior (i.e., at lag 0), and the husband's subsequent Complaint response (i.e., at lag 1). The prototypical transition of interest appears in the shaded portion of the diagram shown earlier. This type of analysis is accomplished straightforwardly using the log-linear methods described earlier. From a transition table perspective, this multiway table would be described as follows: 2 (lag 0: Cw/~ Cw) × 2 (lag 0: Lmh/~ Lmh) × 2 (lag 1: Ch/~Ch).

The different views described earlier both utilize event sequential data, but a more complex set of circumstances arises when the interaction is recorded using timed event sequential data. The use of timed event sequential data also allows the investigator to tailor the construction of a transition table to the specific needs of the research question when one is using Bakeman and Quera's (1995a) program GSEQ. A bit of syntax from Bakeman and Quera's SDIS and GSEQ programs are presented for this illustration.

The interaction sequence discussed earlier may be descriptively presented as follows:

Husband's data stream: ├─Ch─┤ ├─Lmh─┤ ├─Ch─┤ ├──Ph──┤ ├─Lph───┤...
1"–6" 6"–9" 9"–14" 14"–23" 23"–30"

Wife' data stream: ├──Lnw─┤ ├──Cw───┤ ├─Lmw─┤ ├─Lpw───┤ ├─Pw─┤...
1"–5" 5"–11" 11"–16" 16"–24" 24"–30"

This dual-stream representation of a couple's behavior could be recorded using SDIS syntax as a timed event sequence in the following way (Bakeman & Quera, 1995a): Ch,1–6; Lmh, 6–9; Ch, 9–14; Ph, 14–23; Lph, 23–30; & Lnw, 1–5; Cw, 5–11; Lmw, 11–16; Lpw, 16–24; Pw, 24–30 (the "&" allows for reading and storing of time codes in the second stream for which the timing overlaps with those in the first, a situation that usually prompts an error condition in SDIS). Coding and recording the data in this form provides several opportunities, most notably the definition of a new type of event based on a time window. Suppose, for example, that an investigator believes that the important aspect of "Complaint" reciprocity is a response from the other spouse within 5 sec of the beginning of a Complaint. Thus, using the WINDOW command in GSEQ, the investigator could define the given behavior of interest as the onset of the Wife's Complaint plus 5 sec, calling this new code "wComplaint5." After this redefinition, using GSEQ, it is then possible to construct the transition table using wComplaint5 as the given behavior, and the onset of the husband's complaint as the target behavior. For purposes of our transition table, GSEQ will make a tally for every onset of a husband's Complaint behavior coded during the 5-sec window starting with the onset of the wife's Complaint behavior code. One such window is depicted in the shadowed portion of the data stream shown earlier. There is a range of other possibilities. The window might be defined as the duration of the wife's complaint behavior plus 5 sec, or 5 sec after the offset of the wife's Complaint behavior, and so on. Depending on how the husband→wife or wife→husband sequences were defined, there are many types of tables that do not result in structural zeros in the resulting transition tables. See Bakeman and Quera (1995a) for a complete description of data analysis procedures and the syntax used. Ideally, an investigator would determine optimal windows during a piloting phase of the research, so that data analysis could be conducted on a dataset without testing a variety of windows on the same dataset.

SUMMARY AND CONCLUSIONS

Summary

This chapter has focused on the forms in which observational data are stored and the major strategies for analyzing observational data. These forms of data representation, usefully defined by Bakeman and Quera (1995a) and titled as the "Sequential Data Interchange Standard," include event sequential data, state sequential data, interval sequential data, and timed event sequential data. It is often possible to transform data recorded in one SDIS data type to another, to simplify data analysis, or to ask research questions more suited to a different type of data. Data analyses of rates, probabilities, or average durations of behaviors address the basic question of "how much" of specific types of behaviors occur in a couple's sample of communication. The use of one or the other of the indices just listed may depend on the type of data available, the investigator's needs, and other constraints.

Sequential analysis often addresses the subsequent likelihood of specific types of target behaviors, taking into account the occurrence of a given behavior. These patterns are often examined for series of two behavior sequences in streams of data for behaviors that occur over time. It is possible, however, to examine questions for sequences longer than two behaviors, although the demands for the amount of data needed rise exponentially. In this way, sequential analysis addresses the question of the connection of two behaviors occurring in the interaction unfolding between two spouses. Because we may detect a statistical relation between two types of behaviors, we cannot conclude that the first type of behavior causes the second. We can, however, identify meaningful sequences of behavior that are associated with relation dysfunction in the present, or in the future.

Yule's Q and phi have emerged as particularly useful indices of the strength of sequential connection between two behaviors for several reasons—they are easily interpretable, unbiased, and unaffected by the number of tallies that are entered into the analysis. Most questions involving sequential analysis also can be approached using log-linear data analysis methods. The advantages of log-linear analyses include the following: (a) that problems and solutions for these methods have been well developed, (b) that they accommodate sequences longer than two behaviors, and (c) that they also can handle cross-classified events, wherein an event is coded or rated on more than one dimension. Time-series analyses also address the interrelation of spouses' verbal or affective behavior across time. Time-series analyses, however, require ratings based on a continuum or dimension, such as ratings of the intensity of negative affect.

Weaknesses in the Analysis of Observational Data

There are other procedures still in use that have significant limitations, including the use of the z score for determining the strength of sequential connection. Values of the z score are clearly understood to reflect both the strength of sequential connection as well as the total number of tallies entering into the analysis. Also, given the need for greater stability of sequential indices, some investigators aggregate data across couples within groups (i.e., for distressed vs. nondistressed comparisons). Many couples researchers recognize, however, that couples exhibit significant heterogeneity in their interactional styles, so that aggregation potentially masks important variation.

Unexplored Areas

The reader now likely sees the flexibility of the different forms in which observational data can be recorded and represented for analysis, as well as the possible effects that these forms have on the conclusions drawn from the analysis. This is perhaps the least examined issue in the analysis of observational data. Some of the decisions of data recording are made by the coding system developers; other decisions are made after data are recorded, by transforming data from one type to another (e.g., , interval sequential data to event sequential data). Investigators are encouraged to examine the effects of the data type (i.e., event sequential data vs. time event sequential data) on the results by testing several data representations. The general effects of a decision to represent and analyze data one way versus another are difficult to predict. The bottom line is that investigators should understand the nature of the phenomena they are examining and use the methods that preliminary observation and analysis suggests would best help answer their question.

Conclusions

Many methods are available for the data analysis of observational data. Selecting and mastering the techniques in this form of data analysis can be daunting. Careful study of this chapter and the resources cited here give the investigator with no previous exposure a start on learning these methods. In addition, there are many decisions the developer of a coding system may make that have an impact on the analyses conducted. It is best for an investigator to have the most important research questions clearly in mind before proceeding with data analysis. Sequential analyses, however, also can be used in a more exploratory fashion in areas with little previous existing empirical research as a way to generate hypotheses about a phenomenon. The widespread availability of videotape, computer, and software resources make the analysis of observational data especially accessible and rewarding to couples researchers.

II

Problem Solving and Communication

5

Rapid Marital Interaction Coding System (RMICS)

Richard E. Heyman
State University of New York at Stony Brook

The Rapid Marital Interaction Coding System (RMICS) is an event-based system designed to code observed dyadic behavior. Behavior is defined broadly to include all observable actions (i.e., affective, motoric, paralinguistic, and linguistic). The RMICS was designed to measure frequencies of behavior and behavioral patterns (i.e., sequences) between intimate partners during conflicts. As is discussed later, the RMICS is the second-generation extension of the Marital Interaction Coding System (MICS), the oldest and most widely used couples observational system (Heyman, 2001). The RMICS has been used in approximately 20 separate investigations with a range of ages (primarily adult married couples, but also preteen siblings, high school dating couples, and engaged couples), populations (e.g., general married population, marital clinics, cancer patients and their spouses, families at risk for adolescent drug abuse, Vietnam veterans), and research purposes.

THEORETICAL FOUNDATIONS

As a descendent of the early MICS coding system, the RMICS shares most of the theoretical precepts that inform both the MICS itself and the paradigm that evolved to evoke the behaviors operationalized in the MICS. To understand these precepts, however, one should understand the scientific zeitgeist that existed during the MICS's conception.

Prior to the late 1960s, the dominant approach to couple and family problems was psychodynamic (with the nascent family systems approach beginning to garner attention). During the behavioral revolution of the 1960s, clinically-oriented researchers began investigations that fundamentally altered research and clinical practice in this area. Four facets of this research are noteworthy in understanding all coding systems that followed. First, as clinicians, their focus was on the etiology and maintenance of relationship dysfunction, not on the creation and nurturing of optimal relationship health. Second, as behaviorists, they held that clinical endeavors had to be founded on science, and that science required measurement, not inference. Thus, there was a heavy emphasis on both parsimony (i.e., observable, not inferred, concepts) and psychometric soundness (i.e., reliability and validity).

Third, they believed that each partner's pleasing and displeasing behaviors are shaped by the other's contingent responses (i.e., positive and negative reinforcement). Two implications for coding this worldview were as follows: (a) coded observations were likely a more valid measure of such patterns than were self-reports, because fine-grained assessment of behavioral frequency and patterns is beyond the capacity of most people (especially those already engaged in complex, on-going human interaction) and is subject to various heuristic biases; and (b) microanalytic coding systems, which could describe the stream of behaviors that could be subjected to sequential analysis, were preferable to global systems.

Finally, such systems were designed to be flexible tools to describe emitted behavior. As members of the original team wrote: "We were behaviorists and our strategy was to obtain data first and then develop a theory if one were justified" (Patterson, Reid, & Dishion, 1992, p. 1).

MICS: Development and Refinement of the First Generation System

The MICS was developed at the University of Oregon as a variant of the original Family Interaction Coding System (FICS). Rather than have the researchers dictate what behaviors to include in the FICS, a group led by Gerald Patterson let the behaviors dictate which should be included. Patterson (1982) has written about how he and his group observed families in their homes while wearing gas mask-like face mask microphones to narrate the behaviors of families in the home. The most common and/or theoretically important behaviors were included in the FICS. The MICS adapted FICS codes for use with couples.

In the late 1960s, Patterson and his colleagues, Robert L. Weiss and Robert C. Ziller, cleverly convinced the Office of Naval Research that marital conflict was a convenient way to study small group conflict relevant to naval vessels. Graduate students Hyman Hops, Thomas Wills, and Marion Forgatch were instrumental in the development and implementation of the first MICS. The original version of the

MICS (Hops, Wills, Weiss, & Patterson, 1972) was deposited with the National Auxiliary Publication Service in 1972.

Over the ensuing decades, with Robert L. Weiss solely directing the MICS, it underwent several revisions. MICS–II (1979) reflected the collaboration of Gayla Margolin and Gary Weider and included some changes in code definitions and usage. MICS–III (1983) reflected the collaboration of Darien Fenn and Kendra Summers. Changes (described in detail in Weiss & Summers, 1983) included splitting several codes, refining the way the MICS defined sequences, and declaring the primacy of behavior codes for use in sequential analyses (i.e., affect and form codes were ignored when coded in the same unit as behavior codes). Although the MICS had always coded behavior in dual, ongoing streams (see Fig. 5.1 for an example of a dual stream coded RMICS data sheet), MICS–III clarified how to organize such data. That is, statistics for four sets of sequences were produced: (a) Husband→Husband; (b) Wife→Wife; (c) Husband→Wife; (d) Wife→Husband. Taking into account the four sequences inherent in dual stream data obviated the need to artificially impose a single sequence of Husband→Wife→Husband→Wife ... on the data. MICS–IV (1989) reflected the collaboration of this author and J. Mark Eddy. Among other changes (described in detail in Heyman, Weiss, & Eddy, 1995) were the addition of withdrawal and dysphoric affect codes and the establishment of a hierarchy to select the most theoretically important code for sequential analysis (i.e., affect codes were no longer ignored when coded in the same unit as behavior codes).

The MICS and similar systems (e.g., Couples Interaction Scoring System, CISS, Gottman, 1979; Notarius & Markman, 1981; Kategoriensystem für partner- schaftliche Interaktion, KPI, Hahlweg, Reisner et al., 1984)[1] generated a substantial body of replicated findings. As part of a comprehensive review (Heyman, 2001), I recently summarized the literature as follows:

> Across coding systems, countries, studies, spouses, and researchers, several "stubborn facts" (Notarius & Markman, 1989) about observed couple processes have emerged: Distressed partners, compared with nondistressed partners (a) are more hostile, (b) start their conversations more hostilely and maintain it during the course of the conversation, (c) are more likely to reciprocate and escalate their partners' hostility, (d) are less likely to edit their behavior during conflict, resulting in longer negative reciprocity loops, (e) emit less positive behavior, (f) suffer more ill health effects from their conflicts, and (g) are more likely to show demand → withdrawal patterns. Furthermore, both partners in distressed relationships characterized by husband-to-wife aggression, compared with distressed/nonaggressive relationships, are more hostile and reciprocate hostility more. (p. 6)

The accomplishments of such microbehavioral systems notwithstanding, there are several serious problems with such systems. First, they are very expensive to

[1]Other than some differences in number and content of codes, the primary difference between the MICS and the CISS/KPI is that the latter code content and affect (positive, negative, neutral) separately, whereas the MICS embeds affective cues in its code definitions.

use, especially in terms of time and training. Coding a single 10-min interaction takes at least 1½ to 2 hr (Markman & Notarius, 1987), and coder training takes up to 6 months. Second, despite the enormous amount of effort expended, it is difficult, if not impossible, for observers to use 30 or more discrete codes reliably (i.e., Cohen's kappa = .28; Heyman, Vivian, Weiss, Hubbard, & Ayerle, 1993). Symptomatic of this, reliabilities of individual codes are almost never reported. Third, individual codes usually occur too rarely to analyze individually. Researchers thus combine codes into categories. However, there are almost as many ways of collapsing MICS codes as there are observational studies (Heyman, 2001). Thus, much of the coding effort is wasted by coding at the ultramicro level yet combining the codes for analysis (sometimes into only positive–negative– neutral categories). It would be far more efficient (and probably more reliable and valid) to code at the level of detail that one can analyze. Fourth, constructs are often not simply the sum of their parts. For example, when using an ultramicroanalytic system, a researcher must decide whether disagreement, all disagreement, is constructive or nonconstructive, because all instances of "disagreement" must be collapsed with other codes. An entire special issue of *Behavioral Assessment* (Sher & Weiss, 1991) was devoted to the vagaries of such "negative" behavior. Systems that measure constructs of interest, such as hostility, may be able to deal more parsimoniously with such issues than ultramicroanalytic systems because they can operationalize the construct (e.g., RMICS's hostility code) rather than arrive at the construct additively (e.g., a construct comprising MICS codes of put-down, criticize, negative voice tone, and disagree).

Global systems are on the opposite side of the continuum from ultramicroanalytic systems; during the 1980s, several were developed to provide fast ratings at the construct level (e.g., the MICS–Global, Weiss & Tolman, 1990; Rapid Couples Interaction Scoring System, Krokoff, Gottman, & Haas, 1989; Interactional Dimensions Coding System, Julien, Markman, & Lindahl, 1989). A strength of global systems is their use of the existing knowledge base to identify the core constructs on which to concentrate. Although faster in training and coding, global systems cannot provide information about behavioral patterns or sequences and typically demonstrate only modest reliabilities. Thus, Markman and Notarius (1989, p. 5) concluded that, "Despite the increasing popularity of global systems, we believe that the field of observational research can best progress by use of microanalytic strategies that have the potential, unlike global strategies, to reveal complex patterns of interaction that cannot be detected by human judges."

DEVELOPMENT OF THE CODING SYSTEM

Convinced that both ultramicroanalytic and global strategies have severe drawbacks, Dina Vivian and I set out to combine the advantages of the established ultramicroanalytic systems and their newer global offshoots while minimizing their drawbacks. For practical reasons, we believed that a system that was more efficient to train and to code than the established ultramicrobehavioral systems would represent a major improvement. We saw it as wasteful to train coders on more than 30 codes, only to collapse codes for any meaningful analysis. We believed that although such specificity was necessary at the dawn of microanalytic coding (i.e., when Patterson, Weiss, Gottman, and their students were first describing family dysfunction), it was now necessary to learn from that body of knowledge and create a streamlined system. We began with a factor analysis of 1,086 couples coded with the MICS (Heyman, Eddy, Weiss, & Vivian, 1995). This analysis suggested that the MICS comprised four factors. The first three (Hostility, Humor, and Constructive Problem Discussion or Solution) were suitable to use as coding constructs. The fourth factor, Discussing Responsibility, was seen as an example of the more mainstream construct of attributions. We drew on the literature on expressed attributions (Holtzworth–Munroe & Jacobson, 1988) and split this factor into distress-maintaining and relationship-enhancing attributions codes. Although positive codes failed to form a factor (perhaps because of their low base rates), we recognized their theoretical importance and included two codes from the KPI, self-disclosure and acceptance. Two codes that were added to the MICS–IV, withdrawal and dysphoric affect, were included to make the system more exhaustive. (Most of the 1,086 interactions were coded with the MICS–III, which did not include these codes). Finally, after several years of RMICS use and in response to studies from the University of Washington group (e.g., Jacobson et al., 1994), we believed that the RMICS's hostility code was not sensitive enough to capture the intensity and quality of abusive couples' negativity. Thus, we carved a psychological abuse code out of the older hostility code.

In short, we created a MICS–descended system that coded at the category level, rather than at the ultramicroanalytic level. Coders learn the definitions of the MICS codes that constituted the categories (to ground constructs such as "Hostility"), but RMICS constructs, rather than the original ultramicrobehavioral codes, to code the utterances.

TASK AND SETTING

The RMICS's constructs are broadly descriptive of the kinds of behaviors that people emit during interactions with close others. Although originally designed to code conflict behavior, the RMICS has been used to code a wide range of dyadic conversations (e.g., analogue problem-solving tasks [such as planning a hypothetical vacation or discussing what home improvements would be made if given $15,000, Aron, Norman, Aron, McKenna, & Heyman, 2000]; social support tasks, and sibling conversations). Researchers often have compelling reasons for using a system such as the RMICS for tasks and settings other than couples' conflicts (e.g., comparing behaviors in supportive versus conflict tasks; comparing parent–parent, parent–child, and sibling–sibling behaviors). However, such use requires careful thought before embarking on coding and extra attention to validity issues during data analysis (see Bakeman & Gottman, 1997, and Heyman, 2001, for lengthier discussions of what questions researchers must ask themselves before choosing a coding system).

In my review of the psychometrics of couples observational coding (Heyman, 2001), I expressed dismay that researchers introduced unnecessary error variance by exerting too little experimental control in the selection of discussion topics and gender of person whose topic is discussed. I recommended that researchers (a) select the topics to be discussed, (b) narrow down broad topics such as communication through either a play-by-play interview (Gottman, 1996) or a specific questionnaire such as the Areas of Change Questionnaire (Weiss, Hops, & Patterson, 1973), (c) standardize (within and/or across studies) communication task instructions to couples and report them in published studies, and (d) experimentally control the gender of the complainant by either choosing two topics (e.g., the top female and male topics from a problem list) or by keeping the complainant's gender constant. An example of the instructions used in our lab for a recent National Institute of Mental Health-funded observational study can be found in Heyman and Slep (2003).

DESCRIPTION OF THE CODING SYSTEM

The RMICS comprises five Negative codes, four Positive codes, one Neutral code and one Other. Definitions and examples of these follow.

Negative Codes

Psychological Abuse (PA) is defined as follows: "A communication intended to cause psychological pain to another person, or a communication perceived as having that intent" (Vissing, Straus, Gelles, & Harrop, 1991, p. 225). (Corresponds to MICS code of put down). Examples include verbal statements of disgust (e.g., "You make me sick."); contempt, belittling, or mocking (e.g., "You couldn't balance the checkbook if you tried, genius." "Aww, you poor thing." [said sarcastically]); belligerence (e.g., "What are you going do about it? Huh? Huh?"); threatening ("Don't push me. You know what happens when you push my buttons."); domineering (e.g., playing district attorney), devaluing or negating partner's opinions or ideas (not simply disagreeing; e.g., "That's a stupid idea."); and "gaslighting" partner (i.e., trying to make partner think he or she is crazy, that his or her basic instincts or perceptions are wrong, or that he or she couldn't possibly function alone; e.g., "What do you mean I beat you up last month? I've never laid a finger on you"). PA also can be coded for nonverbal behaviors, such as glowering, physically intimidating, or talking very quietly or through one's teeth, in a threatening or menacing manner.

Distress Maintaining Attribution (DA) is coded when (a) the speaker offers an explanation for a negative event that is blameworthy or intentional on the part of the partner/self, or (b) the speaker offers an explanation for a non-negative event that the partner/self caused involuntarily or unintentionally. (Corresponds to MICS codes of accept responsibility, deny responsibility, mindread negative.) Examples include explanations of negative events (e.g., "I always feel like I'm on a leash when I'm coming home from work because if I'm not there within 15 minutes, you're waiting for me at the door ready to bawl me out.") and explanations of non-negative events (e.g., "You're only being nice so that I'll have sex with you tonight.").

Hostility (HO) includes all angry or irritated negative affect and statements with strong negative content, excluding behavior that is codeable as psychological abuse. (Corresponds to MICS codes of turn off ["a nonverbal response that communicates displeasure, disapproval, or disagreement, and is usually in reaction to something the other partner is saying or has just said," Oregon Marital Studies Program, OMSP, 1990, p. 26]; negative voice tone, criticize, mind read negative; also, disapprove, disagree [said with negative affect or in a way that does not further the discussion. Note that disagreements that further discussion or explain a partner's point of view in a non-negative way are coded as PD]). Examples may be non-content-based (e.g., negative/hostile voice tone; rolling eyes, exasperated sighs indicative of criticism, not dysphoric affect, cross or sour facial expression), content based (e.g., "I don't give a damn what you think;") or nonconstructive disagreements (e.g., She: "I think we should go to the movies tonight." [PD]→ He: "I don't think we should." [PD]→ She: "Well, I do." [HO]→ He: "Well I don't." [HO].

Coders should attempt to adjust their coding to the interactional style of the couple. For example, for some couples, loud speaking is a discussion style, rather than a sign of hostility. For these couples, their typical style would be coded as Constructive Problem Discussion or Solution (PD). For others, loud speaking is a clear break from their typical style and therefore would be coded as HO. On the other hand, couples who are nasty from the beginning of the interaction should be coded as HO throughout—blatant hostility is not an interactional style.

Dysphoric Affect (DY) is defined as sad or depressed expressed emotional states. (Corresponds to MICS code of dysphoric affect.) Examples include depressive complaints, whiny voice tone, dysphoric (sad) affect (i.e., commnicating sadness, despondency, or depression), and self-derogatory statements or attributions (note that DY trumps DA in this case; e.g., "We can't afford to send the kids to camp because I am too stupid to get a good job" [said with sad voice tone].)

Withdrawal (WI) is defined as behaviors that imply pulling back from the interaction, walling off the partner, or not listening to the speaker. (Corresponds to MICS code of withdrawal.) Withdrawal does not consist of any one behavior, and it is not cued by any set cluster of behaviors of affective signs. Rather, the coder must make a judgment, based on the flow of the conversation and the verbal and nonverbal cues, if someone is withdrawing. This definition was derived after having dozens of participants watch their recently completed videotaped interactions and indicate when they were withdrawing. Participants were then interviewed about what cues they used that indicated that they were withdrawing at the indicated moments (Heyman, 1988). Withdrawal may be indicated verbally, for example: "I don't want to discuss it anymore!" "Oh god, I'm not going to listen to this." "Sure ... you're right ... you're right." (when meant to block discussion and "shut up" partner). Other cues of WI include the following: (a) closed-off body language (e.g., folded arms, moving body away from partner), especially when there is a change from a more open position during a turning point in a discussion; (b) failure to respond (verbally or nonverbally) to the partner's question; (c) muscular tenseness or rigidity; (d) facial and verbal indications of holding back emotions; (e) nonverbal expressions that indicate that the listener is not listening (e.g., no eye contact, direct but glazed eye contact, turning away from speaker); and (f) a sudden decrease in listener back-channel behaviors.

Positive Codes

Acceptance (AC) is defined as active listening skills that help the partner feel understood and validated, including paraphrasing (restating partner's statement in one's own words), reflecting feelings (voicing what one thought the partner's underlying feelings were), giving positive feedback, and expressing caring, concern, or understanding of the partner's experience. (Corresponds to MICS codes of paraphrase/reflection, positive physical contact, approve, agree.) Examples include the following: "So my untidiness is a real problem for you." "... And that depressed you? (said with caring tone)." "I like how you have been handling the kids lately." Note that the paraphrase or reflection need not be correct, as long as it appears that a good faith attempt at understanding was being made.

Relationship Enhancing Attribution (RA) is defined as an explanation for the causes of (a) a neutral or positive event that implicates the self or partner as having acted intentionally, or (b) a negative event that exempts the partner/self from having caused it in a blameworthy manner. (Corresponds to MICS code of accept responsibility, deny responsibility, mind read positive.) Examples include the following: "You're short with me because you've had a hard day." "I was mad because your boss kept you late at work." "You help my dad out because you're a really sweet guy."

Self-Disclosure (SD) is defined as statements about the speaker's feelings, wishes or beliefs. SD can also include acceptance of responsibility not phrased as an attribution (e.g., "I was wrong to blame you."). (Corresponds to MICS code of accept responsibility.) Examples include the following: "I am always glad when we have company." "I feel very uncomfortable when we are at your parents' house." "I feel it is our responsibility to pay for the damages." Note that excluded are feelings of anger and disgust with "you" as an object and meant to hurt or criticize the receiver (these are coded as HO or PA). For example, "I feel insecure when you talk with other women at parties" is coded as SD, whereas, "It pisses me off when you talk with other women at parties" is coded (HO).

Humor (HM) includes statements that are clearly intended to be humorous. HMalso includes genuine smiling and laughing (not nervous smiling and laughing). Sarcastic humor directed at the partner is coded as hostility, not humor. (Corresponds to MICS codes of humor, smile and laugh.) Examples include the following: "I'll bet if we sold the kids and moved to the moon, we'd get some privacy." "We were so drunk we didn't know if we were lost or the neighbor repainted his house." "Let's shave our heads and sell flowers at the airport for extra income." Note that HM is coded regardless of whether the coder thinks that the comment is funny.

Neutral Code[2]

Constructive Problem Discussion/Solution (PD) is defined as all constructive approaches to discussing or solving problems, including elaborated disagreements. (Corresponds to MICS codes of problem description (internal), problem description (external), agree, compromise, disagree, positive solution, negative solution.) Examples include the following: "I think we should start saving more money." "You should go out more often." "When are the kids going to camp?"

Other Code

Other (OT) is defined as discussing something other than a personal or relationship topic. OT is most often coded when the experimental situation itself is discussed. OT is coded conservatively; the statement must be clearly out of bounds. If the couple strays from the appointed topic, but is talking about anything relevant to their lives or marriage, use another code. (Corresponds to MICS codes of talk, i.e., unintelligible speech, and off-topic.) Examples include the following: "Is that the camera?" "I don't like the painting they have on the wall." "How long has it been? Has it been 10 minutes yet?"

EXCERPTS FROM THE CODING MANUAL

To better illustrate the RMICS, a sample of a coded interaction is presented here. Joe and Allison, married 7 years, presented for couples treatment following several years of increasing arguments. Joe was 40 years old and employed as a laborer.

[2]Although most PD utterances appear to be neutral, the validity data presented in Table 5.1 indicates that PD has the second strongest overall relation to marital adjustment scores, and the strongest positive relation. Thus, the RMICS more correctly can be said to comprise "negative" and "non-negative" codes.

Allison, 38 years old, was a homemaker who cared for their four children (ages 8, 5, 3½, and 1). Joe and Allison met at a local bar and dated for 9 months prior to Allison getting pregnant. They moved in together after the birth of their first child, and got married 9 months later.

Allison's top problem topic was that she wanted Joe to communicate his needs and feelings more clearly. The following is a transcript of the conversation. The accompanying RMICS coding sheet can be found in Figure 1.

Allison (00.00): Sometimes when you come home from work, I say, "Do you want–" PD

Joe (00.05): (interrupts) Is that after working 11 hours a day? PD

Allison (00.09): Well– PD

Joe (00.10): (interrupts) Being up since 5:00 in the morning? Is that when you're asking the question? When I come home from work? PA

Allison (00.20): But I'm not– PD

Joe (00.23): (interrupts) or when I'm sitting down relaxed? When is the question asked? PA

Allison (00.30): But I'm– PD

Joe (00.32): (interrupts) As soon as I walk in the door. [Joe's frequent interruptions are taking on the belligerent quality of a district attorney (cf., Gottman, 1996.] PA

Allison (00.38): I might ask you a simple question, like "Do you want cheese on your hamburger," and you'll scream "Who's thinking about food?" [Said dispassionately] PD

Joe (00.45): Why would you ask a question when I always take cheese on my hamburger? Why would you ask something so stupid like that: (derisively) "Do you want cheese on your hamburger?" PA

Allison (01:00): I just wish that when you came home from work you'd just say, "I had a really rotten"– PD

Joe (01.09): (interrupts) I have a really rotten day every day. Then you'll come up and ask me a really stupid question to tick me off, like do I want cheese on my burger. If someone comes home from work and they're boiling already, why do you have to add fuel to the fire? Why? Because you just like to fight. You love to get me going. (Allison: rolls eyes; HO listener code) Isn't it nice for you to just not say anything when I came home? But no, you want me to scream more, to express myself more. You want to hear more hollering and more screaming. PA

Allison (01:30): No [Allison looks down, looking sad and defeated]. DY (Joe rolls his eyes; HO listener code)

Joe (01:35): That's what you love. You love more screaming and hollering. When someone has a bad day, you should just leave them alone, [bitterly sarcastic] but nooooooooo, you want to hear more and more. You get me going, like you're doing right now. You're getting me going. [glares] PA (Allison continues to avert her eyes and look sad; DY listener code)

Allison (01:50) I don't know what to say to you. I want you to talk about what's really bothering you, not– PD

Joe: (02:00) (interrupts) You've already heard that a million times. My job. What I am and what I've become, and how I cannot provide for the family. Why do you need to hear that over and over and over? Do you think that I'm happy everyday going to work? No, but it pays the bills. So I'm a miserable type person, so don't ask me the same stupid questions over and over. HO

Allison (02.20): Then why don't you look for a different job? PD

Joe (02.25): Because it's too late for me. What am I going to do, go to college? How can we possibly afford it? We can't afford the tuition. We can't afford me working less. I'm stuck. I have seniority and a chance to get a miserable pension, but at least it's something. It's too late for me to start over at the bottom. I've got mouths to feed. Plus, can you see me in management? I hate those bastards. There's no way that you'll see me become one of them [This turn took 35 seconds]. RA–PD

Allison (03.00): I don't know. I just feel like we have to make things a little bit better. PD

Joe (03.10): I don't see any problems [Joe is gaslighting Allison here]. I'm the same as when you met me. You're the one who fell in love with me; you're the one that wanted all this. So you got everything that you wanted, and now you're complaining? Now you're complaining? PA

Allison (03.24): You keep– PD

Joe (03.26): (interrupts) I've always been this way and I will always be this way. This is me. I feel stressed and agitated and I don't hide it. SD

Allison (03.36): You say that– PD

Joe (03.38): (interrupts) There are a million other guys out there that you could have married, but you met me, and you got what you wanted, and now you're complaining. I'm the same guy. HO

Allison (03:53): (quietly) No you're not [looking down at floor, long pause, looking distant and disconnected but not sad]. WI

Joe (04:15): Maybe I'm not the same, because when I first met you, we didn't have a house full of kids, we didn't have a mortgage, we didn't have two cars to pay for, we didn't have all these bills, all the medical problems, we didn't have anything. So yeah, I was a young guy, and I didn't have problems, so yeah, [bitterly] I was different back then, yes. I had a little apartment to rent, I was very happy, and now, now, you expect me to be the same guy as 9 years ago? HO

Allison (04:29): I–

Joe (04:31): (interrupts) Nine years ago? You expect me to be the same person? [Very sarcastically, waving hands] Sorry, those newlywed days are long gone. This is reality. PA

Allison (04:43) But you're so nasty. HO

Joe (04:45): I'm so nasty? PD

Allison (04:48):	You are. PD
Joe (04:51):	Why do you continue to stay with me then? I've always asked you that. If I'm so nasty and so abusive, then why are you still with me? PA
Allison (05:00):	Because– PD
Joe (05.01):	(interrupts) Belligerently, challengingly] Break yourself free. PA
Allison (05.08):	I don't want to break free. I just want our relationship to be more like it was (Begins to cry). DY

CODER TRAINING

Undergraduates constitute the bulk of our coders. Graduate students and professionals can be trained, but often tend to overinterpret behavior. Potential coders must possess both emotional and intellectual intelligence; those high on only one tend to have difficulty reaching the reliability criterion.

Training involves the following steps: (a) assigning reading of coding manual (homework); (b) in-class didactic training on coding process and the codes themselves, including demonstrations with conflict videos; (c) assigning memorization of the coding manual and in-class quizzes on code definitions; (d) in-class demonstration of and practice in identifying speaker turns (i.e., the RMICS' basic unit); (e) assigning homework on identifying speaker turns; (f) providing specific feedback on where homework assignment matched and deviated from master coding protocol; (g) in-class demonstration of coding; (h) assigning coding homework; (i) providing specific feedback on where coding homework matched and deviated from master coding protocol; and (j) repeating steps (g) through (i) until Cohen's kappa > .60 for at least two consecutive assignments.

Undergraduates typically enroll in supervised research for credit, committing to code 6 hr a week (2 hr in-class and 4 hr of homework). At this intensity, it takes approximately 3 months to train coders to meet the reliability criterion. There is a great deal of variability, however.

Currently, training is conducted through a combination of didactic training, Socratic questioning, practice, and feedback, all conducted at the State University of New York (SUNY) at Stony Brook. No offsite training materials, other than the manual, are currently available. Some researchers, wishing to set up their own RMICS coding laboratories, have arranged for a brief (e.g., weekend) didactic training, followed by telephone consultation with SUNY master coders until reliability with the SUNY coders was reached. Occasional reliability calculation and telephone consultation was arranged to help avoid coder drift at the external site. The manual is available at www.psy.sunysb.edu/marital or by email from the author.

CODING PROCESS

The basic coding unit for the MICS was the "thought unit," defined as "behavior of homogeneous content, irrespective of duration or formal grammatical accuracy, emitted by a single partner. Every change in behavior is coded and every behavioral unit is bounded by a different behavior" (Weiss & Summers, 1983, p. 89). Speakers often were coded with multiple thought units during a single speaker turn. However, disagreement on unitization among MICS coders was substantial (Heyman et al., 1993), whereas RMICS coders have little trouble distinguishing speaker turns. Furthermore, Dina Vivian and I believed that the natural unit during conversations was the speaker turn, not the thought unit. To deal with long monologues, we start a new unit every 30 sec that a speaker continues to hold the floor.

Another difference between the RMICS and MICS is that the MICS had coders record multiple codes within a speaker turn (i.e., an interruption in the form of a question that was a problem description with negative voice tone). As mentioned earlier, all codes except for one had to be discarded for sequential analysis. Which code to keep was based on a hierarchy of theoretical importance, with negative codes highest, positive codes next, and neutral codes last. In keeping with the parsimony philosophy of the RMICS, we also employ an a priori hierarchy, but have coders record on the coding sheet one code only (the hierarchically highest) per turn/30-sec. The codes were presented earlier in hierarchical order. The hierarchy is based on both communication theory and substantial research which demonstrates that negative, followed by positive, followed by neutral, codes are of decreasing importance in understanding marital conflict (see Weiss & Heyman, 1997).

RMICS coding can be done in approximately real time (i.e., 10–15 min. coding for a 10-min. interaction). Coders code both partners simultaneously, occasionally noting the times that a coding unit began to aid in matching protocols for calculation of reliability coefficients.

Although we have experimented with more sophisticated coding interfaces (and may one day move toward it), coders use paper-and-pencil to record their codes. Figure 5.1 displays a sample RMICS coding sheet. Basic technological interfaces are employed (either TV and standard VCR or digitized video on CD-ROM with Windows Media Player to play, pause, fast forward, and rewind).

RELIABILITY

Inter-Rater Agreement

Cohen's kappa, a measure of inter-rater agreement, is calculated on a random subset of couples. Two coders are randomly assigned to code the same tape; they remain blind as to which tapes are being used for reliability testing. Our standard procedure is to assign 25% of the interactions for reliability testing. The average overall Cohen's kappa per couple for 17 RMICS studies was .59 (SD = .17, n = 469), which is considered good for complex coding such as this. Table 5.1 displays the reliabilities for each RMICS code. To accomplish this, (a) a single confusion

PA	Psychological Abuse
DA	Distress Maintaining Attribution
HO	Hostility
DY	Dysphoric Affect
WI	Withdrawal
AC	Acceptance
RA	Relationship Enhancing Attribution
SD	Self-Disclosure
HM	Humor
PD	Constructive Problem Discussion/Solution
OT	Other

RMICS Coding Sheet

Couple #: 9999A

Coder: Gayle

Date: 5/15/02

Total # of sheets: 1 of 1

H	1	00:05 2 PD	3	00:10 4 PA	5	00:23 6 PA	7	00:32 8 PA	9	00:45 10 PA	11	01:09 12 PA	13	01:35 14 PA	15	02:00 16 HO	17	02:25 18 RA	02:55 19 PD	20
W	00:00 PD		00:09 PD		00:20 PD		00:30 PD		00:38 PD		01:00 PD	(HO)	01:30 DY		01:50 PD		02:20 PD			03:00 PD
H	03:10 21 PA	22	03:26 23 SD	24	03:38 25 HO	26	04:15 27 HO	28	04:31 29 PA	30	04:45 31 PD	32	04:51 33 PA	34	05:01 35 PA	36	37	38	39	40
W		03:24 PD		03:36 PD		03:53 WI		04:29 PD		04:43 HO		04:48 PD		05:00 PD		05:08 DY				
H	41	42	43	44	45	46	47	48	49	50	51	52	53	54	55	56	57	58	59	60
W																				
H	61	62	63	64	65	66	67	68	69	70	71	72	73	74	75	76	77	78	79	80
W																				
H	81	82	83	84	85	86	87	88	89	90	91	92	93	94	95	96	97	98	99	100
W																				

FIG. 5.1 Sample RMICS Coding Sheet to Accompany Transcript on pages 76–79.

matrix was created by collapsing the confusion matrices across all 469 couples, (b) 2 x 2 matrices were calculated for target code versus all other codes, (c) Cohen's kappa was calculated, and (d) because kappa is overly conservative in low base rate situations, *V* (which provides a better approximation of reliability in such situations; Spitznagel & Helzer, 1985) was also calculated. Agreement on all codes was good ($\kappa = .58$ to .82), with the possible exception of the most infrequent code (psychological abuse, $\kappa = .46$, which constituted about .10% of the observed behavior).

Reliability (Internal Consistency)

Reliability of the RMICS, using the Spearman–Brown split-half correlation, was presented in Heyman, Chaudhry, et al. (2001) for married (nondistressed community), married (clinic), and engaged couples. They found that most coefficients were above .90 in each group, indicating that individual RMICS codes were reliable for some of the most widely used populations (i.e., coded units demonstrate internal consistency; Mitchell, 1979).

VALIDITY

As will be discussed in further detail, most studies to use the RMICS have yet to appear in print; thus, extensive validity data for RMICS codes will be publicly available shortly. In this section, I limit discussion of validity to a cross-investigator[3] data set of over 1,000 couples and published RMICS studies.

Discriminative Validity

Data were combined from 11 studies ($N = 1{,}131$) for which investigators provided Dyadic Adjustment Scale (DAS; Spanier, 1976) or equivalent[4] scores. We used the standard cutoff of 97 and below as the criterion for relationship distress (Eddy, Heyman, & Weiss, 1991). As shown in Table 5.1, most RMICS codes discriminated both men and women in distressed and nondistressed relationships (except for relationship-enhancing attributions and the rare codes of psychological abuse and dysphoric affect). Relationship-enhancing attributions (i.e., those that attribute good intentions to one or both partners) perhaps did not discriminate because they seem to be used as commonly to justify purported bad behavior as to offer an attribution that is truly relationship-enhancing.

In addition, Heyman, Feldbau–Kohn, Ehrensaft, Langhinrichsen–Rohling, and O'Leary (2001) reported that, as hypothesized, hostility and distress-maintaining

[3]Studies that contributed data to the cross-investigator sample are indicated in Table 5.2.

[4]Marital Adjustment Test (Locke & Wallace, 1959) or Quality of Marriage Index (Norton, 1983) were converted to DAS scores using formulae found in Heyman, Sayers, and Bellack (1994).

TABLE 5.1
Inter-Rater Agreement and Validity of (RMICS) Codes

	Inter-Rater Agreement[a]		Validity[b]						
			Distressed		*Nondistressed*				*DAS*
Code	κ	*V*	*M%*	*SD*	*M%*	*SD*	*t*	*df*[c]	*r*[d]
Psychological Abuse	0.46	0.71							
Men			0.22	1.40	0.07	0.71	2.1	751.57	–0.04
Women			0.18	1.27	0.02	0.26	2.62	540.82	–0.11*
Distress-maintaining attributions	0.59	0.71							
Men			1.58	2.64	0.94	2.42	4.18***	1079.31	–0.21***
Women			2.74	4.45	1.53	2.81	5.57***	1103.61	–0.29***
Hostility	0.72	0.75							
Men			19.07	22.18	5.38	10.63	13.8***	985.86	–0.47***
Women			23.35	23.79	8.08	13.80	13.6***	1073.33	–0.48***
Dysphoric affect	0.61	0.79							
Men			0.15	1.13	0.14	1.18	0.14	1129	0.01
Women			0.71	2.98	0.33	2.01	2.52	1119.59	–0.08
Withdrawal	0.55	0.72							
Men			0.64	3.15	0.09	0.58	4.33***	708.29	–0.08
Women			0.49	2.16	0.14	0.81	3.81***	875.61	–0.14***
Relationship-Enhancing attributions	0.67	0.75							
Men			3.04	3.99	3.32	4.78	–1.06	922.02	0.04
Women			2.92	3.74	3.16	4.19	–0.97	964.35	0.04

TABLE 5.1 (cont.)

	Inter-Rater Agreement[a]		Validity[b]						
			Distressed		*Nondistressed*				*DAS*
Code	κ	*V*	*M%*	*SD*	*M%*	*SD*	*t*	*df*[c]	*r*[d]
Acceptance	0.58	0.69							
Men			0.66	2.05	1.21	3.50	–3.03*	720.44	0.03
Women			0.48	2.08	0.99	2.45	–3.71**	930.19	0.12**
Self-Disclosure	0.62	0.71							
Men			5.33	8.01	6.94	9.18	–3.07*	950.36	0.03
Women			5.05	7.06	7.66	9.20	–5.18***	867.07	0.13**
Humor	0.73	0.79							
Men			2.69	4.77	5.05	6.50	–6.73***	840.05	0.20***
Women			2.61	4.73	5.52	7.34	–7.59***	766.89	0.26***
Constructive problem discussion and solution	0.68	0.69							
Men			63.57	22.96	72.73	16.98	–7.71***	1129	0.35***
Women			58.63	23.77	68.54	18.11	–7.95***	1128.02	0.35***
Other	0.82	0.38							
Men			3.40	8.74	4.38	9.19	–1.82	1004.90	0.12**
Women			3.30	8.41	4.26	9.21	–1.79	979.41	0.12**

TABLE 5.1 (cont.)

Note. All tests are one-tailed, with Bonferroni family-wise correction applied ($p/12$).
$^{*}p < .05$, $^{**}p < .01$, $^{***}p < .001$.
[a] $n = 469$ couples randomly assigned to two coders, [b] $n = 650$ distressed and 481 nondistressed couples for all codes except for Psychological Abuse (PA); $n = 491$ distressed and 404 nondistresed couples for PA (PA was added to RMICS later). [c] *dfs* are lower if Levene's test for equality of variance was significant, indicating that pooled *dfs* were not appropriate. [d] $n = 838$ men, 835 women (all codes except for PA); $n = 608$ men, 612 women (PA).

attributions discriminated spouses meeting proposed diagnostic criteria for relationship distress from those who did not meet criteria.

Convergent Validity

The RMICS's convergent validity was demonstrated through the correlations between RMICS code frequencies and DAS scores. For women, all codes except for relationship-enhancing attributions and dysphoric affect were associated with relationship satisfaction in the expected directions. For men, all codes except for psychological abuse, dysphoric affect, and three of the four positive codes (RA, AC, SD) were associated with DAS scores. DAS and RMICS significant associations were also published by Baker et al. (2000) in their study of marital adjustment and hypertension.

Predictive Validity

RMICS variables were found to predict improvement in group treatment for partner aggression (at posttest and at 1-year follow-up) and to predict dropout (Heyman, Brown, Feldbau, & O'Leary, 1999).

Construct Validity

In addition to the findings noted earlier, topic-specific hypotheses of RMICS variables were supported for couples engaging in novel or exciting activities (Aron et al., 2000) and women with breast cancer and their partners discussing cancer and noncancer topics (Manne, Ostroff, Sherman, Heyman, & Ross, 2002).

GENERALIZABILITY

As shown in Table 5.2, the RMICS has been used with a wide range of North American couples[5]. (Coding is also known to be underway at two European sites.) Participants' ages have ranged from midteens to late 70s and their education has ranged from middle school to earned postgraduate degrees. Income and socioeconomic status have ranged from very low to very high. As detailed in a subsequent section, investigators' topic areas have necessitated recruiting participants from a broad swath of couples and problems experienced (e.g., physical health problems, mental health problems, relationship problems). Race and ethnicity of participants has been largely White, although hundreds of interactions of racial and ethnic minorities have been successfully coded. Thus, although our experience in coding leads us to believe that the RMICS has good generalizability across ages, problems, and races or ethnicities, generalizability can only be in-

[5]In addition to romantic couples, preteen sibling pairs have also been coded reliably.

TABLE 5.2

Studies with Rapid Marital Interaction Coding System-Coded Interactions

Investigator	*Type/Participants*	*Age Range*	*Years Education (years)*	*Ethnicity*	*Situation or Setting*
Aron, Stony Brook	Type: C 35 married couples C[1,3]	21–46, mean = 32.4			Setting: Lab Situation: Two 5-min. 4* Topic: Planning vacation; home improvements
Baker, Univ. Of Toronto	Type: C 23 couples, one partner with elevated blood pressure	20–65			Setting: Lab Situation: 10–15 min. 1[a]
Cedar Collaborative Univ. Of Pittsburgh[v]	Type: C 42 families in three groups (SAF, NF, PDF): C[1,2,3,6]	M = 30–48, mean = 37.86 W = 28–46, mean = 35.64	M = 10–17, mean = 13.57 W = 9–17, mean = 13.59		Setting: Lab Situation: 10-min. 1[a]
Epstein, Rutgers	Type: T, L 12 couples, male with drug abuse or dependency diagnosis	M = 22–56, mean = 38.8 W = 19–55, mean = 37.95	M = 11–18, mean = 14.00 W = 12–18, mean = 14.29	M = 33% Wh; 46% AA, 21% H W = 42% Wh, 46% AA, 13% H	Setting: Lab Situation: 10-min. 1[a] at up to 3 time points
Heyman and Slep, Stony Brook	Type: C 264 couples: (239Ma 25LT); C[4]	M = 21–75, mean = 42.3 W = 20–75, mean = 40.4	M = mean 14.68 years W = mean 14.56 years	M = 79% Wh, 7% AA, 6% H, 5% NA, 2% A, 2% O W = 84% W, 7% AA, 6% H, 2% NA, 1% A, 1% O	Setting: Lab Situation: Three 10-min.: two 1[a], one 3[a]

TABLE 5.2 (cont.)

Investigator	*Type/Participants*	*Age Range*	*Years Education (years)*	*Ethnicity*	*Situation or Setting*
Jordan, Univ. Of Washington	Type: C 23 couples transitioning to parenting: C				Setting: Lab Situation: 10-min. 1[a]
Kiecolt–Glaser, Ohio State	Type: C 30 married couples C[1,2,3]	M + W = 18–75		Primarily White	Setting: Lab Situation: 30-min. 1[a]
Langhinrichsen–Rohling, Heyman, Ehrensaft, SUNY Stony Brook[v]	Type: C 75 married couples: C[1]	M = 23–70, mean = 34.32 W = 24–63, mean = 31.94	M = 10–19, mean = 13.82 W = 8–18, mean = 13.80	M = 86% Wh, 5% H, 1% AA, 1% A, 4% O, 3% MIS W = 81% Wh, 7% H, 5% AA, 1% A, 3% O,3% MIS	Setting: Lab Situation: Two 10-min.: 1[a]4[f]
Leisring, Stony Brook	Type: C 40 couples (39Ma, 1LT) Have child 24–47 months, report occasional quarreling with spouse, C[1]	M = 22–46, mean = 33.82 W = 22–46, mean = 32.58	M = mean 13.55 W = mean 14.485	Only child ethnicity given: 93% Wh, 7% Mixed race	Setting: Lab Situation: Two groups (1) 10-min 1[a] (2) 10-min 2[a]
Lidsky, Yale University	Type: C 26 couples with one family member with OCD or TS: C-participants in family study at Yale				Setting: Lab Situation: Two 10–15 min. 1[a], 2[c]

TABLE 5.2 (cont.)

Investigator	*Type/Participants*	*Age Range*	*Years Education (years)*	*Ethnicity*	*Situation or Setting*
Manne, Fox Chase Cancer Center, Philadelphia	Type: C 183 couples F suffering from breast cancer (169Ma, 7LT, 7mis): CL[1]	M = 26–80, mean = 51.39 W = 29–72, mean = 50.06	Not given	M = 91% White W = 88% White	Setting: Lab Situation: Two 10-min 1[a] 2[b]
Mezzich, Univ of Pittsburgh	Type: L 70 couples (8Ma, 62D) F had SUD or CD at 14: CL[3]	M = 17–47, mean = 24 W = 18–24, mean = 20.97	M = 8–16, mean = 12.9 W = 9–15, mean = 13.28	M = 70% Wh, 28% AA, 1% O, 1% MIS W = 81% Wh, 17% AA, 2% O	Setting: Lab Situation: 12-min 1[a]
Miller, Stanford University	Type: L 40 married couples, F suffering from breast cancer: C-recruited from previous breast cancer study	M = 30–78, mean = 57.6 W = 42–72, mean = 57.3	M = 12–20, mean = 16.35 W = 12–20, mean = 15.95	M = 95% Wh, 5% A W = 85% W,h 5% A, 5% H, 5% O	Setting: Lab Situation: Two 10-min, one 15-min. 2[b]
Mongrain, York Univ. Canada	Type: C 92 couples (3Ma, 89D) F DEQ scores (19DP, 11SC, 18 MX, 19CT) C[5]	M = 18–36, mean = 21.54 W = 18–36, mean = 20.15	Not given but were university students		Setting: Lab Situation: 8-min. 1[a]
O'Leary, SUNY Stony Brook[v]	Type: T 63 married couples Report two or more M to W aggression on CTS past year: C[1]	M = mean 38.4 W = mean 36.24	M = mean 13.56 W = mean 13.54	M = 98% Wh, 2% AA W = 97% Wh, 1.5% AA, 1.5% H	Setting: Lab Situation: 10-min.1[a]

TABLE 5.2 (cont.)

Investigator	*Type/Participants*	*Age Range*	*Years Education (years)*	*Ethnicity*	*Situation or Setting*
Pasley and Clingempeel, Univ of NC–Greensboro and Medical Univ of South Carolina[v]	Type: L 33 dating couples C[5]	M = 16–22, mean 19.58 W = 17–22, mean = 18.79	M = 10–22, mean 13.53 W = 10–22, mean = 14.31		Setting: Lab Situation: 10-min. 1[a]
Riggs, Boston VA	34 male Vietnam Veterans and their female partners				Setting: Lab Situation: Three 10-min. 1[a], 4[d]
Vivian, SUNY Stony Brook[v]	Type: T 197 couples presenting for couples therapy C[1], 50 happily married control couples: C[1]	M = 20–75, mean = 37.9 W = 18–35, mean = 35.5	M = mean 13.88 years W = mean 13.79 years	Not collected, but predominantly White	Setting: Lab Situation: 15-min. 1[a]
Walitzer, Research Institute on Addications, Buffalo[v]	Type: L 93 couples (73Ma, 20LT) One member seeking treatment for alcohol dependence: C[1,2]	M = 24–69, mean = 42.01 W = 21–65, mean = 39.26	M = mean 15.00 W = mean 15.18	M = 97% Wh, 1% H, 1% AA, 1% NA W = 96% Wh, 2% H, 1% AA, 1% NA	Setting: Lab Situation: Two 10-min 1[a], 4[e]
Waters, SUNY Stony Brook[v]	Type: L 157 engaged couples 3 months prior to wedding: C[1,6]	M = mean 24.7 W = mean 23.3	14.8 years (across M + W)	96% Wh, 3% H, 1% AA (across M + W)	Setting: Lab Situation: 15-min. 1[a]

TABLE 5.2 (cont.)

Investigator	*Type or Participants*	*Age Range*	*Years Education (years)*	*Ethnicity*	*Situation or Setting*
Wolfe, Univ of Ontario	Type: C 30 adolescent dating couples	Mid to late adolescents	8–12 years		Setting: Lab Situation: Two 10-min

Notes: M = men; W = Women; Univ. = University; SUNY = State University of New York

Study: V = Study included in the validity analysis presented in this chapter

Type: C = Cross-sectional; L = Longitudinal; T = Treatment

Participants: Sampling used: Community: C^1 = advertising-newspaper, C^2 = advertising-TV, radio; C^3 = advertising-flyers, posters; C^4 = random digit dialing; C^5 = college students; C^6 = advertising-other; CL^1 = clinical inpatient; CL^2 = Clinical outpatient; CL^3 = clinical outpatient (group home, juvenile court, etc.); NW = Offspring of normal fathers (average risk); PDW = Offspring of psychiatrically disturbed fathers; OCD = Obsessive Compulsive Disorder; SAW = Offspring of substance abusing fathers (high risk); TS = Tourette's Syndrome; DEQ = 4 groups (high–low dependency × self-criticism) based on women's Depressive Experiences Questionnaire score

Couple Status: M = married; L = Living together in a relationship; D = Dating; Mis = missing

Ethnicity: Wh = White; AA = African American; H = Hispanic; NA = Native American; A = Asian; O = Other

Situations: 1 = Conflict; 2 = Neutral; 3 = discuss "at your best;" 4 = other

Topic: [a] = relationship disagreement; [b] = breast cancer topic; [c] = child rearing; [d] = war experience; [e] = thoughts about drinking; [f] = area of agreement.

ferred after a large body of studies has been published. Finally, given the culturally-bound nature of extracting meaning from couples' interactions, the RMICS and its findings may not be generalizable beyond industrialized countries that share cultural norms regarding relationships.

CLINICAL UTILITY

Pretreatment and posttreatment (and sometimes follow-up) observational assessment, with systems similar to the RMICS, has been used in outcome studies to assess couples' learning of communication skills (e.g., Gottman, 1979; Hahlweg, Schindler, Revenstorf, & Brengelmann, 1984; Jacobson, 1977, 1978; Sayers, Baucom, Sher, Weiss, & Heyman, 1991). The RMICS could be employed for such formal assessments of treatment efficacy.

Such uses are extraordinarily time-consuming and expensive, and are thus not practical for typical clinical use (see Mash & Foster, 2001). However, familiarity with both the observational literature and a relatively simple coding system such as the RMICS can be of high clinical utility. For example, in clinical practice it is important (and becoming increasingly mandatory) to record a formal treatment plan that incorporates observable treatment goals (O'Leary, Heyman, & Jongsma, 1998). Observing communication during initial assessment and then during the course of treatment is necessary to assess the success in meeting the goals. (This, of course, will depend on both the goals and the therapists' functional analysis of what is promoting and maintaining the distress. Communication's importance, and thus the importance of assessing it, will vary across couples.) Informal observation costs nothing other than time in pretreatment and posttreatment assessment in clinical practice. For example, while watching couples' conversations during assessment sessions, I ask myself the following questions: How does the conversation start? Does the level of anger escalate? What happens when it does? Do they enter repetitive negative loops? Do they indicate afterward that what occurred during the conversations is typical? Is their behavior stable across discussions? Do their behaviors differ when it is her topic versus his? Do they label the other person or the communication process as the problem?

To summarize, because most forms of marital therapy include attempts at modifying couples' communication behaviors, being familiar with the basics of communication processes is useful if one is to recognize communication difficulties and, importantly, set appropriate treatment goals (e.g., teaching partners how to monitor and exit negative loops rather than admonishing them not to behave hostilely).

CONCLUSION

The RMICS was designed as a second-generation coding system. We built on the established MICS literature and used both empirical and theoretical guidance to create a system that would be more reliable and valid despite being faster and easier to train and code. Early indications point to success, although more published studies are necessary to establish the RMICS codes' validity more firmly.

I'd like to conclude with a caveat from Bakeman and Gottman (1997):

> We sometimes hear people ask: Do you have a coding scheme I can borrow? This seems to us a little like wearing someone else's underwear. [Using] a coding scheme is very much a theoretical act, one that should begin in the privacy of one's own study, and the coding scheme itself represents a hypothesis, even if it is rarely treated as such. (p. 15).

The mere reading of this book implies a keen interest in the intricacies and implications of choosing a coding system. One must choose carefully, recognizing that coding systems are tools to investigate particular constructs. Thus, there is no "best" coding system, despite the hopes of many that their search can be magically abridged. My hope is that an exposure to the breadth of available coding systems will, as often as possible, help put the right tool in the right hands to answer the right questions.

STUDIES USING THE CODING SYSTEM

Table 5.2 lists 19 studies that have used the RMICS and have had their data coded or analyzed at Stony Brook. At least four other investigators are known to the author to be coding with the RMICS at their own institutions. As a relatively new system, most of these studies have not yet appeared in print. Topics of investigation reflect a very broad range: alcohol abuse or dependence, cancer, cardiac rehabilitation, couples therapy, dating violence, drug abuse or dependence, longitudinal course of relationships, novel or exciting activities, parenting, partner aggression, and combat-related Posttraumatic Stress Disorder, among others.

ACKNOWLEDGMENTS

Preparation of this chapter was supported by the National Institute of Mental Health (Grant R01MH57779) and National Center for Injury Prevention and Control, Centers for Disease Control and Prevention (Grant R49CCR218554–01).

Thanks to the following investigators for allowing their data to be used for the reliability and validity analyses presented here: Art Aron (SUNY–Stony Brook), Brian Baker (University of Toronto), Glen Clingempeel (Medical University of South Carolina), Miriam Ehrensaft (SUNY–Stony Brook; now at Columbia University), Pam Jordan (University of Washington); Jan Kiecolt–Glaser (Ohio State University), Jennifer Langhinrichsen–Rohling (SUNY–Stony Brook; now at University of South Alabama), Penny Leisring (SUNY–Stony Brook; now at

Quinnipiac University), Ilana Lidsky (Yale University), Sharon Manne (Fox Chase Cancer Center), Ada Mezzich (University of Pittsburgh), Myriam Mongrain (York University), Kay Pasley (University of North Carolina– Greensboro), Dan O'Leary (SUNY–Stony Brook), David Riggs (Boston Veteran's Administration Medical Center; now at University of Pennsylvania), David Spiegel (Stanford University), Dina Vivian (SUNY-Stony Brook), Kimberly Walitzer (Research Institute on Addictions, Buffalo, NY), Everett Waters (SUNY–Stony Brook), David Wolfe (University of Western Ontario), and the CEDAR collective (University of Pittsburgh).

Coding is an especially collaborative enterprise, and several important contributions should be acknowledged. First, Bob Weiss not only generously allowed me to adapt the MICS but taught me (most of) what I know about couples and couples coding. Second, Dina Vivian collaborated with me on the development and launching of the RMICS, including cowriting the coding manual (Heyman & Vivian, 1993). Third, Shari Feldbau–Kohn influenced RMICS coding heavily during her 5-year tenure as head coder and coder trainer. Fourth, Joe Lengfellner (assisted by Dawn Canfora) was responsible for obtaining supplemental data from investigators and combining it with RMICS data that allowed me to conduct the analyses reported here. Fifth, RMICS coders and coding trainers, particularly Crista Ayerle, Dianne Orlando, and Joe Lengfellner, spent thousands of hours staring at video screens. Finally, thousands of anonymous couples and families agreed to be observed discussing some of their most difficult and intimate problems; without their bravery, this entire book would not exist.

6

The MICSEASE: An Observational Coding System for Capturing Social Processes

William A. Griffin
Arizona State University

Shannon M. Greene
University of Texas-Austin

Amy Decker-Haas
Arizona State University

The MICSEASE is a behavioral coding system developed in the mid 1980s by William Griffin to capture verbal codes and nonverbal behaviors as they occur concurrent to real-time self-report affect during lab-based dyadic interactions. Although initially derived from the popular and well-developed Marital Interaction Coding System (MICS), the MICSEASE has only a few of the original codes, coding procedures, and code compilation methods associated with its predecessor. Codes include verbal content (e.g., problem solving), nonverbal behavior (e.g., eye gaze), and a way of allowing each interactant to record his or her affect. Over the past two decades, a variety of studies have employed the MICSEASE to examine affect expression in marital (Griffin, 1993a) and postmarital interaction, the role of disease in marital (e.g., Parkinson's; Greene & Griffin, 1998) and family (e.g., asthma; Griffin, Parrella, Krainz, & Northey, 2002) interactions, postdivorce parent–child interactions with the custodial (Wolchik et al., 2000) and noncustodial (Verman, 2001) parent, and interactions in a bereaved sample of parents and children (Sandler et al., 2002). The MICSEASE is fluid: codes are selected, added, or even modified as needed to answer the relevant research questions associated with each study. The constancy across projects, especially in the last decade, has been the code selection process and the coding and reliability estimation procedures. Recently, coding emphasis has shifted from cataloging the probabilities associated with individual behaviors to the creation of behavioral domains that permit the reconstruction, visualization, and pattern classification of dyadic interactions. We are developing code combination algorithms that form indices sensitive to the intricacies of change in the dyadic interaction; in turn, these are used in traditional summary statistics (e.g., ANOVA) or as data points in pattern recognition and data visualization software (see Griffin, 2000, 2002).

THEORETICAL FOUNDATIONS

Code structures in the MICSEASE reflect basic assumptions associated with the common social interactional and general systems models found in the social sciences. Each behavior is coded, strung together sequentially, and laid out to provide two vital pieces of information about the behavior: its occurrence and its timing. Multiple strings of parallel data are created when each interactant generates a behavioral record. Although this strategy is typical of most dyadic coding systems, the MICSEASE creates parallel behavioral strings with the purpose of subsequently combining them into a single process code. Instead of two data points per unit of time, there is one—essentially capturing a dyadic level process. These data, at a composite level, capture the interactional dynamics between and among members of a system, generating a characteristic profile or signature that discriminates between categorically different groups, or shows variation within a group along a continuum. If we assume, for example, that distressed couples interact differently than nondistressed couples, then relevant coded features that form a summary index of the interaction can be manipulated via differential weighting of codes, adding or removing codes from the index, and so on, until the index provides maximum power to distinguish subgroupings. It is assumed that each code captures some relevant dimension of the system that contributes to this discriminating signature. In aggregate, these profiles are multidimensional vectors representing a real-time multivariate index conveying relevant information about the system—ranging from its size, complexity, uniqueness, evolution, and possible trajectory. In effect, if we allow each code to represent a unique dimension (i.e., minimum redundancy of information conveyed) of the dyadic system, when a code is combined with another code, a unique joint code emerges (much like two individuals forming a dyad). It is assumed that this joint code better captures process nuances than either code individually; of course, whether it does is an empirical question. Joining codes together creates a multidimensional vector, where each vector element is assumed to contribute unique information, and more importantly, each should be sensitive to changes in the observed process. Discovering how to join two or more codes conceptually and quantitatively forms the basis of our work of finding discriminating signatures between population subgroupings. We assume that the greater the number of unique sources (i.e., codes) used, their combined utility, and ease of interpretation should allow investigators to differentiate among dyadic subgroupings, observe their evolution over time, and possibly predict their trajectory into the near future. This combinatorial strategy is consistent with the increasingly complex models of social behavior (Fogel, Lyra, & Valsiner, 1997; Newell & Molenaar, 1998). Thus, MICSEASE codes, as discrete entities, are subservient to this conceptualization of the need to capture process, hence their propensity to change regularly, although not indiscriminately, depending on the research question.

Other disciplines, most notably ethology and computer science, have found that a few simple bits of relevant information extracted from a larger body of data are sufficient to reproduce complex processes. For example, ethologists have shown that very simple algorithms specifying behavioral reactions to the near neighbor can explain very complex behaviors in schools of fish or flocks of birds (see, e.g., Shaw, 1970). If we assume similar rules of parsimony apply to dyadic and familial processes, then the selectively coded salient data reduced using an efficient algorithm should reproduce the observed behavioral process. Our objective is to create models that accurately reproduce the process with a minimum number of codes. Depending on the research question, relevant codes are typically drawn from our existing catalog of codes, or we generate an ethogram of the relevant behavior.

As each unique study or research population arises, we generally modify the codes in accord with four conceptual building blocks. Initially, we code the behavior of individual interactants; these codes are the behavioral indicators. Behavioral indicators then collapse into specific behavioral domains that represent unique aspects or dimensions of the individual. Next, behavioral domain data reduce into a single index, collectively representing the behavioral state of the individual. Finally, behavioral process emerges by combining the behavioral states among all interactants (see Griffin, 2000, for greater detail).

Determining and Coding Behavioral Indicators

The initial step in this process is coding the individual. Every social process has defining features that foreshadow the process trajectory. If either member of a dyad, for example, brings a high magnitude negative act into the behavior stream, when their respective streams are combined, the joint process projected into the future has a higher likelihood of having a negative exchange, at least within the same experimental situation and across a specified window of time. The objective initially is to capture the sequential description of the features, referred to as behavioral indicators, shown by each individual. A code is assigned to each indicator, and each individual is described by *n*-codes at time t_x. These codes reflect an observable or inferred disposition of the individual during the unitized time period and are derived from theory, the conceptual model, or the research question. After selecting the relevant domains, we then determine how many different indicators of the domain are codeable. For example, we assume that during adult dyadic interaction, the listener's nonverbal or paralinguistic monitoring behavior is an important dimension of the process and that we can reliably code three indicators of this domain: head nod, back channel, and eye gaze.

Next, we decide whether to score each indicator as nominal or as quantitative. This decision is important because it determines how the indicators eventually collapse to form the behavioral domain index. Although nominal scoring is restrictive to a dichotomous outcome (e.g., on–off; present–not present), it allows us to meaningfully tally the score values over a domain. For example, if each indicator within a domain is scored in the same direction (i.e., *good* = 1, *bad* = 0), then a simple sum provides an informative index. If the number of indicators exceeds 3 or 4 and each is in the same direction, then a proportion also provides a good summary index. Similarly, if the domain has indicators that reflect contradictory behaviors or valences (e.g., listener head nod vs. listener eye roll), an interpretable summary index is constructed using difference, absolute difference, odds (i.e., ratio), or (ln) odds (i.e., natural log or log to the base *e*; 2.71828).

To illustrate, two recent theses conducted at the lab at Arizona State University involved creating indices that were designed to capture the quality of the relation within dyads. Gunnell (2002) used the ratio of the speaker affect rating over the listener nonverbal behaviors, with differential weightings based on the literature. Similarly, Verman (2001) created a summary index that tallied the behaviors of a noncustodial father conversing with his child; the index was a linear function of the verbal statements (i.e., valence at each talk turn) plus differentially weighted nonverbals (e.g., mutual laughter received double the value of only one person laughing) minus negative behaviors.

An illustration of various summary index combinations and their results are in Table 6.1. Note that each combinatorial method produces a range of values. The best index to use depends on indicator format, construction, and clarity of interpretation relative to the research question.

A quantitative indicator, reflecting a rating or scale, provides additional information not available with nominal scoring. However, quantitatively scored indicators are difficult to combine meaningfully with other indicators, either nominal or quantitative (e.g., adding or multiplying two scale values is difficult to interpret). Thus, quantitative indicators usually represent a single domain (e.g., Negative Affect level). Although it is possible to have two quantitative indicators of the same

TABLE 6.1

An Illustration of Domain and State Index Construction at Three Time Periods for Two Subjects Across Multiple Indicators, Domains, and Valences

Domain[a] Valence Indicator		*Nonverbal[b]*					*Verbal[b]*				
		Positive		*Negative*			*Negative*	*Positive*			
Time	*Subject*	*HN*	*BC*	*EG*	*ER*	*Index[c]*		*Agree*	*PS*	*Index[d]*	*Behavioral State*
t_0	i	1	0	1	1	2,1	3	0	0	3,0	2,1,3,0
	j	1	1	1	1	3,1	4	0	0	4,0	3,1,4,0
t_1	i	1	1	0	0	2,0	1	1	1	1,2	2,0,1,2
	j	0	1	0	0	1,0	2	0	0	2,0	1,0,2,0
t_2	i	0	1	1	1	2,1	1	1	0	1,1	2,1,1,1
	j	0	0	0	0	0,0	5	0	0	5,0	0,1,5,0

[a] = Nominal scoring except for Verbal Negative which is quantitative (1-5).
[b] = HN = Head Nod; BC = Back Channel; EG = Eye Gaze; ER = Eye Roll; PS = Problem Solution.
[c] = Index reflects the sum of the summed Positive Nonverbals and the single Negative Nonverbal.
[d] = Index reflects the quantitative Verbal Negative and the summed nominal Verbal Positives.

behavioral domain, they should be contradictory or at least different enough such that their differences or odds are interpretable. For example, dividing a positive and a negative rating during the same time unit estimates the odds index of these valences.

Finally, it is possible to weight any indicator or indicator summary (either nominal or quantitative) score, justifying the weight by theory or past experience with the data. For example, assume the domain of interactant listener consists of head nod, back channel (i.e., paralinguistic cues indicating attention by the listener; e.g., a "uh-huh"), eye gaze, and eye roll. All indicators except eye roll are considered facilitators of conversation, hence the best summary index would be a difference score or the odds (i.e., ratio) between the three positive indicators and eye roll. Assume that all four indicators were scored 1 at t_x, producing a difference score of 2 (3–1) or an odds of 3 (3:1). The utility of this score assumes, of course, that positive and negative listener behavior has equivalent impact on a conversation. Available evidence indicates that negative behavior has a greater detrimental effect on a conversation than positive behavior has on improving a conversation (Noller, 1984); this is especially true for eye roll (Gottman, 1994). Thus, we can justify weighting the negative indicator more heavily.

It is also possible to weigh same valence behaviors differentially within the same domain. If back channel, for example, has been shown to be more influential (i.e., changes conversation trajectory) than other similar valence codes within the same domain, then it can be weighted proportion to its expected influence. Gunnell (2002), for example, in the thesis cited earlier, doubled the value of gaze and allowed eye roll to negate positive nonverbal communication.

Constructing Behavioral Domains

After we decide on the relevant indicators, their scoring and weighting, we develop the behavioral domains. A behavioral domain is a multicode composite index representing a unique dimension or feature of each study participant. Although it is possible to have a single, usually quantitative, indicator for a domain, most often the investigator wants numerous indicators per domain because each domain is an inclusive description of a specific aspect or dimension of the interactant. Table 6.1 illustrates a simple example of four domains (Nonverbal Positive: head nod, back channel, eye gaze; Nonverbal Negative: eye roll; Verbal Negative; Verbal Positive: agree, problem solution) with two participants (i,j) over three time units (t_0–t_2). The time unit here is arbitrary; it could reflect talk turns or discrete intervals (e.g., 5s or 1s). Verbal Negative is a rating with a range of 1 to 5, the other indicators are nominal (1/0). Table 6.1 shows how the individual indicator scores produce the domain index.

Although every behavioral domain index is subsequently collapsed into the behavioral state score, each independently represents a specific behavioral feature, and as such, can be used in traditional sequential or time series analyses. It is assumed that reliability is obtained at the indicator level and, when separate indicators are combined, the resulting domain is reliable.

Defining the Behavioral State

Whereas a behavioral domain provides an index of n-indicators within a subject, the behavioral state is an array of behavioral domain values within a subject (see Table 6.1). The behavioral state encompasses the behavior of an interactant and produces an interpretable behavioral array; it is a vector, an n-tuple of real numbers in an n-dimensional Euclidean space. In this form, it represents the individual's behavior state in the behavioral process at t_x—it is the interactant's signature. Although it might appear to have little utility beyond simply being a collection of domain values, it is unique because the investigator can alter its composition depending on the research question. In effect, the behavioral state, not its constituent components, is the unit used for analysis. And by varying the inclusion or exclusion of specific domain values, the array can be used in various data analytic strategies that employ multidimensional scores; for example, data visualization techniques that require x, y, and z coordinate values, plus additional values that represent magnitude or color (see Griffin, 2000).

Creating the Behavioral Process

When combining behavioral states across subjects, we have two options: retain either a domain-by-domain comparison or collapse over domains into a single process index. By retaining a domain-by-domain comparison, an array of domain values across subjects is available for analysis. Consequently, there is less information loss, and multiple data points are available for analysis. Our recent work, however, has focused on collapsing across domains to create a single index that provides an accurate summary indicator of the process. Griffin (2000) provided an overview of possible methods of creating theses indices. A summary index is more useful for traditional statistical analysis because it is more tractable than the domain-by-domain comparison. Time-series analysis, for example, can trace the behavioral trajectory over time, or if the study requires a group comparison, then the averaged index score over some unit of time is an interpretable behavioral process score for any particular dyad or unit. Assume that we want to calculate a single index representing listener nonverbal behavior using gaze, head nod, back channel, and eye roll. A simple index can be created by summing the proportions of each of the three positive listener behaviors that occupy each talk turn and then taking the average (see Gunnell, 2002). A nonverbal score of zero occurs when no positive or negative listener behaviors take place, or it may result from some combination of positive and negative behaviors, hence we add a constant of .1 to the positive behaviors to remove this ambiguity. And if we assume that a negative behavior such as an eye roll can counteract positive behaviors, we can effectively negate the influence of the positive nonverbals by multiplying the score by .01. To illustrate, if a listener's average head nod, back channel, and gaze scores were 0, .25, and .50, respectively, the listener's nonverbal score for that talk turn would be (.75/3) + 0.1, or .35. If an eye roll also occurred during the talk turn, the nonverbal score is ((.75/3) + 0.1) * .01, or .0035. Notice that with no positive and only the eye roll, the score would be .001. This method of estimating the nonverbal allows credit for the positive nonverbal, yet shows the pervasive effect of negative nonverbal. Of course, each coded behavior can be differentially weighted depending on theory or investigator rationale.

These indices are also appropriate for the more exotic, but very relevant, pattern recognition and classification strategies used in bioinformatics, image analysis, and audio and video engineering (Duda, Hart, & Stork, 2001). For example, Griffin (2002), using Hidden Markov Models as a pattern recognition procedure, showed that it is possible to discriminate distress from nondistressed couples using score vectors (e.g., [2 ,3, 9], as described earlier) generated during a 15-min interaction. Instead of verbal and nonverbal codes, he used affect scores and duration to populate the vectors, where each vector represented a dyadic state (i.e., unique value combinations) as the couple shifts states during the course of the interaction. He found that couple distress level differentiates the likelihood and transition of states in a distinctive way, thus permitting pattern discrimination. Although he used affect and duration in the vectors, any combination of coded behaviors that form a unique (i.e., behaviorally informative) vector set is appropriate.

DEVELOPMENT OF THE CODING SYSTEM

In 1983, the MICSEASE was developed at Auburn University under the direction of William Griffin. Brenda James compiled the manual and training procedures, and Thomas Hannan forwarded the reliability estimates and analysis suggestions. In 1989, the MICSEASE manual was revised and Shannon Greene at Arizona State University added some of its current definitions. In the early 1990s, Amy Decker–Haas codified the coding guidelines and reliability procedures described later in this chapter.

Initially, the number of codes was reduced from 28 to 30 to 15. Some of the original MICS codes were retained; others were modified or combined, and some were dropped. We added self-reported affect to the MICSEASE in 1989. Affect is collected using a modified version of the Gottman and Levenson (1985) procedure; instead of using a rating dial without visual feedback to report affect recall (as in the Gottman lab), couples use a computer mouse to report affect in real-time during recall where each mouse movement corresponds to an affect rating guide on the video monitor. These ratings, collected independently from the husband and the wife after the marital interaction, become a code with an associated string of data. And when combined with the nonverbal codes, also collected second-by-second, their amalgamation constructs a real-time data stream that, when partitioned into verbal code delineated talk-turns, produces a data source rich with analytic possibilities.

By the early 1990s, the MICSEASE had retained a few very specific nonverbal codes (e.g., eye gaze) and dropped most of the standard verbal codes found in marital interaction research because they either failed to discriminate between populations or else the combination of specific nonverbals with self-reported affect reduced the need for many other codes. It was during this period that our coding interests and emphasis shifted from considerations of code inclusion to code manipulation and stricter coding procedures. Code manipulation became paramount in the early 1990s when we had a funded study to examine the role of Parkinson's disease on marital quality. Using a single-case study (Griffin & Greene, 1994), we discovered that subtle but very important physiological changes can occur to a Parkinson's patient (husband in this study) during marital interaction, especially if the spouse is distressed. Capturing these physiological nuances became a coding challenge: it was important to capture the facial features that telegraph change to the nondiseased spouse so that we could discriminate those couples with and without a distressed partner. To assess changes in functioning, we targeted the symptom of orofacial bradykinesia (i.e., extreme slowness of movement) by creating an index that combined estimates of eye blink and mouth closure. These two discrete facial features were combined as a single bradykinesia index because synergistically they interacted to capture the essence of the deterioration. For both, occurrence or nonoccurrence was assessed at each 30th of a second interval, and then separate occurrence probabilities for each were estimated for every 5-sec interval. These probabilities were summed (minus joint occurrences) and then subtracted from 1, providing a probability of nonmovement. Cohen's kappa was .93 for eye blink, and .88 for mouth closure. To determine the wife's role in the interaction, we used the Verbal Negative code for each wife utterance to determine if it fell into either negative (1) or nonnegative (0) valence. The occurrence probability of a verbal negative was then calculated for each 5-sec interval. Cohen's kappa was .80. This index effectively indicated the point of physical deterioration during the conversation, and established the foundation for code development for our subsequent larger study with Parkinson's patients (Greene & Griffin, 1998).

The final evolutionary step during the early 1990s was standardization of the coder training, progress documentation, and reliability acquisition procedures for large multiwave, multiyears studies. Noteworthy achievements during this time were our efforts to standardize training across studies, institute coder pretesting, manualize recalibration procedures, have each coder specialize only on one code, always code against a criterion coder (rather than between two general coders), have a separate code sheet for each code and each study participant, and finally, in the last several years, we have made extensive use of spreadsheets for code sheet construction and data entry, electronic data transfer and database storage, and coding from video CDs. This infusion of coding standardization and technology integration has allowed us to maintain high reliability (e.g., approximately between .8–.9 on all codes) while coding at a very high rate (e.g., over 400,000 seconds of dyadic interaction from 1996–2000).

TASK AND SETTING

All coded interactions occur in the Marital Interaction Lab at Arizona State University, a suite of two rooms designed to resemble a living room, with the requisite prints of pottery and cacti. Two unobtrusive, partially concealed, remotely controlled cameras are mounted on the walls at head level behind each chair. All audiovisual and mixing equipment is controlled from a room adjacent to the interaction. Video signals are combined producing a split-screen image; audio is obtained from lavaliere microphones worn by each spouse.

Depending on the population and the research question, the task varies slightly—but in general, the objective is the same: get the couple to talk about something that each partner agrees is distressful in their relationship for 12 to 15 min. We generally seek to invoke a relevant and affectively laden conversation topic in each study population. For example, with the Parkinson's disease population, we asked that they discuss the following: "How has the Parkinson's disease affected your marital relationship, your relationship to immediate family members, and your relationship with friends?" Given the devastating effects of this disease on the spouse and each family member, this simple question generated ample codeable data.

For married couples, the negative task is always the same. Couples initially are given the Areas of Disagreement questionnaire (i.e., standard Strodbeck's revealed differences task; see Gottman, 1979). Each marital partner selects a list of potential disagreement areas typically associated with marital relationships and ranks the items according to the level and duration of disagreement. Couples are then instructed on how to use the Affect Generation computers in the lab. After they become familiar with the procedure, they return to their chairs. With the lab assistant's help, the couple selects the three most common topics from the list of problem areas, ranks them from most to least distressing, and agrees to discuss them. The lab assistant then instructs the couple to engage in a 12- or 15-min discussion (depends on the study) and attempt to resolve the issues according to their rankings. The assistant leaves the room and uses a visual or audio signal to tell the couple to commence their discussion. After the allotted time expires, each dyad member immediately and independently rates his or her affect.

The videotape is played back using a software generated overlay with a 9-point color-coded vertical scale that appears on the computer screen. This overlay was positioned beside the face on the monitor of the individual reviewing the tape. The affect rating ranges from extreme negative (red; monitor bottom), through neutral (gray; monitor middle) to extreme positive (blue; monitor top), and is controlled by a computer mouse. The width of the bar varies at each affect level (5 pixel increments) corresponding to the intensity of the affect, neutral being the thinnest. The widest affect level is 28 pixels wide (1.5 cm). As the reviewer moves the mouse, the affect bar is highlighted corresponding to the degree and direction of the affect. For example, as the individual's affect rating becomes more negative (positive), the mouse is pulled back (pushed forward) and the appropriate affect level becomes highlighted, and as the highlighted area moves further from neutral, the width of the level expands to reflect intensity. During the review of the tape, and viewing only his or her own rating, each individual is asked to move the mouse to reflect affect experience during the interaction (i.e., "How were you feeling at each moment?"). Software records the location of the bar position every second, providing a continuous measure of affect throughout the interaction.

For divorced couples, we took the question in a slightly different direction: instead of asking the couple to talk about their problems, we asked that they discuss postdivorce issues that arise from having to share custody of a child or children. We gleaned items from several focus groups of divorced parents, created an inventory of 10 items, and when they arrived at the lab, each parent listed the top three items that he or she felt was most problematic in the current postdivorce environment. Items ranged from "scheduling pick-up and drop-off times and locations" to "friends and relatives of mine, or my ex-spouse, who spend time with my child." Couples were asked to jointly agree on the top three items, and the following statement was made by the lab assistant: "I'd like for you to discuss how these issues concerning your children currently affect your relationship and discuss the possibility of resolving, or at least improving, the problems associated with these issues." As with the married couples, after 15 minutes the couple stopped the interaction and proceeded to the Affect recording phase of the task.

We also code parent–child dyadic interactions. A typical interaction is 12 to 15 minutes long, and depending on the study, occurs either in the home or in the lab. One study examining the relationship between a parent whose spouse had died and a targeted child, sought to assess the effectiveness of an intervention program for these at-risk children. To ensure consistency across settings, we took lighting, chairs, and a card table to each home; these were arranged (e.g., distances to camera and lighting) according to guidelines we established to provide optimal coding reliability. The parent and child were read the following statement:

> "We are trying to learn how a family changes after a death in the family. When a parent dies, families go though changes, and since each family is different, we need you to answer the following questions about your family. Please spend 3-4 minutes answering each of the following questions: (1) How have things changed around the house since the death? (2) What changes have been hardest for you during the past month?

(3) What things have you done during the past month to make things better? (4) What things can you do in the future to help make things better?"

In another recent intervention study involving noncustodial divorced fathers and their children, the lab assignment required the father to help the child in an age-graded building block task, but the task was interrupted twice so that the father could ask two questions, drawn from separate envelopes, that were given to him prior to beginning the task. After about 6 to 8 min, the first question was asked: (Father Name) will you please ask (Child Name) the following question: "What did you do either by yourself or with a friend in the last several days that you enjoyed very much?" This conversation lasted 5 min and the building block task resumed for 8 more minutes. Next, the father was asked to read the following question from the second envelope: (Father Name) will you please ask (Child Name) the following question: "Please talk with me for a few minutes about the things that you and your mother did during this past week." This latter question sought to raise the intensity of the conversation, especially in postdivorce families characterized by postmarital animosity. This conversation lasted 10 min, followed by an additional 3 min of the building block task.

DESCRIPTION OF THE CODING SYSTEM

The basic elements used to code adult interaction in the lab setting are as follows: Talk Turn, Nonverbal Behaviors (eye gaze, head nod, back channel, eye roll), Verbal Behaviors (problem solution, negative, agree), and Self-Report Affect. These are the primary codes used in most of the current projects that involve coding adult dyadic interaction, although additional MISCEASE codes include the following: Accept Responsibility, Deny Responsibility, Complain, Humor, Interrupt, Mind Read, Question, Command, Solution, and Problem Description. We typically use only a few verbal codes, and when combined with nonverbal codes, the combination is usually effective in discriminating population subgroupings. Depending on the population or research question, these basic codes can change slightly, either with deletions or additions, or changes in definition. Most recently, we had to modify our definition of Verbal Negative when we started coding formerly married couples. We were surprised at the lack of overt negativity expressed in this population, especially compared to the amount seen in distressed married couples. Yet when the interactions were viewed, negativity clearly was being broadcast within the dyad, but its expression took a different form than we had seen in married couples. We eventually revised the Verbal Negative code to include a Hidden Negative component to capture the various innuendos or private messages that occur in this population. Reliability on this code was adequate: kappa = .84 for women and .82 for men.

As we have noted throughout this chapter, we do not use many codes. The first code is always Talk Turn; it delineates the conversational structure. But more importantly, it determines the construction and interpretation of each data point. Consequently, talk turns take priority in our lab. After reliability is established (kappa averages mid-.9s), we use the talk turn data to create unique Microsoft Excel codesheets for each member of the dyad and each code or code category.

After Talk Turn, the next category is Nonverbal. This is a listener category containing three positive attending behaviors (i.e., eye gaze, head nod, and back channel) and one negative contemptuous behavior (eye roll). (We also code gaze for the speaker to examine if the speaker is looking when talking.) Basically, we include this category to determine if the speaker has reason to perceive the listener as not listening, being disrespectful, or worse, being contemptuous. This impression by the speaker may or may not be evident by his or her action, but it usually influences the affect rating, which then provides an opportunity to compare (e.g., ratio) the speaker versus listener values in either real time or averaged across the talk turn.

Similarly, by using the Verbal codes, we add additional dimensionality by assessing whether the speaker is being generally helpful or facilitating (i.e., Problem Solution, Agree) or destructive (i.e., Negative; e.g., a hostile statement expressing unambiguous dislike or disapproval of a specific behavior engaged in by the partner; a comment intended to demean or embarrass the other person.). These are also compared to the listener attending behavior, or examined for internal consistency with the self-reported affect. In effect, at each unitized time point, either a talk turn or in real time, we have knowledge of how each person was feeling, the presence or absence of constructive or destructive statements, and attending behavior by the listener. In composite form, these coded behaviors form an index of the process at time t_x; this time frame can slide forward or backward to examine any lead or lag relations in the data.

CODER TRAINING

We use the following criteria to select coders; these are most applicable in situations when students seek coding experience for course credit rather than as a campus job. Although these criteria are without empirical support, by adhering to them we have been able to maintain a stable, highly productive coding lab consisting of between 16 and 23 coders per semester since the mid-1990s:

1. Student Status Undergraduate students are generally better coders because they "interpret" behavior less and are willing to be trained to the code definition. Graduate students, especially those from clinical programs, tend to infer too much and thus make poor coders.

2. Academic Standing Students must have a minimum grade point average of 3.0 on 4.0 scale, and junior or senior standing.

3. Academic Major Students must have an interest in social sciences. Majoring in psychology, family studies, anthropology, or sociology is helpful but not required.

4. Interest in the Subject Matter Potential coders need some purpose in participating in research other than earning course credit; for example, interest in graduate school.

5. Female versus Male Coders Male coders perform very well on low inference highly specific codes, such as eye gaze. Female coders tend to pick up on behavioral nuances more quickly than male students, but sometimes their personal interpretations influence reliability. When this is addressed early in training, they perform well with social codes (e.g., problem solve).

6. Time Commitment We request an academic year regardless if they are seeking course-credit or volunteering.

7. Paying Coders Paid coders provide consistency across semesters, whereas those needing research experience to apply for graduate school are usually more motivated. Reliability, however, does not differ across the two groups.

New coders require approximately 20 hr to learn most of our codes; codes requiring more precision (e.g., eye gaze) and inference (e.g., negative), however, usually take 30 hr. Coding shifts are limited to 2 hr per day to minimize coder fatigue and distraction. Prior to training, coders become familiar with the code sheets, equipment use, and data cataloging. Each coder is assigned one code and only has one definition to learn; consequently they become highly proficient at finding that behavior in a data stream. Before viewing tapes, a new coder must score 100% on a 7 to 10 question written test on the definition of the assigned code. To train new coders, we maintain a library of 6 to 12 interactions per code; these training sets are newly created for each project so that the coders are viewing training material with the appropriate population using correct lighting and audio. These data are drawn from the pilot study, or the sample population during actual interactions, but for various reasons cannot be included in the data analysis. Initially, the lab supervisor and the new coder observe at least one interaction together and then discuss the correspondence between the observed behaviors and the definition. Coders then observe and code the remaining training vignettes.

Reliability is calculated on 15% of each of the training tapes. Coders must attain minimum kappa reliability of 0.7 before commencing coding. On most codes we prefer, and regularly attain, a minimum training kappa of 0.8, but accept 0.7 on codes that are more difficult (e.g., negative).

If reliability slips below 0.7 during data coding, the coder is pulled from the data coding pool and retrained on the code. He or she reviews the problem tape(s) with the lab supervisor, discusses the elements of the behavior that are problematic, and then recodes the tape(s) just as if it were a training tape(s). These interactions are removed from data coding for that particular coder and subsequently recoded by another coder. Once acceptable reliability levels are reestablished, the coder returns to the coding pool.

More detailed information about the coding manual, definitions, procedures, spreadsheet macros, and all other questions about the coding system may be directed to the first author at william.griffin@asu.edu.

CODING PROCESS

Each coder generally completes 6 to 10 hr per week in the lab. In general, coding a 15-min interaction for a single verbal behavior (i.e., Verbal Agree) takes approximately 30 to 40 minutes (or a 2:1–3:1 ratio). Talk turns require greater precision, taking from 40 minutes to an hour to code (i.e., 4:1), depending on floor switch frequency. Eye gaze coding also occurs at a rate of about 4:1 per interactant.

The coder initially reviews the entire interaction prior to commencing coding; this allows the coder to observe any participant idiosyncrasies that might influence reliability. Each coder is responsible for only one interactant per pass through the data. Again, this procedure was meant to minimize coder error by requiring them to focus on one behavior and one subject at a time. We create separate codesheets for each code and each interactant. This prevents bias among coders by not allowing them to see other data collected for the same interaction.

RELIABILITY

As we noted earlier, the MICSEASE has been used to code videotaped interactions between adults, adults with children, and dyadic exchanges during a family conversation. Most of the interactions have been recorded in the laboratory, although two studies were conducted in the home, and one occurred in a large institutional room. Irrespective of population and taping location, we have consistently maintained high levels of reliability (kappa). For example, with adult dyads in the lab, reliability for verbal codes range from .78 (Problem Solution) to .9 (Critical Comments), and for the nonverbals, the kappas range from .73 (Back Channel) to .93 (Blink). Of course, across studies the kappa values vary, but the average value for a nonverbal code is .84 (range: .73–.93) and .82 (range: .77–.9) for verbal. With parent–child dyads, the average nonverbal is .86 (range: .8–.94) and the verbal is .84 (range: .76–.96). These values were generated using coders specializing in one code measured against a criterion coder. Specific reliability estimates by study, population, and code can be found at www.public.asu.edu/~atwag.

VALIDITY

The MICSEASE codes have been used with adult dyads, parent–child dyads, family triads, and entire families. Emphasis is always on selecting the most salient features assumed to characterize the population, code them, and then determine if they distinguish between putative subgroupings. Within the framework of Criterion validity, we were able to discern Parkinson's disease couples with and without a maritally distressed partner (Greene & Griffin, 1994), distressed from nondistressed couples (e.g., Griffin, 1993, 2002; Gunnell, 2002), families with and without an asthmatic child (Griffin et al., 2002; Northey et al., 1998), and most recently, intervention effectiveness evidenced by changes in parent–child interactions (Sandler et al, 2002; Wolchick et al., 2000). Although we have been able to discriminate between subtypes within a population, only recently have we moved toward the arena of construct validity by attempting to create a behavioral index measuring relationship quality between a noncustodial father and his child (discussed earlier in the Task and Setting section). We were able to correlate a behavioral index (i.e., [Talk + Gaze + (Talk * Gaze) + Laughter – (Sum of Child Negative) + Father Supportive] using father and child codes per talk turn) with the father's report of his relationship with the child (i.e., family fun time, visitation quality, child acceptance) and his coparenting relationship (Verman, 2001). This index in now being used to test for intervention effects in a large study of noncustodial fathers (see Braver & Griffin, 2000).

GENERALIZABILITY

The MICSEASE has demonstrated its utility across a wide variety of populations. A large proportion of the coding, coding procedures, and index creation algorithms evolved from examining the interactions of distressed and nondistressed married couples (Griffin, 1993, 2000), marital partners with Parkinson's disease (Greene & Griffin, 1998; Griffin & Greene, 1994), and most recently, divorced couples. It has also been used with parent–child conversations conducted in the lab and the home (Sandler et al., 2002; Verman, 2001; Wolchik et al., 2000). Children in these studies have ranged in age from 4 to 16. Also, a modified version of the MICEASE (i.e., Family Interaction Scales; Griffin, Krainz, & Northey, 1994) was used to examine family interactions patterns in the home among families with and without an asthmatic son (see Griffin et al., 2002; Northey Griffin, & Krainz, 1998). The MICSEASE also has influenced development of coding procedures for tetradic family systems involving both nondivorced and stepfamily arrangements (Anderson & Greene, 1999).

Study participants have been predominantly middle and lower income. Most of the participants have been White, with approximately 10% being Mexican–American. Although we have not specifically attempted to ascertain reliability or coding differences as a function of ethnicity or income, we have had no difficulty implementing the MICSEASE across the populations or settings. This broad applicability is likely possible because most of the codes used are basic to dyadic interaction (e.g., Verbal Agree, Head Nod, Gaze).

CLINICAL UTILITY

As we have maintained throughout this chapter, the MICSEASE emphasizes the importance of capturing behavioral processes. Process is a key component in most of the systems-based clinical theories (see Griffin, 1993b; Griffin & Greene, 1999). Previous work with populations at risk for clinical manifestations (i.e., depression among the recently divorced, the bereaved, and those with a chronic illness) suggests that the MICSEASE would be an excellent tool to assess targeted clinical change. For example, it specifically delineates what behaviors constitute "good listening'—head nod, back channel, eye gaze—thereby providing clinicians with a means for assessment and instruction. Of course, the implementation of this or any other behavioral observational coding system requires a substantial investment in time, money, and personnel. With minimal or no research funding, the clinician would need to restrict his or her assessment of change to a few basic interactional features that should be sensitive to the desired or expected changes (e.g., reduced negative statements [Negative]; increased agreement [Verbal Agree]; modify attending behavior [Gaze, Head Nod]).

STUDIES USING THE CODING SYSTEM

When coding dyadic interaction, we assume that only a few theoretically determined codes are needed to distinguish distressed from nondistressed couples, or any specified subgroupings within a population of couples. This, of course, requires that the theory driven codes are reasonable, present in the interaction, definitions are clear, and the behavior can be obtained reliably. In the early 1990s, we focused on features that distinguish distressed from nondistressed marital dyads (Griffin, 1993); this evolved into finding distinctive marital quality features among married couples who had one spouse with Parkinson's disease (Greene & Griffin, 1994; Griffin & Greene, 1994).

In the mid-1990s, we extended our lab-based data acquisition of dyadic behavior into the home and expanded the subject unit to dyads within a family. Specifically, we coded the behaviors of dyadic exchanges in families with and without an asthmatic child to determine if and how these families might differ according to Salvador Minuchin's Psychosomatic Model (see Griffin et al., 2002, for details).

During this same period, we further extended the coding from adult dyads to parent–child dyads; the coding of the parent–child dyads was part of two large interventions studies, and the behavioral data were used to determine the effectiveness of the intervention of parental skill acquisition and general relationship quality. The first study examined the effects of a postdivorce custodial parent (i.e., mother) intervention that attempted to modify child adjustment to divorce; behavioral data indicated that it successfully altered the mother–child interaction (see Wolchik et al., 2000). The other study, instead of attempting to modify a child's risk associated with divorce, sought to reduce the risk that occurs following the death of a parent; again, behavioral data indicated that the intervention was successful (see Sandler et al., 2002). In each study, we used basic codes (e.g., laughter, positive statement) that reflected the parenting behaviors taught in the intervention and are generally associated with a good parent–child relationship. Similarly, to assess the effectiveness of a postdivorce intervention for noncustodial fathers (see Braver & Griffin, 2000, for details), our most recent work involves coding the basic interactional features of formerly married partners and the noncustodial fathers in those dyads conversing with a targeted child. Preliminary analyses indicate that we can create a behavioral index that accurately assesses the quality of the father–child relationship, and a coding structure that successfully captures intervention effects in the divorced couples.

ACKNOWLEDGMENTS

Numerous grants have supported the observation coding associated with the evolution of the MICSEASE. These include the following: National Institute of Mental Health, MH51184-01A1 (with Sanford Braver), MH39246-11 (Center for the Prevention of Child and Family Stress Renewal), and MH49155 (Child Bereavement Program); the Arizona Disease Control Research Commission (Contract Number 82-0682); and an Arizona State University Research Incentive Award and Faculty Grant in Aid award. We would like to thank Gordon Gunnell for reviewing earlier drafts of this chapter.

7

The Interactional Dimensions Coding System: A Global System for Couple Interactions

Galena H. Kline[1], Danielle Julien[2], Brian Baucom[1], Scott Hartman[1],
Katy Gilbert[1], Tondeleyo Gonzalez[1], and Howard J. Markman[1]
[1]*University of Denver*
[2]*University of Quebec at Montreal*

This chapter presents up-to-date conceptual and empirical information on the Interaction Dimensions Coding System (IDCS; Julien, Markman, & Lindahl, 1989). The purpose of the IDCS is to provide an efficient means of coding both positive and negative dimensions of couple interactions. It is global in nature, so that it can capture the entirety of an interaction, including affect and content components, yet the system is based on research findings from microanalytic coding systems such as the Couple Interaction Scoring System (CISS; Notarius & Markman, 1981) and the Marital Interaction Coding System (MICS; Summers, 1983). The system provides nine individual codes (i.e., each partner receives a separate rating) and five dyadic codes (i.e., the couple is rated as a whole). For all 14 codes, the entire interaction is the unit of analysis. To date, this system has mostly been used to code heterosexual couples' discussions of problem areas in their relationships, yet it is applicable to a diverse set of couples and tasks.

THEORETICAL FOUNDATIONS

When the IDCS was initially developed at the Center for Marital and Family Studies (CMFS; see Julien et al., 1989), global coding systems, as opposed to microanalytic systems, were just beginning to become widely used (Markman, 1992). As a global system, it was designed to be more efficient and economical than microanalytic systems. In addition, the developers aimed to tap theoretically relevant communication constructs that had been neglected in other systems and to assess danger signs (e.g., withdrawal, invalidation) identified in years of research using microanalytic systems that were associated with and predictive of marital distress and divorce (see Markman, Stanley, and Blumberg, 2001, for an overview of research on danger signs). Julien and colleagues (1989) explained the original and theoretical foundations of the IDCS in detail; therefore, only a brief summary from their discussion is presented in this chapter.

Broadly speaking, the developers of the IDCS based the coding system on dimensions that are consistent with theories of family distress (see Markman and Notarius, 1987, for a review). In addition, the system is based on communication behaviors and patterns that have been shown to discriminate between functional and dysfunctional family communication processes (Hetherington & Martin, 1972; Jacob, 1975; Schapp, 1984).

Given that negative behaviors have been shown to effectively distinguish distressed couples from nondistressed couples (Schapp, 1984), the IDCS was designed to include five codes for different types of negative behavior: Conflict, Withdrawal, Dominance, Denial, and Negative Affect. Specifically, there is a code for conflict because many theories of marital functioning highlight the importance of conflict-management skills and because research has shown that distressed couples show more behaviors that provoke conflict (e.g., blaming and nagging) than do nondistressed couples (Gottman, Markman, & Notarius, 1977; Revenstorf, Vogel, Wegener, Hahlweg, & Schindler, 1980). Likewise, withdrawal is coded because research indicates that withdrawing from interactions is common in distressed couples (Komarovsky, 1967; Margolin, 1984; Raush, Barry, Hertel, & Swain, 1974; Spanier & Thompson, 1984). Because withdrawal is considered a mostly physical tactic, denial is also coded, so that verbal tactics of ending the interaction can be assessed. Dominance is central to many theories of communication and is therefore included in the IDCS as well; it provides an assessment of "asymmetries in floor control" during interactions. The final negative dimension of interactions that the IDCS examines is negative affect. Justification for inclusion of a negative affect code comes from research that indicates that nonverbal negative behaviors serve to discriminate distressed from nondistressed couples (Jacob, 1975; Schapp, 1984).

There are four positive codes included in the IDCS: Communication Skills, Problem-Solving Skills, Support/Validation, and Positive Affect. A rating of communication skills was included because many theories of marital distress show the importance of communication skills deficits. Furthermore, studies indicate that satisfied couples display behaviors that are inherent to good communication skills such as metacommunicative statements, self-disclosure, and clarification of requests (Hahlweg, Reisner, et al., 1984). Because some research has emphasized that happy couples use tactics aimed specifically at solving problems effectively (Beier & Sternberg, 1977; Gottman et al., 1977; Margolin & Wampold, 1981; Revenstorf, Hahlweg, Schindler, & Vogel, 1984), a code for problem-solving skills was included. A separate code was developed to assess support and validation, as some theories suggest that members of functional families validate one another frequently (Alexander, 1973). In addition, research has indicated that satisfied couples are supportive of one another (Lieberman, 1982; Paykel, Emms, Fletcher, & Rassaby, 1980). Finally, although the research on positive affect and marital relations is less conclusive than the research on negative affect (Gottman et al., 1977; Hahlweg, Revenstorf, & Schindler, 1984; Margolin & Wampold, 1981; Revenstorf et al., 1984), a code for positive affect displayed during the interaction was also included as the IDCS is intended to be comprehensive in nature.

In addition to the nine individual-level codes, there are five dyadic codes. The first is Negative Escalation, referring to a pattern of negative behaviors by one partner being followed by negative behaviors by the other. This code was included because research indicates that negative escalation is an indicator of marital distress (Gottman, 1979; Gottman et al., 1977; Revenstorf et al., 1980). The second dyadic code is Positive Escalation, a construct that has received little attention in research on marital communication, but seems useful because it is the reciprocal of negative escalation. The last three codes, which were added since the development of the original coding system, do not assess communication patterns between partners. Codes for current commitment, future satisfaction, and future stability were added to assess raters' abilities to predict these important relationship phenomena based on viewing just one interaction. However, these three codes have not yet been systematically analyzed and, therefore, their validity is unknown at present.

DEVELOPMENT OF THE CODING SYSTEM

The coding system was developed to assess both behavioral and affective components of couple interactions. In addition, it aims to provide a global system for coding interactions that can be used in a time-efficient manner. The developers drew from other global coding systems (e.g., Communication Skills Test; Floyd & Markman, 1984), microanalytic systems (see Schapp, 1984), and from the developers' experience with the CISS when devising the examples of behaviors and affect cues that are provided for each code.

TASK AND SETTING

Although other researchers have used the IDCS to code various types of interactions (e.g., Black, 2000), the primary purpose of the IDCS at the CMFS has been to code couples' discussions of problem areas in their relationship. In research at the CMFS, couples are asked to identify their top problem area using the Marital Agendas Protocol (Notarius & Vanzetti, 1983) and discuss the issue for 10 to 15 min during a lab visit. These problem discussions are videotaped and coded later.

DESCRIPTION OF THE CODING SYSTEM[1]

Following are definitions of each of the 14 codes. The coding manual also provides example behavioral cues for each code:

Individual Codes

1. Positive Affect refers to positivity expressed through facial expressions, body positioning, and tone of voice. Positive affect is not the same as absence of negative affect.

2. Negative Affect refers to negativity expressed through facial expressions, body positioning, body positioning, and tone of voice. Negative affect is not the same as absence of positive affect.

3. Problem-Solving Skills refer to an individual's ability to define a problem and work toward a mutually satisfactory solution for the problem. Ratings are assigned based on the individual's ability to try to solve the problem, not on whether the problem was actually solved.

4. Dominance refers to an individual's ability to control or influence his or her partner. Dominance may be identified through forceful, monopolizing, or coercive behaviors. Ratings are assigned based on whether the individual achieves dominance over his or her partner.

5. Support and Validation refers to positive listening and speaking skills that an individual uses to demonstrate support and understanding to his or her part-

[1]Since the inception of the original version of the Interaction Dimensions Coding System with newlywed couples at the Center for Marital and Family Studies, Julien and her team have used the system with various groups of French–Canadian dyads. Three modifications were made to the original set of individual and dyadic codes (Chartrand & Julien, 1994). First, Denial was abandoned because it consistently yielded low reliability scores in French–Canadian samples. Second, Dominance was changed from an individual code to a dyadic because it required a judgment on the dyad for establishing a score. Finally, Positive Escalation was abandoned and replaced by Interactional Synchrony. Using the empirical findings and theoretical frameworks of studies in behavior adaptation during communication (e.g., Burgoon, Stern, & Dillman, 1995), Julien's team felt that positive spiraling or snowballing (as opposed to negative affect cycles) was empirically and conceptually meaningless, and that partners' attunement to each other's behavior (synchrony) during interactions had stronger roots both in empirical findings and theories relating communication to relationship outcomes. Intercoders' reliability for Interactional Synchrony was .66 or higher in all the studies in which it was used.

ner. Close synonyms for this code are encouragement, acknowledgement, and acceptance.

6. Conflict refers to behaviors that encourage arguing. The level of tension, hostility, oppositionality, antagonism, and negative affect that an individual displays identifies conflict.

7. Withdrawal refers to attempting to avoid an interaction or discussion through body language or stating a desire not to discuss a topic.

8. Denial refers to an active rejection of a problem's existence or of personal responsibility for the problem.

9. Communication Skills refers to an individual's ability to convey thoughts and feelings in a clear, constructive manner.

Dyadic Codes

10. Negative Escalation refers to a pattern in which a negative behavior of one partner is followed by a negative behavior of the spouse and so forth, creating a snowball effect. Consecutive negative chains of behaviors are the essential elements that must be observed. This means that unrelated negative behaviors in an interaction do not constitute the spiraling effect, and such an interaction must be rated low on Negative Escalation, although one or both partners may receive moderate or high scores on Negative Affect. To be rated very highly on Negative Escalation, both partners must not only display a high frequency of negative verbal and nonverbal behaviors, but also give the impression of triggering each other's negative behaviors.

11. Positive Escalation refers to a pattern in which a positive behavior of one partner is followed by a positive behavior of the other partner and so forth, creating a snowball effect. Consecutive positive chains of behaviors are the essential elements that must be observed. This means that unrelated positive behaviors in an interaction do not constitute the spiraling effect, and such an interaction must be rated low Positive Escalation, although one or both partners may receive moderate or high scores on Positive Affect. To be rated very highly on Positive Escalation, both partners must not only display a high frequency of positive verbal and nonverbal behaviors, but also give the impression of triggering each other's positive behaviors.

12. Commitment refers to how willing a couple is to make their relationship a priority and to work on improving their relationship. How personally dedicated are they to their relationship? Do they put their partner's needs or the rela-

tionship's needs above their own at times? Do they think of themselves as a team ("we" versus "I")?

13. Future Satisfaction refers to the coder's prediction of how happy a couple will be five years from now. How rewarding will this relationship be for the couple? How pleased will they be with the relationship?

14. Future Stability refers to the coder's prediction of how likely it is that a couple will be together 5 years from now. Ratings are based on the level of dedication, satisfaction, patterns of behavior, and amount of constraints (forces that keep people in relationships regardless of their desire to stay in relationships; Stanley & Markman, 1992) that the couple exhibits during the interaction.

CODER TRAINING

Coders at the CMFS are currently graduate students and staff members who have at least a Bachelor's degree. However, advanced undergraduate students also have been successful coders. Coder training requires approximately 50 hr. Coders in training begin by reading the coding manual and attending coding meetings, during which trained coders and coders in training watch videotaped interactions together and discuss their ratings thoroughly. We suggest that coders-in-training watch at least five interactions with trained coders before coding alone. Next, we suggest that coders in training code at least 10 previously coded interactions to check for reliability. These last 10 interactions should be discussed with the previous coders if reliability appears to be low, and additional training may be necessary.

At the CMFS, coders-in-training have always received training directly from trained coders, not simply by reading the manual. However, the revised manual has examples of ratings and provides anchors for ratings. Thus, it might be possible for coders to learn the coding system simply by reading the manual. The manual can be obtained from the first author. The CMFS might also be able to provide training videos and notes on assigning ratings for these videos. A complete set of updated training videos and notes for use by other research teams is currently being constructed.

CODING PROCESS

The coding process is simple and straightforward. The instructions that follow describe, step-by-step, how a coder should go about coding a videotaped interaction. The IDCS manual suggests that coders divide each interaction into three equal time segments, rating each segment individually before assigning an overall rating for the entire interaction. Coding in segments assists coders in recalling the entire interaction when calculating the overall ratings for each code. The coding process is described in detail:

Steps for Coding

1. Watch the entire problem discussion once. Notes of both content and affect cues should be made on a form, such as the simple note-taking sheet that is included in the coding manual. No ratings should be assigned yet. The purpose of the initial viewing is to get a feel for the couples' overall interaction.

2. Obtain the total time for the interaction and divide this time into three equal time segments.

3. Watch the first segment and take notes on the coding note-taking sheet. Stop the recorded interaction. Using the notes and the manual, make ratings for each of the nine individual dimensions (see Table 7.1 for an example of a coding sheet). It is unlikely, especially when first becoming familiar with the coding system, that coders will be able to rate all of the dimensions after just one viewing of a segment. Thus, coders should watch the segment as many times as needed to confidently assign ratings for the codes.

4. Repeat step 3 for the second and third segments.

5. Having rated each third of the interaction separately, coders now assign an overall rating for each of the nine dimensions for each partner. Calculating an overall rating essentially means "summing over" the three ratings made for each dimension to reach one rating that the coder feels best describes the overall, global evaluation of each particular code. The final rating for a dimension usually reflects either the modal rating (i.e., most commonly assigned rating; 5, 5, 6 corresponds to an overall rating of 5) or the mean of the three segment ratings (i.e., the average rating; 4, 5, 6 corresponds to an overall rating of 5). The coder has some discretion in departing from this custom. The overall score is meant to reflect the entirety of the interaction and it may seem, on reflection, that the interaction is most accurately represented by only one of the three segments ratings (i.e., 3, 4, 5 corresponds to an overall rating of 5) rather than a statistical average of the three segment ratings.

6. Lastly, rate the couple (as a dyad) on the five dyadic dimensions, using the entire interaction as the coding unit.

When coders are fully trained and comfortable with the coding system, each interaction usually only needs to be viewed twice. Thus, the total time for coding an

TABLE 7.1
Coding Sheet

Date ____________ Session: Pre Post FU1 FU2 FU3 FU4 FU5

Couple Number __________ Coder __________________________

Affect Codes					
Positive Affect	Male				Overall Score
	_____	_____	_____		_____
	Female				Overall Score
	_____	_____	_____		_____
Negative Affect	Male				Overall Score
	_____	_____	_____		_____
	Female				Overall Score
	_____	_____	_____		_____
Content Codes					
Problem-Solving Skills	Male				Overall Score
	_____	_____	_____		_____
	Female				Overall Score
	_____	_____	_____		_____
Denial	Male				Overall Score
	_____	_____	_____		_____
	Female				Overall Score
	_____	_____	_____		_____
Dominance	Male				Overall Score
	_____	_____	_____		_____
	Female				Overall Score
	_____	_____	_____		_____
Combined Codes					
Support Validation	Male				Overall Score
	_____	_____	_____		_____
	Female				Overall Score
Conflict	Male				Overall Score
	_____	_____	_____		_____
	Female				Overall Score
	_____	_____	_____		_____

TABLE 7.1 (cont.)

Withdrawal	Male			Overall Score
	____	____	____	____
	Female			Overall Score
	____	____	____	____
Communication	Male			Overall Score
	____	____	____	____
	Female			Overall Score
	____	____	____	____

Dyadic Codes

Positive Escalation___ Negative Escalation___ Commitment___
Satisfaction___ Stability___

interaction with the IDCS is approximately twice the length of the couples interaction, plus 5 to 7 min of extra time to assign ratings.

RELIABILITY

As noted in the Coding Process section, each interaction is divided into three equal time segments, and each segment is coded separately. This procedure is employed to increase the reliability and validity of the overall score. The overall score is designed to represent the entire interaction, so it is essentially an average of the three time segments. At this point, we have not statistically examined the relation between the three segment scores and the overall score. At the CMFS, we only use the overall rating for each of the 14 codes (as opposed to using any of the three time segment codes). Reliability is thus reported only for these overall ratings for each of the 14 codes. Julien et al. (1989) reported reliability in terms of intercoder Pearson correlations. These correlations ranged from .05 to .71 for the 14 codes. Combining all individual codes, the Pearson correlations were .70 for men and .74 for women. For the two dyadic codes included in the original article, the Pearson correlations were .69 for Negative Escalation and .49 for Positive Escalation. The low reliability scores reported in the original article were attributed to the small variance in levels of behaviors with the particular sample of newlywed couples. The original authors suggested that the IDCS may be most useful with populations that show high variance in dyadic adjustment and that, eventually, micronalytic coding systems may fare better with populations showing less variance in adjustment (i.e., pairs of friends). More recent estimates of reliability have shown higher rates of agreement, even with similar populations of newlywed couples. The most recent reliability analyses were based on 16 videotaped-interactions that were coded by the three current coders at the CMFS. Intraclass correlations ranged from .66 to .95, with a median correlation of .87. In addition, in a recently published article from the CMFS, weighted kappas for the IDCS codes ranged from .80 to .92 (Stanley et al., 2001). However, in another recent study, reported median weighted-kappas were somewhat lower (e.g., .64 to .71; Schilling, Baucom, Brunett, Allen, & Ragland, 2003).

It should be noted that in most research at the CMFS, we use positive and negative composite scores that tap overall positive and negative dimensions of couple interactions (see Stanley et al., 2001). If used, these composite scores should be based on factor analyses computed for the overall ratings or strong theoretical rationale, both of which may differ across studies. Other researchers have also used positive and negative composite scores and report reasonable reliability for the composite scores (e.g., Cox, Paley, Burchinal, & Payne, 1999).

VALIDITY

Evidence for validity of the IDCS was presented in Julien et al.'s (1989) article in which the authors examined the IDCS's association with a microanalytic coding system, self-report measures of relationship quality and severity of problems, and with marital satisfaction 4 years later. In relation to convergence with other coding systems, many of the negative codes correlated with the negative affective dimensions of the microanalytic CISS (Notarius & Markman, 1981), although the positive IDCS codes did not correlate with the positive affective dimensions of the CISS. There were many differences in definitions of codes for the IDCS and the CISS, and Julien et al. (1989) suggested that these differences may account for the lack of similarity for the positive dimensions. In addition, the many methodological differences between global and microanalytic codes (Floyd, 1989) could also account for the nonsignificant findings.

In relation to self-report measures, Julien et al. (1989) reported that for men, some of the negative and the positive codes were correlated with self-report measures of relationship adjustment and severity of relationship problems. However, women's IDCS scores were not significantly correlated with self-report measures. More recently, it has been suggested that for both men and women, the IDCS negative codes are moderately correlated (.30 and .56) with a self-report measure of negative interactions skills (Communication Skills Test; Saiz, 2001) that examines similar dimensions of interactions (Kline, Low, & Stanley, 2002). Because of a small sample size ($N = 36$), these results should be interpreted with caution.

Predictive validity was established for two of the dyadic codes in the original study. Positive and Negative Escalation both predicted marital satisfaction 4 years after the initial interaction (Julien et al., 1989). In a more recent study, composite scores for positive and negative IDCS individual-codes changed over the course of a weekend premarital communication-training workshop (Schilling et al., 2003).

Furthermore, these changes predicted risk of marital distress at later follow-ups (Schilling et al., 2003).

The IDCS distinguishes between couples in several ways. First, distressed couples have been shown to have more negative interactions than nondistressed couples, as assessed with the IDCS (Prado & Markman, 1999). Second, couples who received premarital education (Prevention and Relationship Enhancement Program, PREP; Stanley, Blumberg, & Markman, 1999) delivered by a clergy or lay leader showed more positive and less negative interactions than those receiving naturally occurring premarital training (Stanley et al., 2001). Third, married couples who lived together prior to engagement had more negative interactions than those who lived together only after engagement or not until marriage (Kline et al., 2003). Fourth, IDCS positive and negative codes discriminated between married partners' attachment styles (as measured with the Adult Attachment Interview; Bouthillier et al., 1998).

A study by Chartrand and Julien (1994) suggested that their French–Canadian version of the IDCS is also valid and reliable. The French–Canadian version was correlated with similar interaction measures. For example, a composite of the positive codes was associated with a concurrent observational measure of intimacy behaviors (Chartrand & Julien, 1994) and with observed social support of couples in a support task (Julien, Chartrand, Simard, Bouthillier, & Bégin, 2003). In addition, the French-Canadian IDCS predicted marital satisfaction 1 year later (Chartrand & Julien, 1994).

GENERALIZABILITY

It is likely that the IDCS can be employed in a variety of couple interaction tasks, but thus far the IDCS has been used mainly for couples' discussion of problems in their relationships. Very recently, we have begun examining reliability and validity of a modified version of the IDCS that is focused on couples' friendship talk, rather than problem discussions. Couples who take part in the Family Stability Project at the CMFS complete a 10 to 15 min videotaped discussion in which they are asked to simply "talk as friends." Codes for affection, playfulness, and boredom have been added to this modified version of the IDCS and some less applicable codes, such as Problem Solving and Denial, were excluded. More information on the friendship-talk version of the IDCS can be obtained from the first author.

Julien and her colleagues have made similar modifications to design coding systems assessing support tasks (e.g., Cormier & Julien, 1996; Julien et al., 2003) and pleasant tasks (Simard, Julien,Bouthiller, & Dubé, 2002). These systems have shown good concurrent validity with dyadic adjustment measures. However, except for the contribution of synchrony in the support task, the information they provided did not explain unique variance in dyadic adjustment beyond what was already captured with the IDCS in the problem discussion (Julien et al., 2003;

Simard et al., 2002). In other words, social support and playful situations might be relevant for couples' adjustment, but Julien and colleagues (2003) suggest that much of the information we get in analyzing them is already captured with the IDCS in the classic problem discussion.

In terms of generalizability to other populations, the IDCS has mainly been used with heterosexual newlywed couples at the CMFS. Our sample has a diverse age range (17 to 53), although couples in our study are primarily White (78%). We have not systematically examined the utility of the IDCS with different minority groups. However, Julien and her colleagues have successfully used the IDCS with gay and lesbian couples (Julien et al., 2003).

With certain populations, it might be important to modify the rating scale when using the IDCS. For example, if the IDCS were used with a subpopulation of verbally abusive couples, it may be important to shift the anchors to prevent floor or ceiling effects. Additionally, it would be important to examine the validity and reliability of the IDCS carefully if it were to be used in a different language or with different cultures, as Chartrand and Julien (1994) have done with the French–Canadian version.

CLINICAL UTILITY

Although we are unaware of the IDCS being formally used for assessment of couples seeking treatment, it could be quite useful in a clinical setting. For example, the interactional processes of couples seeking therapy could be assessed quickly with the IDCS. Couples could be asked to discuss a problem area, and a therapist or a coder could then code the interactions. The coding process could illuminate specific areas, such as problem-solving skills or regulation of negative affect, in which a couple seeking treatment may need special training. Additionally, couples could be asked to complete the same task throughout the therapy process to examine improvement. The drawback in formally using the IDCS in a clinical setting as an assessment tool is the amount of time it requires to be trained in coding.

With the time it takes to become fully trained in the IDCS in mind, it may be useful for clinicians to simply be familiar with the communication dimensions presented in the IDCS rather than becoming fully trained. Understanding how specific dimensions, particularly negative dimensions, such as withdrawal and negative affect, may reflect danger signs for the future of relationships would be useful for clinicians. The examples provided in the IDCS of behaviors that define particular dimensions of communication could be used rather informally to evaluate danger signs in therapy-seeking couples' relationships.

Chapter 5 of *We Can Work it Out* (Notarius & Markman, 1993) provides a framework for understanding how therapists might be able to apply their knowledge of the IDCS dimensions to evaluating couples' interaction patterns. Although the chapter does not use the IDCS, it presents several definitions of interaction terms similar to IDCS definitions and describes several examples of couples' interactions with commentary on how each of the definitions apply. We envision clinicians using the IDCS in a similar manner, evaluating couples' interactions with the dimensions of the IDCS in mind.

In addition to these potential uses in couples' clinics, the IDCS is currently being used at the CMFS as part of a longitudinal study examining the long-term effectiveness of premarital training (PREP; Stanley, Blumberg, & Markman, 1999). PREP teaches couples communication skills that can be examined easily with the IDCS. As noted previously, the IDCS has been shown to be a valid measure in this longitudinal study.

STUDIES USING THE CODING SYSTEM

In recent years, the IDCS has been used in a variety of ways, although it has mainly been used for coding heterosexual couple problem discussions. Presented here is a sampling of studies that have used the coding system. The presentation of these studies is meant to augment what has already been presented in earlier sections.

As described earlier, several studies at the CMFS have used the IDCS in examining marital interactions (Kline et al., 2003; Markman, Renick, Floyd, Stanley, & Clements, 1993; Stanley et al., 2001). In addition, Paley, Cox, Burchinal, and Payne (1999) have used codes from the IDCS (positive affect, negative affect, and withdrawal) in examining the relation between marital interactions and adult attachment styles. Researchers have also used the IDCS in transition to parenthood studies. For example, Cox, Paley, Burchinal, and Payne (1999) found that the transition to parenthood was associated with changes in both positive and negative interaction behaviors. Cordova (2000) found that positive and negative dimensions of interactions were associated with self-report measures of teamwork for first-time parents.

A few studies have used modified versions of the IDCS for other types of interactions. Some have modified the IDCS for use with adolescents. For example, modified versions have been used to code adolescents' behavior during conflict resolution tasks with their friends (Black, 2000; Black & McCartney, 1997). In addition, Furman and his colleagues have modified the IDCS for adolescent romantic-partners' discussions (Sabina Low, personal communication, August 19, 2002). Also, Julien and her collaborators have used the IDCS to assess communication in mothers and adolescent-daughter dyads (Dubé et al., 2001, Dube et al., 2003). Positive behaviors in the discussions between mothers and their daughters discriminated daughters' attachment style 5 years later (Simard et al., 2003). Additionally, negative couples' interaction, as measured by the IDCS, predicted negative communication between mother and daughter and predicted daughters' social contacts with friends outside the family (Dubé et al., 2003).

In summary, the IDCS provides a global and efficient means of coding nine individual-level dimensions of interactions and five dimensions at the dyadic level. Most studies using the IDCS have focused on marital interactions. Recent estimates of intercoder reliability suggest that the IDCS is an adequately reliable coding system. Future research should be conducted to extend the validity of the IDCS because the results in the original article were mixed. The IDCS does appear to discriminate between several types of couples (i.e., distressed and nondistressed, premaritally-educated or not), and it has been shown to predict marital satisfaction (Julien et al., 1989; Schilling et al., 2003).

ACKNOWLEDGEMENTS

We wish to thank Francesca Harper and other Interactional Dimensions Coding System coders for their dedication to coding interactions and for training new coders. Support for this research and for preparation of this manuscript was provided in part by a grant from the National Institute of Mental Health: Division of Services and Intervention Research, Adult and Geriatric Treatment and Prevention Branch, Grant 5–RO1–MH35525–12, "The Long-term Effects of Premarital Intervention" (awarded to Howard J. Markman, Scott M. Stanley, and Lydia M. Prado).

8

Kategoriensystem für Partnerschaftliche Interaktion (KPI): Interactional Coding System (ICS)

Kurt Hahlweg
TU Braunschweig, Institut fuer Psychologie

The KPI (Kategoriensystem für Partnerschaftliche Interaktion; English version: Interactional Coding System ICS; Hahlweg & Conrad, 1983) was developed by Hahlweg, Reisner, et al. (1984) to provide a detailed understanding of the verbal and nonverbal behaviors that occur during marital or family problem-solving interactions. The KPI was designed to evaluate the effects of behavioral marital therapy (BMT). Therefore the major objective is to measure the communication and problem-solving skills taught in BMT and similar therapy programs. Furthermore, the KPI is also used to analyze family interactions with more than two persons. The reliability, validity, and generalizability seems to be established. The KPI has been used with a variety of community and clinical couples and families (ranging from schizophrenia to asthma) in different countries.

THEORETICAL FOUNDATIONS

Perhaps the most common complaint presented by couples who seek marital therapy is "lack of communication" or "lack of problem-solving" ability. Families are often referred to family therapy for the very same reasons. Taking this into account, some form of Communication Skills Training (CT) is germane to many treatment programs for relationship problems. Accordingly, in most Behavioral Marital and Family Therapy (BMFT) programs (published between 1970 and 1985, the time of the development of the KPI), CT and Problem-Solving Training (PST) were an integral part of the intervention. This focus on communication is not only due to the obvious needs of the clients but follows directly from theoretical assumptions borrowed from Social Learning Theory (Bandura, 1974). This model suggests that a critical skill in determining a successful marriage and family is skill in conflict resolution.

Although the CT and PST components of the various BMT interventions differ somewhat with regard to content and technique, there are some common assumptions: General communication will be enhanced when the spouses are using the following skills, which have been derived by combining different sources, especially CT (Berlin, 1975; Guerney, 1977), Systems Theory (Watzlawick, Beavin, & Jackson, 1967), and BMT (Hahlweg, Schindler, Revenstorf, & Brengelmann, 1984; Jacobson & Margolin, 1979; Weiss, Hops, & Patterson, 1973).

The aim of the KPI is to assess empirically the speaker and listener skills that are the basis of CT and PST:

1. Speaker skills Use "I" messages, describe specific situations and behaviors, and stick to the "here and now."
2. Listener skills Listen actively, paraphrase, ask open-ended questions, and give positive feedback.

Partners who employ these skills also should avoid blaming, criticizing, and sidetracking, as well as increasing their mutual understanding, and generating specific solutions to their problems. The core skills are reciprocal self-disclosure of feelings, attitudes, and thoughts, either about a specific problem in the relationship or about a general point of discussion, and accepting (not necessarily agreeing with) the speaker's utterances. The codes of the KPI were defined along these lines.

DEVELOPMENT OF THE CODING SYSTEM

In the 70s, at least five behavioral observation systems for coding marital interaction had been reported in the literature:

1. Marital Interaction Coding System (MICS; Hops, Wills, Patterson, & Weiss, 1972).
2. Coding System for Interpersonal Conflict (CSIC; Raush, Barry, Hertel, & Swain, 1974).

3. Marital and Family Interaction Coding System (MFICS; Olson & Ryder, 1975).
4. Couple Interaction Scoring System (CISS; Gottman, 1979; Notarius & Markman, 1981).
5. Kategoriensystem für Interpersonelle Kommunikation (KIK; Wegener, Revenstorf, Hahlweg, & Schindler, 1979; Category System for Interpersonal Communication).

Because all these systems had some conceptual or psychometric problems, the development of a new system seemed justified. Some of the problems were as follows (Hahlweg, Reisner, et al., 1984):

1. Coding unit—One of the major decisions in devising a system is the definition of the coding unit. Both the CSIC and the MFICS employed the "floorswitch" as a coding act, which is defined as the "The statement or action of one person bounded by the statement or action of the other" (Raush et al., 1974, p. 214.) This often leads to difficulties in coding when the speaker emits two or more utterances which differ in content (double coding), which in turn may lower the reliability of the system. Therefore, the coding unit of the KPI was defined as a "thought unit" (a verbal response that is homogenous in content or theme without regard to its duration or syntactical structure), as used by the CISS, MICS, and the KIK.

2. Discriminative validity—The coding system should discriminate between distressed and nondistressed couples. The discriminative validity of the MFICS seemed very questionable, and the CISS verbal codes alone did not discriminate between the groups.

3. Independent coding of nonverbal behaviour—Nonverbal behavior had been shown to be a powerful discriminator between distressed and nondistressed couples, but only the CISS assessed this dimension independently.

4. Content validity—To establish the content validity for a system, it is necessary to describe the theoretical assumptions underlying the development of the code definitions. Unfortunately, with the exception of the KIK, none of the other systems gave a rationale for defining the codes.

5. Double coding—When analysing stimulus-response chains by sequential analysis, double coding should be avoided. Instead, it seems more appropriate to code the responses of the partners in an alternating manner. None of the systems satisfactorily handled this problem.

6. Summary codes—At least seven different schemes for summarizing the MICS categories had been published. Because of this, interpretation from different studies was difficult.

Some conclusions could be drawn with respect to the systems:

1. CSIC, MFICS—Definition of coding unit unsatisfactory, unknown or questionable discriminative validity, nonverbal behavior not assessed.
2. MICS—Definition of some nonverbal codes questionable, no common definition for summary codes.
3. CISS—No discriminative validity for verbal codes.
4. KIK—Nonverbal behavior not assessed.

These conclusions led to the development of a new system, the KPI. The verbal KPI categories have been derived primarily from assumptions about effective communication and were supplemented by some of the more salient categories and definitions from other coding systems, notably the MICS (Hops et al., 1972), the CISS (Gottman, 1979; Notarius & Markman, 1981), and the CSIC (Wegener et al., 1979).

TASK AND SETTING

The task most often used is a discussion of a relationship problem selected by the couple. To help the couples to decide conjointly on the topic, one approach is to have the partners complete the Problem List (Hahlweg, Schindler et al., 1984). It contains 23 possible areas of relationship conflicts, for example, communication, sexuality, social activities, finances, or alcohol problems. Each problem area is rated by each partner using the following categories: 0 = *no problems*; 1 = *problems, but we can usually solve them*; 2 = *problems we cannot find solutions for, and we often quarrel*; 3 = *problems we cannot find solutions for, and don't discuss any more*. Couples select a problem of moderate intensity from those areas rated by the partner as 2 or 3. The couple is then asked to discuss the problem for 10 to 15 min in the video-laboratory with the experimenter not present. Partners are instructed to describe their feelings, attitudes, and wishes toward the problem and to try to arrive at a solution.

A variant of the task, which was developed by Goldstein (1985), has also been used, especially in family studies. Each family member is interviewed individually to generate problem issues that focus on the family relationship. After an issue has been identified, the interviewer directs the family member to pretend that the person to whom the problem is directed is sitting across from him or her, and to briefly verbalize a statement about the issue. This statement is audiotaped and taken to the respective family member, who listens to the statement and is asked to respond to it on the tape. The family is then brought into the video-lab and listens to the audiotaped statements. The family is directed to discuss the problem, express thoughts and feelings about it, and try to solve the issue.

DESCRIPTION OF THE CODING SYSTEM

Verbal and nonverbal behaviors are assessed directly from couples' videotaped discussions. The basic coding unit is a verbal response that is homogenous in content or theme without regard to its duration or syntactical structure. The KPI consists of the 11 verbal categories, which can be summarized into positive, neutral, and negative. To ensure easier coding, the categories are broken up into 26 subcategories, which are shown in Table 8.1.

For each content code, a nonverbal rating (positive, neutral, negative; see Gottman, 1979; Notarius & Markman, 1981) is assigned (discussed later). In a hierarchical order, first the facial cues of the speaker or listener are evaluated as positive, neutral, or negative, using a list of descriptions (see Table 8.2). If the coder is unable to code the utterance as positive or negative, the tone of voice is evaluated, followed by the body cues. Then the appropriate rating is applied. In case of a sequence of codes from one speaker, a Listening (LI) code with the nonverbal rating is assigned to the listener, thus guaranteeing alternate coding.

To apply sequential analysis and to reduce the number of significance tests, the 11 categories can be collapsed into either 6 (Reduction 1) or 4 (Reduction 2) summary codes. The reductions are based on content and correlational analysis.

Reduction 1–Self-disclosure and problem solving are collapsed into Direct Expression (DE); acceptance of partner, agreement, and positive or neutral listening are condensed into Acceptance and Agreement (AA); criticism and negative solution are collapsed into Critique (CR); disagreement, justification, and negative listening are condensed into Refusal (RF); and problem solving and metacommunication are collapsed into Neutral Information (NI). The rest of the category is maintained separately.

Reduction 2–The positive codes DE and AA are collapsed into Positive Communication (PC), and the negative codes CR and RF are collapsed into Negative Communication (NC). Neutral information and the rest of the codes remain as separate categories.

Statistical Analysis

Base Rate Analysis. With the KPI data, base rate analysis is possible without any alterations, for example, using analysis of variance procedures. Because there

TABLE 8.1

Positive Verbal KPI Categories

Category	*Subcategory*	*Example*
Self-disclosure (SD)	Expression of feelings (SDF)	"I am too angry to listen to you at the moment."
	Expression of wishes and needs (SDW)	"I would like to go fishing tomorrow."
	Expression of attitudes, behavior (SDB)	"When I first meet a person, I get very quiet."
Positive Solution (PS)	Specific, constructive proposal (PSP)	"Let's keep a list of our expenses in the future."
	Compromise suggestions (PSC)	"I'll sweep the floor if you'll play with the kids."
Acceptance of the other (AC)	Paraphrase (ACP)	"You are saying that the kids are too young to go to kindergarten."
	Open question (ACQ)	"Are you still unhappy?"
	Positive feedback (ACF)	"I liked the way you started the discussion."
	Understanding for the other (ACU)	"You must be feeling sad now."
	Direct agreement (AGD)	"Yes, that is right."
Agreement (AG)	Acceptance of responsibility (AGR)	"I was responsible for the quarrel."
	Assent (AGS)	"Yes" or "ok."

Neutral Verbal KPI Categories

Problem Description (PD)	Neutral description of the problem (PDD)	"I think we've got a problem with the kids."
	Neutral Questions (PDQ)	Did the car break down yesterday?"
Meta Communication (MC)	Clarifying requests (MCC)	"Would you say that again, please?"
	Related to topic (MCT)	"We are getting away from the issue."
Rest category (RC)	(RCC)	Statement does not fit any other code or is inaudible.
Listening (LI)	(LIS)	LI is coded when double-coding of speaker occurs

TABLE 8.1 (cont.)

Negative Verbal KPI Categories

Category	*Subcategory*	*Example*
Criticize (CR)	Devaluation of partner (CRD)	"You make me sick!"
	Specific (CRS)	"I get home and the house is a mess; you've done nothing!"
Negative Solution (NS)	Destructive solution (NSD)	"If you're so unhappy, why don't you just jump in the river and get it over with?"
	Demand for omission (NSO)	"We'd get along better if you would stip criticizing everything I do."
Justification (JS)	Excuse of own behavior (JUB)	"I had a lot to do yesterday."
	Denying own responsibility (JUD)	"I never said I would take out the trash!"
Disagreement (DG)	Direct disagreement (DGD)	"No, that is not true."
	Yes–but (DGY)	"Yes, I could go back to school part-time, but it would take me too long to graduate."
	Short disagreement (DGR)	"No" or "What?"
	Blocking off (DGB)	"I have had enough; I'm not talking with you about this anymore!"

Note. KPI = Kategoriensystem fur Partnerschaftliche Interaktion

is often notable variation in the number of codable behaviors emitted by each participant in the interaction, it is often necessary to correct the raw frequency for each coding category by the total number of codable behaviors emitted. Therefore, the score for each KPI code is expressed as a proportion of codable units of that person. For verbal codes, the proportion is calculated without the listener code.

Sequential Analysis. Base rate analysis of communication behaviors does not allow the investigation of the structure of the communication process. Here, the best method is to look for probability rules using sequential analysis. Because the responses as coded last only for 6 sec on the average, computation of simple stimulus reaction patterns (Lag 1 contingencies) seems inadequate to depict a meaningful interaction pattern of spouses. Therefore longer sequences should be considered. The difficulty with considering longer sequences is the increasing

TABLE 8.2

Cues Used to Code Nonverbal Behavior (see Gottman, 1979; Notarius & Markman, 1985)

Nonverbal Channel	*Cue*	
	Positive	*Negative*
Face	Smile, empathetic expression, head nod	Frown, sneer, fearful, glare, angry expression.
Voice	Caring, satisfied, warm, soft, happy.	Cold, blaming, sarcastic, tense, accusing, depressed.
Body	Touching, attention, forward lean.	Rude gestures, pointing, inattnetion, arms akimbo.

paucity of data points with longer sequences. There are two ways to overcome this handicap. One way is to use lagged sequential analysis (Gottman & Bakeman, 1979), where responses are considered in relation to antecedents more than one step back in time, irrespective of what is happening in between. Unfortunately, it is doubtful whether the resultant behavior sequences realistically portray what is occurring in the interaction.

The other possibility is to look at real, but generalized, behavior patterns using what we have called K-Gramm analysis (Revenstorf, Hahlweg, Schindler, & Vogel, 1984). The following behavior sequence demonstrates how the data are analyzed. The first letter indicates the person, husband (H) or wife (W). The second and third letters represent the summary code. The observed behavior sequence was as follows:

HDE		HNI		HRF	
	WAA		WCR		WRF

The sequence is analyzed by looking at the frequency of the following patterns:

- 2-Gramm—HDE/WAA, WAA/HNI, HNI/WCR, WCR/HRF, and so on.
- 3-Gramm—(HDE/WAA)/HNI, (WAA/HNI)/WCR, and so on.
- 4-Gramm—(HDE/WAA/HNI)/WCR, (WAA/HNI/WCR)/HRF, and so on.

For each K-Gramm pattern, the conditional probability is computed. Because the number of observations for each couple is rather small (100 codes per couple in a 10-min problem discussion), most sequential analyses are based on aggregate data: data are summed across couples in each group, for example, distressed or nondistressed. Unfortunately, statistical evaluations of the differences between groups, therefore, are not possible. The results are interpreted descriptively regarding the data as exploratory. For example, Hahlweg et al. (1989) could show that in high expressed emotion (EE) critical families, participants engaged in long-lasting negative escalation sequences of 20 successive reactions, whereas low EE families escalated only briefly up to a sequence length of six reactions.

The K-Gramm analysis requires dyadic data. For triadic families (e.g., mother, father, identified patient), it becomes necessary to combine the responses of two of the persons. For example, the investigator might decide to combine the two parents such that parent-patient dyads are analyzed sequentially.

man		LIS^-								
1 time	1:30		1:35							
woman	SDF^0		CRD^-							
face		–								
voice										
body		–								

CODER TRAINING

Coders can be undergraduate or graduate students. Our experience is that female coders are somewhat better at grasping the rationale than male coders. Coders are asked to read the extensive coding manual and see two coded training tapes. Next, the first coding meeting is conducted and coding is practiced. Coder training in groups of maximum of four coders lasts for about 40 hr. Our experience is that it is best to conduct the training intensively for 4 to 6 hr per day over a 2-week period instead of having shorter training sessions, for example, weekly 2-hr sessions. Thereafter, coders individually rate training tapes at home and meet for brief review sessions. In total, the training lasts for 60 to 80 hr. In any case, personal consultation seems to be necessary to obtain sufficient reliability. The coding manual is available from the author in either German or English. Although training tapes are available (in German), they are confidential and only may be used within our laboratory.

CODING PROCESS

During the video recording, a time signal (minutes and seconds) should automatically be recorded onto the tape. The beginning time for each code should be noted. This simplifies the coding and can be used for checking reliability.

Transcripts are not necessary for coding. However, for the purpose of training raters, some tapes with transcripts are helpful.

The video recording should first be seen in entirety, so that the rater can obtain an overall perspective of the interaction and the individual style of the couple's communication. The coding unit is not limited by time, but relies on the unity of its content (thought unit). These units could consist of a word ("No"= DGR), a sentence ("I am glad that you looked after the cat." = SDF), or a longer description, as long as the content is consistent.

Nonverbal behavior is added as an index (positive [+], neutral [0], or negative [–]) to each verbal category (e.g., DPQ^{+}). To reach the utmost reliability for coding nonverbal behavior, do not use one's own system of reference, but use the examples for face, voice, and body as shown in Table 8.2.

Retaining the Alternating Sequence

Often the speaker's comments fit into several code units; for example, : A: "You haven't paid any attention to me during the entire evening; that makes me both sad and angry (SDF) but that is how you are, careless and selfish! (CRD). After each code for partner A, a code for partner B should follow. In the instance in which partner B silently listens to A, the LI category is used with the nonverbal index for partner B's behavior (face: avoids eye contact; body: arms akimbo).

After sufficient training, coding of 15 min of interaction will require approximately 2 to 3 hr, depending on the quality of the tape recording, the total number of codes, and how often partners interrupt each other, which leads to difficulties in understanding who said what. In general, coding cannot be done in real time. In the coding process, the rater looks at a 30-sec block (for coding ease only; codes are not based on 30-sec units), codes, and rewinds the tape to check the coding. Afterwards, the tape is reviewed two or three more times to apply the nonverbal codes.

RELIABILITY

In the study by Hahlweg, Reisner, et al. (1984), interobserver agreement was investigated using four randomly selected interactions, which were coded by one reliability checker and five coders. As a first analysis, place-to-place agreement was computed, comparing each trainee with the reliability checker, showing averages of 86% agreement for verbal and 76% for nonverbal codes, respectively. The agreement for the verbal codes ranged from 78% (RC) to 94% (JU).

In a second analysis, Cronbach's alpha (see Gottman, 1979, chapter 5) was computed using the same four tapes and six coders. For the verbal codes, α ranged from .85 (PD, RC) to .99 (DG), demonstrating that all verbal codes had high generalizability coefficients. For the nonverbal codes, the results were quite good for positive ($\alpha = .82$) and negative behavior ($\alpha = .89$), but not for neutral behavior (α= 52). This may be due to the fact that the nonverbal codes are not independent of one another, thus enhancing residual (error) variance for the neutral code. In addition, Cohen's Kappa coefficients were computed; these ranged from .70 (nonverbal neutral) to .96 (DG).

Since its development, the KPI has been used in many studies in Germany, the United Kingdom, the United States, and Australia, with a great variety of subjects (see sections on Validity and Studies Using the Coding System). In general, the levels of inter-rater agreement have been satisfactory for frequency and sequential analysis, yielding significant Kappas of over .70 for verbal and nonverbal behavior in most studies.

VALIDITY

The discriminative, criterion, predictive, and construct validity, as well as the sensitivity to monitoring change, have been investigated, showing support for the validity of the KPI.

Discriminative Validity

Distressed Versus Nondistressed Couples. Hahlweg, Reisner, et al. (1984) compared the interactional behavior of $n = 29$ distressed and $n = 12$ nondistressed couples when discussing a relationship problem. Nondistressed couples emitted significantly more nonverbal positive behavior, self-disclosure, acceptance of partner, agreement, and neutral problem description and significantly less negative nonverbal behavior, criticism, disagreement, justification, and negative solution statement than distressed couples.

In two cross-cultural studies, the discriminative validity of the KPI was investigated. Hooley and Hahlweg (1989) compared marital satisfaction and communication in German and English couples, finding striking similarities in distressed and nondistressed couples. Halford, Hahlweg, and Dunne (1990) compared the communication of Australian and German couples using frequency and sequential analysis. Across cultures, distressed couples engaged in significantly higher rates of negative verbal and nonverbal behaviors, and were more likely to engage in coercive escalation patterns. Some cultural differences were evident: the German couple had higher rates of criticism and justification than the Australian couples. Overall, although there were some cultural differences, communication associated with marital distress seems to be consistent in both cultures.

Construct Validity

In several studies, the construct validity of the KPI has been investigated, showing expected correlations with a variety of self-report measures of marital quality, conflict, and sexual behavior (e.g., Braukhaus, Hahlweg, Kroeger, Fehm– Wolfsdorf, &

Groth, 2001; Hahlweg, Reisner, et al., 1984; Hooley & Hahlweg, 1989; Kaiser, Hahlweg, Fehm–Wolfsdorf, & Groth,1998; Kroeger, Hahlweg, Braukhaus, Fehm–Wolfsdorf, & Groth, 2000; Thurmaier, Engl, & Hahlweg, 1999).

Factorial Validity. Remen, Chambless, Steketee, and Renneberg (2000) conducted a factor analysis with KPI data from n = 121 couples' discussions in which one partner had an anxiety disorder. A three (Varimax) factor solution accounting for 50% of the variance emerged. The factors were Negativity (disagreement, criticism justification, negative solution, negative nonverbal, and—negatively correlated—positive nonverbal), Problem-Solving Focus (problem description, agreement, positive solution), and Emotional Engagement (self-disclosure, metacommunication, acceptance of other).

Sensitivity to Monitoring Change

The KPI has been used as a criterion variable in several interventions studies. Hahlweg, Revenstorf, and Schindler (1984) investigated the effectiveness of BMT in a randomized controlled study with treatment ($n = 29$) and waiting list control couples ($n = 14$). Partners discussed a relationship problem before and after the intervention or waiting period. Treatment was effective in changing the base rates of couple's communication skills in the expected direction and, when compared to the behavior of nondistressed couples, to a clinically significant extent. Changes became even more apparent when sequential analyses were conducted. The interaction patterns of the treated couples closely resembled the patterns exhibited by the nondistressed couples, whereas the waiting list couples did not change at all.

The KPI was also sensitive to change after Behavioral Family Management (BFM), conducted with schizophrenic patents and their relatives to reduce relapse (Falloon, Hahlweg, & Tarrier, 1990; Rieg et al., 1991). In the U.S. (Falloon) and German studies, families were asked to discuss a family conflict before and after 3 (U.S.) or 6 (German) months of receiving BFM. Frequency analysis showed the expected improvement in communication and problem-solving behavior. When compared to the control condition in the Falloon study, effects were still significant at the 2-year follow-up.

Finally, the KPI has been used to assess the effects of preventive interventions with couples. Thurmaier et al. (1999) conducted a prospective longitudinal study evaluating the effects of the Ein Partnerschaftliches Lernprogram (EPL, A Couples Learning Program) for couples planning marriage (universal prevention). In a controlled trial, $n = 55$ EPL couples and $n = 17$ control couples were asked to discuss a relationship problem before and after the intervention, and 1.5, 3, and 5 years afterward. Significant differences in the communication behaviors emerged at every measurement point after the intervention favoring the EPL couples. In a randomized controlled study, the efficacy of the EPL when used with longer married couples was investigated (Kaiser et al., 1998). After the intervention, EPL couples emitted more positive and fewer negative communication behaviors than control couples.

GENERALIZABILITY

The generalizability of the KPI system seems to be high. The KPI has been used with a wide variety of distressed and nondistressed community couples and families in different countries, for example. Germany, England, Austria, Australia, and the United States, and of different social classes. It seems well suited to investigate couples and families with a wide variety of disorders, for example, schizophrenia, depression, anxiety disorders, asthma, and atopic dermatitis (see Studies section). Furthermore, it seems to be valid not only for partner interactions but also for the analysis of mother–child interactions, at least for children older than 7 years. However, with regard to ethnicities, mainly White participants have been assessed.

CLINICAL UTILITY

The KPI is useful as a clinical tool for conducting marital or family therapy. In our outpatient clinic, marital or family interactions are taken during the assessment phase prior to the beginning of therapy. These recordings are analyzed clinically and not microanalytically because this is too time consuming. However, therapists looking at the discussion will get a far better understanding of the couples' communication patterns, for example, whether the partners show some form of acceptance reactions, try to generate positive solutions, or use personal criticisms. This macroanalysis helps with treatment planning in that the therapist makes informal notes about the overall communication patterns based on KPI knowledge.

To employ this approach, marital and family therapists should obtain brief KPI training not focussed on microcoding. However, a more detailed understanding of the key constructs (self-disclosure, acceptance, criticism, justification, negative solution, and disagreement) will help to monitor more closely the actual interaction of the couple during treatment. This will foster more immediate therapist interventions when necessary, for example, when one partner emits a criticism instead of a self-disclosure.

STUDIES USING THE CODING SYSTEM

Expressed Emotion and Family Interaction

Levels of family expressed emotion (EE) have repeatedly been found to predict relapse in schizophrenic and depressed patients 9 months after hospital discharge

(Butzlaff & Hooley, 1998). The chance of relapse increases by a factor of about 2.5 (schizophrenic patients) and of about 4 (depressed patients) when a patient returns to a family environment marked by high levels of criticism or emotional overinvolvement. The number of critical comments emitted during the Camberwell Family Interview (CFI), which is conducted with a relative to assess EE during the hospital stay of the patient, is counted and the degree of emotional overinvolvement rated. Relatives are classified as high EE if they show evidence of excessive criticism or overinvolvement.

Because the CFI measures the relative's attitudes toward the patient, little is known in what ways these attitudes are also expressed in face-to-face contact with the patient. One approach to investigating the construct validity of EE is to systematically analyze the behavior of high and low EE relatives as they interact with the patient at home.

Schizophrenia

In a study by Hahlweg et al. (1989) conducted at the University of California, Los Angeles, the KPI was used to analyze the interactional behavior of $n = 43$ families with a schizophrenic patient during a family's conflict discussion. High EE relatives were more negative than low EE relatives. Sequential analysis indicated that high EE critical families showed extreme negative escalation patterns. Patients' reactions to high EE critical relatives were characterized by justification and nonverbal negative behavior. These results were replicated in a study conducted in Munich, West Germany, with $n = 42$ schizophrenic patients and $n = 11$ community control families using the same methodology (Müller et al., 1992).

Depression

In a study with depressed patients and their spouses conducted in Oxford, England, Hooley (1986) analyzed the couple's interaction using the KPI. Again, high EE spouses behaved significantly more negatively than low EE partners, replicating the findings cited earlier. Low EE couples were characterized by a predominantly positive style of interaction, whereas high EE couples showed mostly negative communication patterns (Hooley & Hahlweg, 1986).

Anxiety Disorders

In a study with families of obsessive–compulsive and agoraphobic patients, Chambless, Bryan, Aiken, Steketee, and Hooley (2001) used structural equation modeling to predict expressed emotion. A direct path between relatives' low rates of KPI observed problem solving and their hostility toward the patients was found.

Schizophrenia and Depression

In an attempt to investigate whether interaction patterns are disorder-specific, Schröder, Hahlweg, Fiedler, and Mundt (1996) compared marital communication in couples with a depressed ($n = 28$) or schizophrenic ($n = 29$) patient. Results showed that depressed dyads behaved significantly less negatively than schizophrenic couples. In particular, criticism was very rare among couples with one depressed partner. These results point to the heightened interpersonal sensitivity of depressed patients and call for a different approach when conducting marital therapy.

Agoraphobia

Twenty-two married couples with a female agoraphobic spouse were compared to 21 community control couples on self-report and KPI observational measures of marital interaction (Chambless et al., in press). Consistent with hypotheses, husbands of agoraphobics were more critical of their wives than were control husbands, and clinical couples were less likely to engage in positive problem solution. Contrary to hypotheses, clinical husbands were not less supportive than control husbands.

Somatic Illness

Hermanns, Florin, Dietrich, Rieger, and Hahlweg (1989) investigated maternal EE attitudes and mother–child communication in $n = 25$ families with an asthmatic child and in $n = 25$ community control families. The mother and child dyad discussed a problem of mutual concern. KPI analysis showed that mothers with an asthmatic child made significantly more critical remarks than control mothers. High EE critical dyads showed longer sequences of negative verbal interaction than low EE dyads.

Atopic Dermatitis

Exacerbations of atopic dermatitis (neurodermitis) may be related to stressful social interactions. Wenninger, Ehlers, and Gieler (1991) compared the problem discussions of such patients ($n = 20$) with their partners and community control couples ($n = 20$). As predicted, patient dyads made more KPI verbal and nonverbal negative and fewer positive statements than control dyads. Furthermore, patient dyads showed longer negative and shorter positive escalation patterns than controls.

ACKNOWLEDGEMENTS

The development of the Kategoriensystem für Partnerschaftliche Interaktion (KPI) was supported by grants from the Deutsche Forschungsgemeinschaft (DFG

RE/Ha 402/1–6; Ha 1400/1–4), the Bundesministerium für Forschung und Technologie (BMFT; nr. 0701620 S), and the Max-Planck-Institut für Psychiatrie.

The author is grateful to the many students and colleagues who helped to develop and improve the system: Dianne Chambless, Marylin Conrad, Heijo Dürr, Anke Ehlers, Jochen Engl, Gabriele Fehm-Wolfsdorf, Thomas Groth, Kim Halford, Jutta Hermanns, Jill Hooley, Andrea Kaiser, Guljit Kohli, David Miklowitz, Jim Mintz, Ulla Müller, Sebastian Naumann, Babette Renneberg, Dirk Revenstorf, Claudia Rieg, Marianne Römer, Ludwig Schindler, Brigitte Schröder, Gail Steketee, Franz Thurmaier, Bernd Vogel, Kerstin Wenninger, and the late Hans Brengelmann, Irmela Florin, Michael Goldstein, and Lillith Reisner.

9

Communication Skills Test (CST) Observational System for Couples' Problem-Solving Skills

Frank J. Floyd
Georgia State University

The Communication Skills Test (CST) assesses the communication and problem-solving proficiency exhibited by partners when they interact together to resolve a disagreement or solve a relationship problem. The coding system focuses on the process of the dyadic interaction and judges the quality of the behaviors in terms of the goal of solving a relationship problem. The system is used by assigning a rating to each speech turn, defined as all behaviors by one person that occur between floor switches. The turn is rated very positive, positive, neutral, negative, or very negative, depending on how facilitative the statement is in meeting the problem-solving goals of the conversation. The choice of a rating is based on a set of guidelines about levels of problem-solving proficiency outlined in the manual. When the coding is completed, the ratings can be summarized and analyzed in several ways, including (a) the frequency of each of the five ratings given to each partner, which indicate the rates of negative and positive behaviors by the partners; (b) the mean of all ratings given to each partner, which indicates the general level of communication proficiency exhibited during the interaction; or (c) sequential patterns of positive, negative, and neutral exchanges between the partners.

The coding procedure is designed to provide a relatively economical, efficient alternative to more micro-analytical measures of couples' communication process, while also retaining information about the sequence of exchanges between the partners. The CST focuses on many of the same features as micro-analytic systems; however, it requires the coders to consider verbal and nonverbal features of behaviors and integrate information on the timing, sequence, and context of actions to produce a single rating of communication proficiency for each speech turn. Although in most cases, coders work from videotaped recordings of couples' problem-solving discussions, the procedure was designed so that, with experience, coders could evaluate interactions live, as they occur, to make the coding system practical for use in clinical or field settings.

THEORETICAL FOUNDATIONS

The rating criteria for the CST system are based on research and clinical theory about the effects of couples' communication and problem-solving behaviors on relationship functioning. The criteria address three general aspects of these behaviors.

First, the criteria address the ability to use behaviors that focus the problem discussion so that it can lead to effective problem solutions. The initial source for these criteria was a communication manual written by Gottman and colleagues (Gottman, Notarius, Gonso, & Markman, 1976), and the skills are also advocated in more recent guides for couples and marital therapists (e.g., Epstein & Baucom, 2002; Jacobson & Christensen, 1996; Notarius & Markman, 1993). Focused problem-solving means that it is important for couple members to be able to openly state their opinions or concerns about problem issues. However, they should do so in a way that minimizes defensiveness from the partner. Also, the CST system assumes that, in most cases, effective problem-solving proceeds, at least loosely, in phases from initial statements of concerns and problem definition, to clarification of opinions, solution proposals, and finally, compromise and decision making. Research on couples interaction shows that specific skills used by successful couples include positive actions such as requesting specific changes and suggesting solutions (e.g., Birchler, Clopton, & Adams, 1984), and resisting, or "editing," negative actions that cause defensiveness and exacerbate conflict, such as blaming, put downs, and attacks on each other's character (Notarius, Benson, Sloane, and Vanzetti, 1989; Weiss & Heyman, 1997).

Second, the CST coding criteria incorporate Rogerian principles of warmth, acceptance, and genuineness as applied to couples communication in the form of empathic responding and effective expressor behaviors (Guerney, 1977; Halford, 2001). The coding system assumes that showing support, understanding, and acceptance for the partner facilitates cooperation. Furthermore, managing hostile affect keeps arguments from escalating, whereas expressing vulnerable and warm emotions elicits empathy, caring, and positive regard. For example, research shows that marital satisfaction is associated with open discussion of problem areas and concerns (Christensen & Shenk, 1991), and the expression of mutually supportive behaviors such as approval, assent, and empathy (Birchler et al., 1984; Margolin & Wampold, 1981; Schapp, 1984).

Third, the coding system uses affective tone as an important cue in judging communication proficiency. Couples research shows that nonverbal affect is particularly salient in determining the impact of communication on couple members (Gottman, Notarius, Markman, et al., 1976; Noller, 1984) because nonverbal features of interactions influence the meaning of verbal statements. Additionally, studies demonstrate that happy couples exchange gleeful and warm emotions (e.g., Revenstorf, Hahlweg, Schindler, & Vogel, 1984), whereas relationship distress is strongly predicted by hostile affect in the form of contempt or sulking withdrawal (Gottman, 1994).

DEVELOPMENT OF THE CODING SYSTEM

There are two properties of the CST system that explicitly guided the development of the system and distinguish it from other couples' coding systems: the nature of the unit of measurement, and the evaluation of goal-focused process.

Unit of Measurement

To make the coding system efficient yet rich in information about patterns of interchanges, the first decision in designing the system concerned the unit of measurement. It was important to use a unit of measurement that is large enough so as not to impede or distract the coder during live observations, but small enough to capture sequences of exchanges between the partners. The intention was to develop a measure that required limited coder effort in recording observations, so that coders could code quickly, without either repeatedly reviewing recordings to capture specific onsets and offsets of behaviors, and without needing to have transcripts of the couples' verbal behaviors. Ideally, with experience, observers should be able to code either while observing the couple live or during a single viewing of a recorded discussion.

The challenge in developing the CST was to find a way that coders could make relatively complex inferential judgments of interaction process while preserving information that would allow the investigator to analyze the flow of the discussion and the nature of exchanges between the couple members. Micro-analytic systems that assess couples' interactions are expensive and time-consuming because they focus on small units of behavior and require coders to record details about verbal and nonverbal actions. Additionally, when micro-analytical systems are used, the investigator usually evaluates the effectiveness or quality of actions only after the data collection is completed, when micro-units are combined into larger evaluative categories. Live coding is almost impossible with micro-analytical systems unless the coding system assesses behaviors that are overt actions which are relatively unidimensional and require little inferential judgment on the part of the coder. An alternative to micro-analytical systems that has been used to assess more complex features of interaction involves the use of macro-analytical, global rating scales, completed at timed intervals or at the close of the entire discussion. However, macro-analytical ratings provide only general impressions of the interaction, and preclude further sequential or pattern analysis of the data.

An alternative to the limitations of both micro-analytic and macro-analytic methods is to use a midsized unit of observation, which Mahoney and colleagues (Mahoney, Coffield, Lewis, & Lashley, 2001) called a "meso-analytic" approach to observation. Accordingly, the unit of measurement for the CST is a talk turn, or speech turn, which is defined as the period of time during which a speaker has the floor between speeches by the other partner. This unit was selected for several reasons. Most importantly, it met the criteria of both manageable recording demands and sufficient detail to evaluate patterns of exchanges between the partners. Additionally, it appeared to be a "natural" way to parse the ongoing flow of the discussion. Speech turns are usually obvious both to the couple and to outside observers. In earlier work with couples, we used a "communication box" device to have the listeners rate the positiveness of their partner's preceding speech turn each time the speaker completed a turn (Floyd & Markman, 1983). We found that the spouses could complete this rating quickly and efficiently, with little interruption in the flow of the discussion. Also, the spouses were usually comfortable with summarizing their impressions during the entire speech turn, and did not feel that too many events had taken place to make a summary rating meaningful. Additionally, experience with more micro-analytical observational coding systems suggested that evaluations could be summarized at this level as well, without mixing disparate impressions into a summary code that was essentially meaningless because it combined incongruent elements (i.e., individuals rarely made both highly facilitative and high disruptive comments during a single speech turn).

The speech turn also is an ideal level of reduction for the purposes of sequential analysis of exchanges between the partners. Research on the sequential analysis of couples' transactions emphasizes the nature of transitions from one speaker to the next (e.g., Cordova, Jacobson, Gottman, Rushe, & Cox, 1993; Margolin & Wampold, 1981); that is, how preceding behaviors elicit subsequent responses from the partner. With micro-analytic systems in which several codes might be given to a speaker during one speech turn, sequential transitions between the partners (at lag 1) concern the last code given to the initial speaker and the first code given to the respondent. However, it seemed possible that the last or first microbehavior within a speech turn might not adequately capture the overall impact of the communication during that turn. For example, a spouse might embed a put-down within neutral problem talk during the same speech turn, which would go unnoticed in a sequential analysis of the micro-analytic codes that occurred only at transition points. In contrast, a single evaluation of the entire speech turn would take into account this negative action.

Because the CST uses an entire speech turn as the unit of measurement, the coding process involves attending to and noting instances of relatively facilitative, disruptive, and neutral behaviors, then using this information to produce one rating of communication and problem-solving proficiency for the entire speech act. In this regard, the system actually uses a relatively micro-analytic unit of observation (i.e., the specific actions the coder attends to), but a larger unit of recording (i.e., the output the coder produces). For the purposes of evaluating the reliability and validity of the data obtained, the unit of recording is the relevant unit of measurement. However, for the purposes of understanding the phenomena accounted for by the coding system, it is important to recognize the unit of observation (Floyd, 1989). That is, coders do not merely form a vague, general impression of the entire speech turn; they note the quality of specific actions and use this information to formulate an overall rating of the entire unit.

Goal-Focused Process

A second guiding principle behind the development of the CST system is that all actions are judged relative to the goal of resolving a disagreement or solving a problem. Thus, the criteria for the assignment of ratings have been adopted from guidelines about effective and ineffective problem solving, as well as effective communication skills in speaker and listener roles. Using the Gottman, Markman, and Notarius (1977) problem-solving manual as a framework, the CST coding criteria assign positive ratings to statements that include skills or actions recommended for effective communication and problem solving (e.g., summarizing and validating the partner's opinions, suggesting specific solutions or compromises), and negative ratings to behaviors proscribed because they obstruct problem resolution (e.g., blaming the partner, dogmatically repeating an opinion or position, denying responsibility, displaying hostile affect).

By focusing exclusively on the communication and problem-solving process, the CST intentionally ignores other constructs or features evident in couples' interactions that may be relevant to relationship functioning, but either cannot be reliably discerned or are not directly related to problem-solving effectiveness per se. For example, self-disclosure could be considered a facilitative communication skill. However, whereas self-disclosure may be reliably coded when observing strangers interacting, with intimate partners it is impossible to discern if statements that appear to be personal opinions reflect a disclosure of new information, or are merely restatements of information already known to the other partner. Another example is relationship power dynamics, which has received attention in research on couples' problem-solving discussions (e.g., Lindahl & Malik, 1999). In recent research, we reclassified many of the specific actions included in the CST into new categories that reflect power dynamics (Daugherty, Floyd, Zucker, Fitzgerald, & Bingham, 2001; Floyd, Harter, & VanWidenfelt, 2001). However, the original CST rating categories ignore characteristics of interpersonal power dynamics, including equality, control, and dominance. It would be possible for a couple to display an imbalanced power dynamic, in which one spouse assumes the lead in determining the nature of the decision making and the other spouse concurs in a submissive manner, while both partners receive relatively positive ratings for the communication proficiency of their behaviors.

In assessing communication/problem-solving proficiency, the CST treats agreements and disagreements between the partners somewhat differently than other coding systems that evaluate problem-solving behaviors. A common practice is to evaluate agreements as positive events and disagreements as negative events, which means that the overall assessment of a discussion can be highly affected by the sheer amount of agreement or disagreement between the partners rather than the quality of their behaviors in managing disagreements. To avoid having the ratings unduly influenced by the severity of the problem or the amount of disagreement, the CST judges statements of agreement or disagreement in terms of the skillfulness of the communication exhibited rather than the mere fact that the content reflects an agreement or a disagreement. Because, in problem solving, couples are encouraged to identify areas of agreement and disagreement, statements that explicitly identify and label either agreements or disagreements are both facilitative to the discussion, and are considered positive in the CST system. Only when disagreements are stated in a dogmatic manner, with no explanation for the disagreement, are these behaviors considered negative. Similarly, statements of opinion that agree with the partner's opinion receive positive evaluations only when the agreement is noted explicitly by the speaker. That is, the assignment of positive or negative ratings depends on the quality of the statement as a communication or problem-solving act, not simple whether the partners are in conflict about an issue.

TASK AND SETTING

The CST uses the same problem-solving task commonly employed in research on couples' interaction. Specifically, the couple is asked to identify an important current problem area in their relationship; a topic about which they disagree, not just a source of mutual stress about which there is no disagreement (e.g., money or job pressures). Couples can be helped to find an appropriate topic by rating their level of disagreement for each of a list of common marital problem areas (Knox, 1971), selecting an area of disagreement reported on the Dyadic Adjustment Test (Spanier, 1976), or asking them to recall a recent argument about a topic that is as yet unresolved. The couple is then instructed to discuss the problem for 10 min, and to attempt to reach a mutually satisfying solution to the problem. It is essential that the couple understand that they are supposed to problem solve together about a specific issue so their actions truly represent efforts to resolve a conflict and solve a problem. Otherwise, the ratings of communication and problem-solving proficiency would have little validity as reflections of the couple's best efforts. If the couple understands that they should attempt to solve the problem, then behaviors that fail to maintain a focus on the issue at hand, such as changing the topic to an irrelevant issue or being unresponsive to the partner's questions, can be understood as avoidance behaviors. Otherwise, a couple may ramble simply because they do not understand the goal of their discussion, and the interaction segment will be an invalid assessment of their ability to problem solve together.

This procedure is robust for identifying patterns of interaction that discriminate distressed from nondistressed samples, including couples in which one spouse has a clinical disorder (Weiss & Heyman, 1997). Although some investigators have used either warm-up discussions to have couples become familiar with the task, or preliminary interviews about the problem area to ensure the spouses' involvement in the discussion, there is no evidence to indicate that these additional procedures improve on the data obtained from the standard procedure. In fact, some evidence indicates that problematic interaction patterns emerge within the first 5 min of the interaction, and that distressed couples can be reliably detected even when they are instructed to "fake good" (Vincent, Friedman, Nugent, & Messerly, 1979).

It is important that the couple complete the discussion without interruption, and preferably without anyone else present. When an interviewer or therapist is in the room, couple members frequently address their comments toward this third person rather than communicating only with each other. Thus, if observations must be conducted with live coders, it might be useful to complete a warm-up task to have the couple habituate to the presence of the observer.

The CST has been used to evaluate couples' behaviors in research laboratories, clinical offices, and home settings. There is little research evidence about whether the setting for the couples' interaction has an influence on their behavior. Both couples' reports and cross-setting observations suggest that couples' interactions during the laboratory tasks are consistent with their behaviors in the home, although the laboratory behaviors may be somewhat less aversive overall (Gottman, 1979; Weiss & Heyman, 1997). Of course, in the home it is important to find a separate room and arrange for privacy from interruptions by children or other household activities.

DESCRIPTION OF THE CODING SYSTEM

The CST coding manual lists and defines 40 verbal and nonverbal actions, which are classified into five general categories: very negative, negative, neutral, positive, and very positive. The specific behaviors in each category are given in Table 9.1. In most cases, the definitions for specific actions were directly borrowed from well-known and well-tested micro-analytic coding systems such as the Marital In-

TABLE 9.1

Communication Skills Test Rating Categories and Specific Behaviors

VERY POSITIVE (5)

(a) Summarize other or both—Reflecting the partner's point of view.
(b) Checking out—Verifying the accuracy of a summary
(c) Opinion or feeling probe—Asking the partner's opinion.
(d) Solution Proposal—Suggesting a reasonable, well timed solution.
(e) X, Y, Z—feedback—A behaviorally anchored, focused complaint.
(f) Back on Beam—Returning to the topic.
(g) Metacommunication—Discussing the communication process.
(h) Validation—Acknowledging the reasonableness of the partner's point.

POSITIVE (4)

(a) Feeling statement—Expressing an emotion.
(b) Agree—Explicitly noting an agreement with the partner.
(c) Disagree with rationale—Noting a disagreement and justifying it.
(d) Plan suggestion—nonspecific—Offering a plan early in the discussion.
(e) Compliment—Noting a positive quality or behavior.
(f) Clarification Request—Trying to better understand the partner.
(g) Accept Responsibility—Acknowledging a role in creating the problem.
(h) Empathy—Recognizing the partner's feelings.
(i) Summarize self—Concise attempt to clarify own opinion.
(j) Humor—Appropriate joking.
(k) Positive nonverbal—Conveying positive emotion nonverbally.

NEUTRAL (3)

(a) Problem-talk—Offering an opinion about the issue at hand.
(b) Question—Asking for factual information.
(c) Information—Providing relevant factual information.

NEGATIVE (2)

(a) Confused problem-talk—Illogical speech.
(b) Opinion without rationale—Dogmatic statement.
(c) Disagree without rationale—Dogmatic disagreement.
(d) Disruptive extraneous comments—Brief statement that is off-topic.
(e) Avoidant question—Answering a question with a question.
(f) Negative nonverbal—Conveying negative emotion nonverbally.
(g) Leading question—Question with an implied correct answer.

TABLE 9.1 (cont.)

VERY NEGATIVE (1)

(a) Off Beam—Moving the conversation away from the topic at hand.
(b) Kitchen sinking—Answering a complaint with a complaint.
(c) Mind reading—Assigning negative intent to the partner.
(d) Put Down—A condescending criticism.
(e) Summarizing self—Dogmatically restating a point of view.
(f) Blaming—Accusing the partner of causing the problem.
(g) Character Assassination—Insulting the partner generally.
(h) Deny Responsibility—Denying own role in the problem.
(i) Command-patronizing—Telling the partner what to do.
(j) Very negative nonverbal—sarcastic, condescenting tone of voice.
(k) Avoidance or Withdrawal—Unresponsive and "tuned out."

teraction Coding System (MICS; Weiss, Hops, & Patterson, 1973) and the Couples Interaction Scoring System (CISS; Gottman, 1979; Notarius & Markman, 1981). The behaviors included in the most extreme categories of very positive and very negative behaviors are those specifically targeted by couples therapists (e.g.; Baucom & Epstein, 1990; Gottman et al., 1977; Halford, 2001; Notarius & Markman, 1993), and include, respectively, the behaviors prescribed for effective problem solving, and those proscribed as ineffective and combative. In addition to these specific skills taught by therapists, there are many other behaviors frequently noted in the literature on couples interaction (see review by Heyman, 2001) that tend to either facilitate or hinder problem-solving discussions. The CST incorporates these behaviors into the criteria used for assigning ratings of either 4 = *positive* (e.g., displaying positive affect, noting areas of agreement, describing one's feelings) or 2 = *negative* (e.g., failing to explain an opinion or disagreement, making disruptive comments). Finally, behaviors are rated as 3 = *neutral* when they involve discussing and offering opinions about the topic at hand, or dealing with relevant factual information. These behaviors meet the minimal demands of the problem-solving task.

As described later regarding the coding process, the most complex feature of the CST coding scheme is the need to arrive at one rating of "communication proficiency" for speech turns that include both positive and negative elements. Many therapists (Guerney, 1977; Jacobson & Christensen, 1996) explicitly encourage couples to use such statements by including a positive compliment when making a complaint about the partner, to cushion the negative impact of the complaint by acknowledging other positive qualities. Although it is possible to state complaints or concerns in nonhostile and nonthreatening ways, simply including a positive element does not usually erase the negative impact of hostile statements. An exploratory analysis we conducted to prepare a set of data for sequential analysis (VanWidenfelt, Harter, & Floyd, 1996) suggests that spouses may be highly sensitive to the negative impact of criticisms embedded within positive comments. In this analysis, speech turns that included only positive or only negative behaviors were significantly likely to be reciprocated in kind with positive or negative behaviors by the spouse. However, speech turns that included both positive and negative behaviors were significantly likely to elicit only negative responses by spouses. It seems that the spouses attended only to the negative content of these mixed statements, and responded negatively to what they perceived to be negative statements. Thus, in the CST system, mixed statements are likely to receive a "negative" or "very negative" rating if the negative features of the statements, such as a hostile or condescending tone of voice, or blaming or dogmatic elements, effectively nullify the impact of the positive features. A subtler problem occurs when the spouses' behaviors are ambiguous or equivocal. Most notably, some spouses embed critical digs within apparently innocent, or even caring statements (e.g., "I know that you're trying hard to be less rude toward my friends"). Other spouses laugh and joke while they say demeaning things to each other, so that it is impossible to discern whether this is truly meant as joking, or whether the laughter is a cover for hostility or embarrassment. Such statements are uncodable with the CST system, so the entire talk turn is simply treated as an uncodable unit, similar to inaudible units.

CODER TRAINING

Because most of the work with the CST has been conducted in university settings, most CST coders have been undergraduate students. However, there is no reason to suspect that college course work in psychology is a prerequisite to becoming a reliable coder. There has been no systematic research on coder characteristics that predict proficiency with the CST, but two qualities that seem to be relevant are sensitivity to interpersonal dynamics and the ability to understand how one's personal emotional reactions and interpretations are similar to and different from the coding criteria specified in the CST manual. These qualities usually become apparent within a few training sessions. In those instances in which a new coder fails to show signs of "catching on" after two or three meetings, additional training sessions typically have not been helpful. Also, therapists with experience in another theoretical framework may struggle with the need to suspend this framework to adhere to the CST criteria.

On the whole, coder training for the CST system follows guidelines commonly recommended for behavioral observation (e.g., Floyd, Baucom, Godfrey, & Palmer, 1998; Haynes & O'Brien, 2000). In brief, coders first become familiar with the coding criteria by reading the manual thoroughly, then they are "tested" in a series of face-to-face meetings with a trainer in which videotapes of couples' discussions are observed, and the coder rates each speech turn and explains the rationale that guided the rating. The trainer acknowledges and elaborates on accurate ratings, corrects and explains inaccurate ratings, and encourages the coder to ask questions about any points that seem to be confusing. After one or two 1.5-hr training sessions, the coder rates entire 10-min interaction sequences independently between meetings. Agreement with the trainer's codes is calculated, and the training meeting consists of providing feedback about accuracy and reviewing the tape to discuss the rationale for coding decisions and to correct inaccurate ratings. Training meetings continue until the new coder reaches 80% to 90% agreement with the trainer on the independent ratings. For research purposes, we check agreement with the coder trainer on approximately 20% of all interactions, and hold a weekly group meeting in which the coders review videotapes together and resolve coding disagreements.

Because the CST system requires considerable judgment on the part of the coder about the proficiency of couples' behaviors and the quality of their interactions, it is advantageous for coders to become as knowledgeable and sophisticated as possible about couples' problem-solving interactions. The coders are encouraged to read the Gottman et al. (1977) manual and other books about couples interactions, and to share this information, as well as their experiences about couples they observed, with other coders during the group meetings. Although we make every effort to keep coders blind to specific research hypotheses concerning, for example, couples membership in various subgroups that should relate to problem-solving skills, they are not blind to the evaluative nature of the coding, that is, that behaviors can be either effective or ineffective toward the goal of solving an interpersonal disagreement.

The CST has been used successfully by several investigators not affiliated with the author (e.g., Cappelli et al., 1994). In some cases, we have provided feedback about one or two interaction sessions coded with the system to help investigators ensure that their coding is consistent with our approach. In contrast, there has been at least one instance in which another investigator could not obtain reliability among new coders after sustained effort and consultation with the author. In this case, experienced coders who have worked with the CST system also had great difficulty with coding the interaction sessions from that study. Thus, it is likely that the poor agreement among the new coders was due to the unusually complex behaviors by the couples in that study, most of whom were highly distressed but in stable long-term relationships, with one member who demonstrated significant individual psychopathology.

CODING PROCESS

The coder attends to each speech turn as it occurs, and uses the definitions and criteria for the 40 behaviors in the CST manual to determine the specific types of behaviors that occurred during a speech turn. At the end of the speech turn, the coder uses the classifications listed in Table 9.1 as guidelines to determine the appropriate rating for the entire speech turn on the 5-point scale of proficiency. There are five rules of thumb that guide the coders' decision making for producing the 5-point ratings.

First, the most common behaviors seen in the problem-solving task are statements of opinion about the issue at hand, which are classified as neutral in the CST system. The coders are instructed to scan the speech turn for the presence of other actions that are classified as positive, very positive, negative, or very negative by the CST criteria. If none of these actions occurs, the entire speech turn is given a rating of 3 = *neutral*.

Second, if the speech turn contains any other form of behavior apart from neutral behaviors, the turn is rated in accordance with that behavior. That is, turns that include any of the behaviors in the very negative, negative, positive, or very positive categories shown in Table 9.1 receive ratings in accordance with those classifications. For example, a turn that consists of an opinion probe, which inquires about the partner's ideas or feelings, would receive a rating of 5 = *very positive* (see Table 9.1).

Third, it is common for turns to include neutral problem talk along with another non-neutral behavior. In these cases, the entire turn is rated in accordance with the non-neutral behavior. For example, a statement of neutral problem talk that ends with an opinion probe would receive a rating of 5 = *very positive* to reflect the use of a highly facilitative type of behavior.

Fourth, by extension, if multiple types of behavior occur, the speech turn should be rated in accordance with the most extreme form of behavior exhibited, defined as the type of behavior that most deviates from the neutral category. For example, a speech turn that includes actions categorized as both positive and very positive, as well as neutral problem talk, would be rated 5 = *very positive* to reflect the most extreme form of behavior exhibited.

Fifth, occasionally a speaker exhibits both positive and negative behaviors during the same speech turn. When this occurs, the coder must judge which behavior is dominant in influencing the course of the discussion, and should rate the entire statement in accordance with that behavior. Coders are discouraged from merely rating such statements as neutral. In this way, neutral ratings are preserved only for statements that contain no other actions but neutral actions. For example, a brief summary of the partner's point (a "very positive" action), followed by an accusation that blames the partner for the problem (a "very negative" action) might be rated 1 = *very negative* to reflect that the blaming action was prominent. In contrast, a summary and validation of the partner's opinion (a "very positive" action), followed by a brief comment that the speaker still disagrees with the opinion (a "negative" action) might receive a rating of 5 = *very positive* if the validation is perceived by the coder as prominent.

Generally, ratings are made quickly so that the coder can attend immediately to the next speech turn. Ratings can be written in list form on a sheet of paper, prepared with alternating "H" and "W" prefixes to indicate that the speaker is the husband or wife, respectively. Currently, we use the Observer observational software (Noldus, 1991) to enter ratings directly into a computer file using the terminal keyboard. Software systems are also available for live coding with a hand-held keyboard device. Originally, we developed the CST procedures with the intention that the rating system would be efficient enough to use in live observation situations (Floyd & Markman, 1984). However, the majority of applications have involved coding from videotapes of couples' interactions. In this situation, the coders have the convenience of replaying segments to aide in their decision making. New coders often do so repeatedly, so that a 10-min interaction session takes nearly 1 hr to code. However, experienced coders rarely replay segments, and usually do so only because of poor sound quality of the recording, so that they are able to code a 10-min segment within 15 to 20 min.

RELIABILITY

Reliability has been assessed in terms of interobserver agreement both for ratings of individual speech turns and for the mean scores calculated from all ratings given to a person during the problem-solving discussion. CST coders undergo training until they are able to agree with a master coder on 80% of the individual ratings they make, and achieve a kappa of at least .70. For reliability checks, the coders must achieve 70% agreement, with kappa = .60. The interobserver agreement for the mean CST scores has been assessed in terms of the correlations between scores obtained from independent observers on reliability checks. Across studies with three different samples, the mean correlations were $r = .82$ (Floyd & Markman, 1984), $r = .78$ (Floyd, O'Farrell, & Goldberg, 1987), and $r = .86$ (Haynes et al., 1992). Additionally, in a study that examined negative reciprocity of CST codes (Floyd & Zmich, 1991), a negative reciprocity score was calculated for each spouse by computing a lag-sequential z score to indicate the extent to which the spouse responded negatively to negative behaviors by the partner, beyond what would be expected by chance (Bakeman & Gottman, 1997). The z scores computed from the CST codes produced by independent observers were correlated $r = .73$.

VALIDITY

Two studies have been conducted to evaluate the validity of the CST scores; both the relative frequency scores for the five categories of behaviors, and the CST overall mean scores. In the initial investigation to develop the coding system (Floyd & Markman, 1984), construct validity was supported when these scores were shown to be sensitive measures of pretreatment to posttreatment improvements in communication skills for premarital couples who completed a cognitive–behavioral relationship enhancement intervention. In the second study (Floyd et al., 1987), convergent and discriminant validity were assessed by comparing the CST scores with scores obtained from the MICS (Weiss et al., 1973), an observational coding system that examines more discrete, molecular events. The positive and negative scores from the two measures showed little convergence, but both coding systems successfully discriminated distressed couples from happily married couples. The effects were most apparent for the CST negative and very negative ratings, but for the MICS codes for positive behaviors.

Other research that shows expected effects on CST scores provides further evidence for the construct validity of the measure. For example, mean CST scores have been shown to correlate with marital satisfaction for older married couples (Haynes et al., 1992), and CST-coded marital discussions were shown to be less positive and more negative for couples raising a child with a developmental disability as opposed to couples with typically developing children (Floyd & Zmich, 1991). Spouses' mean CST scores and the negative reciprocity of CST coded behaviors were correlated with negative parent–child interactions concurrently (Floyd & Zmich, 1991) and predicted increases in negative parent–child interactions over time (Floyd, Gilliom, & Costigan, 1998).

GENERALIZABILITY

Studies with the CST have included ethnically diverse samples, with up to 25% of subsamples including people of color (e.g., Floyd & Zmich, 1991). However, no specific evaluations have been conducted to examine possible ethnic or cultural group differences on this measure. Because the coding criteria provide positive ratings for direct discussion of problem areas, openness about opinions and concerns, and overt expressions of emotions, researchers should consider whether this type of behavior is culturally appropriate for their samples. Several studies have involved special groups, including retirees (Haynes et al., 1992), male alcoholics and their wives (Floyd et al., 1987), premarital couples (Markman, Floyd, Stanley, & Storaasli, 1988), and couples with children who have developmental disabilities (Floyd & Zmich, 1991).

CLINICAL UTILITY

The strongest evidence for the clinical utility of the CST comes from a study of the effectiveness of a premarital intervention (Markman et al., 1988) designed to teach couples effective communication/problem-solving skills to prevent the development of relationship distress. The short-term outcomes showed increases in the positiveness of CST scores from pretreatment to posttreatment, which suggests that the couples learned the skills taught in the program. These improvements were later associated with less relationship distress and divorce up to 2 years later.

Thus, it seems that the CST sensitively measures the types of skills that couples learn in this type of intervention.

Apart from detecting group-level changes, the CST can be used as an assessment tool for individual couples to determine whether the presence of excessive negative behaviors or the absence of positive skills should be a focus of intervention with the couple. Although we regularly use the measure in this way and have described this type of use in family assessments (Floyd, Weinand, & Cimmarusti, 1989), to date, there are no studies that explicitly document that this type of assessment improves clinical practice.

STUDIES USING THE CODING SYSTEM

In addition to the research described earlier, another study addressed the association of CST scores with partners' evaluations of each others' behaviors (Floyd, 1988). In this study, observers' used the CST to rate every communication turn by each couple member. The participants also used a 5-point rating system to evaluate the "positiveness" of their cognitive–affective reactions (i.e., "how it makes you feel") to every statement emitted by their partners. In general, the observers' CST ratings of behaviors showed only modest correlations with the partners' ratings of those same behaviors, which confirmed an earlier study (Floyd & Markman, 1983) that showed that insiders' impressions of marital interactions differ from outside observers' evaluations.

ACKNOWLEDGEMENTS

Research with the Communication Skills Test has been funded by grants R01 HD24205, R01 HD35988, and K04 HD01023 from the National Institutes of Health, a grant from the AARP Andrus Foundation, and a BRSG grant from the Illinois Institute of Technology. Coders who have worked with the system over the years have greatly contributed to its development and refinement, particularly Kalpana Dwarikesh, Glen Phillips, Cindy Windham, and Lindsay Ogden. This chapter was prepared when the author was a Visiting Professor at the University of Hawaii at Manoa.

10

Observational Coding of Demand–Withdraw Interactions in Couples

Mia Sevier, Lorelei E. Simpson, and Andrew Christensen
University of California, Los Angeles

For many years, "communication" has been identified as an important issue in relationships. Whether in popular culture, self-help books, or psychological research, communication has been cited frequently as one of the main problems among distressed couples and as a focus for couple therapy (e.g., Weiss & Heyman, 1997). Despite this emphasis on communication, our understanding of this construct has rarely gone beyond stating that positive communication is good for relationships, whereas negative communication is bad. A more specific understanding of the dyadic interactions underlying this construct and the effects such interactions might have on relationship satisfaction has not been explored nearly as much as the broader focus. However, one specific area of communication that has received more in depth focus is the demand–withdraw pattern. This pattern, extensively researched by Christensen and colleagues (e.g., see reviews by Christensen & Heavey, 1993; Eldridge & Christensen, in press), focuses on the tendency for one partner to criticize, blame, and demand change whereas the other withdraws, emotionally, physically, or both. Demand–withdraw, which can become increasingly polarized over time, is related to lower levels of relationship satisfaction (Eldridge & Christensen, in press).

The purpose of the Couple Interaction Rating System (CIRS; Heavey, Gill, & Christensen, 1998) is to rate this behavior pattern in observed couple interactions. The CIRS has a distinct advantage over self-report measures of the demand–withdraw pattern, such as the Communication Patterns Questionnaire (Christensen & Sullaway, 1984), in that it allows for an independent perspective on relationship interactions. Self-report measures, although useful, require individuals to recall and rate interactions with their partner, an activity that can be easily biased by relationship dissatisfaction and negative feelings toward the partner. The CIRS has been used to rate observations of couples discussing problems in their relationship as well as individual issues. It is most applicable to couple interactions around some sort of conflict or disagreement in their relationship, as this is the time when the demand–withdraw pattern is most likely to occur.

THEORETICAL FOUNDATIONS

As mentioned earlier, the CIRS was designed to tap the demand–withdraw interaction pattern in couples. In this dyadic pattern, partners play off of each other, with one person blaming and demanding ever more strenuously for change, and the other avoiding and withdrawing from any discussion just as strenuously. This pattern can leave the demanding person feeling that their partner never listens to him or her, doesn't care about his or her thoughts, feelings, or needs, and doesn't want to put effort into the relationship. The withdrawer, on the other hand, may feel that their partner is always nagging, is constantly critical, blames him or her for little mistakes, and won't let issues go. It is easy to see how such feelings could be related to relationship distress, especially when this pattern happens repeatedly, as it frequently does among unhappy couples (Christensen & Shenk, 1991).

Clinicians have been aware of the demand–withdraw pattern for many years and have described it variously as the pursuer–distancer pattern (Fogarty, 1976) and the rejection–intrusion pattern (Napier, 1978), as well as the demand–withdraw pattern (Wile, 1981). Researchers have found evidence for this demand-withdraw pattern among both opposite-sex and same-sex couples (Walczynski, 1997), in dating couples and married couples, and among couples in cultures as diverse as the United States, Brazil, Italy, and Taiwan (Christensen, Eldridge, Grasshoff, Lim, & Santagata, 2003). The prevalence of this pattern, especially when combined with its association with relationship distress, emphasizes the need to understand its occurrence and its implications for couple therapy.

A number of studies have demonstrated that the most common pattern is woman-demand-man-withdraw, although man-demand–woman-withdraw does occur, and is particularly likely to be seen in violent relationships (Babcock, Waltz, Jacobson, & Gottman, 1993). The greater likelihood of woman-demand–man-withdraw as opposed to man-demand–woman-withdraw has been found in studies of married couples, dating couples, happy and unhappy couples, couples entering therapy, and divorcing couples (Christensen & Shenk, 1991; Walzcynski, Schmidt, Christensen, & Sweeney, 1991).

In their review of the research on demand–withdraw, Eldridge and Christensen (in press) described four theoretical explanations for this gender difference. The first, labeled the gender differences perspective, focuses on the different socialization experiences of men and women as well as potential physiological differences. According to this view, heterosexual couples may experience conflict due to socialization experiences that encourage women to be affiliative and expressive and to place a high value on relationships, whereas men are encouraged to be independent and unexpressive (Chodorow, 1978). These different values can lead women to seek more closeness whereas men seek more independence, which can create cyclical interactions in which women pressure men for more intimacy, and men respond by withdrawing to gain independence, which leads to greater pressure for intimacy, and so on (Christensen, 1987, 1988). Gottman and Levenson (1986, 1988) also suggested that the woman-demand– man-withdraw pattern may result from greater physiological reactivity in men. This physiological arousal then results in increasing physical discomfort, leading men to avoid the emotional conflicts which spark that arousal. In contrast to these findings, however, a recent review by Kiecolt–Glaser and Newton (2001) demonstrated that a number of studies have actually found women, rather than men, to experience greater physiological reactivity in the face of relationship conflict. These studies suggest that there may be a relationship between physiological arousal and the demand–withdraw pattern, but that greater arousal may not lead simply to greater withdrawal.

The individual differences perspective suggests that the greater prevalence of woman-demand–man-withdraw is not due to gender differences, but rather to individual differences that may be associated with gender. According to this view, regardless of gender, the partner who desires more closeness in the relationship is more likely to be demanding, whereas the partner who desires more independence is more likely to withdraw. Individual characteristics, particularly femininity (also called expressivity), have been found to be related to demand behavior. Walczynski (1997) found that demand–withdraw communication occurred just as frequently among same-sex couples as among opposite-sex couples and that the person who was more often the demander tended to be higher on personality characteristics like femininity.

Third, the social and marital structure perspective attributes the woman-demand–man-withdraw pattern to more macroscopic social factors. This view emphasizes the larger social structure and roles of men and women. Advocates of this view suggest that the discrepancies in power and status that favor men make them more reluctant to change in relationships and that they maintain their power by resisting women's efforts to create change (Noller, 1993). Women, on the other hand, have much more to gain through change, so are more likely to pressure for it (Peplau & Gordon, 1985). This perspective also focuses on the structure of traditional marriage, in which men benefit more than women in a number of ways. In such relationships, women are more likely to pressure for change, whereas men seek to maintain their more powerful position.

Finally, the conflict structure perspective attributes the gender differences in the demand–withdraw pattern to characteristics of the conflict, rather than characteristics of the individual or the couple. Christensen and Heavey (1990, 1993) have suggested that it is the topic of discussion that predicts who will demand and who will withdraw. If the topic is one in which the woman wants change from the man, she will be more likely to demand while he will withdraw, but if it is a topic in which the man wants change from the woman, the pattern will be reversed. This pattern occurs because the partner who wishes to maintain the status quo does not have to do anything to get what he or she wants, whereas the person who wants change must have the cooperation of his or her partner for this to occur. The woman-demand–man-withdraw pattern is more likely to occur because women seek change in relationships more often than do men. Christensen and Heavey (1993) have also suggested that because women's concerns tend to be around more serious relationship issues than men's, and because women are more likely to agree to make changes that their male partners desire, women's concerns are more likely to become long-standing sources of greater conflict. The history surrounding a particular issue can lead partners to be more polarized around it, resulting in demand–withdraw communication.

DEVELOPMENT OF THE CODING SYSTEM

The Communication Patterns Questionnaire (CPQ; Christensen & Sullaway, 1984) was developed as a self-report measure of demand–withdraw communication. The impetus for developing the CIRS was to have an observational measure of this pattern. It has undergone a number of changes throughout its development including the addition of other communication items. However, this chapter focuses exclusively on the demand–withdraw codes as they are the basis of the system and are what make it unique.

Although the CPQ was designed, in part, to measure demand–withdraw in general situations (i.e., items ask couples to rate how they interact in conflict situations), the CIRS was designed to assess demand–withdraw in a particular interaction. Some of the wording of the observational codes was taken from the wording of the CPQ items. However, as withdraw behaviors that can occur in a naturalistic setting (e.g., getting up and leaving the room, watching TV or reading a book) cannot occur in the laboratory interaction, a wider range of withdraw behaviors is available for a self-report questionnaire than for observational coding. As such, more subtle nonverbal items, such as looking away and silence, as well as some verbal behaviors, such as refusing to discuss a particular topic, changing the topic, or being vague, were included to assess withdraw in the coding system.

A strategic decision was made to have coders rate the overall interaction rather than have them conduct micro-analytic coding of specific behaviors. This decision was made for several reasons. First, there are many ways that one can be demanding or withdrawing, and a full catalogue of all those possibilities was not available. Second, it was felt that coders could understand the concepts of demand and withdraw and would be able to rate a variety of behaviors that might indicate these constructs. Third, the rating system was designed to capture the intensity of the behaviors rather than their frequency (e.g., one high intensity behavior might be worth several low intensity ones). Finally, a macro-analytic rating system would require less time and expense in training than a complex micro-analytic coding system. By choosing a rating system rather than a micro-analytic coding system, the possibility of looking at the sequential relationship of demand and withdraw behaviors was forfeited. However, an easier and more ecologically valid assessment of demand–withdraw may have been gained.

TASK AND SETTING

Demand–withdraw communication is most likely to become apparent during discussions of areas of conflict or disagreement. In particular, theory predicts that the structure of the conflict influences the roles that partners may assume in the demand–withdraw asymmetry. Hence, in our research, each partner is asked to generate a relationship topic that is of personal concern to that individual. Then, in counterbalanced order, couples are asked to engage in a 10-min, videotaped interaction about each topic. Although, ideally, couples would be observed in natural settings, for practical reasons, our coding system is designed for coding interactions gathered in the laboratory. Videotaping takes place in a simple room designed to simulate a small living room or family room.

Before engaging in discussions, partners separately complete a questionnaire, the Problem Areas Questionnaire (PAQ; Heavey, Layne, & Christensen, 1993), where they rate on 7-point scales how satisfied or dissatisfied they are with various aspects of their relationship. The PAQ assesses diverse areas of marriage including topics such as household tasks, in-laws, child care, religion, moodiness, and sex. This questionnaire will later serve as the basis for choosing relationship discussion topics; however, the couple is not aware of the purpose of the questionnaire while they complete it.

After completing the PAQ, the partners are brought together into a videotaping room and are seated directly facing each other. The following prompt is used to initiate the interaction:

> "We're going to leave the two of you alone to discuss two topics that are important in your marriage. The discussions should be about issues in your marriage that you have different opinions about or that are a source of tension or disagreement for you. We'd like you to have two separate discussions. In the first discussion, both of you will talk

> about a topic that is of concern to (name) and together you will discuss that issue for 10 minutes. We'll knock on the door to let you know that time is up. Then you will spend 10 minutes discussing a topic that is of concern to (name). Is that clear? Now on this form (the PAQ is handed to each partner), you indicated the aspects of your relationship that you are more or less satisfied with. Would each of you be willing to reveal and discuss the area you are most dissatisfied with?"

Topics that one partner does not want to discuss are eliminated until a suitable topic is determined. Partners are required to choose different topics. Then, the first discussion is initiated with the following prompt:

> "Please discuss the issue of (topic A) for the next ten minutes. Try to stay on the topic of (topic A) for the entire time, and try to understand and resolve this issue as best as possible. Talk to each other as you would at home, not to the cameras or to us. After 10 minutes we will knock and get you started on the next discussion."

The researcher leaves the room and videotaping begins. After 10 min, the researcher stops the video equipment, knocks, enters the room, and initiates the second discussion with the following prompt:

> "Now we'd like you to discuss (topic B), the topic that (name) identified, for 10 minutes. Again, stay focused on the topic, talk to each other as you would at home, and try to understand and resolve this issue as best as possible. After 10 minutes we will knock and end your discussion."

DESCRIPTION OF THE CODING SYSTEM

The CIRS (Heavey, Gill, & Christensen, 1998) is a global rating system used to rate an individual as he or she interacts with his or her partner. Each item is rated on a scale of 1 (*none*) to 9 (*a lot*). Raters make judgments based on the extent to which the target individual displays the behavior in question relevant to other individuals in similar interactions. Complete descriptions of each dimension can be found in Table 10.1.

Two dimensions are used in capturing demanding communication: Blaming and Pressures for Change. Blaming represents the target partner's accusations, criticism, and assignment of the other as the causal agent for the problem or target's reactions. Pressures for Change includes positive or negative and implicit or explicit pressure for change in the partner. Demanding communication is computed by averaging Blaming and Pressures for Change.

Withdrawing communication is represented by three dimensions: Withdrawal, Avoidance, and Discussion. Withdrawal represents nonverbal passive behavior indicating a lack of interest or energy to discuss the topic. Avoidance includes active behavior that serves to avoid engaging in the discussion. Discussion represents level of engagement and involvement in discussion of the topic.

TABLE 10.1

Couples' Interaction Rating System Codes

Blaming	Blames, accuses, or criticizes the partner, uses critical sarcasm; makes character assassinations such as "you're a real jackass," "all you do is eat," or "why are you such a jerk about it?" Explicit blaming statements (e.g., "you made me do it" or "you prevent me from doing it"), in which the spouse is the causal agent for the problem or the subject's reactions, warrant a high score.
Pressures for Change	Requests, demands, nags, manipulates, seduces, or otherwise pressures for change in the other partner. This pressure can be either positive or negative (critical, or complimenting and supportive). This pressure can be implicit as well as explicit. In other words, it need not be as explicit as "I want you to play with our son." It must, however, carry in it an implicit should statement, which clearly indicates what the partner "should" be doing. Examples of this include "You never play with our son," and "If you spent more time at home, our child would probably not act out as much at school." These statements both carry implicit "shoulds" that the parent should carry out his or her parental duties by spending more time with the child. Many strong implicit statements warrant a high rating. Remember, character assassinations do not belong here; "you're a jackass" does not carry any clear implicit suggestions as to what should be done to correct or lessen this condition.
Withdrawal	More passive than Avoidance and generally non-verbal. Acting in ways that suggest the individual is emotionally or psychologically withdrawn from the discussion. Generally speaking, how much does the person seem to be withdrawn from their partner and the discussion. Withdraws, becomes silent, refuses to discuss a particular topic, looks away, refuses to argue or fight about the issue, does not actively defend self, pulls back, retreats, disengages self from the discussion, does not offer solutions or assist in the discussion, does not respond to the partner, does not follow or pay attention to what the partner says.
Avoidance	More active than Withdrawal, using energy to avoid. Any behavior that serves to avoid engaging in the discussion. Generally speaking, how much is the person trying to avoid discussing the issue at hand rather than actively engaging in the discussion. Includes minimizing the importance of the problem being discussed, denying the existence of the problem, shifting the focus or changing the topic of the discussion away from the problem, purposefully being vague or making ambiguous comments about the problem to obscure the discussion or confuse the partner, hesitating, diverting attention, or delaying the discussion.

TABLE 10.1 (cont.)

Discussion	Tries to discuss the problem, is engaged and involved in the topic, approaching, interested, willing to discuss the issue (whether it makes them happy or upset). Active listening can count as engagement in the discussion. Discussion reflects how interested the partner is in the topic. This rating should not include how interested the individual is in including their partner in the discussion, (i.e., an individual who intently lectures on the topic without leaving room for their partner to interject would receive a high score.)

Withdrawing communication is computed by averaging Avoidance, Withdrawal, and the reverse score of Discussion.

Individual measures of woman-demand, woman-withdraw, man-demand, and man-withdraw can easily be computed by following the aforementioned procedures separately for each partner. Couple level communication patterns can be computed as follows: woman-demand–man-withdraw:[1] the average of the woman's demand composite and the man's withdraw composite; man-demand– woman-withdraw, the average of the man's demand composite and the woman's withdraw composite; and demand–withdraw communication, the average of the woman-demand–man-withdraw and man-demand–woman-withdraw composites.

Several aspects of composite measures may make individual level measures more useful than the couple level measures. First, composites represent totals of each partner's behavior and do not necessarily represent totals of observed, contingently-related, demand–withdraw behavior. Although our theory suggests that withdraw behavior elicits demand behavior and vice versa, in the course of a 10-min interaction, a couple may not show a clear tit-for-tat contingency between the two. For example, a couple might get a high score on woman-demand–man-withdraw simply because the man was withdrawn during the entire interaction. Although his withdrawal did not seem affected by whatever level of demand the woman showed, the couple would get scores based on the total of his withdrawal and her demand. Our theory might assume that his withdrawal is related to her history of demand (and vice versa), but a high score on demand–withdraw does not necessarily support that notion. Second, it is important to note that, by averaging the two partner scores in composite measures, very different patterns can be represented by identical couple level scores. For example, the same score could represent a woman with moderate demand and a man with moderate withdraw or alternatively, a woman with high demand and a man with low withdraw. Hence, individual measures have advantages over couple level measures as they do not carry any implication of a contingency based on partner's behavior and avoid the problem of obscuring different patterns within similar couple level scores.

[1]These patterns can easily be applied to same-gender couples by assigning partners labels such as partner 1 and partner 2 and substituting these labels for the woman and man labels.

CODER TRAINING

The CIRS was designed for use by naïve raters who are fluent in English and have a layperson's understanding of human interaction in general, and of demand and withdraw behaviors in particular. A training period is undertaken to fine-tune each rater's conception of these concepts. Training in coding demand–withdraw can be done with the CIRS manual in conjunction with training tapes.[2] Novice raters read descriptions of each dimension and then rate a series of videotaped interactions which have been selected to exemplify both high and low ratings of each dimension. Raters view tapes and compare their own scores to master scores. Training also occurs through discussion with expert raters, who help new raters evaluate the use of items in regard to specific interactions. Ratings of study tapes begin once raters demonstrate a reasonable level of reliability, which can typically be expected after approximately 15 hr of total training.

After initial training, raters continue to attend weekly 2-hr training meetings to prevent drift and maintain high reliability. Each week, the team leader computes inter-rater reliability for recently coded data. Items with the lowest reliability are chosen for rescoring and discussion at the training meeting. Original rating sheets are returned to raters so that they may assess their own consistency over viewings. Group discussion focuses on definitions of inconsistent items and specific application to the interaction just viewed. Raters are encouraged to share their reasoning behind item usage. Discussion can involve lively debate and ends with an agreement on the proper item rating.

CODING PROCESS

Teams of three to four raters independently rate one partner in each interaction. Each rater views an entire 10-min interaction before rating. Raters are encouraged, but not required, to take notes while viewing the tape. If, while viewing an interaction, raters do not understand what occurs during a segment, they immediately stop the tape and replay the segment. After viewing an entire interaction, raters evaluate whether they have enough information to make ratings on all of the categories. To keep rating time to a minimum and to keep ratings global rather than remembrances of specific incidences, raters are permitted to review the entire discussion only once more, at which point all ratings must be made. With fully trained raters, assigning ratings can be accomplished in approximately 1 min. To prevent biases, raters are kept blind to study structure and purposes and code interactions that are ordered randomly (e.g., the order of an interaction on the man's topic and an interaction on the woman's topic or the order or pretreatment and posttreatment interactions are determined randomly).

[2]A sample of four staged interactions for training purposes can be obtained from Andrew Christensen and Mia Sevier at the University of California, Los Angeles.

RELIABILITY

Previous work using slightly different versions of the CIRS demand–withdraw codes has demonstrated acceptable levels of reliability (Christensen & Heavey, 1990; Heavey, Christensen, & Malamuth, 1995; Heavey et al., 1993; Holtzworth-Munroe, Smutzler, & Stuart, 1998; Shoham, Rohrbaugh, Stickle, & Jacob, 1998; Walczynski, 1997). Using demand–withdraw coding from the CIRS described in this chapter, an analysis of data from a study in progress, the Couple Therapy Project,[3] was conducted to examine reliability. Eight teams were involved in coding a total of 1,764 10-min interactions. At the item level, the teams demonstrated the following range of inter-rater reliability: Blaming, .86 to .94; Pressures for Change, .76 to .88; Withdrawal, .60 to .87; Avoidance, .62 to .84; and Discussion, .69 to .83. At the subscale level, Demand inter-rater agreement ranged from .87 to .93, and Withdraw inter-rater agreement ranged from .75 to .88. Internal consistency was also assessed using Chronbach's alpha; we obtained an alpha of .80 for the Demand subscale and .73 for the Withdraw subscale ($n = 78$ couples).

VALIDITY

Evidence for construct validity of the CIRS has been gathered in several studies. Demand–withdraw, as measured by the CIRS, relates to satisfaction in predicted ways (Eldridge, 2000; Heavey et al., 1995; Heavey et al., 1993) such that greater satisfaction is related to low levels of demand–withdraw and more flexibility in which partner engages in demand and withdraw across interactions. In addition, CIRS demand–withdraw has been demonstrated to vary in theoretically predictable ways across topics such that woman-demand–man-withdraw is more likely in the woman's topic, and man-demand–woman-withdraw is more likely in the man's topic (Christensen & Heavey, 1990; Eldridge, 2000; Heavey et al. 1993). In addition, CIRS demand–withdraw varies across type of discussion, such that the highest levels are present in conflict discussions rather than social support discussions (Eldridge, 2000).

The CIRS is not highly correlated with the self-report CPQ. For purposes of comparison, correlations between the CIRS and CPQ were computed in a subset of data from 78 distressed treatment-seeking couples from the Couple Therapy Study. CIRS woman-demand–man-withdraw correlated .26, $p = .02$ with woman CPQ reports, and .21, $p = .07$ with man CPQ reports. CIRS man-demand–woman-withdraw correlated .47, $p = .00$ with woman CPQ reports, and .42, $p = .00$ with man CPQ reports. CIRS total demand–withdraw communication correlated .35, $p = .00$ with woman CPQ reports, and .17, $p = .13$ with man CPQ reports. These

[3]The Couple Therapy Project is a two-site clinical trial of couple therapy at the University of California at Los Angeles and the University of Washington under the direction of Andrew Christensen and Neil S. Jacobson (and William George since Jacobson's death).

moderate to low correlations are not surprising given that the domain of assessment varies across methods. The CPQ asks about communication patterns in general, whereas the CIRS focuses on a specific topic discussion. Importantly, despite moderate associations between assessment measures, the pattern of results across the CPQ and CIRS have been consistent. For example, both measures have shown that satisfaction levels are associated with demand–withdraw communication. Also, both measures have demonstrated that demand–withdraw interaction shifts as the topic of conflict shifts (see Eldridge & Christensen, in press, for a review).

To assess the construct validity of the CIRS, a factor analysis was conducted on a sample of 169 married couples from the Couple Therapy Project, who completed the 10-min interactions described earlier. Principal components analyses with varimax rotation were conducted with factors defined by an eigenvalue greater than 1. As interactions within couples were correlated, the factor analysis was run separately for wife and husband behavior in the wife topic interaction and wife and husband behavior in the husband topic interaction, resulting in four separate analyses. Across all four analyses, the demand items loaded heavily on one factor and the withdraw items loaded heavily on a second. Furthermore, the demand items did not load on the withdraw factor, and the withdraw items did not load on the demand factor. For the wife topic analyses, 70% of variance in the items was explained by the demand and withdraw factors for wife ratings and 80% was explained for husband ratings. For the husband topic analyses, 74% of variance was explained in the wife ratings and 72% of variance in the husband ratings.[4]

GENERALIZABILITY

Evidence for the generalizability of the observational coding of demand–withdraw during problem-solving discussions has been gathered across different samples of dyadic relationships. Theoretically consistent results linking demand–withdraw to satisfaction or demonstrating variations across topics and discussion types have been demonstrated in samples of married couples (Christensen & Heavey, 1990; Eldridge, 2000; Heavey et al., 1995; Heavey et al., 1993; Holtzworth–Munroe et al., 1998), dating couples (Heavey et al., 1995), same-sex couples (Walczynski, 1997), violent couples (Holtzworth–Munroe et al., 1998), couples in treatment for alcoholism (Shoham et al., 1998), and distressed, treatment-seeking, married couples (Eldridge, 2000).

Recent work has expanded the focus of research from problem-solving discussions to an inclusion of personal concern discussions (Eldridge, 2000). Instead of discussing relationship issues, partners each choose a topic that is a personal concern that they would like to work on or change about themselves. These discus-

[4]Further data from these analyses is available from the authors on request.

sions generally contain lower levels of demand–withdraw, but this communication pattern continues to relate to relationship satisfaction and to appear in theoretically consistent ways. For example, those couples who show a rigid pattern of demand–withdraw communication across both problem-solving and social support interactions tend to be more unhappy.

Research to date using this type of observational coding has primarily focused on predominantly Northern American, White, middle-class, college-educated couples. However, small groups of minority couples (sometimes composing up to 25% of the sample, i.e., Shoham et al., 1998) have been present in some studies. Research on demand–withdraw communication using other assessment methods has demonstrated the presence of this pattern in couples in Germany, Brazil, Italy, and Taiwan (Christensen, Eldridge, Grasshoff, Lim, & Santagata, 2003; Hahlweg, Kaiser, Christensen, Fehm–Wolfsdorf, & Groth, 2000).

CLINICAL UTILITY

The CIRS was originally developed for research purposes as an observational assessment of couple interaction and to track changes in communication over time. The Couples Therapy Project is using this measure to evaluate treatment effectiveness and the process of change in communication. Outside of research, other contexts in which this measure might be used could include assessment of communication patterns prior to therapy and evaluation of treatment effectiveness in couples therapy. Clinicians are unlikely to use this measure in a formal manner because it requires coders who are blind to a couple's history, videotaping, and multiple raters for reliability. However, clinicians could use it informally to guide their observations of couples' demand–withdraw behavior. In our experience and as demonstrated by the CPQ, couples can understand demanding and withdrawing communication. Clinicians could provide useful feedback to couples about their demand–withdraw communication and relate this pattern to the problems they are experiencing, how they express their distress, and how that communication might change over time. A focus on demand–withdraw communication could also be useful in identifying the conflicts that are most troubling and long-standing for couples. Finally, informal CIRS use might provide a useful addition to the self-report measures often used by couple therapists to track changes and provide feedback to couples over the course of treatment.

STUDIES USING THE CODING SYSTEM

A series of studies has been conducted to examine demand–withdraw using varying versions of the CIRS. Several studies investigated the effects of gender and social structure on demand–withdraw. Christensen and Heavey (1990) demonstrated that gender and conflict structure interact such that woman-demand–man-withdraw was more likely than man-demand–woman- withdraw only in discussions of woman topics. Heavey et al. (1993) found additional support for the interaction of gender and conflict structure such that women were more demanding than their male partners, and men more withdrawing than their female partners in the woman's topic, but not in the man's topic. Eldridge (2000) further confirmed that gender-related roles emerged in topics selected by women, but not in topics selected by men.

Demand–withdraw has also been related to relationship satisfaction using the CIRS. Cross-sectionally, higher levels of demand–withdraw communication are found in distressed couples than among nondistressed couples (Christensen & Shenk, 1991; Eldridge & Christensen, in press). Eldridge (2000) uncovered an interaction between relationship satisfaction and conflict structure such that highly dissatisfied partners rigidly remained in demanding or withdrawing roles across topics, whereas moderately dissatisfied and happy couples shifted roles in response to changes in topics. Longitudinally, Heavey et al. (1993) discovered that woman-demand–man-withdraw predicted a decline in wives' satisfaction 1 year later. Heavey et al. (1995) found that male withdrawal and woman-demand–man-withdraw during women's topics predicted declines in the women's satisfaction 2.5 years later.

Using same-sex couples, Walczynski (1997) investigated individual differences in demand–withdraw unrelated to gender. She discovered that personality characteristics, such as femininity, are related to role assignment and that partners desiring more relationship closeness tended to be more demanding, whereas partners desiring more independence tended to be more withdrawing.

The study of demand–withdraw has also been expanded to explore violence in relationships, treatment dropouts, and changes in response to therapy. Holtzworth-Munroe et al. (1998) discovered that man-demand–woman-withdraw communication is more prevalent among couples with male generated relationship violence than in couples with no violence. Shoham et al. (1998) found that couples with high woman-demand–man-withdraw were more likely to drop out of cognitive behavioral treatment for the husband's alcoholism. The authors hypothesize that the treatment may mimic the demanding pattern of the woman and hence, prompt a withdrawal of the alcoholic male from treatment. Eldridge (2000) demonstrated a reduction in overall levels of demand–withdraw in response to both Traditional Behavioral Couple Therapy and Integrative Behavioral Couple Therapy.

ACKNOWLEDGEMENTS

This research was supported by National Science Foundation graduate student fellowship to Mia Sevier and a grant from the National Institute of Mental Health awarded to Andrew Christensen (MH 56223) and Neil S. Jacobson at the University of Washington (MH 56165) for a two-site clinical trial of couple therapy. After Jacobson's death, William George served as Principal Investigator at the University of Washington. We would like to acknowledge Kathy Eldridge for her work supervising the University of California, Los Angeles coding team in the beginning years and the work of the undergraduates who have served on the coding teams, including Anthony Berryman, Gabriela Bravo, Cheyenne Henderson, and Angelica Hormann.

11

System for Coding Interactions in Dyads (SCID)

Neena M. Malik and Kristin M. Lindahl
University of Miami

The System for Coding Interactions in Dyads (SCID) is a global coding system, designed to capture elements of dyadic and individual communication behaviors within the context of couples' problem discussions. Recent work has suggested that it is important to study specific elements of couple communication that go beyond constructs of positivity and negativity (Fincham, 1998). As such, this system was primarily designed to focus on dynamics of power and control within couple relationships, in addition to behaviors that are linked with overall couple stability and relationship quality. The SCID includes an assessment of power behaviors such as verbal aggression, coerciveness, and control. It also assesses elements of couple behavior and communication that may be related to domestic violence and other indicators of relationship power dynamics. These elements include negative escalation, conflict management style, and balance of power. The SCID also assesses behaviors related to the overall quality of couple relationships, such as support, problem-solving communication, and cohesiveness. There are both individual codes and dyadic, couple-based codes within the system.

The SCID has been found to be reliable with Anglo, Hispanic, and Black (including African American and Caribbean American) couples. It was designed for use with typical couple problem discussion tasks and assesses strategies and behaviors potentially employed during couple disagreements.

THEORETICAL FOUNDATIONS

Several areas of research have guided the development of the SCID. These include a large body of research on couple communication and conflict (Bradbury & Karney, 1993; Gottman, 1994), describing both the positive and negative aspects of couple communication and how observed behaviors are empirically linked to relationship quality and stability; couple power dynamics and relationship quality, including domestic violence (Babcock, Waltz, Jacobson, & Gottman, 1993; Gray–Little & Burks, 1983); and cross-ethnic research on couple communication and relationship values (Marín & Marín, 1991).

As reflected in this volume, a variety of coding systems have been developed to understand the various dimensions of couple relationship functioning. Although the SCID shares elements with many of the other existing systems, one of the primary unique perspectives guiding the development of the SCID is theoretical and empirical work on what is referred to as "family power" or "relationship power," most broadly defined as the expression and exertion of influence of one partner over the other (Blood & Wolfe, 1960; Goode, 1971; Gray–Little & Burks, 1983; Huston, 1983). Empirical work consistently links power dynamics with relationship satisfaction (Gray–Little & Burks, 1983), and a growing literature has shown power dynamics to be linked with domestic violence (Babcock et al., 1993; Claes & Rosenthal, 1990; Malik, 1998). Theoretical work in domestic violence posits that a quest for power is a driving force behind spousal abuse, and that violence is the most extreme expression of relationship power (Murphy & Meyer, 1991). As noted in a recent review by Gottman and Notarius (2002), although the study of power dynamics is critical to research on couples, little is written about power dynamics in the study of marital interaction. The SCID, although also focusing on constructs relevant to couple functioning overall, was developed primarily to fill the gap and focus observation efforts on the study of power dynamics.

There are three primary subconstructs defined within the overall construct of relationship power (Cromwell & Olson, 1975; Huston, 1983), including power bases, power processes, and power outcomes. Power bases typically refer to those individual characteristics that impute authority or status, such as education, high level socioeconomic status, or material wealth. Power bases in an individual may also be those characteristics that others perceive them to have, such as high levels of persuasive abilities or communication skills, or even perceptions that an individual belongs to a racial, ethnic, or gender group with elevated social status.

In a relationship, when one partner perceives the other to have better communication skills or persuasive ability, it is considered an indicator of a power base for the partner perceived to be more skilled. When such communication skills are observed, they are also considered to be power processes. Power processes have been defined as behaviors that individuals engage in as "attempts to gain control in the negotiation or decision-making process" (McDonald, 1980, p. 843). Power processes are essentially those observable behaviors that an individual employs to assert authority or gain control in interaction with others. Power outcome, considered the third of the subconstructs of relationship power, is generally described as the ultimate result of utilization of power bases and processes, referring to who, in the end, is the decision maker or dominant member of a dyad (Cromwell & Olson, 1975; Huston, 1983).

Of the theoretically defined subconstructs of power, including power bases, power processes, and power outcomes, most measures have been limited to power bases (Huston, 1983; Malik & Lindahl, 1998). Power dynamics, particularly power processes, although theoretically considered to be quite important to couple functioning and domestic violence in couple relationships, have presented major measurement challenges. This has led many researchers to study more concrete elements of power such as power bases, or give up the study of power altogether in favor of less abstract couple dynamics (Gottman & Notarius, 2002; Huston, 1983; Murphy & Meyer, 1991). As noted earlier, the SCID has been designed in part to fill that measurement gap and focus on the behaviors that relate to how the processes of power are played out in couple communication. In particular, the individual codes of Verbal Aggression, Coerciveness, Attempts to Control, and Problem Solving Communication, and the dyadic code of Balance of Power, are designed to examine power process behaviors as they are engaged in by partners in intimate relationships.

The research on relationship power that does exist has largely focused on its link with relationship satisfaction (Gray–Little & Burks, 1983). Although research was mainly conducted in the 1960s and 1970s and focused primarily on Anglo couples, data were consistent in indicating that imbalances between partners across dimensions of relationship power were related to lower levels of relationship satisfaction. Later research, although again largely limited to Anglo couples, provided data to suggest that power imbalances also are related to domestic violence (e.g., Babcock et al., 1993).

In addition to attempts to control and other individual power processes, there are couple level dynamics that are relevant to power, violence, and relationship quality and are included in the SCID. The couple demand–withdraw pattern has been linked with power, violence, and other elements of relationship quality (Babcock et al., 1993; Berns, Jacobson, & Gottman, 1999; Christensen & Shenk, 1991; Gottman, 1993; Gottman & Notarius, 2002). Withdrawal is often seen as a stonewalling tactic to enforce the status quo in a relationship, where the demander or pursuer is the individual seeking change, which is an inherently less powerful position. As such, the demand or pursuit–withdrawal pattern may be seen as indicative of a power struggle in a couple interaction. Similarly, negative escalation is a consistent indicator of couple distress and relationship dissolution, and it is also a pattern linked to domestic violence (Burman, Margolin, & John, 1993; Gottman, 1994). Among the more common theories of domestic violence is that violence is the highest intensity expression of power (Murphy & Meyer, 1991), and the highest intensity of violence is at risk for occurring in escalating conflict situations (Yllö, 1993). Therefore, dyadic codes of Negative Escalation and Pursuit–Withdrawal Pattern are included in the SCID, with additional individual ratings of Withdrawal.

An additional theoretical and empirical perspective employed in the development of the SCID, which was designed to assess power dynamics as well as other elements of relationship quality, is Gottman's (1993) work on couple typologies. Gottman's findings indicate that levels of engagement, positivity, and negativity are linked with stability or instability in couple relationships. These longitudinal results suggest that there are two overall categories of couples, stable or unstable, and that overall rates of positivity or negativity determine whether relationships are likely to succeed or dissolve. Among the stable couples are those who are either positively engaged with each other in either a calm, harmonious way or a volatile, expressive, but still overall positive way. There is also a group of stable couples whom Gottman describes as having somewhat low rates of engagement or interaction rates but who nonetheless are not negative with one another. The unstable couples may or may not have high levels of engagement, but in the case of both types of unstable couples, Gottman found that there were more negative than positive changes overall in both unstable groups, whom he described as either hostile engagers or hostile detached partners. Based on the work of Gottman (1993), the SCID includes ratings of engagement, positivity, negativity, and a typology of how couples manage their conflict.

The SCID codes were developed so that the system can be sensitive to variations in couple dynamics across ethnic groups, as power and communication dynamics in the marriage are likely to vary by ethnicity (Marín & Marín, 1991). Research suggests that Anglo couples tend to value egalitarianism, shared roles, and democratic interaction and decision making (Ho, 1990; Wagner, Kirchler, Clack, Tekarslan, & Verma, 1990), whereas Latino and Hispanic couples value *familism*, complementarity in family roles, and hierarchical decision making (Vega, 1990). The Balance of Power code, therefore, has four categories that include assessments of different ways in which power is distributed in couple interactions (i. e., male or female dominant, balanced, or conflictually imbalanced). Based on literature examining relationship values across ethnic groups, it might be expected that the balanced and conflictually imbalanced ratings would relate to indicators of relationship well-being and domestic violence similarly across ethnic groups. For example, it is likely that couples observed to be balanced in problem discussions will also be happier and less violent, whereas couples who fight for control with each other may also be less happy and more violent (Malik & Lindahl, 1998). Male or female dominance, however, may be related to more negative relationship functioning in Anglo couples but not, for example, in Latino and Hispanic couples. In addition, the coding system has distinguished straightforward attempts to control or tell partners what to do in a dominant fashion from more negative, threatening, and coercive attempts to dominate a partner. Although coerciveness may relate to negative relationship functioning and violence across ethnic groups, this may not be the case for straightforward attempts to control.

DEVELOPMENT OF THE CODING SYSTEM

The original version of this coding system was developed in 1996, in conjunction with and as a companion to two other coding systems. These include a triadic family coding system, the System for Coding Interactions and Family Functioning (SCIFF; Lindahl & Malik, 2001), and the System for Coding Interactions in Parent–Child Dyads (SCIPD; Lindahl, 1996). These systems were all developed to assess similar constructs across various family subsystems, including the couple dyad, parent–child dyads, and family triads (both parents and child). Therefore, certain codes are common across all coding systems, with each system containing additional codes specific to the family subsystem it assesses. The systems were developed based on the research and theory on couple communication, family systems, family power, and cross-cultural family dynamics.

The SCID is a global coding system, designed to capture multiple qualities of couple interaction. Impressive micro-analytic coding systems already exist in couple observational research and therefore, in developing the SCID, we attempted to create a system that would assess couple dynamics—particularly power dynamics—that are distinct from those well-captured by micro-analytic systems. For example, to observe the overall balance of power or dominance in a couple, a more molar observational method is likely to yield a fuller picture of the dynamics than a micro-analytic examination might. Although there is clear utility to parsing interactions by utterances or moment-by moment interactive behaviors, power dynamics in a couple are difficult to capture using micro-analytic methodology. A good example is the balance of power dynamic (which was found in one other study that utilized a global method of rating; Gray–Little, Baucom, & Hamby, 1996). Although there may be a higher frequency of decision-making statements by one partner in an interaction, it requires only one or two decision making statements or ultimatums of high intensity to create an imbalance of power in a couple's relationship. This is also true of verbally aggressive behaviors. Unless a careful and potentially burdensome weighting system is employed, therefore, a micro-analytic approach would be misleading in this scenario. A global system, therefore, allows for a more qualitative analysis of behavior. Family systems theorists have long noted that the whole is greater than the sum of its parts, and this adage likely holds true for a construct as complex and systems-based as the dynamics of power and control in intimate relationships. Clearly, however, other types of individual and couple level communications may best be understood through more micro-analytic means of coding.

TASK AND SETTING

As noted earlier, the SCID is designed for observations of couples' problem discussions, rather than observations of interactions that are more positive in nature. Typically, the method used to set up the problem-solving task is to have each partner individually fill out the Marital Agendas Protocol (MAP; Notarius & Vanzetti, 1983), which asks partners to individually rate the severity of problem areas in their relationship (such as money, in-laws, sex, communication, or other conflict areas) and rank order the top three problem areas. Couples are then asked to choose a top problem area to discuss on videotape for approximately 12 to 15 min. This process may or may not entail partners actually sharing their responses to the MAP with one another. In studies in our laboratory, these interactions have constituted the final stage of data collection and follows questionnaire data collection.

If needed, a researcher will stay in the observation room with the couple and help them mutually decide on a topic. This is not typically necessary but can occur. The researcher will then state, "Go ahead and talk with each other about the topic you've chosen. We will ask you to talk together for about 12 to 15 minutes. We will knock on the door to let you know when a minute is left. We'll then come back and let you know when the time is over." It is not uncommon for some couples to request a few extra minutes to discuss the matter they are dealing with, and this is something we always allow in our laboratory.

One of the reasons we have the observational task at the end of any other data collection is to allow this additional processing time to occur, and to allow for a complete debriefing of the interaction once it is completed. Debriefing includes processing with the couples how it felt to talk about their issues if it is needed, in addition to monitoring the level of conflict that arose. With couples for whom the task created minimal stress or conflict, the debriefing tends to be quite short (a few minutes). Debriefing may be lengthier to reduce levels of tension and conflict with couples who have had strong reactions to the interaction. Any questions about the study are also addressed at that time. One of the primary goals of debriefing, particularly with violent couples, is to ensure that the conflict has not exceeded a level of comfort or safety for the participants. At times, particularly with violent couples, debriefing may occur in separate rooms initially and may include a safety interview.

DESCRIPTION OF THE CODING SYSTEM

The SCID is divided into two sections: codes of individual behavior, and codes that reflect the dyadic aspects of the interaction (see Table 11.1). The first set of codes are rated twice, once for each member of the dyad. These include specific power dynamic codes, including Verbal Aggression, Coerciveness, and Attempts to Control; and codes related to communication skills and affect, including Problem Solving Communication, Support, Negativity and Conflict, Withdrawal, Dysphoric Affect, and Positive Affect. Couple or dyadic codes include Negative Escalation and Pursuit–Withdrawal Pattern, Cohesiveness, Conflict Management Style, and Balance of Power.

Thirteen of the fifteen codes are rated on a 1 to 5 point Likert scale with a paragraph of descriptors serving as an anchor for each point on the scale. These an-

TABLE 11.1

System for Coding Interactions in Dyads

Code	*Construct Measured*	*Indicators*	*Measurement*
Individual Codes			
Verbal Aggression	Power processes	Hostility, insults, put-downs, demeaning remarks	5-point Likert scale
Coerciveness	Power processes	Threatening, manipulative statements or body language	5-point Likert scale, frequency count
Attempts to Control	Power processes	Overt commands or demands to change partner's thoughts, feelings, or actions	5-point Likert scale, frequency count
Negativity and Conflict	Communication skill	Anger, frustration, irritation, blame (without aggression or control)	5-point Likert scale
Withdrawal	Communication skill	Avoidance or distance, tone, body language, attitude	5-point Likert scale
Problem Solving Communication	Communication skill	Constructive facilitation of discussion and problem solving	5-point Likert scale
Support	Communication skill	Attunement, sensitivity, validation	5-point Likert scale
Dysphoric Affect	Affective state	Sadness, grief, remorse	5-point Likert scale
Positive Affect	Affective state	Affection, joy, satisfaction through tone, body language, facial expression	5-point Likert scale

TABLE 11.1 (cont.)

Code	*Construct Measured*	*Indicators*	*Measurement*
Dyadic Codes			
Negative Escalation	Couple level communication dynamics	Escalating, reciprocal negative behaviors	5-point Likert scale
Pursuit-Withdraw Pattern	Couple-level communication dynamics	One partner actively seeks, the other withdraws or shuts down, communication	5-point Likert scale
Cohesiveness	Couple level communication and affective characteristics	Unity, closeness, teamwork	5-point Likert scale
Conflict Management Style	Couple level conflict dynamics	Relational styles in conflict discussion	Categorical code
Balance of Power	Couple level power processes	Distribution of power, dominance, control in interactio	Categorical code

chors typically describe ratings based on both frequency and intensity of behaviors. Two of these codes, Coerciveness and Attempts to Control, are Likert-type ratings but are based on frequency counts only of these specific behaviors. Because coercive and controlling statements are relatively rare but can be quite meaningful, the frequency of these statements does not have to be high to merit a rating of a 4 or 5 in the coding system. The two categorical codes include Conflict Management Style, which rates the overall style with which couples appear to manage negative affect and communication, and Balance of Power, which rates the overall balance of authority in the dyad. There are six categories in Conflict Management Style (Female Pursuit–Male Withdrawal; Male Pursuit–Female Withdrawal; Harmonious, High Conflict-Expressive, High Conflict-Hostile, and Disengaged), based on Christensen and colleagues' work on demand–withdraw (Christensen & Shenk, 1991) and Gottman's typologies (1993). Four categories are included in Balance of Power: Balanced, Male Dominant, Female Dominant, and Conflictual Imbalanced, the latter suggesting that a power struggle is observed in the dyad.

CODER TRAINING

One of our goals was to develop a coding system that could yield meaningful data about complex couple dynamics while still being simple enough for undergraduate students to learn. We have found that undergraduates can become quite reliable coders. Training, however, is extensive for undergraduates, whereas graduate students require less training time to become reliable coders. Therefore, if appropriate graduate students are available, we recommend graduate students as coders. In our lab, however, we most frequently involve teams of undergraduates as coders for several reasons. First, although they take substantially more time to train and supervise, a team of undergraduates eventually is able to complete more coding because they tend to be available in greater numbers than graduate students. Second, our research involves multi-ethnic samples of families, many of whom are bilingual. When doing multi-ethnic observational research, it is important to have the ethnicity of the coders reflect the ethnicity of the study participants, as much as possible.

The original studies for which the SCID was developed were conducted in Miami, Florida, where the majority of the population is Hispanic. Studies thus far have included samples that are therefore primarily Hispanic, including couples that are Cuban American as well as couples from Central and South America. Study samples have also included Anglo, Black (including African American and Caribbean American), and to a lesser extent, Asian couples. As such, coders have primarily been Hispanic and Anglo, with efforts made to include coders who are African American or Caribbean American in ethnicity. Many couples in our samples are more comfortable speaking Spanish than English during interactions;

therefore, coders who are bilingual are important team members. In general, when conducting observational research with multiple ethnic or cultural groups, coding team members who are familiar with the ethnicities and cultures of the participants allow for increased understanding of cultural issues, behaviors, and dynamics, and allow for more accurate coding.

The first step of the training process is for coders to read the coding manual (Malik & Lindahl, 2000), and for meetings to take place to review the manual in its entirety, including the theoretical background, the codes, and the anchors that describe each point on each scale. This manual review typically takes between 3 and 4 hours. For each code, the manual provides a general description that is a half a page to a page long. The general descriptors are followed by detailed descriptions of each of the five anchor points on the 5-point, Likert-type scales of the continuous codes, and detailed paragraphs describing each of the categories of couple behavior related to the Conflict Management Style and Balance of Power codes.

Following discussions about the manual, the second step includes reviewing, item by item, four or five tapes that have been coded jointly by the authors of the manual (the "gold standard" tapes, used with all trainees). Third, as a group, the trainees code two or three criterion tapes with one of the authors of the SCID present (this may also be done with a skilled graduate student who is reliable on the system). Each code is discussed, with coding errors reviewed and explained. This process helps clarify any misunderstandings with the codes. The next step in training is to assign two to three tapes that each coder will code individually, and coding is reviewed as a group in meetings that are usually weekly and take place over the course of approximately a month.

Trainees are instructed to watch each tape at least three times, and at the outset of training, four times. First, the interaction is watched in its entirety, with no coding done. Second, the tape is watched, starting and stopping as needed, to code the individual and dyadic codes that do not require exact frequency counts. During training, trainees are asked to write down their justifications for each code. Their reasons for their coding choices must include verbatim quotes and detailed behavioral descriptions (such as, "the husband said 'you are an idiot' to his wife, which is an instance of Verbal Aggression," or "there were no A-B-A negative escalation cycle behaviors in the interaction"). The third viewing of the tape is done to code the frequency-count codes, Coerciveness and Attempts to Control. Prior to reaching reliability, trainees are instructed to watch each tape a fourth time to ensure that they have coded the interaction accurately and have written down all the information needed to justify their coding. At this stage of training, it is not uncommon for coders to require up to an hour and a half to code an interaction. Once an adequate level of reliability is reached (.70 minimum correlation or kappa, depending on whether the code is continuous or categorical), coders are assigned two to three tapes a week and are instructed to watch the tapes three times. This typically takes about 1 hr per interaction. Ideally, each tape is coded individually by two coders.

Posttraining, weekly group meetings are held to discuss problematic items, review disagreements, and prevent observer drift.

To train users of the SCID in other labs, the most efficient way of ensuring accuracy and reliability of coding is to have consultation from our lab. Coerciveness and Attempts to Control tend to be the most difficult for trainees. Consultation has been conducted formally, via training of other labs over the course of 2 to 3 days, followed by reliability checks of tapes, or more informally, via the telephone or e-mail, when problems arise. We do not currently have training tapes that we make available outside our own coding lab, but in consulting with others who use the SCID, we have coded tapes from others' labs for the purposes of establishing reliability. Researchers have achieved good reliability by using the manual, primarily, including the method of watching tapes three times, with only informal consultation from our lab (Cohan & Kleinbaum, 2002). The coding manual is available for downloading in PDF form at www.psy.miami.edu, using the faculty Web sites for either of the authors of the manual.

CODING PROCESS

The coding process requires an experienced coder to watch the tape two to three times (ideally three) and is therefore unlikely to be reliable or valid if coding is attempted in real time. Split screen views are not necessary for coding, but taping should be done in such a way that the facial expressions of each partner are observable. In our lab, we have used a simple analog videotaping procedure, with one camera, typically behind a one-way mirror. With appropriate lighting, this procedure is perfectly acceptable for valid and reliable coding. We are currently upgrading our system to digital videotaping, and we are beginning to use a dual-camera procedure to allow for split screen viewing and coding directly onto the computer. These procedures increase efficiency by increasing video quality and reducing error in data entry, but they are not necessary for accurate coding.

RELIABILITY

Two studies have examined the reliability and validity of the SCID. The first reliability study was conducted with a sample of 50 couples who were 44% Anglo American, 32% Hispanic American, and 24% Black (including African American and Caribbean American couples). All individual codes had adequate reliability and ranged from a low of r =.70 for female Support, to a high of r = .91 for male Verbal Aggression (with Pearson correlations). The three continuous dyadic codes, Negative Escalation, Cohesiveness, and Pursuit–Withdrawal Pattern, all had acceptable reliability, as well (rs = .80, .84, and .70, respectively). The categorical codes of Conflict Management Style (all six categories) and Balance of

Power (all four categories) were adequately reliable, with Kappa coefficients of .80 and .71, respectively.

In the second study to evaluate reliability of the SCID, tapes of 90 couples were coded (35 Hispanic American couples, 35 Anglo American couples, and 20 Black couples). Good inter-rater reliability was found for most of the SCID codes. Reliability analyses were calculated separately for the three ethnic groups in the validation study, as well as for the group as a whole. Similar reliability figures were found across ethnic groups for most of the codes, although some differences were detected. Adequate inter-rater reliability was found, collapsing across ethnic groups, for the following individual and dyadic codes: Verbal Aggression ($r = .84$ for male partners, $r = .80$ for female partners), Attempts to Control ($r = .76$ for men, $r = .71$ for women), Negativity and Conflict ($r = .79$ for men, $r = .87$ for women), Dysphoric Affect ($r = .75$ for men, $r = .83$ for women), Positive Affect ($r = .86$ for men, $r = .80$ for women), Negative Escalation ($r = .79$), Cohesiveness ($r = .75$), and Pursuit–Withdrawal Pattern ($r = .66$).

Differences were found across the ethnic groups for the following codes. Coerciveness was reliably coded for female partners across ethnic groups (average $r = .75$) and for Hispanic American and Anglo American males (rs = .69 and .74, respectively), but it was less reliable for African American males ($r = .55$). The reliability coefficient for Hispanic females was slightly less than for all others ($r = .60$ vs. rs = .71–.81).

With regard to the dyadic, categorical codes, both Conflict Management Style and Balance of Power were coded reliably across all three ethnic groups. Collapsing across ethnic groups, for Conflict Management Style, a Kappa of .61 was found when all six categories were used. Reliability increased when some of the categories were collapsed. For example, when four categories were used (pursuit–withdrawal, disengaged, high conflict, harmonious), a Kappa of .71 was obtained, and when two categories were used (harmonious and not harmonious), a Kappa of .90 was obtained. For Balance of Power, a kappa of .72 was found when all four categories were used and .94 when two categories were used (balanced, not balanced).

VALIDITY

An initial validation study of the SCID as a measure of concurrent power dynamics was conducted with 50 couples (as noted earlier, 44% Anglo American, 32% Hispanic American, and 24% Black; Malik, 1998). In this study, SCID codes of Coerciveness, Verbal Aggression, and Negativity and Conflict were combined into a summary code of Verbal Abuse. This summary code and the independent code of Attempts to Control were summed across partners. Both of these codes were significantly related to questionnaire data on power dynamics, including which partner makes the ultimate decisions in the relationship and which partner is more satisfied with the decision making in the relationship. In addition, a chi-square analysis of the association between observed Balance of Power and self-reported balance of power outcome was significant, $\chi^2(1, N = 50) = 10.00, p < .01$).

SCID codes also were related to concurrent reports of domestic violence, as measured by combined partner report on the Conflict Tactics Scale (Straus, 1979). Both male and female Verbal Aggression were related to higher levels of overall couple domestic violence ($r = .55, p < .001$ for male Verbal Aggression, and $r = .30, p < .05$, for female Verbal Aggression). Higher levels of female Coerciveness related to higher levels of overall couple violence ($r = .38, p < .01$) as well as both partners' reports of female violence ($r = .44, p = .001$). Male Coerciveness and female Attempts to Control were significantly related to female violence only ($r = .34, p < .05$, and $r = .33, p < .05$, respectively). Utilizing the Balance of Power code, collapsing across Male Dominant, Female Dominant, and Conflictual Imbalance, to yield two categories of Balanced or Imbalanced, it was found that power imbalanced couples reported over 3 times the level of domestic violence than did couples who were not observed to have imbalances in the power dynamics.

With regard to couple relationship satisfaction, multiple codes of the SCID were related to concurrent reports of male and female reports of relationship satisfaction on the Locke–Wallace (Locke & Wallace, 1959). Observed couple Cohesion was strongly related to increased levels of satisfaction, and Negative Escalation was negatively related to satisfaction (*r*s in the .6 range for Cohesion and male and female satisfaction, and *r*s in the –.3 to –.4 range for Negative Escalation). With the exceptions of female Dysphoric Affect and Male Withdrawal and Attempts to Control, all other SCID codes were related in expected directions to male and female reports of relationship satisfaction (*r*s ranging from .28 to .59). Please see the section, "Studies Using the Coding System," for further information.

GENERALIZABILITY

The SCID was originally designed to explicate power differences between violent and nonviolent couples and has now been used with a wide range of adult couples whose relationships vary in length, stability, and quality. This coding system has been used reliably with married and nonmarried heterosexual couples who have been of Anglo, Hispanic, and Black (including African American and Caribbean American) racial and ethnic groups. It has been reliably used to rate problem discussion behaviors with couples speaking English or Spanish. All couples who have participated in studies using the SCID have been together for at least 1 year, even the couples in their late teens and early 20s. It is also likely that this system could be used with teen dating couples, although reliability and validity data are not available with such couples based on the studies conducted thus far. This system has been used reliably with couples across socioeconomic status, as poor, middle class, and wealthy couples have participated in research studies using the SCID.

Although the SCID thus far has been used only in studies of heterosexual relationships, the theory and empirical work on which the SCID is based are likely as relevant with gay and lesbian couples, as well, and therefore would likely be as useful a measure with homosexual couples as it is with heterosexual couples. One of the limits of this coding system is its focus on conflict discussions rather than on communication behaviors in couples more generally. The SCID, therefore, is likely to yield important data regarding couple relationships when coded from problem discussions rather than from positive communication tasks.

CLINICAL UTILITY

Although the coding system as a whole is likely to be too cumbersome to utilize as a tool in regular clinical practice, there are a number of elements in the coding system that may have significant clinical utility. For example, power struggles are often an issue in couple relationships and may bring couples into therapy. Rarely, however, are couples able to concretely describe the power dynamics in their relationship, even when they can discuss that control or decision making can be a problem. One of the more useful elements of the SCID for clinical purposes is the manner in which it makes concrete and distinct many of the dynamics of power that couples struggle with in their efforts to communicate and achieve intimacy with one another.

Should these issues be of clinical concern, the coding system, or elements of it, may be quite useful for tracking the process of therapy. For example, a therapist might use the Coerciveness code initially as a way of helping clients recognize the ways in which they undercut or demean their partners. By videotaping sessions and coding that construct with clients as therapy progresses, the therapist may explicate some of the dynamics and assess change over the course of therapy. In general, probably the most useful aspect of the SCID for therapeutic purposes is its operationalization of power dynamics in couples. Knowledge regarding how couples may play out these dynamics may be of use to clinicians as they observe and interact with couples therapeutically, whether or not the coding system is actually used.

STUDIES USING THE CODING SYSTEM

As noted earlier, the SCID was developed in conjunction with a family coding system, the SCIFF (Lindahl & Malik, 2001). Utilizing the SCID Conflict Management Style and Balance of Power codes, we conducted a study to examine the moderating effects of ethnicity and relationship distress on links between observed marital functioning and observed family functioning in a sample of 113 families with school-aged boys (Lindahl & Malik, 1999). This study focused on two ethnic groups, Hispanic American (58% of the sample) and Anglo American (42%). In this study, we found that Conflict Management Style (using only Harmonious, Disengaged, and High Conflict/Hostile categories) was related to maternal withdrawal in a family problem discussion, as well as to paternal withdrawal and coerciveness, rejection, and lack of support with sons. Findings showed that parents in High Conflict marriages were less positive in triadic interactions than were parents in Harmonious or Disengaged marriages. Observed marital power imbalances also were related to more negative parenting behavior in the triadic family interaction. These results suggest that problematic behaviors observed in the couple relationship can also be observed and linked to problematic behaviors in other family subsystems. Therefore, as expected, perturbations across family subsystems are observable with the SCID and the SCIFF.

Ethnicity was found to moderate many of the relations between the observed marital and family behaviors. Although we had not expected that ethnicity would affect the relation between balance of power in the marriage and parenting behavior in the triad, results indicated that when marriages involved power struggles (Conflictual Imbalance), Anglo American but not Hispanic American fathers were more withdrawn in triadic family interactions (Lindahl & Malik, 1999). This may indicate that power imbalances overall (including male and female dominance and conflictual imbalance) may be less relevant to the relation between marital and parenting behaviors in Hispanic families.

A second wave of data collection has yielded a sample of over 250 families (38% Hispanic, 29% Anglo, 19% Biethnic Hispanic–Anglo, and 14% Black). Results thus far indicate that observed couple behaviors are significantly related to multiple areas of concurrent, self-reported couple functioning, including relationship satisfaction and verbally and physically aggressive behavior. Further analysis will likely reveal numerous mediating and moderating effects, but preliminary results also indicate that couple functioning as measured by the SCID is related to parental reports of child internalizing and externalizing behavior. In particular, the power codes of Verbal Aggression, Coerciveness, and Balance of Power are linked to child maladjustment. For example, a one-way analysis of variance was conducted to examine how marital Balance of Power is related to maternal and paternal reports of children's internalizing and externalizing behaviors on the Child Behavior Checklist (Achenbach, 1991). Across the four parental reports, Balance of Power was significantly related to child behavior, $Fs(3, 231)$ range from 3.04 to 5.59, ps range from .03 to .001. Across the board, mothers and fathers in Conflictual Imbalance relationships reported that children were exhibiting the most internalizing and externalizing behaviors when compared with Balanced, Male Dominant, and Female Dominant relationships (Malik & Lindahl, 2001).

Outside our laboratory, the SCID has been used to assess for premarital cohabitation effects (Cohan & Kleinbaum, 2002). In a study of 92 mostly Anglo American couples, Cohan and Kleinbaum (2002) found that premarital cohabitation experiences were related to higher levels of Coerciveness and Attempts to Control when husbands' problems were discussed. Cohabitation was also related to higher levels of Verbal Aggression and, with the dyadic codes, higher levels of Negative Escalation in the observed problem discussion. These results indicate that the SCID can reliably distinguish different types of couples from one another across codes relevant to power dynamics and other elements of relationship functioning.

ACKNOWLEDGMENTS

Funding for the research described in this chapter was in part provided by Grant MH54631 R03 from the National Institute of Mental Health.

III

Affect and Intimacy

12

The Specific Affect Coding System (SPAFF)

Alyson F. Shapiro and John M. Gottman
University of Washington

The Specific Affect Coding System (SPAFF) is designed to code specific emotions in marital and family interactions. This coding system categories affect at the level of the emotion, and yields codes that are descriptive of the emotional communication in any interaction over time. SPAFF is a gestalt coding system, which uses a holistic approach to recognizing and categorizing affect, through integrating a physical features approach with a cultural informant approach. The physical features approach allows a detailed recognition and categorization of facial, physical, and verbal cues currently known to be related to specific emotions. The cultural informant approach allows the coder to be a cultural informant to use his or her subjective understanding of emotions in identifying specific affects. The synthesis of these two approaches allows the coding system to draw on the wealth of research information on emotional expression, training observers to become aware of cues typically associated with discrete emotions, and allows the observer to bring to the coding the wealth of his or her experience as an emotional being to further aid in accurately identifying specific affects.

SPAFF can be used to examine any discussion between two (or more) people. (For example, it has been used to code group interaction in breast cancer support groups.) Although it has been used most extensively to capture emotional communication when couples are discussing an area of disagreement, it has also been used to study parent–child interactions, sibling interactions, couples discussing the events of the day or a positive topic, and couples naturally interacting in an unstructured apartment laboratory setting.

THEORETICAL FOUNDATIONS

The idea behind the development of SPAFF is that emotions are expressed in a large variety of ways. They are not only evident in the face or the voice, or the content of a conversation, but in all of these ways and are even evident in what one is trying to conceal as well as what one is freely expressing. Emotions are expressed in ways that are culturally universal and quantifiable through affective cues (Ekman & Friesen, 1975), and in ways that are culturally specific, and can only readily be recognized and coded by a cultural informant (the coder). Categorizing emotions goes beyond the quantification of physical cues such as the action of a facial muscle or the distance between one's cheek and shoulder. Thus, SPAFF categorizes specific emotions at the gestalt level, of the emotion itself, rather than the level of the verbal or nonverbal cues. Furthermore, emotions do not occur naturally in categories of negative, positive, and neutral, but in the form of specific affects, and can be coded as specific affects to reveal many of the nuances that distinguish qualitatively different relationships from each other. For example, the look and smile with which one greets a coworker is likely to be very different from the look and smile with which one would greet one's spouse.

DEVELOPMENT OF THE CODING SYSTEM

The SPAFF grew out of the Couples Interaction Scoring System (CISS) and Ekman and Freisen's (1978) Facial Action Coding System (FACS). The CISS affect system was designed to have coders scan hierarchically for a set of specific cues. The observer would look first in the face, then in the voice, and finally in the body, ignoring the content of the conversation and focusing on the nonverbal communication. Observers would then make either a positive, neutral, or negative judgment for both the speaker and the listener during each speaker turn in a conversation. The CISS is described in detail in Gottman (1979), and a detailed account of the development of the SPAFF can be found in Gottman, McCoy, Coan, and Collier (1996).

Through careful examination of couples' conflict discussions, John Gottman became convinced that the CISS system was inadequate. The cues the CISS system was designed to tap were not extensive enough to capture all of the emotion moments in a conversation. Secondly, he was convinced that the content of a couple's conversation, as well as their nonverbal cues, communicated emotion, and the CISS system did not capture the emotion in the script a couple used. Finally, Gottman felt that lumping emotions into positive, neutral and negative was too crude to adequately describe and examine family interactions. Negative affect in the CISS, for example, lumped anger, sadness, contempt, disgust, and fear into the same category despite the different impact the expression of any of these emotions could have on the relationship. Another example of this is that negative reciprocity in the CISS system would be coded any time a negative code from one spouse was followed by a negative code for the other spouse, despite the fact that a relationship in which anger is followed by contempt is clearly different from one in which anger is followed by fear or sadness. The development of a new coding system was essential to capture these important differences.

In 1980, Gottman consulted with Ekman and Friesen about their new Facial Action Coding System (FACS). The FACS is designed to categorize the Action Units (AUs) produced by each facial muscle, which produces the changes in facial appearance seen during what we recognize as expressions of emotion (Ekman & Freisen, 1978). This system is very detailed and objective and can be used to describe any set of facial actions, and the combination of several of these AUs typified the expression of basic emotions. Continued observation of couple's interactions, however, led Gottman to realize that the FACS codes alone were both too detailed and also not adequate to describe the richness of specific emotional moments found in couple's natural interactions. He started noting additional cues that he saw couples using to communicate affect. The task of listing all possible physical features that could serve as cues of emotional expression, however, proved to be virtually impossible. One example illustrated this dilemma particularly well.

A husband and wife were discussing a disagreement in which he accused her of being jealous of all the women in his car pool. She responded in a very interesting and compelling way. She gently rubbed her face against her soft looking white cashmere sweater, tilted her head, and looking at her husband with wide eyes said, "That's not true." This was clearly a request for love and affection, and her husband responded with affection and reassurance saying, "Now you know, none of those women are as beautiful to me as you are." She was reassured and beamed with joy.

This wife's request for support and affection could be recognized by other cultural judges, but could not easily be coded by defining specific cues used to express emotions. In this instance, what was the critical cue or set of cues to be coded? Was it the rubbing of the face against the sweater, the tilting of the head, the head-to-shoulder velocity, or the wide eyes? Any of these things alone, however could be part of other emotional expressions, or completely unrelated to emotional expression. Scratching one's face against ones shoulder, for example, could be part of a request for affection such as the one described earlier, but is likely to more often reflect that someone has an itch they are trying to quell. The infinite number of gestures that could be used to express emotion, and the infinite meanings of physical features of actions that could reflect gestures of emotions (or gestures that were not emotional) simply made the task of categorizing all cues of emotional expression unwieldy. Cultural informants, in contrast, could be used to identify culturally clear gestures of specific emotions. This approach is typically used by anthropologists studying new cultures, and can be validated by the use of independent judges to establish reliability.

In revising the CISS system, Gottman endeavored to include the verbal content of a couple's conversation into the coding of emotional expression as well as recognizing a gestalt of cues including the voice, face expression, gestures, timing words, stress, movement, and the relationship of one person to another as is communicated in theatre emotions. The final result of Gottman's labors in developing SPAFF was a gestalt coding system designed to categorize specific emotions using verbal content, facial, vocal, and cultural cues. This coding system bridges an objective and subjective approach through the synthesis of a physical features and a cultural informant approach. The SPAFF system was designed to systematically teach coders about cues that typically reflect specific affects, while going beyond these cues to use their judgments as socially competent cultural judges and code specific affects that were recognizable from a cultural rather than physical features perspective.

TASK AND SETTING

The Specific Affect Coding system has been used to code parent–child interactions, sibling interactions, natural couple interactions in an apartment laboratory, and most extensively used to code couples having a discussion of a disagreement. Several versions of SPAFF have been developed with various levels of detail. The most recent version, which we currently use in our laboratory to code discussions of disagreements, is a 20-code version that includes 13 negative codes, 1 neutral code, and 6 positive categories.

In our research, we prepare couples for these conflict discussions through using the Play-By-Play Interview (Hooven, Rushe, & Gottman, 1996). This interview is designed to help all couples (both happily and unhappily married) find a real area of continuing disagreement to discuss, and to help them remember the issues surrounding the disagreement such that the discussion can be as natural as possible. This interview process begins with each couple being asked to complete the Knox Couple's Problem Inventory (Knox, 1971), which measures the severity of various marital problems. Items include standard marital problem areas such as in-laws, finances, and sex. Each item is rated on a scale from 0 to 100, with higher scores signifying that the problem is considered more severe.

The interviewer then reviews items that the couple rated as being most problematic to help the couple choose several issues to use as the bases for a discussion of disagreement. Specifically, the interviewer is looking for areas that are current, have emotional content, and are disagreements in which the husband and wife both have a side to argue. The Play-By-Play Interview is designed to avoid the problem of happily married couples not actually discussing a real marital issue; this problem plagued early marital interaction research in which structured tasks (such as the Inventory of Marital Conflicts; Olson & Ryder, 1970) created real conflicts only in unhappily married couples. The goal of the play-by-play procedure was to examine differences in ecologically valid discussions of real disagreements for all couples.

Once topics for the discussion have been chosen, couples are asked to discuss their chosen conflict topics for 15 min while they are videotaped. In our laboratory, we use two cameras that are integrated into a split screen view with one camera focused directly on the face and upper body of each spouse (to adequately be able to code facial expressions, a full face shot, or close to it, is required), and we recommend that others use this approach. It is important that the cameras face the couples directly, being mounted at or only about a foot above their heads.

When research visits are conducted in the couples' homes, or some other setting where integrating two camera views into one split screen view is difficult, we ask the husband and wife to sit facing each other at a 45-degree angle, and use one videocamera to videotape both the husband and wife. We recommend staying away from videotaping the husband and wife separately as two videotapes can be difficult to synchronize, and it is important for the coder to be able to see the husband and wife simultaneously for coding. We also recommend staying away from profile views if possible as they make coding difficult from the standpoint of using facial cues for that coding.

DESCRIPTION OF THE CODING SYSTEM

Coding manuals and training audiotapes and videotapes are available from Lawrence Erlbaum Associates, Inc. in Mahwah, NJ. Each emotion is coded at the level of the specific affect itself, rather than at the level of the cues a coder may use to identify a specific emotion. SPAFF uses a gestalt approach to identifying emotions, which combines training coders in the physical/facial, vocal, and verbal content cues related to each specific affect, with the use of a cultural informant approach that allows each coder to act as a cultural judge in making judgments about the expression of specific emotions. Specific emotion codes are associated with facial and vocal cues in the content of the conversation that coders are trained to use to identify each emotion in addition to being instructed to use their own intuition and code a specific emotion if they feel that it is justified by their background as a cultural judge.

This SPAFF-20 code version includes 13 negative, 1 neutral, and 6 positive categories. These negative codes are as follows: Disgust, Contempt, Belligerence, Domineering (divided into High and Low Domineering codes), Criticism, Anger, Tension, Tense Humor, Defensiveness, Whining, Sadness, and Stonewalling. The positive codes are as follows: Interest, Validation (divided into High and Low Validation codes), Affection, Humor, and Surprise/Joy. The one Neutral code categorizes affect that appears neither clearly positive or clearly negative in nature. Each of these specific emotion codes is described briefly.

Disgust reflects the underlying feeling of revulsion, and includes the verbal and nonverbal rejection of something the person considers noxious. This disgust is usually seen in response to something their partner does or says he or she likes. This code is different than contempt in that it reflects more of a physiological revulsion than an attitude of superiority toward one's spouse. This is usually an involuntary reaction, and reflects distaste or an aversion. Verbally, disgust is expressed through statements such as "yuck, yuck," or "Oh, that makes me sick." Physically, the expression of the disgusted spouse is one of nausea and can take the form of a gagging gesture or wrinkling of one's nose as if the person has smelled something very sour.

Contempt is an attempt to put one's partner down through an insult or lack of respect that is otherwise communicated. It tends to have an icy quality with a sense of superiority, and can be communicated verbally or facially. Verbal expressions of contempt include sarcasm, mockery, insults, and hostile humor. Facially, contempt can be expressed by a dimpling on one side of one's mouth (the muscle buccinator pulls the left lip corner laterally and creates a dimple) or an eye roll.

Belligerence is coded when a person appears to be trying to provoke a fight with their partner. This is often done by challenging one's partner or delighting in their discomfort. Examples of this include asking taunting questions, using unreciprocated humor, and daring ones partner or using interpersonal terrorism through testing the agreed limits of the relationship. Examples of this type of dare are, "What would you do if I did?" and "What are you going to do about it?"

Domineering is the act of trying to dominate one's partner. This can be seen through one trying to dominate the conversation or force compliance from their partner. Low intensity domineering includes patronizing, lecturing, incessant speech, invalidation, and low-balling. Low-balling involves getting ones partner to say "yes" to the simplest facts, and then slowly escalating like a salesman in an attempt to draw their partner into agreeing to things that are far from their initial point of view. Examples of high intensity domineering are threats or ultimatums.

Criticism goes a step further than a simple complaint in that it involves attacking one's partner's personality or character rather than a specific behavior, and almost always involves blaming or the insinuation of blame. It is important to distinguish this code from a complaint, which usually involves a specific situation, and is a specific statement of anger, displeasure, or distress. Criticism makes a complaint global and pervasive. Criticism can be distinguished from contempt in that it is usually focused around a global issue (such as never helping around the house) rather than directly putting down one's partner (such as saying that they are a slob).

Anger is coded when the person sounds or looks like they are "fed-up." This can include irritation or annoyance, using a raised voice, direct statements of anger, and signs of constrained anger. Physical cues associated with anger include involuntary twitches, having a tight jaw or clenched teach, and one's voice being lowered or raised beyond the limits of normal tone. Note that anger is often blended with other negative emotions such as belligerence and contempt, and that the other negative codes take precedence over anger in the SPAFF such that the anger code reflects only expressions of pure anger.

Tension results from feeling worried, anxious, or fearful, and is usually the result of an uncomfortable topic being brought up in one's conversation. Tension is clear through stammering and the use of repetitive "uhs" and "ahs," a voice that moves from a chest to a head register (fundamental frequency shift upward in pitch), fidgeting, shifting, or nervous smiling and laughter that do not seem appropriate to the situation.

Tense humor is coded when both partners in a conversation share in a bout of tense laughter or tense joking.

Defensiveness is coded when people act as if they are trying to communicate that they are blameless. Defensiveness usually includes either an innocent victim stance and communicates, "It's not my fault, why are you picking on me?" or a righteous indignation stance, or both. Defensiveness can take the form of excuses, "yes-but" statements, counter criticisms, and even aggressively defensive statements such as a strong, loud, "No, I did NOT do that." Defensiveness often involves denying any personal responsibility for the problem being discussed.

Whining is coded when the voice quality, although airing a complaint, has a very nasal, high pitch, singsong sound. This whining sound is often drawn out as in the example, "Whyyy? I like watching that show."

Sadness is characterized by a marked decrease in energy, passivity, sighing, pouting, crying, or expressing hurt feelings through words, vocal quality, or facial expression. The underlying feeling that accompanies this affect is one of depression, hopelessness, dejection, regret or grief.

Stonewalling refers to the total lack of listening behaviors in couple's interactions. Usually a listener watches the speaker, nods from time to time, and gives occasional verbal assents to the speaker such as "Uh-huh," "yeah," or "um." When someone is stonewalling, that person gives none of these listener cues, looking like a stone wall rather than an interactive partner in the conversation. Often one will focus on something trivial to avoid eye contact (such as playing with hair or hands), and have a monitoring gaze where the person glances at the partner occasionally and quickly looks away, as if to see if the ogre is still there.

The Neutral code is the dividing line between negative and positive, and is typically characterized as being nonemotional in nature. Any behavior that does not fit into any of the other SPAFF categories is also coded as neutral to satisfy the requirement of a mutually exclusive and exhaustive coding system.

The positive affects follow.

Interest is reflected in the involvement and positive energy of the listener. This interest is often clear from the questions the person asks seeking elaboration or opinions, and communicates genuine concern about one's partner's thoughts and feelings.

Validation involves acceptance and openness to one's partner's views and feelings that communicates respect, even if they disagree. The SPAFF codes both low-level and high-level validation. Low-level validation involves giving back channels, or positive listening behaviors. These consist of keeping eye contact with the speaker and occasionally responding with head nods or giving verbal assent to let the speaker know the listener is following him or her such as "umm-hum," "yeah," or "um." High-level validation requires a higher level of expressing understanding or acceptance. This can be stated directly, through an apology, by paraphrasing what one's partner has said, or through finishing a partner's sentence to express that he or she is "on the same page."

Affection is coded when a direct expression of caring is clear. These expressions can include direct statements of loving and caring, expressions of tenderness or closeness such as reminiscing about sharing moments, compliments, empathy, and supporting one's partner in a common cause.

Humor is characterized by the sharing of laughter with the underlying feeling of shared happiness rather than tenseness. Joking, good-natured teasing, and exaggeration such that both partners think the joke is funny enough to laugh, can characterize these moments. This shared humor, or having something be funny enough that both people enjoy the joke, is very important in distinguishing this positive affect from the derisive teasing that can be seen in contempt.

Surprise/Joy involves a happy, positive, or emphatic reaction to something in the conversation. Joy can often been seen through a broad, warm smile that appears on one's face after receiving a compliment. Positive surprise is often evident through big smiles and exclamations in reaction to an unanticipated event or remark.

CODER TRAINING

As a preparatory step in learning the SPAFF, coders in our laboratory are first taught the Ekman and Friesen FACS, which identifies each AU in the face. These AUs are what cause the changes in the face's appearance to form what we call facial expressions. This coding system involves close attention to detail in every muscle in the face. This training helps to sensitize coders to minute facial expressions, and ensures that they have a base for associating those AUs with specific emotion.

Once coders have learned FACS, training in the actual SPAFF system begins. Coders are taught to draw on the wealth of information we have about what physical features are typically clues of specific emotions based on research. They are also taught that we want them to go beyond simply using these physical features in their coding, and to make judgments as socially competent cultural informants.

Training starts with a focus on the content of the conversation through reading and coding affect from written transcripts. The next step is to integrate vocal cues with the content and have coders work on listening to and coding from a set of training audiotapes. Finally, using a training videotape, coders are taught about the specific sets of facial actions that tend to be associated with specific emotions, and begin working to recognize and code these cues on videotape. This training is very time intensive, taking approximately 80 hr to learn the FACS, and an additional 40 hr to learn the SPAFF. We also recommend regular weekly meetings reviewing and discussing coded tapes after coders are trained and reliable to ensure that all coders are using the coding system in the same way and not succumbing to coder drift over time.

We train coders in the SPAFF through a coding class that meets several times a week, and are typically able to train coders in a little less than the overall 120 hr of training estimated earlier with this class format. Training, however, can be done through using the training manual and test tapes available in the *What Predicts Divorce: The Measures* book and set of audiotapes and videotapes available through Lawrence Erlbaum Associates, Inc. (Gottman, Coan, & McCoy, 1996). This book features both the 10-category version of SPAFF and the 16-category version of SPAFF, which is very similar to the 20-category system of SPAFF we have focused on here.

We have found that actors tend to be the best SPAFF coders due to their extensive familiarity with specific emotions through their work in portraying those emotions. Graduate students, staff, and undergraduate students, however, can all make excellent SPAFF coders. The important thing is that the coders are sensitive to emotions, and can act as socially competent cultural informants about those emotions. We have found that some people simply can't seem to recognize and thus categorize the emotions. To ensure that the people you select as coders can function as emotionally sensitive cultural judges, we recommend that you have your coding candidates watch a video of a marital conflict discussion with you and discuss the emotions they see. If they can distinguish between basic positive, neutral, and negative emotions, they will probably be able to learn and become reliable using the SPAFF. Another prerequisite for being a reliable SPAFF coder is not being tone deaf; being musical is helpful. One group of potential coders we worked with that simply could not recognize whining turned out to be tone deaf.

CODING PROCESS

SPAFF coding in our laboratory is currently done in real time using an "Affect Wheel," developed by the Instrument Development Lab of the Center for Human

[1]James Long software and hardware can be obtained by writing the James Long Company, 45 Woodland Road, Bedford Hills, NY 10207–1713, telephone 518–835–3734. This software is very general and could be used for any observational coding system.

Development and Disabilities at the University of Washington, and supporting computer software, developed by Catherine Swanson, in our laboratory, specifically for this purpose. Coders first do a preparatory viewing of the interaction they are planning to code to familiarize them with the couple and their conversation. They then begin the supporting computer program and sit down in front of monitors and the dial we call an "affect wheel" to code. While watching the videotape, they code each spouse separately by turning the affect wheel dial that changes a light display under the video monitor as that spouse's facial expression changes. This display is labeled with each of the SPAFF codes, and each change in the position of the display reflects a change in code. The codes indicated on the display are automatically entered into the computer through the affect wheel, preventing data entry errors as well as saving data entry time. This system for collecting data allows codes to be recorded sequentially and records the duration of each code. The entire coding process described here takes as little as 45 min. That includes 15 min for the initial viewing, and an additional 15 min to code each spouse. The coding itself is very efficient, and can be completed before the couple being coded leaves our laboratory. We also believe that this real-time coding is theoretically sound as emotions in the real world are communicated in real time rather than slow motion. One drawback to this system is that it is difficult to make corrections to the coding file once the coding is complete, and if a coder makes a mistake, the easiest way to correct the error is to code the discussion a second time. It is for this reason that we recommend viewing a tape once before coding it to reduce errors in real-time coding.

Two coders code each interaction to ensure reliability. Coders can code either at separate times or simultaneously in our laboratory such that they can instantly check their reliability using a kappa program designed by Catherine Swanson. If the coders have a kappa of .6 or above, the coding file is kept for later analysis. If the coders were not able to get a kappa of .6 or above, however, that interaction is recoded by a different set of coders.

Although we currently do SPAFF coding exclusively in real time, SPAFF has been used in many ways. It has been used for coding with only audiotapes, as well as with videotapes. Initially, verbatim transcripts were used as a coding tool, and the coding was done on paper and later entered into a computer. This system worked well and yielded good reliability, but it took 25 hr on average to code a 15-min discussion. SPAFF coding has also been done without transcripts using a computer-assisted coding station designed by the James Long Company (phone number: 518-835-3734). Similar to our affect wheel system, this system allows for continuous coding, and automates the timing such that the code entered into the computer is synchronized with the corresponding point on the video the computer is connected to. This allowed for computing duration of codes as well as recording the sequence of codes, which makes the use of diverse statistics possible including the use of sequential analysis and nonlinear dynamic modeling. The use of this system for coding and recording the SPAFF also speeded up the coding making it about 75% faster than the older system using transcripts, and coding reliability remained reasonable. This hardware and software is available through the James Long Company.[1]

RELIABILITY

We have been able to obtain reasonable inter-rater reliability using each version of SPAFF described earlier using Cohen's kappa. We recommend having two coders independently code each interaction around the same time to ensure reliability throughout the study. We use this procedure in our laboratory and accept coding only for interactions in which the Cohen's kappa is above a .6. This method ensures that even the most difficult videotapes are coded reliably as well as tracking ongoing reliability. Although a kappa value is only considered acceptable in our studies if they are above a .6, they typically range from .6 to around .98 with the average kappa varying from study to study In the spouse abuse study Gottman did in collaboration with Neil Jacobson, for example, kappas ranged from .75 to .95 with an average kappa of .86 (Gottman, McCoy, et al., 1996). To ensure that coding is reliable for sequential analysis, we need to show that observers are coding the same affect at the same time. We use a 3- to 5-sec window in the confusion matrix from which the kappa is calculated for this purpose. This means that a code is considered as being coded reliably if the second rater records the same code plus or minus 1 to 2 sec (plus or minus 1 sec for the 3-sec window, and plus or minus 2 sec for the 5-sec window).

VALIDITY

The validity of the SPAFF is clear from the multiple studies using SPAFF codes successfully to predict divorce and relationship satisfaction (Cook et al., 1995; Gottman, 1994; Gottman, Coan, Carrére, & Swanson, 1998; Gottman, Swanson, & Murray, 1999). Studies using SPAFF coding have been able to predict divorce with over 90% accuracy, and up to 14 years longitudinally (Gottman & Levenson, 2002). Several of these studies are described later in this chapter.

The special utility of this coding system to examine the specific affects that are most important in relationships was demonstrated by research revealing that not all negative behaviors were equally corrosive or damaging to a couple's relationship. Specifically, four emotions grouped together and called the "Four Horsemen of the Apocalypse" were particularly predictive of divorce. These specific affect were Criticism, Contempt, Defensiveness, and Stonewalling. When using these four codes in combination with other measures assessing the couple's marriage, we have been able to predict divorce with 90 percent accuracy (Gottman, 1994).

The SPAFF is also validated by its high correlations with the other measures of marital quality. Specifically, the SPAFF has been validated with the Oral History Coding System (Buehlman, Gottman, & Katz, 1992), and the Rapid Couples Interaction Coding system (Krokoff, Gottman, & Hass, 1989). The Oral History Coding system has been able to predict divorce with between 90% and 94% accuracy, (Buehlman et al., 1992; Carrére, Buehlman, Coan, Gottman, & Ruckstuhl, 2000), and has also been used to predict stability versus decline in marital satisfaction as couples become parents (Shapiro, Gottman, & Carrére, 2000). Additionally, it is reliable with the Rapid Couples Interaction Coding system (Krokoff et al., 1989), which, like the SPAFF, has been used for predicting divorce through nonlinear mathematical modeling (Cook et al., 1995).

GENERALIZABILITY

In theory, the SPAFF should be generalizable across cultures, with the stipulation that the coder is a cultural informant for the culture he or she is coding. This is the case because the coding system is designed around combining the physical cues of universal emotional expressions with the judgments of a cultural informant. This premise is supported by the fact that the SPAFF has been successful in describing the interactions of all the types of relationships and ethnicities we have attempted to examine it with to date. Further research, however, is needed to confirm the validity of using SPAFF across cultures.

The SPAFF system has been used to code emotions in married couples, gay and lesbian couples, between parents and children, and between adult siblings (Gottman, 1994, 1996; Gottman, Levenson, et al., 2003; Shortt & Gottman, 1997). It has been used not only to code conflict discussions, but also neutral or positive conversations (Gottman & Levenson, 1999). These studies not only support the validity of the SPAFF, but also illustrate that the SPAFF codes are generalizable across all of these groups and types of interactions. This summary is based on six different longitudinal studies with a total of 667 married couples. As required by the National Institute of Mental Health, each of these studies matched the major racial and ethnics groups of the area in which the research was conducted. The samples we have coded, six different longitudinal studies with a total of 667 married couples, reflected the ethnic distribution of the area from which each sample was recruited. These samples included a largely White Midwestern sample, more diverse and representative samples from the Seattle, WA area, and diverse and representative samples from the San Francisco Bay area. Approximately, 30% of the total sample across all six studies was from non-White ethnic groups. Although our sample includes ethnic minorities, we do not make racial distinctions in our summary. This kind of future research would require oversampling a particular ethnic group to observe differing patterns in couple interactions. Although the ethnic diversity we have been able to include in our samples suggests that the SPAFF coding is generalizable across ethnic groups within the United States, this is an area where further study is needed.

CLINICAL UTILITY

The SPAFF has demonstrated utility for clinical use. Simply learning the SPAFF will likely aid clinicians in their work by helping them to readily recognize affective cues in their clients and increasing their sensitivity. The SPAFF is also likely to be particularly useful as a diagnostic and treatment tool in marital and family therapy. Therapists could quite easily ask couples to discuss a disagreement for assessment or engage in an everyday conversation and have that discussion videotaped. These discussions could then be coded using SPAFF, and a report including even simple frequencies of specific affects could be used to give couples feedback on the way they resolve conflict and support in changing patterns that are predictive of marital distress and divorce. A summary of SPAFF codes, or notes about specific codes made by the clinician could aid in generating ideas for interventions specific to the difficulties each couple exhibits. The "Four Horseman of the Apocalypse," Contempt, Criticism, Defensiveness, and Stonewalling, are the primary negative codes that clinicians would want to look for in identifying warning signs. Clinicians may also want to look for the lack of positive affect in everyday conversations, because it was this lack of positive affect in everyday conversations that Gottman and Levenson (1997) found most predictive of divorce.

It may be useful to help the couples themselves recognize criticism, contempt, defensiveness, and stonewalling, so that they can work on steering away from them and focusing on increasing the positivity in their conflict discussions. Following are what we believe are the antidotes of each of the four horsemen that couples can use to strengthen their marriage. If a couple expresses a lot of criticism, we recommend working with that couple to complain without blame such that their partner doesn't feel criticized. Because the expression of contempt reflects a lack of respect for ones partner, we believe that the antidote for contempt is fondness and admiration for ones spouse. Thus, we recommend that in combating contempt, clinicians work help couples to build a strong fondness and admiration system through things such as rediscovering their initial attraction for each other, and trying to recognize the positive things each spouse does that they appreciate. Couples who have a lot of defensiveness can work to accept some responsibility for the issue in question. Being able to start the conflict discussion in a soft, nonthreatening way can also help couples eliminate defensiveness from their conflict. Finally, when couples experience stonewalling, or withdrawal, we recommend couples learn to recognize that this is a sign the stonewaller is emotionally flooded or over stimulated. In these cases, we recommend that couples take a 20-minute break, and then return to their discussion when they are calm.

One method for summarizing SPAFF data that may be useful to clinicians involves the use of a nonlinear mathematical model designed to examine marriage. This math model provides a qualitative description of the couple's interactive world and yields parameters that aid in pinpointing where couples are having difficulty in their relationship (Cook et al., 1995; Gottman, Swanson, & Murray, 1999; Gottman, Swanson, Swanson, Murray, & Tyson, 2002). Information this model helps us identify includes: each spouse's predisposition to their partner in the context of a conflict discussion; how open to their partner's influence each person is; how they influence their partner, and the affective states couples tend to drift toward, or get stuck in, during their interactions. This math model of marriage takes only about 15 min to analyze once SPAFF coding is complete, and is designed for analysis at the level of the individual couple making it a practically feasible tool for therapy with the aid of a computer program to yield the parameters from the math model from the SPAFF coding.

To demonstrate the clinical utility of the math model, some detail follows. Each spouse enters an interaction with the partner with a certain predisposition that is reflected in their initial emotional state. We call this the "uninfluenced steady state" in our math model. This affective predisposition is particularly important because it tends to influence the direction the conversation will take before influence processes take effect, and we have found that it is highly predictive of divorce versus stability in the marriage (Cook et al., 1995). Thus, identifying each spouse's predisposition at the beginning of a marital conversation through looking at the value of the "uninfluenced steady state" yielded from the math model may be extremely valuable for treating an ailing marriage. A negative uninfluenced steady state value, for example, would be a cue for a therapist to work with a couple on approaching conflict in a softer, more positive manner.

Each person also has a certain amount of "emotional inertia," or tendency to stay in the same affective state they were in at the beginning of the conversation. High inertias in a marital conversation have been found to reflect distress. Thus, identifying that one or both spouses in a relationship have a high emotional inertia could cue the clinician to work with that couple on accepting influence from each other.

We have used a combination of a SPAFF frequency report and a report of the SPAFF coding based on this mathematical model to design interventions for couples in our laboratory and believe that both these methods are useful tools. The SPAFF frequency report is helpful in identifying warning signs in the specific affects themselves, and the mathematical modeling is helpful in identifying the strengths and problem areas in couple's interactive dynamics. Further information about the marriage model and the therapeutic interventions based on the marriage model are provided in Ryan, Gottman, Murray, Carrére, and Swanson (2000).

Repeated use of these SPAFF frequency reports and mathematical modeling reports can be a useful tool in measuring the progress a couple is making in a treatment study. For example, in one case, Gottman worked with a couple that started out with a negative steady state of interacting. After the intervention, the couple had moved to an unstable but positive steady state, which meant that although the couple had made great progress, they would need to work to keep from sliding back to their initial more negative pattern. When this couple returned 2 years after their initial visits, they had a positive and stable steady state indicating that they had not only been able to change their marriage in a positive way, they had also successfully been able to maintain and firmly establish a new positive and stable pattern of discussing conflict.

STUDIES USING THE CODING SYSTEM

The SPAFF has been used for a variety of purposes across a multitude of studies. Although the SPAFF has been used most extensively to capture emotional communication during conflict discussions, it has also been used to examine everyday conversations and positive conversations in marriages (Gottman & Levenson, 1997, 1999). In addition, it has been employed with parent–child and sibling interactions (Gottman, 1994; Shortt & Gottman, 1997). It has been used for examining specific affects and by assigning weights to each affect and grouping positive and negative coding together (Gottman, 1994; Gottman et al., 1999), and has been used both inside and outside of our laboratory (Dufore, 2000). Summaries of a small selection of studies utilizing SPAFF coding are presented in this section.

A study predicting martial happiness and stability in newlyweds used SPAFF coding of conflict discussions to examine several types of process models of marriage (Gottman, Coan, et al., 1998). The models explored were as follows: (a) anger as a dangerous emotion, (b) active listening as important for the marriage, (c) negative affect reciprocity, (d) negative wife start up, (e) husband physiological soothing, and (f) de-escalation. Results did not support an active listening model, a negative affect reciprocity model, or a model that posits that anger is a dangerous emotion. Indeed, this research revealed that anger does not appear to have any negative outcomes longitudinally provided that the anger is not blended with other negative emotions such as contempt, domineering or belligerence. Active listening exchanges rarely occurred, and were not predictive of differential marital outcomes, and reciprocation of high-level negative affect did not predict marital instability and unhappiness.

Support was found for the negative wife start up, positive affect, de-escalation, and physiological soothing models tested. Specifically, harsh start up by the wife, absence of de-escalation on the part of either the husband or the wife, lack of physiological soothing of the husband, and the husband rejecting his wife's influence, all predicted divorce. Marital satisfaction was predicted with 80% accuracy, and divorce with 83% accuracy (Gottman, Coan, et al., 1998). Through using the SPAFF, this research was able to identify specific affects that were problematic, and distinguish them from those that were not problematic such as anger. Additionally, the sequential nature of the coding collected enabled the researchers to examine dynamics of the conflict discussion such as how the discussion was started, and whether influence was accepted.

The ability of SPAFF to capture the dynamics in couples with abusive relationships was illustrated by a 1996 study examining the longitudinal course of these relationships (Jacobson, Gottman, Gorner, Berns, & Shortt, 1996). Again, coding from marital conflict discussions were used to predict the course of the marriage. This study revealed that husbands who tended to be highly domineering, emotionally abusive, and globally negative during their initial visit tended to remain severally abusive if they were still married 2 years after their initial visit to our laboratory.

The utility of the SPAFF across populations is illustrated by a study conducted by Shortt and Gottman (1997) to examine the closeness of sibling relationships. Adult siblings were videotaped while having both a conflict discussion and a discussion of an enjoyable nature. This study revealed that close sibling relationships were characterized by empathy as well as overall higher positive affect and fewer power struggles.

Finally, we have used SPAFF coding in conjunction with nonlinear dynamic modeling to describe the dynamics of the couple's relationship and to predict relationship success (Gottman et al., 1999). The advantages of using mathematical modeling are as follows: (a) This approach provides a new language for thinking about the changing dynamics of the couple's interaction over time, (b) once a model has been created for the marriage, it can be used to simulate a variety of situations to test the model and the corresponding theory (Cook et al., 1995), and (c) the parameters yielded from modeling each couple's interaction yields valuable information about the quality of the couple's relationship and has the potential to inform clinicians as well as researchers about what type of intervention is needed to help couples improve their relationships.

SPAFF coding can be analyzed through the use of nonlinear mathematical modeling by assigning theoretically based weights to each code such that there is a numerical value for each time. These numerical codes can then be analyzed using a model we have developed specifically to describe marriage. This technique was used in a study to predict divorce in a sample of newlyweds. Factors that predicted divorce were as follows: (a) both husband and wife having more negative predispositions, or uninfluenced steady states; (b) husbands being influenced negatively by their wives, or having more negative influenced steady states; and (c) having lower negativity threshold, or having a lower tolerance to negativity before a change in affect is seen (Gottman et al., 1999).

ACKNOWLEDGEMENTS

We would like to acknowledge the couples that participated in our research and the grants that have made the development and use of the Specific Affect Coding System (SPAFF) possible, including the National Institute of Mental Health (NIMH)

Grant ROI PHS MH42722, and Research Scientist Award IK02MH00257 to John Gottman. Additionally, we would like to acknowledge the students who have contributed to the development and evolution of the SPAFF over the years, who include Jim Coan, Kim McCoy, Holly Collier, and Erica Woodin.

13

Turning Toward Versus Turning Away: A Coding System of Daily Interactions

Janice L. Driver and John M. Gottman
University of Washington

The Turning Toward Versus Turning Away Coding System (Turning System) was created for the study of the unique interactions of couples in their everyday lives. This system was designed to measure subtle, microlevel behaviors in everyday interaction. We designed the Turning System to gain a better understanding of the ways in which couples initiate interactions and respond to each other in a semi-natural environment. The codes were created from daily interactions in a broad range of situations from watching TV to cooking dinner. As a result, they capture daily interactions whenever they occur.

THEORETICAL FOUNDATIONS

Approximately 12 years ago, we built a studio apartment laboratory at the University of Washington as a way to collect everyday interactions that a couple might experience on a typical weekend day. There were no instructions about what a couple could or could not do in the 24 hr they spent in the lab. They could make phone calls, work, listen to music, watch videos, and take walks in the park that surrounded the apartment lab. We were trying to tap into everyday, primarily nonconflict, interaction.

As we analyzed these data over the next decade, we realized that there were a number of reasons why one might be interested in obtaining such a sample of everyday marital interaction. First, in analyzing 14-year longitudinal data, we recently reported (Gottman & Levenson, 2001, 2002) that at Time 1 there were two dysfunctional patterns of conflict resolution, a high conflict and escalating attack–defend pattern, which predicted early divorcing (an average of 5.6 years after the wedding), and a pattern of emotional disengagement and suppressed negative affect, which predicted later divorcing (an average of 16.2 years after the wedding). The emotional disengagement pattern was best characterized by a lack of shared positive affect, such as affection, humor, interest, and playfulness. We wanted to know whether these two dysfunctional patterns of marital interaction were related to patterns of everyday nonconflict interaction in the apartment lab. That is, we were curious about whether marital conflict might be, to some extent, a failure of intimacy or emotional connection in the couple's everyday lives. Gottman and Levenson (2002) collected interaction data by having couples meet in the laboratory at the end of their day after having been apart for at least 8 hours. They were asked to talk about the events of their days for 15-min. Immediately after this interaction, the couple had a 15-min conflict discussion on an area of disagreement in their relationship. From this study, we found that disinterest and irritability during the events of the day led to a "harsh start up" during the conflict interaction. On the other hand, interest and engagement in one another's descriptions of their days were precursors of much less negativity during the conflict.

Second, with a newlywed sample (Gottman, Coan, Carrére, & Swanson, 1998), we found that the amount of positive affect during conflict not only predicted divorce, but it also predicted whether a couple would be happy or unhappy if they did not divorce. This was the only observational variable able to make both predictions. Hence, the amount of positive affect during conflict turned out to be a critical variable that needed to be understood. A review of outcome research in marital therapy studies by Gottman (1999) also suggested the hypothesis that lasting change beyond 1 year after termination is best predicted by three factors: (a) a reduction of negative affect during conflict, (b) an increase in positive affect during conflict, and (c) an increase in positive affect in nonconflict contexts (mostly accomplished by behavior exchange interventions). The problem to be solved was that although many interventions accomplish a reduction of negative affect during conflict, few interventions also accomplish an increase in positive affect during conflict (Vincent, Friedman, Nugent, & Messerly, 1979). Hence, increasing positive affect during conflict would seem to be an important puzzle to solve. If it were controlled by nonconflict interaction, behavior in this context might be easier to modify than behavior during conflict, where couples might be in a state of fight or flight.

Third, there is reason to be interested in positive affect in its own right. In a recent chapter on the role of conflict in marriage, Bradbury, Rogge, & Lawrence (2001) asserted that marital research has primarily focused on interpersonal conflict to the virtual exclusion of other relationship factors. This focus may be disproportionate compared to the amount of actual disagreements the couples experience in their everyday lives. Bradbury et al. (2001) wrote, "A strong focus on conflict has led to an incomplete and inadequate portrayal of marital functioning, and perhaps more inadequate than is typically recognized" (p. 62).

This emphasis on negative affect and on conflict is pervasive in studies of marital interventions. Most marital and premarital interventions concentrate on reducing negative affect by improving couple communication and conflict resolution. Christensen and Heavey (1999) reviewed the three most effective treatments in couple therapy research: behavioral, cognitive behavioral, and emotion-focused. Each of these therapies, in their own way, concentrated on improving the marital relationship by changing the way the couples communicate while they attempt to resolve conflict. Their assertion is that if the therapy can improve arguments and communication styles, the couples' overall relationship will improve as well. Although the results of these studies often show improvement in relationship satisfaction (which is not the same as positive affect), Jacobson and Addis (1993) suggested that many marital intervention effects are small.

Similarly, Bradbury et al. (2001) cited two longitudinal treatment studies by Hahlweg, Markman, Thurmaier, Engl, and Eckert (1998) that found couples who were trained in problem-solving and conflict communication skills did not show stronger relationship satisfaction over time. Each of these target couples greatly improved in their conflict and communication skills, but were not more satisfied in their long-term marital relationships.

This is not to suggest that communication during conflict is not important. In fact, most of our own research has focused primarily on conflict interactions (i.e., Gottman, Coan, & McCoy, 1996; Gottman, Coan, Carrére, & Swanson, 1998; and Gottman, Markman, & Notarius, 1977). It does, however, stress the need to emphasize research in other areas of the marital relationship. Seligman and Czikszentmihalyi (2000) suggested that psychology as a science has focused predominately on healing the damage life creates (p. 5). Although this focus is important, they suggested that it is limited in its ability to enhance the necessary positive qualities for a thriving individual or relationship.

Unfortunately, little research has been conducted on the development of positive interactions in marriage outside the conflict and communication realm. Because we do not fully understand the marital development or extinction of positive interactions, it is difficult to target these behaviors for intervention.

Fredrickson (2001) has developed a theory for positive affect called "The Broaden-and-Build Theory of Positive Emotions." She believes that the mechanism for positive affect is opposite to negative affect. With negative emotions, there is a triggering event with an immediate response. Fear, for example, produces an instantaneous change in heart rate, a narrowed, attentive focus, and the urge to act or to escape.

Positive emotions, on the other hand, are often built on a series of positive interactions over a period of time. They may or may not have a triggering event. For example, contentment often develops over days or weeks with a series of small enjoyable events. A person has just finished a major project at work, her children are playing outside, she is sitting on the porch in the sun and feels content. All of these events contribute to the positive emotion, but are not immediate causes. Positive emotions, she suggested, need to be cultivated.

On the other hand, D. H. Baucom (personal communication, November 6, 2002), suggested that perhaps disgust and contempt are also cumulative, rather than reactions to momentary events. This may be the reason that they are better predictors of eventual relationship outcomes than other, more momentary negative affects (such as anger). If both positive and negative emotions are cultivated outside of conflict, the study of daily behaviors is vital to our understanding of marital relationships.

Problems in Studying Positive Affect

Although several studies have shown that negative behaviors during conflict are malleable (Butler & Wampler, 1999), positive emotions are more challenging to change directly. Simply admonishing a distressed couple to increase positive affect during conflict does not create a more positive interaction (Vincent et al., 1979). Because it is difficult to directly influence positive affect, we believe there may be an indirect method through daily interactions.

Consistent with Fredrickson's idea of cultivating positive emotions, we suggest that the way a couple responds to everyday, fleeting exchanges may have a cumulative effect on their overall relationship, including conflict and communication. Seemingly mundane, everyday comments such as "Your sister called," can be met with a variety of responses from an irritable groan to a positive discussion about the sister. If a couple can learn to see these ordinary interactions as opportunities to build a positive relationship, they may successfully change the trajectory of their marriage. This foundation, along with conflict and communication training, may effect lasting, positive marital satisfaction. If positive affect were controlled by nonconflict interaction, behavior in this context might be easier to modify than behavior during conflict, where couples might be in a state of fight or flight.

Our starting assumption was that we needed to collect some basic observational data. Thus, we began our attempt to understand these daily interactions by observing couples in their daily lives in our apartment lab. We reasoned that once we understood the mechanisms for ordinary moments, we could then examine them in relation to conflict and communication patterns. Toward this end, we created a coding system to study these everyday moments

DEVELOPMENT OF THE CODING SYSTEM

The studio-type apartment in which this research took place had a kitchenette, dining table, and a small living room with an entertainment center. Fifty newlywed couples agreed to live in this apartment for 24 hr. With three cameras mounted near the ceiling, we videotaped them for 12 of the 24 hr they lived in the lab. They were allowed to bring their own groceries, CDs, books, videos, or work. Their only instructions were to live as they would at home.

We were surprised by the data we collected. Our original expectation from the apartment lab was to capture major events in the couples' everyday lives. We wanted to film moments of self-disclosure, emotionally charged discussions, and naturally occurring conflict. Instead, we discovered an unexpected difficulty—subtlety. Couples did not interact in overt and exciting ways in their everyday lives. Most of their interactions involved "hanging out." In fact, when we tried to code these interactions using the Specific Affect Coding System (SPAFF; Gottman, 1996), we found that most of the interactions were neutral. Our observations in previous studies had involved couples in conflict, so we were not accustomed to hours and hours of mostly neutral interactions. At first, these tapes seemed dull and unimportant compared to the fervor of conflict.

We eventually noticed, however, that some couples engaged in neutral interactions differently from others. None of the exchanges were charged with emotion, but there were subtle differences in the ways the couples interacted. We noticed that some people regularly made bids for emotional connection from their partners, which seemed to indicate another unit of intimacy. This observation challenged us to create a new coding system that would capture small and often insignificant moments in daily life.

In the book *Observing Interaction*, Bakeman and Gottman (1986) suggested that clear observational coding systems need to originate from the participants' interactions. With this in mind, we began watching the apartment lab tapes and recording any behaviors that seemed new or interesting. For example, a husband would get up from the dining table to sit on the couch next to his wife. Or a wife might ask her husband for something to drink. For many months, we simply recorded these descriptions on a log sheet. After hundreds of observations, we began to categorize the interactions based on common themes. The resulting system is summarized in Table 13.1.

TASK AND SETTING

The Turning System was designed to capture natural or semi-natural exchange in everyday life. It was designed to be used to code any daily-type behaviors with two or more people. Currently, this system is being modified to be used to examine the daily interactions of parents with their autistic children.

TABLE 13.1

The Specific Bids, Responses, and Aways for the Turning Toward Versus Turning Away Coding System

Code	*Description*	*Example*
Bids		
Silent	Nonverbal action that the partner can notice and acknowledge	Points to the salt shaker.
Low Comment	Comment containing information exchange	I'm going to lunch with Kate.
High Comment	Comment containing opinions, thoughts, or feelings	Kate is a wonderful friend.
Low Question	Question of general interest or information	Are you going to call Roger?
High Question	Question about opinions, thoughts, or feelings	Do you enjoy doing things with Kate and Roger?
Playful	Involves some physical sparring with good-natured jesting	A husband tries to wrestle a dollar bill out of his wife's hand.
Negative	Initiates an interaction in a negative way using contempt, belligerence, criticism, or defensiveness from SPAFF	Do you have to call your mother again? (sneers)
Reponses		
Passive	It is clear the bid has been received, but minimal effort is taken to reply	Looks at the TV, then back to his book.
Low Energy	Answers the bid only	Looks up and comments, "Yeah."
Attentive	Welcomes the bid. Makes an effort to respond	Stops watching TV, looks at her husband and asks, "Why didn't he call you?"
Enthusiastic	High energy and good eye contact. Effortful response	Walks over to her husband, puts her arms around him and asks, "What?"
Playful	Full of fun and good spirits. Involves some physical sparring with good-natured teasing	Husband bops his wife with a paper plate. She responds by lightly poking him with her fork.

TABLE 13.1 (cont.)

Code	Description	Example
Responses (cont.)		
Turning Against	Based on the SPAFF codes for negative affect. Must include contempt, belligerence, criticism, or defensiveness.	"At least I'm not fat and lazy."
Turning Away		
Preoccupied	Partner is engaged in an activity and doesn't respond	Watching TV , reading, typing.
Interrupt	Partner begins a new bid without acknowledging that her partner is bidding.	H: "Honey, Did you see —?" W: "Where are the pans around here?"
Disregard	Complete lack of response to the bid.	A wife plans with her hair after the husband makes a bid.
Re-bid	Repeat the same bid or a similar bid after an Away.	H: "Are you going to work early tomorrow?" (no response)
Shared Moments	Shared moment where the partner looks at the bidder before responding.	W: "Oh! (Regarding the TV)" H: Looks at his wife, then at the TV and says, "Yeah!"

Note. SPAFF = Specific Affect Coding System.

One important aspect of this system is that the interaction of the participants should be unstructured with little or no direction from the researchers. In fact, our only instruction to the couple was to try to live as they would at home. We have found that participants who are given specific tasks changed their turning behavior. Although this is interesting information, it does not highlight the everyday nature of this observational system.

DESCRIPTION OF THE CODING SYSTEM

Rather than describe each of the 18 codes, we would like to explain the major concepts involved in the Turning System. Each code falls into one of five categories: Bids, Responses, Shared Moments, Turning Away, and Re-bids.

Bids for Interaction

An important concept for the Turning System is the Bid. This term refers to the idea that one partner is attempting to interact with the other. They are bidding for attention or an emotional connection. These bids cover a wide range of interactions from a simple look to a funny story. The bid was coded whenever one partner attempted to engage the other in some type of interaction. In an attempt to initiate interaction, the partners used a wide range of behaviors from a simple look to a funny story. We categorized each of these bids into five possible types (Silent, Low and High Comment, Low and High Question, Playful, and Negative).

Early on in the creation of this coding system, we had trouble knowing when to record a bid. Some couples had staccato-type interactions where the bid was made and quickly answered. Others would begin a conversation and continue it for 2 or 3 min. Both situations involved a single initiation but had very different results. After reviewing the types of conversations couples were having, we realized that they used bids to initiate conversation, but also to continue existing conversations. Bids could be used to encourage further interaction. The following examples show the difference between the two styles.

Bid to Initiate Interaction

Noelle:	Did you get dog food before we left?	[Bid]
Brook:	Yeah. I got it on Wednesday	[Response]

Bid for Further Interaction

Noelle:	Did you get dog food before we left?	[Bid]
Brook:	Yeah. I got it on Wednesday.	[Response]
	It's ridiculous how much we have to pay for it these days.	[Bid for interaction]

Noelle:	Oh. I know.	[Response]
	I didn't realize how expensive animals can be …	[Bid for interaction]

In the second example, Brook responded to Noelle's bid and then encouraged her to interact further. She, in turn, answered his bid and interjected another bid of her own. Although we categorized seven different types of bids, each type had the potential to initiate interaction or promote further interaction.

Comment and Question Bids

As we noted earlier, the specific types of bids are listed in Table 13.1, but we would like to describe one distinction regarding comments and questions. We decided to divide these categories into two types: information-based and emotion-based. Each is content driven. The low-level bids are based on information exchange, and the high-level bids on emotional exchange. The low comment and low question bids were focused on informational content, whereas the high-level comments and questions had an emotional emphasis. The following illustrates this further:

Information Exchange

Kyle:	Have you ever been to Mexico?	[Low Question Bid]
Hayden:	Once when I was a kid. My dad took us there on a car trip. I was carsick most of the time, and my sisters and I kept fighting about sitting next to the window.	

Emotion Exchange

Kyle:	Would you enjoy living in a hot, dry climate?	[High Question Bid]
Hayden:	I think I'd like living in a warmer climate. It would be wonderful to wake up every morning to sunshine and warm weather. I'm not sure about the desert though. Since I'm from Seattle, It may be too hot.	

In the first example, Kyle is asking for information. Hayden's story about her family is interesting, but also information-based. The emotion-based exchange provides Kyle with different information about Hayden as a person. Both types of bids are important to the relationship, but have different goals and results.

Negative Bid

Not all bids during daily interaction were neutral to positive. Some bids were negative, even hostile. These bids were recorded as Negative Bidding and were based on the criteria for the SPAFF coding system (Gottman, 1996). An example of a negative bid would be, "Can't you get it right?"

Responses

In contrast to the bids, the responses were not content-driven. They were more hierarchical and based on effort by the responder. A spouse, who simply muttered a one-word response, would receive a different code than if he or she stopped what he or she was doing and showed some effort to respond. This part of the coding system was more difficult for training, because responses with the same type of content could receive a different code based on the energy of the response. In the following scenario, Ryan is putting the groceries away while Allie is reading the newspaper.

Passive Response

Kevin:	Did you happen to bring paper towels?	[Low Comment Question]
Allie:	Huh? [Continues to read. Doesn't look up.]	[Passive response]

Attentive Response

Kevin:	Did you happen to bring paper towels?	[Low Comment Question]
Allie:	What? [Sets aside the newspaper, turns to her husband and smiles.]	[Attentive response]

The Attentive response gave Allie credit for wanting to interact with her husband. If Allie also got up from the couch to help her husband look for the paper towels, she would be credited with an Enthusiastic response. Although it was a challenge to reliably code these hierarchical responses, this system allowed us to accurately record the subtlety of "Turning Toward."

Turning Against

Some of the responses from the partners seemed irritable or even hostile. We decided to record these behaviors using the SPAFF (Gottman, 1996) criteria for negativity. This allowed us to capture such contemptuous moments as, "If you weren't so lazy, you'd get up and get it yourself." Although "Turning Against" behavior may play a role important to everyday interactions, we did not code it often with the newlywed couples. It would be interesting to look at this behavior in couples who had been married for a longer period of time.

Shared Moments

One code that is related to the couples' responses, but seemed separate from them, was the Bidder Referencing code. When one spouse made a bid, the responder looked at the bidder before commenting. For example, there was a large picture window in the apartment lab that had a view of Portage Bay in Seattle, Washington. Spouses often looked out the window to comment on various boats passing by. One wife was looking out the window when a large yacht sailed by with a small helicopter on the top. The wife pointed out the window and exclaimed, "A helicopter!" The husband, who was reading the paper, first looked at his wife, smiled, and then looked out the window at the yacht. This was bidder referencing.

At first, we thought this code was a "checking in" type of interaction, like social referencing with children (Campos, 1982). Instead, bidder referencing seemed related to sharing the moment with their partner. In the aforementioned example, the husband's first priority was to interact with his wife and then to acknowledge the helicopter. Shared moments such as these only occurred with very happy couples.

Turning Away

On the opposite extreme from shared moments was when partners ignored each other. From our initial observations, we found three ways that partners can ignore each other: Preoccupied, Disregard, and Interrupt. With the "Preoccupied Away" code, the partner needed to be engaged in an activity that was substantive such as working at the computer or reading a book. If he or she was engaged in a trivial activity such as playing with his or her hair, we coded these interactions as Disregard. Although we did not use the term *ignore* because it carried negative connotations for the coders, the Disregard code is most like a traditional ignoring behavior: one partner just does not respond. Finally, the Interrupt code referred to interactions in which one partner interrupted the other with a bid of his or her own. It was as if the first bid never occurred. Again, each of these three codes are defined in Table 13.1.

Re-bidding

Regardless of the type of Away, once a partner was ignored, he or she could potentially repeat the bid again. We labeled these attempts as Re-bids. The Re-bid code was recorded separately from Bids and Responses, because it was a restatement or rephrasing of the original bid. It was as if the bidder is pressing the other person to interact. An example follows:

David:	Would you like milk or water?	[Low Question Bid]
Toni:	[No response]	[Disregard]
David:	Hey Toni. Are you thirsty?	[Re-bid]

When we first began coding, we believed that couples who were distressed would not make re-bids. Happy couples, on the other hand, would feel comfortable re-bidding. Although there was a difference between the two groups, it was surprising that happy couples only re-bid 20% of the time (Driver & Gottman, 2002). Unhappy couples did not re-bid at all. When happy couples did re-bid, it was usually related to necessary information. If a wife asked her husband for his brother's phone number, she would ask again because she needed the number. Aside from this type of information, neither happy nor unhappy couples would ask again.

We are in the process of analyzing this data further to determine whether Turning Aways are comparable to Stonewalling in the conflict discussion. Stonewalling is a code from the SPAFF Coding System (Gottman, 1996) in which one partner simply stops interacting and avoids looking at the other person. It often occurs when the partner is overwhelmed with the conflict and stonewalls to stop the discussion. This type of interaction is one of the predictors of divorce. If being ignored in everyday life is similar to Stonewalling during conflict, the behavior may be too strong to overcome with a re-bid. It may require recovery time or some type of repair interaction.

The Bids, Responses, and Turning Aways from the Turning System can be used to observe couples in a variety of natural situations to better understand the role of daily interactions. We believe that everyday interactions provide an important new dimension to the study of marriage.

CODER TRAINING

We began our coder training with an intensive 5-week course of 6 hr each week to train coders in the Turning System. Each coder was given a manual and asked to study three to four codes per week. The students were then shown videotaped examples in class of the specific codes they were studying. Once the students had seen several examples of the codes in class, they were asked to individually watch a videotape from the apartment lab and to code what they had learned to that point.

For training purposes, we selected tapes that included multiple incidents of the codes they were learning during that week. The beginning of each subsequent training session began with a group discussion of observed moments and questions regarding the codes. The students spent approximately 3 hr per week in class, 2 hr watching tapes, and 1 hr studying the manual. This seemed to keep them from feeling overwhelmed with coding information.

Monthly, we randomly assigned coders to a master tape to check their reliability with that tape. This prevented coder drift and allowed us to maintain consistent standards. If a coder was not reliable with the master tape, we immediately assigned him or her to a retraining session. We were careful to let the student know that this was a natural part of observational coding and common to most coders.

The Turning System manual is available on request from Janice Driver (jdriver@u.washington.edu). Training tapes are not available, but can be created from any natural observation footage.

CODING PROCESS

When the couples came to the apartment laboratory, we did not give them specific instructions for activities or dialogue. As a result, the couples engaged in a myriad of behaviors from playing cards to reading the paper. This created a problem for coding, because we wanted to find similar segments across couples to reduce the possible confounds of time and environment. For example, if we chose a specific time to code all couples, they might be engaged in different activities. One couple might be watching TV whereas the other is napping. Turning behavior would be very different for these two activities.

Simply choosing similar behaviors was also difficult, however, because it tended to create a time confound. If one couple read the paper when they first arrived at 9:00 a.m., their interaction may be very different from a couple who read the paper late in the evening.

One activity that was consistent across couples and was time-specific was the dinner-time segment. We decided to use dinner-time, because all of the couples ate dinner and had lived in the apartment for a minimum of 6 hr (9 a.m. to 4 p.m.). We coded these segments for 10 min from the moment they sat down to eat. Even 10 min was enough of a sample for bids and turning, because these behaviors occur at a high rate during dinner-time conversations.

Once we chose the specific segment to code, we edited each of the videotapes to 10-min sections. The coders used these shortened versions to code the Turning System, so they did not have access to longer portions of the couples' interactions. To begin a coding session, we instructed the coders to watch the entire 10-min segment without recording any bids or responses. They just watched the tape for conversation content and subtle behaviors.

Once the coders had watched the entire segment, they watched it again to record the specific codes using a coding sheet and a pencil. The coders were allowed to pause the tape when they observed a code. They then recorded the time of the bid, the spousal response, and the first few words of the bid. We included the first words so we could match any codes that may be off by 1 or 2 sec, but were exact with the first words. To code in this way, it was necessary to rewind the tape often to capture the beginning of the interaction. Although we had to start and stop the tapes frequently, we are able to code 10-min segments in approximately 1 hr. More practiced coders averaged 45 min.

When they had finished coding the entire segment, the coders woulds enter the data into a Microsoft Excel spreadsheet which was later used to run the free-marginal Kappa program. The data entry files were spot checked weekly for accuracy.

RELIABILITY

We used Free Marginal Kappa (Kn; Brennan & Prediger, 1981; Dunn, 1989) to measure reliability between Turning coders. For each couple, the percentage of agreement between coders needed to be at a minimum of 75% before we would calculate the Kn. Our overall agreement across all the couples was 81% for Bids and 76% for Responses. The Kn across all couples was .88 for Bids and .77 for Responses.

To measure the internal consistency of our coding system, we used the Cronbach alpha generalizability coefficients (Cronbach, 1972; Wiggins, 1977). In our case, the Cronbach alpha was used to assess how well a specific code measured variability between participants as opposed to variability between coders. The closer to 1.0, the more reliable the code, that is, the more the code is doing its intended work of discriminating between couples rather than discriminating between observers. We computed the alphas for each code as the ratio of the mean square for observers minus the mean square error term divided by the mean square for observers plus the mean square error term. The Cronbach alphas for the Turning System ranged from .29 to 1.0, with a mean of .78.[1] The low Cronbach alphas in some categories are a concern. They probably reflect two facts. First, in some instances, we were coding rare events. For example, playful responses by wives only occurred three times across all couples. The coders agreed on one of those three responses, so the Alpha was a low .29. Second, some of our constructs are not uni-dimensional. As we train coders in the future, we will focus on the definition and observation of these rare behaviors, and, as a result, these reliabilities will likely increase.

VALIDITY

Validity of the Bids and Turning codes was assessed in our research on the basis of the ability of these codes to correlate with positive affect during the conflict discussion. In a 14-year longitudinal study of marriage, Gottman and Levenson (2002) identified two dysfunctional interaction patterns: an attack–defend pattern of escalating conflict that predicted early divorcing, and an emotionally disengaged pattern that predicted later divorcing. In a subsequent longitudinal study of newlywed couple interaction, 50 couples were studied in a standard marital conflict interaction and observed in an apartment laboratory. Using the Bids and Turning coding system, dinner-time conversations were coded and data were correlated with variables that indexed these two dysfunctional styles of marital conflict. The hypothesis tested in this analysis was inspired by Wile's (1988) notion that conflictual marital interaction is related to unspoken marital dialogue. Wile proposed the counterintuitive hypothesis that an attack–defend conflict dis-

[1]The Cronbach alpha scores for Bids are as follows: Playful, 1.0; Low Comment, 0.99; Low Question, 0.98; High Comment, 0.95; Silent, 0.92; High Question, 0.91; and Negative, 0.55. Scores for Responses are as follows: Passive, 0.98; Low Level, 0.98; Attentive, 0.97; Ignore, 0.95; Preoccupied, 0.92; Interrupt, 0.87; Against, 0.73; Enthusiastic, 0.41; and Playful, 0.29.

cussion pattern would be related to Turning Away in everyday marital interaction. We extended this hypothesis by proposing that the emotionally disengaged pattern would be related to a Turning Against pattern. We computed the amount of Turning Against and Turning Away observed in the apartment laboratory and the attack–defend or emotionally disengaged patterns during conflict. Table 13.2 provides a summary of these correlations.

Table 13.2 shows that, as predicted, the emotionally disengaged pattern during conflict discussions is significantly correlated with Turning Against in the apartment laboratory, whereas the attack-defend pattern during conflict discussions is significantly correlated with Turning Away in the apartment laboratory.

The amount of positive affect, particularly humor, was a predictor of both marital happiness and stability in the newlywed sample, so we wondered whether everyday interaction in the apartment laboratory was correlated with the amount of humor during conflict. We tested the idea that a couple's access to shared humor during conflict discussions was related to the amount of playful bidding and the enthusiasm of Turning Toward in the apartment laboratory. The husband's humor during the conflict discussion was correlated .65 ($p < .01$) with the number of husband playful bids in the apartment laboratory. The wife's humor during the conflict discussion was also correlated .65 ($p < .01$) with the number of husband playful bids in the apartment laboratory. The husband's humor during the conflict discussion was correlated .60 ($p < .01$) with the number of wife playful bids in the apartment laboratory. The wife's humor during the conflict discussion was correlated .61 ($p < .01$) with the number of wife playful bids in the apartment laboratory. We

TABLE 13.2

Intercorrelations Between Conflict Modes and Apartment Laboratory Turning Codes

Variable	1	2	3	4	5	6	7	8
Husband								
1. Turning Against	1.00							
2. Turning Away	.05	1.00						
3. Attack–Defend	.06	.06	1.00					
4. Withdraw	.47***	.16	.06	1.00				
Wife								
1. Turning Against	.30*	.14	.06	.14	1.00			
2. Turning Away	–.20	.23	.18	–.01	.23	1.00		
3. Attack–Defend	.07	.44***	.49***	.21	.08	.08	1.00	
4. Withdraw	.17	.30*	.09	.48***	.20	.05	.16	1.00

*$p < .05$. **$p < .01$. **$p < .001$

also were interested in whether enthusiastic Turning Toward in the apartment laboratory would be related to the amount of humor in the conflict discussion. We found that this was the case only for wife enthusiastic Turning Toward, which was related to both husband humor (.52, $p < .01$) and wife humor (.68, $p < .01$).

GENERALIZABILITY

The participants in the apartment laboratory were matched to the ethnic diversity of the Greater Seattle region which was as follows: 12% Asian American, 10% African American, 4% Hispanic American, 1% Native American and 73% European American. Although our sample included ethnic minorities, we did not make racial distinctions in our analyses. This kind of future research would require oversampling a particular ethnic group to observe patterns in couple interactions (McGoldrick & & Rohrbaugh, 1987).

CLINICAL UTILITY

We believe that a couple's daily interactions make a valuable contribution to the overall success of a marriage. Major positive and negative events happen in the context of the overall relationship. Many marital interventions ask couples to engage in dating-type events such as partner gifts, date nights, and vacation plans. These events are important, but occur with a history of rejected or accepted bids. For example, a romantic dinner can be a success or failure depending on the quality of the couple's daily interactions. If the wife has consistently ignored her husband throughout the week, he may be more distant and irritable during their date. Hundreds of small moments during the week create a foundation for the major event of the romantic dinner. If these moments turn into missed and miscoordinated interactions, the date is likely to fail because the small, daily moments were not a priority.

Alternatively, small, seemly unimportant moments may create an atmosphere that allows intimacy and positive interaction to flourish. If these daily moments do have an effect on major events, they may be easier to target for intervention. These small moments may be important in influencing the overall tone of the marriage even if they do not influence major events. Gottman (1999) theorized that an accumulation of Turning Toward one's partner would create positive rather than negative sentiment override (Weiss, 1980), and that this would, in turn, determine the effectiveness of repair attempts during conflict interactions. For example, it may be easier to coach a husband or wife to respond to questions during everyday moments than to behave affectionately on a dinner date. This type of intervention, along with conflict and communication training, may create a more stable and satisfying relationship in the long-term.

STUDIES USING THE CODING SYSTEM

The Turning System is currently being used in two different studies in the Gottman Research Laboratory and is being modified by a colleague for a study with autistic children. Earlier in this chapter, we described the original 14-year longitudinal study of newlywed couples in the semi-natural environment of an apartment laboratory. The Turning System was designed specifically for this study to capture everyday interactions in this unstructured setting. Although we have continued to follow these couples for 14 years, we have only recently contacted them to participate in a second natural-environment session. This second session of daily life may provide some insight into the trajectory of the couples' original interactions. This phase of study will only include those couples who have remained married, but will recruit both distressed and nondistressed groups.

A second study from the Gottman Research Laboratory that is incorporating a natural-environment session is the study of couples in the transition to parenthood. These couples are being recruited while they are pregnant with their first child and will be followed for a minimum of 3 years. Although the first sessions with these couples will only involve structured interviews and conflict discussions, a later phase of the study will include extended natural observations with the parents and their children. We hope to capture dinner-time interactions, play exchanges, and bedtime rituals. The Turning System itself is being modified to include the multiple interactions of the family.

Finally, Christopher Jones, PhD, from the University of Washington, is modifying the Turning System to capture the natural interactions of parents with their autistic children. As with the "Transition to Parenthood" study, his modifications to the Turning System will accommodate the more complex interactions of parents with their disabled children.

Our goal as we proceed with future research is to include natural interactions whenever possible. The study of couples, parents, and families in more ordinary environments is an important addition to understanding interpersonal relationships.

ACKNOWLEDGMENTS

This research was supported by National Institute of Mental Health grant MH3943 to John Gottman, Department of Psychology, University of Washington.

14

Repair Attempts Observational Coding System: Measuring De-Escalation of Negative Affect During Marital Conflict

Amber A. Tabares, Janice L. Driver, and John M. Gottman
University of Washington

The role of affect within marital conflict has been important for identifying different processes of communication between happily and unhappily married couples. The focus of many studies on marriage has been the identification of negative behavior patterns that predict divorce or characterize negative communication patterns (Lindahl, Clements, & Markman, 1997; Rugel, 1997). This information has been useful both to therapists and researchers in building relationship theory and has been useful as a means for understanding the mechanisms that underlie patterns predictive of divorce.

What is less clear, however, are the patterns that couples use to prevent negativity and how they attempt to lessen negative interactions once they occur. We propose that the most salient qualitative difference between dysfunctional and functional marriages is the ability to repair communication during a conflict discussion once it becomes affectively negative. This may be related to a suggestion by Gottman (1979) that a critical component of functional marriages is a couple's ability to de-escalate conflict. In this chapter, we describe our new Repair Attempts observational coding system, which was designed to capture the ways in which couples naturally attempt to prevent and reduce negativity during their conflict interactions. Some Repair Attempt codes show one spouse attempting to repair an interaction by introducing positive affect or positive comments to a disagreement. Other codes demonstrate spouses' attempts to stop or decrease negativity by such measures as directly addressing the negativity, redirecting comments, and accepting influence. Each of these types of Repair Attempts and specific definitions for each code is addressed.

THEORETICAL FOUNDATIONS

Our laboratory has conducted extensive studies to understand marital conflict. Using the Specific Affect observational coding system (SPAFF; see Shapiro, Gottman, & Driver, this volume, for further detail), we discovered the specific negative affects and patterns of negative reciprocity during conflict interactions that distinguish couples headed toward early divorce (Gottman & Levenson, 2000).

Although understanding negative affect during conflict has been essential for predicting divorce, we also observed that the disagreements of both happy and unhappy couples contained moments of naturally occurring change. In this context, we realized that an essential difference between these types of couples was the ability to make effective Repair Attempts during discussions of disagreement. Happy couples seemed to be more skilled at using Repair Attempts because they seemed to use them more often and earlier in a conflict discussion. For these couples, Repair Attempts helped prevent later negativity. Unhappy couples seemed to use Repairs less often, later in the conversation, and with seemingly ineffective results. Also, it appeared that distressed couples were far less likely to accept a Repair Attempt; but instead, tended to perceive the Repair Attempt as hostile or manipulative.

DEVELOPMENT OF THE CODING SYSTEM

When we first began to develop the Repair Attempts coding system, we watched many hours of videotapes of marital conflict discussions. We recorded any moments during these discussions where the couples were able to de-escalate negative interactions or prevent negative escalation. To define moments of high negativity, we used the SPAFF (Gottman, 1996), which consists of 14 codes for negative affect, 1 neutral code, and 5 positive affect codes.

As we searched for Repair Attempts, we noticed that repair behaviors would emerge at different points throughout an interaction depending on the couple. The same behaviors we were categorizing as Repair Attempts during high levels of negativity were used by some couples early in their conflict discussion before things became very negative. These couples seemed to be using repair behaviors as a means for preventing negative escalation. This pattern seemed to occur more frequently with happy couples. Unhappy couples, on the other hand, would wait until the conflict was very negative before repairing. To catch both types of Repair Attempts in our coding, we decided to code Repair Attempts any time they occurred throughout the conflict discussion rather than just at periods of high negativity.

TASK AND SETTING

To develop the Repair Attempts coding system, we used the first assessment period from a sample of newlywed couples who participated in a 14-year longitudinal study of marriage. Couples were recruited using newspaper advertisements. To participate in the study, couples had to meet several criteria including the following: they had to be in the 1st year of their first marriage, and they had to be without children. Couples were asked to complete a telephone version of the Marital Adjustment Test (MAT; Krokoff, 1987; Locke & Wallace, 1959) and questionnaires that included measures of demographic characteristics, characteristics of their marriage, and measures of health and well-being. The newlywed sample consisted of 130 couples. From among these couples, we selected the conflict discussions of a sample of couples for whom we have data from a 24-hr apartment laboratory stay. Our couples were grouped into four groups by marital satisfaction: happy stable, moderately happy stable, unhappy stable, and divorced. Because such a small portion of our sample divorced, we included all newlywed couples who divorced regardless of whether they stayed in our apartment laboratory.

As part of the study, couples were then asked to come to our laboratory and participate in a 15-min, videotaped conflict discussion. Before the discussion, couples were given the Couple's Problem Inventory (CPI; Gottman, Markman, & Notarius, 1977) to complete. The CPI asks couples to rate 11 discussion topics previously rated by married couples as the most typical areas of disagreement. Couples rated each of these areas on a scale from 0 to 100 and indicated for how long each issue had been a source of disagreement. Using the completed questionnaire, a member of the research team discussed various issues with each spouse to identify a salient topic that the couple would discuss for 15 min. Once one or two topics were identified, the researcher left the room and allowed the couple to discuss the issue. The Repair Attempts coding system was developed out of these 15-min conflict interactions.

DESCRIPTION OF THE CODING SYSTEM

The Repair Attempts coding system consists of 17 Repair Attempt codes and 11 responses (see Table 14.1). We define Repair Attempts as behaviors aimed at pre-

TABLE 14.1

Descriptions of Repair Attempts

Repair Code	*Description*
Affection	
Affection	Compliments, positive feelings, expressions of caring, and shows of appreciation.
We're Okay and Teamwork	Compliment of the relationship or the reinforcement of the partnership by acknowledging similarities between spouses.
Accepting Influence	
Agreement	Two types: Acceptance of a complaint or a 180° turn-around on an issue presented by the other spouse.
Compromise	An attempt to find middle ground through cooperation by both spouses.
Taking Responsibility	Acknowledgement of own contribution to the conflict.
Process Oriented	
Defining the Conflict	A summary of both spouse's contributions to the conflict.
Guarding	A warning not to continue a specific part of the discussion. A request to back off of a particular issue.
Monitoring the Conflict	Two types: Keeping the discussion on track or addressing negativity in the interaction, including self-correction.
Stop	An intentional end of subject or change of subject; directly stated or implicit.
Partner Focused	
Making Promises	A promise or assurance of a positive change in the future.
Repair Question	A "check-in" question that draws out feelings and opinions of the other.
Request for Direction	One partner tries to gain information from the other about how to improve the situation.
Understanding	Two types: Positive mind reading and the communication of empathy or the sudden realization of the partner's point.
Asking for Empathy	
Self Disclosure	Revelation of personal thoughts and feelings as reasons behind the conflict or negative behavior.
Tooting Your Own Horn	Asking for credit.
Humor	
Humor	An attempt to lighten the conflict with a joke, witticism, or silliness without a malicious intent.
Damage	
Damage	Any repair attempt that is immediately followed by a negative behavior or comment, which in essence ruins the repair.

venting or reducing negativity during conflict. Although the overall purpose of all Repair Attempts is the same, the ways in which couples make Repair Attempts vary. The Repair Attempts codes are grouped into seven categories: Accepting Influence, Humor, Partner-Focused, Affection, Process-Oriented, Asking for Empathy, and Damaged Repairs. Whereas Repair Attempts are coded on an individual basis, the categories provide a useful framework to conceptualize types of Repair Attempts that are made.

Accepting Influence Repair Attempts

Studies of marital conflict have yielded information about the types of conflicts that are typical for couples. We have found that both happy and unhappy marriages have unsolvable as well as solvable problems; yet, what distinguishes successful and unsuccessful couples is their ability to accept influence during conflict. Spouses who accept influence create an atmosphere of acceptance of their partner's viewpoint rather than causing a stalemate or condition of "gridlock" (Driver, Tabares, Shapiro, Nahm, & Gottman, 2003).

We have found that issues in any conflict can be categorized as solvable or unsolvable. Solvable problems have a solution, whereas unsolvable problems are perpetual issues that may never be resolved, such as differences in personality, culture, or religion. There is a distinct difference in the manner in which happy versus unhappy couples handle disagreements over unsolvable issues, with happy couples demonstrating the ability to accept influence. Repair Attempts may be one way to measure accepting influence. The Accepting Influence category of Repair Attempts includes three Repair codes: Agreement, Compromise, and Taking Responsibility.

Although some couples assume adversarial roles during discussions of perpetual issues, other couples use a more positive strategy to discuss perpetual problems. They strive to achieve a level of peace around their perpetual issues rather than attempting to solve the problem. Following is an example of Donna and Jesse during a discussion of disagreement in which they accepted influence from one another by using the Agreement and Compromise codes:

Donna: I thought you were going to start helping with the cleaning around the house. It's been almost 2 weeks since we discussed it and not much has changed.

Jesse: I've had less time than usual with everything that's been going on at work in the last 2 weeks.

Donna: [Agreement—180 degree turnaround] That's true. I hadn't really thought of that.

Jesse: [Compromise] Since I have two more days of this work schedule, could you finish doing both of our lists of chores this week, if I do both lists next week?

Donna started out with a criticism, which could have easily escalated to a position of gridlock with both spouses determined to defend their own positions. Instead, this example showed Donna and Jesse using Repair Attempts to collaborate and acknowledge some part of the other's viewpoint, which enabled them to prevent further escalation of negativity.

Humor Repair Attempts

The Humor category contains only the Humor code. We have found that appropriate humor can have a soothing influence during conflict. These humorous moments are not used to derail the discussion or demean the partner, but to interject positive interaction in an otherwise negative context:

Irene:	… I know you say you pick up the clothes, but I never see it happen..
Malcolm:	Well, maybe you should notice and appreciate when I do things.
Irene:	That would mean you'd have to actually do something … [long pause].
Malcolm:	[Humor] Maybe I could organize a neighborhood work party to help me with laundry. That'd get it done! [They both laugh].

This example illustrates the de-escalating effect of a well-placed (and good-natured) Humor Repair Attempt. In this case, the husband's idea of a neighborhood rally was not only a respite from the negativity but a chance to replace the negativity with lightheartedness that both spouses found funny.

Partner-Focused Repair Attempts

Making Promises, Repair Questions, Request for Direction, and Understanding are the four Repair Attempt codes that create the Partner-Focused category of Repair Attempts. Partner-focused Repair Attempts exhibit spouses' concern for and interest in their partner. They demonstrate a way to learn more about one another during a disagreement. See the following for an example of a Repair Question:

Ron:	It seems like we've already talked about this visit; I thought we had come to a decision that we would both go to visit my family.
Julie:	I guess we did..
Ron:	[Repair Question] Do you not feel like going anymore?

Understanding and Making Promises are Partner-Focused Repair Attempts in which spouses can directly express empathy and concern during a conflict. Ron, for example, could show his concern for Julie with Repair Attempts such as, "I know it's hard for you to go on these trips [Understanding]. I won't leave you alone with my family, I'll make sure we have time together [Making Promises]."

Affection Repair Attempts

Similarly, with the Affection Repair Attempts, spouses are able to communicate concern and empathy, but more importantly they communicate solidarity and fondness in the face of negativity. In this category of Repair Attempts, spouses use the Affection and We're Okay codes to give each other credit for doing things well. With Affection, one spouse gives the other credit for something or communicates fondness toward the partner. The We're Okay code emphasizes teamwork and gives credit to the relationship, for example, "I think we do a really good job of traveling together."

Process-Oriented Repair Attempts

Repair Attempts are not always delivered with positive affect. Often, these behaviors are less intuitive as attempts to repair negativity, but our observations seem to indicate that some of these Repair Attempts may be just as effective in reducing negativity. These types of Repair Attempts are included in the Process-Oriented and Asking for Empathy categories.

Process-Oriented Repair Attempts address the discussion itself in four different codes: Defining the Conflict, Guarding, Monitoring the Conflict, and Stop. Directly or indirectly they address the negativity occurring in the current conversation and the responsibility each spouse has to discuss a certain topic or to manage a certain level of negativity. For example, Monitoring the Discussion and Defining the Conflict Repair Attempts are used to modify the discussion topic and keep negative interactions in check. Monitoring the Discussion can be conveyed on a full spectrum of affects. The self-correction form of Monitoring the Discussion may be delivered with the most positive affect as it seems to carry the speaker's concern for the negative message the listener might have heard:

Daryl and Kim have been having a disagreement over money.

Kim: You have to save more money from each paycheck. [Self-correction] Well, I don't mean you *have* to do that, I meant it more as an option for something you *could* do.

Monitoring the Discussion can also include more direct addresses of process such as, "will you let me finish?" and "we're getting off topic." In both of these instances, spouses are trying to keep the discussion of disagreement at a manageable level, but both messages might be delivered with neutral to negative affect. Similar to Monitoring the Discussion Repair Attempts, Defining the Conflict also serves to narrow the area of disagreement by outlining the boundaries of the conflict as a joint disagreement that both spouses are responsible for creating.

Stop and Guarding Repair Attempts include direct and indirect halts or changes in the topic of discussion. We have observed that these types of Repair Attempts seem to appear at moments of increased tension in the conflict discussion when at least one spouse seems to be flooded. Using our physiological measures taken during conflict, we found that flooding occurs during periods of high arousal. Flooding is marked by an increase in sweat due to stress, shallow or irregular breathing, and an increase in heart rate to over 100 beats per min (roughly the intrinsic pacemaker heart rhythm). With these physiological symptoms, the partner is unable to think clearly or participate in constructive conversation. Conflicts that include high levels of negative affect commonly show one or both partners to be emotionally and physically overwhelmed (Gottman, 1994; Gottman & Levenson, 1983). The primary focus of the flooded spouse is reduced to self-preservation. This is a type of situation in which Stop and Guarding Repair Attempts may be used to reduce negativity by backing away from a currently heated discussion or avoiding a topic that would further escalate negativity.

Stop Repair Attempts can occur with an explicit statement such as, "let's talk about something else" or more implicitly with one spouse just changing the subject. Guarding is always explicit; it comes in the form of a warning such as, "don't go there," from one spouse to another about a topic they should avoid if they wish to escape further negativity. These process-oriented repairs provide a respite from negativity.

Asking for Empathy Repair Attempts

The Asking for Empathy category contains Self-Disclosure and Tooting Your Own Horn Repair Attempts. With these Repair Attempts, one spouse is asking the other for understanding. These Repair Attempts also seem to be delivered with varying levels of affect, but the spouses making the Repair Attempts put themselves in a vulnerable position by looking for understanding and acceptance from the other. During a disagreement about her husband's work schedule, Pilar uses a Self-Disclosure to explain her side of the conflict while implicitly asking for understanding, "It's just that I've been feeling really lonely lately." With the Tooting Your Own Horn Repair Attempt, understanding is asked for more explicitly:

Dan: You have to admit I've been a lot better about calling you from work, haven't I? [Tooting Your Own Horn]

Pilar: Yes, you have. I really appreciate how you've done that for me.

Responses to Repair Attempts

As seen in this last example, the effectiveness of a Repair Attempt is most evidenced by the spouse's response. In fact, the responses to Repair Attempts seem to be the key to classifying different types of couples and identifying specific dynamics of couples' interactions. Taking the last interaction as an example, Pilar's re-

TABLE 14.2

Descriptions of Responses to Repair Attempts

Response	*Description*
Positive	
Repair	A repair attempt by one spouse that is immediately followed by a new repair attempt made by the second spouse.
Accept	A positive acknowledgement of a repair attempt.
Reassure	A statement of encouragement or comfort following a repair attempt.
Resolve	An effort to formulate a plan or come to a solution for the topic of conflict.
Laugh and Smile	A smile or laugh that is positive in nature that does not include mocking or derisive laughter.
Neutral	
Back-channel	Nodding and "mm-hmm" in response to the speaker.
Neutral	Information exchange.
Disagree	A difference in opinion not accompanied by hostile affect.
Negative	
Ignore and Interrupt	A complete lack of acknowledgement of the previous repair attempt.
Reject	Overtly negative response to a Repair Attempt, including the Four Horsement.
Damage	A positive or neutral response that becomes negataive before the end of the speech turn.

sponse to Dan's Tooting Your Own Horn illustrates much about their relationship. First, Pilar recognized that Dan was asking for empathy; second, she demonstrated a willingness to give him the credit he needed. Another spouse might have responded differently, thus painting a very different picture of the interaction. In this way, responses are key to our coding and make up the second half of our Repair Attempts coding system. The coding system includes 11 responses that are classified as positive, neutral, or negative (see Table 14.2).

Positive Responses. In the midst of a heated conflict, it can be difficult not only to express positivity but also to recognize a partner's attempts to express positivity and to acknowledge those attempts in a positive manner. The Positive Responses to Repair Attempts do just that.

We consider a Repair Response the most positive type of response. As seen in the previous example, Pilar positively responded to Dan's Tooting Your Own Horn and made a point to appreciate his efforts with an Affection code, thus responding to his Repair Attempt with her own Repair Attempt. This interaction began to increase the positive affect during their conflict.

The remaining codes of Accept, Reassure, Resolve, and Laugh/Smile are further examples of Positive Responses. The Accept response reflects an active acknowledgement of the other's Repair Attempt, in the form of agreeing, or going along with the repair. The Accept response shows the listener as receiving the Repair Attempt in good faith. Reassures are efforts by one spouse to comfort and encourage the other following a Repair Attempt. A Reassure response might be found after a Self-Disclosure as seen in Ron and Judy's discussion of disagreement:

Judy: [Self-disclosure] I feel bad, but I haven't wanted to start planning our move because I'm scared that it's going to cause a rift between us.

Ron: Really? I'm surprised to hear that, but you don't have to feel bad about telling me. [Reassure Response].

Ron sensed Judy's vulnerability in making this statement. Then he went a step further; he addressed her feelings and reciprocated the positive behavior in their interaction.

Resolve responses were another type of response that we noticed helped de-escalate negative affect during conflict. Resolves occurred as one spouse began to work toward a solution to at least part of the issue as a result of the other's Repair Attempt. Sometimes the Resolves do not contain high levels of positive affect, but they seem to maintain the conversation at a level that prevents further negative escalation.

Neutral Responses. The Neutral category contains the Neutral and Disagree responses. Disagree is coded when a spouse differs in opinion regarding the statement made in the Repair Attempt. If the disagreement is about content only, it is coded a Disagree, but if it is accompanied with hostility or negative affect, it no longer is coded a Disagree response but falls into the category of Negative responses[DHB6].

Negative Responses. The negative responses are Reject, Ignore/Interrupt, and Damaged responses to Repair Attempts. Negative responses may indicate a lack of acknowledgement of the other spouse's Repair Attempts or an intentional disregard for a partner's efforts toward repair. The most openly negative response is the Reject response in which one spouse responds aggressively to the other's Repair Attempt. Reject responses involve the escalation of negativity after a Repair Attempt and generally include one of three "Four Horsemen of the Apocalypse": Contempt, Criticism, or Defensiveness (see Shapiro, Gottman, & Driver, this volume).

Ignore/Interrupt responses communicate a disregard for the previous Repair Attempt. To code Ignore/Interrupt, there must be no indication of acknowledgement of the Repair Attempt. The ignoring portion of the code includes active disregard of the spouse's comments or simply a continuation with a previous subject as if the Repair Attempt was never heard. Ignore/Interrupt may also be coded if a spouse interrupts the Repair Attempt.

As we began using the Repair Attempts coding system, we found that coders were running into difficulty coding certain patterns of Repair Attempts. Often it seemed that couples would begin a Repair Attempt in a positive manner, only to then destroy it with negativity.

In certain situations, it seemed it was just too difficult for spouses to "let go" of their negativity. We decided to call these lost Repair Attempts, "Damaged:"

Mary and Juan discuss her choice to return to school, and Juan illustrates a Damaged Repair Attempt.

Juan: I can see why it's so important for you to go to school, [Damaged Repair Attempt] but I don't think you're disciplined enough to get through it.

In this example, Juan began with the Understanding Repair Attempt, but in the same speech turn followed it up with negativity toward his spouse. The first half of Juan's statement displays his ability to repair, but the ensuing criticism canceled the intent of negative de-escalation. Often the speaker seems to be unaware of having damaged the Repair Attempt and then is surprised at the lack of Positive Response by the partner.

CODER TRAINING

To train coders in the Repair Attempts Coding System, we began an intensive 8-week course of 6 hr each week. Each coder was given a manual and asked to study three to four codes per week. The students were then shown videotaped examples in class of the specific codes they were studying. Once the students had seen several examples of the codes in class, they were asked to individually watch a marital conflict discussion and code what they had learned to that point. We began by training coders on the Repair Attempt codes, without the Response codes. After they became comfortable coding Repairs, we trained the coders on the Response codes and asked them to go back and code a Response code to each previously coded Repair Attempt.

For training purposes, we selected tapes that included multiple incidents of the codes they were learning during that week. The beginning of each subsequent training session began with a group discussion of observed moments and questions regarding the codes. The students spent approximately 3 hr per week in class, 3 hr watching tapes, and 1 hr studying the manual. By the end of each week, coders felt comfortable with the new codes.

Reliable coders were then given four tapes per week to code. Two independent observers coded each videotape for the first few weeks, and the kappas were checked at the end of each coding session. Later, 35% of the tapes were double coded. Those tapes that did not meet our kappa standard were recoded by both observers.

Once per month we randomly assigned coders to a master tape to check their reliability with that tape. This prevented coder drift and allowed us to maintain consistent standards. If a coder was not reliable with the master tape, we immediately assigned them to a retraining session. We were careful to let the student know that this was a natural part of observational coding and common to most coders. The training manual is available from the first author on request (atabares@u.washington.edu)

CODING PROCESS

To begin the coding session, coders are asked to watch the entire 15-min segment for conversation content and subtle behaviors without recording any Repair Attempts or Responses. Next, they watched it again to record the specific codes using a coding sheet and a pencil. The coders were allowed to pause the tape when they observed a code. They then recorded the time of the event or Repair, selected a Repair Attempt, and wrote down the first few words of the Repair. We included the first words so we could match any codes that may be off by 1 or 2 sec but were exact with the first words. To code in this way, it was necessary to rewind the tape often to capture the beginning of the Repair interaction. After the Repair was selected, the coder then recorded the other spouse's response to the Repair. Responses usually occur within 5 to 10 sec of the Repair. We are able to code 15-min segments in approximately 1 hr. More practiced coders averaged 45 min. New coders were given the guideline that each 5-min segment of the conflict discussion should take between 15 and 20 min. Setting goals for shorter coding segments seems to help coders not get overwhelmed and improve their overall coding time.

RELIABILITY

We used the Free Marginals Kappa (Kn; Brennan & Prediger, 1981; Dunn, 1989) to measure reliability between Repair Attempt coders. For each couple, the percentage of agreement between coders needed to be at a minimum of 75% for the Repair Attempts observed, before we would calculate the Kn. To measure the internal consistency of our coding system, we used the Cronbach alpha generalizability coefficients (Cronbach, 1972; Wiggins, 1977). In our case, the Cronbach alpha was used to assess how well a specific code measured variability between participants as opposed to variability between coders. The closer to 1.0, the more reliable the code, that is, the more the code is doing its intended work of discriminating between couples rather than discriminating between observers.

VALIDITY

Preliminary descriptive analysis of a subset of 16 couples indicates that happy couples' Responses to Repair Attempts are critical to understanding differences in communication patterns of happy and unhappy couples. Internal validity of the coding system has been measured by correlations between individual codes and marital satisfaction. In our initial subset of couples, we found that Wives' negative responses to Repair Attempts were negatively correlated to both the Husband's marital satisfaction ($r = -.628$, $p = .01$) and the Wives' marital satisfaction ($r = -.560$, $p .< .05$). We also explored which Repair Attempts were correlated to success and failure. The success of a Repair Attempt was measured as a Repair Attempt that was responded to with the Repair response. A failure was measured as a Reject response. For Husbands, the Defining the Conflict and Repair Question codes seemed to be the most successful. Both codes were significantly correlated with the Wife responding with a new Repair Attempt ($r = 7.12, p < .01$; $r = .650, p =$ 05, respectively). Wives, on the other hand, were successful using Humor as a Repair Attempt ($r = .884$, $p < .01$).

Two of the process-oriented Repair Attempts used by the Wives were unsuccessful with the Husbands. Monitoring the Conflict, ($r = .883$, $p < .01$) and Stop (r – $.544$, $p < .05$) were positively correlated with Reject responses by the husband. For Husbands, a different set of repair codes was positively correlated with Wife Reject responses, Compromise ($r = .542$, $p < .05$) and Request for Direction ($r = .544$, $p < .05$). With the full sample, we plan to compare the successful and unsuccessful responses to the affect codes measured by the SPAFF (see Shapiro, Gottman, and Driver, this volume) including those most predictive of divorce.

GENERALIZABILITY

The participants in the apartment laboratory were matched to the ethnic diversity of the Greater Seattle region which was 12% Asian American, 10% African American, 4% Hispanic American, 1% Native American and 73% European American. We have classified couples into one of three categories: happily married, unhappily married, or divorced. The classification of happy or unhappy was based on the MAT (Krokoff, 1987; Locke & Wallace, 1959) given to each of the partners at the beginning of the study. To understand the generalizability of Repair Attempts, we need to measure Repair across other types of dyads. A strength of our system is that it has been created based on an ethnically diverse sample of couples that represented a range of marital satisfaction. This system can be easily applied to happily married couples as well as highly distressed couples. We have yet to test whether Repair Attempts can be observed in familial or friendship dyads, but we do know repair-type behavior has been measured across development (Krohne, Pieper, Knoll, and Breimer, 2002; Tronick & Gianino, 1986; Zahn–Waxler, Radke–Yarrow,

Wagner, & Chapman,1992), indicating the possibility for using the system in a broader context.

CLINICAL UTILITY

The Repair Attempts observational coding system facilitates an objective view of couples' natural attempts to de-escalate negativity and increase positive affect during conflict interactions. This emphasis on naturally occurring, positive interaction identifies what the couple is doing well, rather than the usual focus on identifying problem areas in couple's communication. Clinicians can identify significant Repair Attempts during an interaction and point out positive aspects of couples' communication in an effort to increase these interactions. Hence, what we do is use a Repair Checklist (Gottman, 1999) to give couples to use as they discuss an area of disagreement.

Learning about Repair Attempts can also be a valuable tool for spouses to give each other credit. If a spouse recognizes a behavior as an attempt by the other to reduce negativity (rather than as a personal attack), the response may be more likely to be positive, thus de-escalating a negative interaction. For example, if one partner changes the subject during a negative interaction, this might be seen by the listener as an attempt to avoid communication and a disregard for the importance of the topic of discussion. Some therapists might even reject these behaviors and direct the couple to get back to the main point. From a Repair standpoint, however, a change of subject is a Stop repair. It is used as a signal that the person wishes to reduce emotional flooding and to take a break from negativity. If the partner allows the change of subject, both could potentially self-soothe and alter the course of the interaction. By reframing their perception of a Stop, the couple may gain a greater awareness of their physiology and communication style.

The Repair Attempt coding system can also be used as a measure of improvement in communication patterns during conflict in assessing the effectiveness of intervention studies. Repair Attempts that increase in frequency over time may be a sign of increased development of adaptive behavior patterns during conflict. An increase in positive responses to Repair Attempts might indicate each partner's increased awareness of the other's emotional state, which is critical to maintaining the marital friendship.

Surprisingly, damaged Repair Attempts may also provide the couple with important information about their interactions. Although damaged Repairs invalidate the positive portion of the comment, the Repair is still imbedded in the interaction. For many couples, it can be helpful to learn that they are already making Repair Attempts, if only they can inhibit the urge to follow-up with negative affect. This emphasis on strengthening their own positive behaviors may be easier to modify in therapy than teaching a completely new skill.

STUDIES USING THE CODING SYSTEM

The Repair Attempts coding system is currently being used in three studies in our lab. In this chapter, we have described the newlywed study which is currently being re-analyzed with the full sample of Repair Attempts data. One of the primary goals of this study was to understand the factors within marital interaction that predict divorce. Because the newlywed study is a 14-year longitudinal study, we plan to code Repair Attempts during the conflict discussions at follow-up intervals to measure changes in Repair Attempts across time. We would like to increase our understanding of the ongoing processes used by the couples who do not go on to divorce.

Another laboratory study we conducted was an intervention study that measured proximal change. In this study, participants completed a 15-min conflict discussion, following the same standardized procedure as the newlywed study. A 20-min intervention and a second 15-min conflict discussion then followed this first conflict discussion. The intervention involved a checklist of positive or negative attributes that each spouse used to describe the other. The participants in this study were categorized into four equal groups based on marital satisfaction measured by the MAT (Krokoff, 1987; Locke & Wallace, 1959). Happy couples were considered to be those in which both spouses scored one standard deviation above the mean on the MAT. The unhappy couples had at least one spouse who scored one standard deviation below the mean. And finally, there were two types of moderate groups; moderates with both spouses falling within one standard deviation of the mean and the mixed-moderates in which one spouse scored in the moderate level and the other scored in the happy category. This sample varied not only across marital satisfaction but also in the number of years married. We are currently beginning to use Repair Attempts to identify differences in these groups of couples.

Currently underway in our laboratory is a longitudinal study of the transition to parenthood. In this study, couples are followed for 3 years beginning at pregnancy and continuing until their children are 2½ years old. At each wave of the study, the couples are interviewed in their homes about their marriage, the pregnancy, the birth, and the transition to parenthood. Each visit also involves a 15-min conflict discussion that has a similar procedure to the previously mentioned studies, and after the baby arrives, parent-child interactions are also obtained. We are beginning to code these conflict discussions for Repair Attempts and also have plans to modify the coding system to measure Repair behavior between the parents and toddlers.

ACKNOWLEDGMENTS

This research was supported by National Institute of Mental Health grant MH3943 to John Gottman, Department of Psychology, University of Washington.

15

Coding Intimacy in Couples' Interactions

Marina Dorian and James V. Cordova
University of Illinois at Urbana–Champaign

Studying intimacy in marriage is both practically and theoretically important. Lack of intimacy is one of the most frequent complaints of couples seeking therapy and is central to the personal goals of most people. At the heart of intimacy are the ways in which partners manage the emotionally challenging vulnerability inherent in close relationships. However, marital interaction research has focused almost exclusively on the behaviors that spouses exchange when attempting to resolve conflict (see Weiss & Heyman, 1997). Studying problem solving has proven to be remarkably productive. Research has consistently found that partners' problem-solving behaviors differentiate distressed from nondistressed couples (Gottman, 1994; Weiss & Heyman, 1997). Although problem solving appears essential to healthy marriages, recent research indicates an only modest association between such behaviors and changes in marital satisfaction, implying that other interpersonal domains may contribute substantially to marital health (Karney & Bradbury, 1995). The field, however, has limited knowledge of other domains of marital interaction (see, however, Pasch & Bradbury, 1998). Theoretically, intimacy processes should contribute substantially to marital health (Cordova & Scott, 2001). However, few efforts have been made to observe intimacy processes in marriage, and little is known about how these processes may differ between distressed and nondistressed couples.

THEORETICAL FOUNDATIONS

Despite widespread agreement that intimacy is an essential facet of marriage (e.g., Prager, 1995), researchers have found it a difficult phenomenon to define. Most thinking in the area has focused on defining the boundaries between what is and what is not intimacy. However, a comprehensive list of necessary and sufficient features differentiating intimacy from other constructs has proven to be elusive. In response, intimacy has been conceptualized as a "natural concept" in which the boundaries separating category members from nonmembers are necessarily "fuzzy" (Prager, 1995, p. 14). Scholars have lacked consensus about what the definition of intimacy is, in part, because it is difficult to specify the features of a natural concept. Intimacy has been referred to in terms of the proverbial elephant where "some researchers must feel some parts of the creature, whilst others probe other areas" (Acitelli & Duck, 1987, p. 306). Intimacy has been variously studied as self-disclosure (e.g., Jourard & Lasakow, 1958), as an interaction (Reis & Shaver, 1988), as an emotion (e.g., Sternberg, 1988), and as a type of relationship (Schaefer & Olson, 1981). Yet these categorical conceptualizations have (a) failed to resolve the structural fuzziness of intimacy, (b) divided the phenomenon of intimacy into several disparate parts lacking cohesion, and (c) failed to clearly postulate the process by which intimacy develops over time.

Our contention is that attempts to study intimacy as a category defined by its formal characteristics have resulted in a premature focus on the products of an interpersonal process, and have missed the forest for the trees. Alternatively, we view intimacy as a process in which behavior vulnerable to interpersonal punishment is reinforced by the response of the other partner. Thus, one shifts the epistemological focus from the problem of "fuzzy boundaries" between categories to the process of development over time. The goal of a unifying theory of intimacy should be to explicate a process, grounded in empirically verified basic psychological phenomena, that integrates all the facets of intimacy into one developmental whole.

Intimate Events

Cordova and Scott (2001) conceptualized intimacy as a process emerging from events in which behavior vulnerable to interpersonal punishment is reinforced by the response of another person. This two-component sequence is called an intimate event. Interpersonally vulnerable behavior is defined as behavior that has been associated with response-contingent punishment by others in a similar interpersonal context. A person learns what classes of behavior will likely result in punishment by (a) engaging in that behavior and being punished, (b) observing someone else being punished for engaging in that behavior, (c) being told that the behavior will be punished, or (d) experiencing punishment for a related behavior.

Vulnerability can be placed on a continuum, from behavior associated with only rare or mild punishment, to behavior associated with frequent or severe punishment. The vulnerability of any specific behavior will vary from person to person depending on their individual history.

The second component of the intimate event is the reinforcing response. By definition, the reinforcement of vulnerable behavior increases the probability of that behavior occurring again in similar contexts. The probability of interpersonally vulnerable behavior occurring again increases principally in relation to those contexts that are functionally or formally similar to those within which the behavior was previously reinforced. For example, if Jack confided to Jill about his insecurities regarding his future career, and Jill reinforced that behavior by validating and normalizing his fears, then Jack should become more likely to engage in that behavior with Jill (and similar others) in the future. Intimate events, therefore, beget the probability of future intimate events between specific pairs of actors. The occurrence of the first intimate event sets in motion a process that, unless derailed, will inevitably develop into an intimate partnership.

Suppressive Events

Interpersonally vulnerable behavior can also be punished. If Jill mocks Jack's insecurities, Jack will be less likely to confide in her and others like her in the future. Such suppressive events interfere with the process of intimate partnership formation by maintaining a low probability of future vulnerable behavior. Our contention, however, is that suppressive events are an inevitable aspect of any developing partnership. As vulnerable behavior increases in frequency and variety, inevitably some vulnerable expressions will be punished, whether intentionally or accidentally.

The development of an intimate partnership involves the accumulation of both intimate and suppressive events. As each event occurs, it is added to the couple's history, which can be represented at any point in time as a ratio similar to Gottman's (1994) positivity–negativity ratio. The more heavily the ratio is weighted toward intimate events, the more likely that vulnerable behavior will continue to occur and that the intimate partnership will be maintained. The more heavily the ratio is weighted toward suppressive events, the less likely that vulnerable behavior will continue to occur and the more likely that the intimate partnership will deteriorate.

Intimate Safety

Intimate partnerships with different ratios of intimate to suppressive events result in different affective climates. If the ratio consists of significantly more intimate than suppressive events, then the partners should describe their relationship as safer and more comforting than if the ratio consists of more suppressive than intimate events. We refer to the feeling of safety and comfort behaving vulnerably as intimate safety, and it is also assumed to be the principal feeling associated with the process of intimacy (encompassing related feelings such as closeness).

The current conceptualization of intimacy allows for the integration of the various components of intimacy through a developing operant process. Intimate events set a process in motion that leads to developing intimate partnerships characterized by an accumulating ratio of intimate to suppressive events and resulting in self-reportable feelings of safety or discomfort.

DEVELOPMENT OF THE CODING SYSTEM

We are interested in how spouses display intimacy through their interactions around issues that make them feel vulnerable. The initial challenge in studying intimate interactions was designing an interaction that would elicit interpersonal vulnerability. We settled on a task inspired by the work of L'Abate (1977) in which each partner was asked to share with the other a particularly salient time when that partner hurt his or her feelings. The sharing of hurts is consistent with the conceptualization of intimacy posited by Cordova and Scott (2001) in which vulnerable behavior is characterized as interpersonal behavior that, due to the individual's particular history, risks punishment by others. We propose that the quality of a couple's interaction around emotionally vulnerable topics has important implications for the overall quality of the relationship and for the depth of intimacy experienced by both partners.

The Intimacy Coding System (Dorian & Cordova, 1999) was created to code couples' behavior during the Hurt Feelings Interaction. We chose to develop a global rating system because, although the nature of intimate and suppressive events is sequential, it is unlikely that such real-world sequences occur in the precise behavior–behavior sequences sought in traditional sequential analyses. Instead, reinforcement of interpersonal vulnerability most likely emerges out of the ongoing transaction between partners as the conversation evolves. Essentially what should emerge is a sense that one partner's expressions of vulnerability were ultimately tolerated and validated versus a sense that they were rejected and invalidated. Traditional sequential analyses might miss this more qualitative character of the interaction by focusing too blindly on the search for one type of behavior immediately following the other at greater than chance levels. Our contention is that such tightly contingent sequences do not accurately represent the complex ways in which partners' interactions develop into those that genuinely reinforce vulnerability versus those that genuinely suppress it.

In addition, developing a coding system based on the assumed function of the observed behavior presents the sticky problem of assuming function based on form. In other words, what functions as vulnerable behavior and what functions to reinforce or suppress that behavior can theoretically vary from individual to individual. Ideally one would have observed the interpersonal history of each partner to determine which behaviors had been made vulnerable. In addition, the reinforcing or punishing function of a sequence of events would be determined by observing an increase or decrease in the target behavior over time within each individual couple. However, such ideals can never be met within the constraints of practical research. Therefore, for the purposes of this research, we made the concession of assuming function from form and defined our coding categories to capture those observable behaviors that one might reasonably assume to be vulnerable, reinforcing, or punishing.

Codes for the Intimacy Coding System were constructed through collaboration between the two authors. Initially, a sample of Hurt Feelings Interactions were observed to determine which behaviors could be reasonably defined as fitting the conceptualization of vulnerability, reinforcement of vulnerability, suppression of vulnerability, and intimate safety. An iterative process was followed in which definitions and examples of each code were developed, informally applied to subsequent tapes, modified, and then re-applied to subsequent tapes until both authors were satisfied with their utility for capturing the phenomena.

TASK AND SETTING

The setup of the Hurt Feelings Interaction required both partners to choose an instance in which the other hurt his or her feelings. Partners were given 15 min to talk about the first partner's hurt and then were given an additional 15 min to talk about the remaining partner's hurt. The order in which partners shared hurt feelings was chosen randomly. The partner whose hurt feelings were being discussed was labeled the speaker, and the other partner was labeled the listener. Speakers were coded for degree of vulnerability. Listeners in turn were coded for degree of reinforcement of vulnerability and degree of suppression of vulnerability. Finally, the couple as a whole was rated for overall level of emotional closeness (i.e., intimate safety).

As noted, to assure that interpersonally vulnerable behavior would occur during the interaction, we developed a task in which each partner was asked to remember a particularly salient time that his or her feelings had been hurt by the other partner. In keeping with the theory's focus on interpersonal vulnerability, the task was specifically designed to require partners to engage in behavior that risked punishment by the other partner. Topics for discussion ranged from hurt feeling about a partner going out with friends while the other was at home sick with the flu to a discussion about a past affair. The task presented a challenge to both the speaker and the listener, as the speaker was required to engage in interpersonally vulnerable behavior, and the listener was presented with a stimulus that could evoke either a suppressive response (e.g., defensiveness) or a reinforcing response (e.g., compassion). The task allowed observation of the comfort with which the speaker engaged in vulnerable behavior, as well as how that behavior was consequated by the partner.

DESCRIPTION OF THE CODING SYSTEM

Partners' interactions were rated for the discloser's degree of vulnerability, the responder's reinforcing response to that vulnerability, the responder's suppressing response to that vulnerability, and the overall closeness between the partners at the end of the interaction. Each variable was rated on a 5-point scale from 1 (*none*) to 5 (*extensive*).

Vulnerability

Vulnerability is defined as behavior that risks punishment by the partner. Vulnerable behaviors include such soft expressions as hurt, sadness, love, loneliness, insecurity, shame, disappointment, and so forth. Note that when one partner expresses his or her hurt in a hostile way, then he or she is less vulnerable than a partner who expresses his or her hurt in a soft way. Note that both the frequency and intensity of the expressed vulnerability is taken into account in the rating. Ratings are not based on the listener's response to the speaker's vulnerability.

Reinforcing Response to Vulnerability

When expressions of vulnerability are not responded to in a harsh manner, then we say that they are reinforced. Sometimes the mere absence of expected punishment can be reinforcing. But often, vulnerable behavior is reinforced positively. Examples include validation ("It's ok to feel that way"), apology, sympathizing, support, normalization ("I do that sometimes too"), active listening, admitting fault, clarifying the situation, and acceptance. Note that in this interaction, we are asking one partner to talk about the last time his or her feelings were hurt by the other partner. The listener may often interpret this disclosure as an accusation and initially respond defensively, only to soften up and apologize later. It is not necessary for a reinforcing response to occur directly following the vulnerable expression. The listener can respond in a punishing way at first and then as the interaction progresses, or he or she can become reinforcing of the initial vulnerable expression. Reinforcement and suppression are rated independently.

Suppressive Response to Vulnerability

If vulnerable behavior is punished, it decreases the chances of the speaker expressing such vulnerability in the future. A suppressive response is usually an expression of negative emotions such as being defensive, critical, invalidating, dominant, and intolerant. Other examples include anger, hostility, sarcasm, contempt, denial, blame, or counterblame. The listener can also be suppressive by withdrawing from the conversation. Note that a punishing response does not necessarily have to be delivered in an angry tone.

Closeness at the End of the Interaction

This code measures how close the couple appears at the end of the interaction compared to how close they appear at the beginning. In other words, coders make a judgement about the degree to which the interaction resulted in increased closeness between the partners.

CODER TRAINING

During the initial study, ratings were conducted by three trained female undergraduate psychology students and the first author (Dorian & Cordova, 2001). Ideally, the coding team should consist of both men and women to have input from both genders; however, only female coders were available for the initial project. Coders should be blind to couples' distress group. Coders are initially trained on a sample of pilot interactions. Coders practice rating sample tapes until they obtain reliability scores as measured by intraclass correlations above $r = .60$ calibrated against the first author's ratings. The training period lasts approximately 7 weeks and consists of weekly 2-hr coding meetings, with coders rating two 15-min sample interactions each week. Coders require approximately 45 min to rate each interaction. Overall, coders spend about 4 hr a week learning the coding system. Once coding begins, weekly calibration meetings are held to maintain consistency. A coding manual is available by request from the authors. Other lab groups should be able to train themselves simply using this manual. "Gold standard" tapes have yet to be developed, however; therefore, there is some risk that different labs will develop somewhat different rating standards.

CODING PROCESS

A typical coding session consists of first viewing a Hurt Feelings Interaction in its entirety. During this first viewing, the coder writes down whose hurt feelings topic is being addressed and what is the subject of the discussion. During the second viewing, the coder notes the behaviors being coded by jotting down quotes from the interaction. The coder then completes his or her rating by marking the single number on the scale best reflecting both the frequency and intensity of the behaviors. Rating each 15-min interaction takes approximately 45 min.

RELIABILITY

Inter-rater reliabilities were assessed on 25% of the interactions that had been randomly selected from a group of 32 distressed and nondistressed couples recruited through newspaper advertisements to participate in a marriage checkup (Cordova, Warren, & Gee, 2001; Dorian & Cordova, 2001). Coders were unaware of which tapes were used to calculate reliability. Intraclass correlations indicated acceptable inter-rater reliability (intimate event: $r = .64$; suppressive event: $r = .63$; closeness: $r = .61$; vulnerability: $r = .77$).

VALIDITY

Criterion validity was assessed by calculating correlations between the intimacy behavior ratings and the partners' self-reported intimacy (Dorian & Cordova, 2001). Two measures of intimacy were used. Intimate safety was assessed with the Intimate Safety Questionnaire (ISQ: Cordova, Gee, Warren, & McDonald, 2002) and a broader definition of intimacy was assessed using the Personal Assessment of Intimacy in Relationships (PAIR; Schaefer & Olson, 1981).

The ISQ is a 14-item self-report scale specifically designed to measure intimate safety. Items include the following: "When I am with my partner, I feel anxious, like I'm walking on eggshells," "I feel like I have to watch what I do or say around my partner," "I feel comfortable telling my partner things I would not tell anybody else," and "I feel comfortable telling my partner my likes and dislikes while we are making love." Respondents rate each statement on a 5-point scale from 0 (*never*) to 4 (*always*). Factor analyses support a single-factor interpretation of the ISQ. Internal reliability has been found to be adequate with alphas of .93 and .96 for men and women, respectively, and test–retest reliabilities over a 1-month period of .83 and .92 for men and women, respectively. On a sample of 60 married Midwestern couples, the ISQ has been found to be significantly correlated with the Personal Assessment of Intimacy in Relationships Questionnaire (Schaefer & Olson, 1981), particularly with the Intellectual Intimacy subscale ($rs = -.78$ and $-.73$ for women and men, respectively) and the Emotional Intimacy subscale ($rs = -.82$ and .80 for women and men, respectively), suggesting that the ISQ and PAIR are measuring very similar constructs. In addition, the ISQ is significantly correlated with the Global Distress Scale of the Marital Satisfaction Inventory (Snyder, 1979; $rs = -.72$ and $-.68$ for women and men, respectively), the Marital Status Inventory (Weiss & Cerreto, 1980; $rs = -.54$ and $-.43$ for women and men, respectively), and partners' attachment styles (Hazan & Shaver, 1987; $rs = .42$ and .43 with secure attachment for women and men, respectively). These results provide preliminary support for the ISQ's construct and criterion validity.

The PAIR was chosen as an alternative measure of intimacy because it is one of the most frequently used measures of intimacy. It is a 36-item measure designed to assess intimacy within five relationship areas (emotional, social, sexual, intellectual, and recreational). Items are assessed on a 5-point scale from 1 (*strongly agree*) to 5 (*strongly disagree*) and are summed to yield a total score with lower numbers indicating greater intimacy. Schaefer and Olson (1981) reported good split-half reliability ($r = .70$ to $r = .77$) and internal consistency (alphas $>= .70$).

For observed reinforcement of vulnerability, husbands' reinforcement of their wives' vulnerability was correlated with husbands' intimate safety and with both husbands' and wives' general intimacy. Wives' reinforcement of their husbands' vulnerability was correlated only with their own intimate safety (Dorian & Cordova, 2001). In general, it appears that observer ratings of partners' reinforcement of each other's vulnerability correspond to their self-reported feelings of intimacy. This should be the case if these types of intimate events genuinely result in greater feelings of intimate safety.

For suppression of vulnerability, the only correlation was between wives' suppression of their husbands' vulnerability and their own level of intimate safety, with greater degrees of suppression being related to lower levels of intimate safety. Thus, wives who reported feeling less safe with their husbands were also more likely to respond negatively to his vulnerable expression.

With regard to emotional closeness, the level of couple closeness observed following the wives' interactions was associated with both wives' and husbands' level of intimate safety and general intimacy The level of couple closeness observed following the husbands' interactions was associated only with wives' levels of intimate safety and general intimacy. Observed closeness appeared to be fairly robustly associated with both husbands' and wives' self-reported intimacy, suggesting that some significant component of partners' private experience of intimacy can be reliably observed in their public behavior.

With regard to level of observed vulnerability, the only association was between husbands' vulnerability and husbands' intimate safety. Contrary to prediction, however, this was a negative association. In other words, husbands who were seen to be engaging in more vulnerable behavior also reported experiencing less intimate safety. Interpretation of this finding is provided later in the chapter.

The strength of the correlations among the intimacy behaviors vary. The strongest appear to be (a) negative correlations between reinforcement and suppression, (b) positive correlations between wives' reinforcement of husbands and the observed closeness of both husbands and wives, and (c) a negative correlation between wives' suppression of husbands' vulnerability and observed closeness during husbands' interaction. Thus, as expected, partners who reinforce vulnerability more tend to suppress it less, and how close partners appear to be corresponds with whether they are generally reinforcing or suppressing of each other's vulnerability.

GENERALIZABILITY

The sample used to create and test the Intimacy Coding System was relatively homogenous in terms of ethnicity (92% White) and socioeconomic status (mostly middle class), limiting generalizability to more diverse populations. In general, the system should generalize well across populations as the principals of reinforcement and punishment of vulnerability are universal. However, it is likely that exactly which behaviors are interpersonally vulnerable and which responses are reinforcing or punishing will vary to some degree from individual to individual and from population to population. It remains an open question, however, to what degree such individual variability will result in lawful differences between ethnic or socioeconomic groups.

CLINICAL UTILITY

The Intimacy Coding System consists of a few well-defined codes that can be assessed in real time. The setup for the Hurt Feelings Interaction can be done either formally outside of a regular session or informally as part of an ongoing session. Therapists can make their own ratings relatively quickly. Current and future research should inform therapists about aspects of the couples' interaction that are particularly clinically relevant. For example, it appears that husbands who can easily think of and discuss incidents in which their feelings have been hurt tend to have higher levels of relationship distress. It may be that incidents where their feelings are hurt do not become particularly memorable to husbands until they become genuinely unhappy in the relationship. Therefore, therapists should consider that couples in which husbands readily talk about past hurts may be particularly vulnerable and that resolving those hurts may be particularly important to the couple's continued stability.

STUDIES USING THE CODING SYSTEM

In the initial study (Dorian & Cordova, 2001), the coding system was used to examine the intimacy interactions of distressed and nondistressed married couples. Thirty-two married couples participated in The Hurt Feelings Interaction and completed questionnaires measuring intimacy and marital distress as part of a study on the effectiveness of a brief couples intervention (Cordova et al., 2001). Husbands' mean age was 42 years ($sd = 12.2$), and wives' mean age was 39 years ($sd = 10.3$). Mean length of marriage was 11.3 years (range = 6 months to 40 years, $sd = 11.5$). The mean number of children was 1.2 ($sd = 1.2$). Husbands had completed an average of 16.9 years of education, and wives had completed an average of 16.3 years.

Marital distress was measured using the 43-item Global Distress Scale (GDS) of the Marital Satisfaction Inventory (MSI; Snyder, 1979). Scores are based on provided *T*-scores (Snyder, Wills, & Keiser–Thomas, 1981) such that individuals can be classified as moderately distressed, severely distressed, or nondistressed. Partners scoring below 50 were placed in the nondistressed group, and those scoring over 50 were placed in the distressed group.

Gender Effects

Husbands and wives were classified as distressed or nondistressed separately, given that partners sometimes did not agree on their distress status. *T*-tests revealed that wives exhibited more interpersonally vulnerable behavior than husbands.

Intimate Events

Although theoretically it is the ratio of intimate to suppressive events that determines the couple's intimate safety, our analyses consider these variables separately because a ratio could not be constructed from what is essentially an ordinal rating scale. Given that all between-group hypotheses were directional, one-tail tests were conducted. Analyses were conducted separately for husbands and wives. *T*- tests revealed that nondistressed husbands reinforced their wives' vulnerable behavior more than did distressed husbands. In addition, the wives of nondistressed husbands reinforced vulnerable behavior more than the wives of distressed husbands. Thus, intimate events occurred more frequently in the interactions involving nondistressed husbands than in those involving distressed husbands.

T-tests between distressed and nondistressed wives revealed that nondistressed wives reinforced their husbands' vulnerable behavior more than distressed wives. The husbands of nondistressed wives, however, did not reinforce their wives' vulnerable behavior more than did the husbands of distressed wives.

Suppressive Events

The wives of distressed husbands suppressed more of their husbands' vulnerable behavior than did the wives of nondistressed husbands. Distressed husbands themselves, however, did not suppress more of their wives' vulnerable behavior than did nondistressed husbands.

Distressed wives suppressed their husbands' vulnerable behavior more than did nondistressed wives. However, distressed wives did not have their own vulnerable behavior suppressed more than did nondistressed wives.

Emotional Closeness

Nondistressed husbands and their wives demonstrated more closeness than did distressed husbands and their wives. Similarly, nondistressed wives and their husbands demonstrated more closeness than did distressed wives and their husbands.

Interpersonal Vulnerability

There was no difference between the vulnerable behavior of nondistressed and distressed husbands. There was also no difference in vulnerable behavior between the wives of nondistressed and distressed husbands. Similarly, there was no difference in the vulnerable behavior of nondistressed and distressed wives, or between the husbands of nondistressed and distressed wives. It is possible that the demands of the hurt feelings tasks resulted in equivalent levels of vulnerability in both groups. In other words, because partners in both groups were required to talk about hurt feelings, the amount of observable vulnerability was roughly the same regardless of distress level. However, it is also possible that genuine differences do exist in the levels of naturally occurring vulnerability of distressed and nondistressed partners when they are free to choose whether to expose vulnerabilities to each other.

Intimate Safety

Nondistressed husbands reported greater intimate safety than did distressed husbands. Nondistressed wives also reported greater intimate safety than did distressed wives.

Taken together, these results suggest that studying intimacy processes in marital interactions can contribute to our knowledge of marital distress. In general, intimate and suppressive events appear to reliably distinguish between distressed and nondistressed partners. Nondistressed partners appear to reinforce their spouses' interpersonal vulnerability more readily, thus theoretically ensuring high levels of intimacy in the relationship. Distressed partners, however, appear to more consistently suppress their spouses' interpersonal vulnerability, ensuring low levels of intimacy and the continued erosion of marital quality.

Interestingly, it appears that how wives respond to their husbands' vulnerability is reflected in both their husbands' satisfaction and in their own marital satisfaction. On the other hand, although nondistressed husbands facilitated more intimate events than distressed husbands, these behaviors were not related to their wives' marital satisfaction. These results may indicate a genuine phenomenon in which wives' behavior toward their husbands' vulnerability has a more consistent influence on their husbands' marital satisfaction than husbands' behavior toward their wives' vulnerability has on their wives' marital satisfaction. Alternatively, the hurt feelings task may have capitalized on women's greater facility with emotional statements (Gottman, 1994), thus biasing the task toward more consistently detecting wives' roles in the intimacy process over husbands' roles. Husbands may have an impact on their wives' marital satisfaction through facets of the intimacy process occurring primarily outside of verbal conversation. If this is the case, then the verbal nature of the hurt feelings task may preclude our ability to observe those facets through which husbands influence their wives satisfaction and intimate safety. In sum, that wives' behavior differentiated between distressed and nondistressed husbands, but husbands' behavior did not differentiate between distressed and nondistressed wives, may indicate that (a) how wives respond to their husbands' vulnerability is more lawfully related to husbands' relationship satisfaction than how husbands respond to their wives' vulnerability, or (b) the verbal nature of the task may have made wives' contributions to their husbands' marital satisfaction more readily observable.

The results also suggest that feelings of safety and closeness are integral to marital health. Nondistressed partners not only report experiencing greater feelings of intimate safety than distressed partners, but actually appear visibly closer than distressed partners. Theoretically, that sense of closeness and safety results from being openly vulnerable with the partner and being reinforced for that vulnerability more often than punished for it.

The results also suggest that partners who feel a greater degree of intimate safety are also more likely to facilitate intimate events (to reinforce the other person's vulnerability). In other words, the safer that both husbands and wives felt behaving vulnerably with each other, the more likely they were to reinforce their partner's vulnerable expression of hurt feelings. In addition, it appears that the less safe wives feel being vulnerable, the more likely they are to suppress their husbands' vulnerable expressions. The current data imply that the likelihood that a person will facilitate intimate or suppressive events is itself a reflection of current feelings of intimate safety.

In addition, the current results suggest that even the most private component of the intimacy process (intimate feelings) involves readily observable public manifestations. Results were fairly consistent in suggesting that partners who rated themselves as experiencing greater feelings of intimate safety also tended to be rated by observers as more visibly emotionally close.

Finally, the current results suggest that husbands who feel higher levels of intimate safety may actually have more difficulty talking about hurt feelings with their wives than husbands who feel lower levels of intimate safety. There was a negative correlation between husbands' reported intimate safety and husbands' vulnerability, and a trend for distressed husbands to demonstrate more interpersonally vulnerable behavior than nondistressed husbands. Thus, not only does it appear that husbands in general engage in fewer vulnerable behaviors than wives, it appears that husbands in healthier marriages engage in less vulnerable behavior than husbands in more unhealthy marriages. It appears both from the current data and from informal observation of the videotapes that nondistressed husbands have a remarkably hard time thinking of and talking about a time when their wives hurt their feelings. Speculatively, it may be that talking about hurt feelings is a very vulnerable and consequently rare type of behavior for husbands. Such behavior may therefore only come to strength under unusual circumstances, such as when a relationship has become so distressing that instances of hurt feelings are readily available and profound enough to warrant talking about as a type of problem-solving attempt.

The study has several limitations. First, the sample size was small, and, therefore, the power to detect differences and associations was limited. Second, the current data are cross-sectional, so the findings do not address the directionality issue. One cannot know if the partners are distressed because they have low intimate safety and more suppressive events, or if their being distressed has led them to engage in more suppressive events and become distant. Finally, the intimacy task did not appear to be as gender neutral as desired. Given these limitations, however, the study provides an initial foray into theoretically driven observational research of the intimacy process that may facilitate further research into this important phenomenon.

ACKNOWLEDGMENTS

This study was supported in part by the University of Illinois at Urbana–Champaign Research Board.

16

Looking in the Mirror: Participants as Observers of Their Own and Their Partners' Emotions in Marital Interactions

Marc S. Schulz
Bryn Mawr College

Robert J. Waldinger
Harvard Medical School

In this chapter, we present a method for enabling participants in couple interactions to provide ratings of their own and their partners' emotional experience during their interactions. At the core of this method is a video recall technique in which participants review a videotape of their couple interactions to cue their memories and are then asked to report what they were feeling and what they perceive their partners to have been feeling during the interactions. In this chapter, we illustrate how we have used this technique to obtain participants' ratings of their overall positive and negative feelings throughout their interactions, as well as self- and partner-ratings of the intensity and quality of specific emotions during key affective moments of their interactions. We have applied this methodological approach to laboratory-based couple interactions, but the general method is applicable to any type of couple or family interaction that can be videotaped.

THEORETICAL FOUNDATIONS

Emotion and its regulation have been widely identified as key determinants of couple well-being and stability (e.g., Gottman, Coan, Carrére, & Swanson, 1998). Because emotion consists of interconnected subjective, behavioral, and physiological responses that shift rapidly (Gross, 1998; Schulz & Lazarus, in press), it presents significant measurement challenges for the researcher. Addressing these challenges is a crucial step toward improving our understanding of the ways that emotional experience, expression, and regulation combine to shape marital quality and stability.

Much progress has been made in the development of coding systems that capture fleeting behavioral and expressive elements of emotion (e.g, Specific Affect Coding System, SPAFF; Gottman, McCoy, Coan, & Collier, 1996; Waldinger, Schulz, Hauser, Allen, & Crowell, in press). In addition, a number of researchers have successfully employed strategies for capturing streams of psychophysiological data (e.g., heart rate) that have been linked with emotional experience in couple interactions (e.g., Levenson, Carstensen, & Gottman, 1994; Levenson & Gottman, 1985). Methods to study participants' subjective experience of emotion in marital interactions are less well developed. Yet studying emotion without gathering information about participants' subjective experience leaves an essential source of data untapped. This is especially true when attempting to learn about how people regulate emotion. What one feels and what one shows to others can be quite discrepant, and these discrepancies may reveal much about strategies for managing emotional arousal.

The measurement of subjective experience relies on participants to remember and represent accurately their experience using words or some other tool of communication (Nisbett & Wilson, 1977; Rosenberg & Ekman, 1997). Obtaining reports of participants' experience in the middle of an interaction is likely to disrupt the natural flow of the interaction, and for this reason, researchers have turned to retrospective methods for recalling key aspects of experience. These methods must address two important challenges to validity (Stone, 1997): limitations in the accuracy of retrospective recall, and the tendency of individuals to distort their memories and reports of affective experiences when these experiences make them uncomfortable (e.g., when one is not comfortable acknowledging feelings of sadness). By replaying videotapes of participants' interactions to cue their memories and allowing them to rate their emotional experience during the interactions as they view it, our approach attempts to minimize inaccuracies that result when participants are asked to recall experience over extended periods of time (Thomas & Diener, 1990). The concrete "evidence" of the videotape and the minimal time available for processing (due to the demand created by continuous rating) help reduce bias but are unlikely to eliminate it fully.

In developing our video recall strategy, we had to decide which aspects of emotion to measure. Researchers disagree about the best way to characterize emotions and emotional experience (Stone, 1997). Some investigators advocate dimensional approaches that emphasize global qualities such as valence (positive vs. negative), intensity and arousal level, or dominance (e.g., Feldman, 1995; Russell & Mehrabian, 1977; Yik, Russell, & Barrett, 1999). Other researchers focus on discrete emotions such as sadness and anger, each of which is believed to have unique qualities or implications. The latter approach is represented in a series of studies by Gottman and colleagues (Gottman, 1994; Gottman, Coan, Carrere, & Swanson, 1998), who found that specific forms of negative affect, such as criticism and contempt, rather than overall negative affect, are particularly deleterious to marital health. We designed an approach to rating participants' emotional experience that incorporates aspects of both the dimensional and discrete emotions perspectives. Second-by-second fluctuations in emotional intensity and valence are captured, along with variation in the specific types of feelings (e.g., anger, sadness) that partners experience during affectively significant moments.

DEVELOPMENT OF THE CODING SYSTEM

Our approach builds on a video recall strategy first employed in marital interaction research by Levenson and Gottman (1983). In their studies, participants used a rating dial to provide continuous reports of affective experience on a single positive–negative dimension while watching a videotape of their marital interaction. Subsequent studies have established the validity of this approach and of similar video recall procedures for obtaining reports of affective experience (e.g., Gottman & Levenson, 1985; Ickes, Stinson, Bissonnette, & Garcia, 1990; Levenson & Ruef, 1992; Rosenberg & Ekman, 1997; Thomas, Fletcher, & Lange, 1997).

We modified the mechanical aspect of the Levenson and Gottman (1983) rating dial by using a slide device rather than a rotary dial. In our device, a small knob rides a channel in the top face of a rectangular box that is 3 in. wide and 10 in. long (see Fig. 16.1 for the face of the box). The knob moves across an 11-point scale that is similar to Gottman and Levenson's (1985) original affect rating scale. Like theirs, our scale ranged from *very negative* to *very positive* with a neutral point in the center. The anchors and bars signifying intensity of positive affectare color coded in blue whereas the negative side is red. The knob is attached to a series of mechanical springs and pulleys that return the knob to the center point ("neutral") if released and that apply increasing tension as the participant moves it further from the center in either the positive or the negative direction. This increased tension provides feedback to the participant about the knob's positioning. Partici-

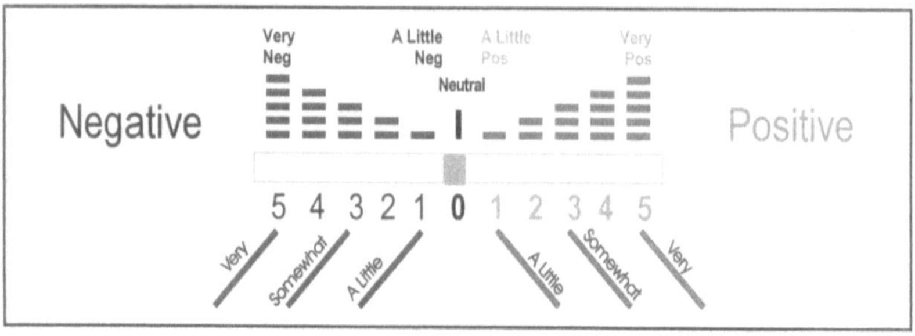

FIG. 16.1. Affect slide.

pants' ratings of the positivity or negativity of their overall emotional experience may be linked with other data that can also be obtained continuously over time, such as psychophysiology variables and observational measures of behavior.

We were interested in combining this coarse measure of affective experience with a more differentiated measure during affectively significant moments. The strategy we pursued was inspired by earlier work by Regina Rushe (as described in Gottman, 1994) and Sally Powers and colleagues (e.g., Powers & Welsh, 1999) that used questionnaires to rate short epochs within the interaction. Like Rushe, we chose to focus in depth on those moments rated as most affectively intense by the participants themselves. We might have chosen affectively intense moments in any of a number of ways, such as selecting the epochs with the strongest physiological response or those with the most intense emotional expression as rated by trained observers. We chose to let participants' affect slide ratings define which moments were most emotionally intense for two reasons: We wanted to rely as much as possible on participants' own perspectives of their emotional experience during the interactions, and we wanted to be able to examine potentially meaningful discrepancies between subjective experiences and other indices of emotional intensity such as physiological arousal and observed expression. We therefore focused on what we term High Affect Moments (*HAM*s)—those epochs of the marital interaction identified by the participants themselves as most emotionally negative or positive. We sampled both positive and negative moments to examine differences in behavior, physiology and reported experience across these poles of affective experience.

Our decision to select 30 sec as the duration of each HAM segment was informed by two primary considerations. We wanted a segment of sufficient length for participants to be able to orient themselves to that particular part of their interaction and to form an accurate judgment of their emotions during that segment. At the same time, we did not want a segment that was too long and likely to contain multiple significant emotional events that would be inappropriately collapsed in a summary set of ratings. Mindful of the need to limit the burden on our participants, we asked them to watch and rate four negative HAMs and two positive HAMs in addition to using the affect slide to rate the entire interaction. This set of compromises resulted in a useful combination of continuous ratings on a single positive–negative dimension and a more differentiated set of ratings of specific emotions for a sample of the most emotionally intense epochs.

TASK AND SETTING

Our procedures were developed specifically for a laboratory-based couples study, but the approach is applicable to any couple interaction that can be videotaped. In our study, we used a variation on the classic revealed differences paradigm (e.g., Gottman, 1994) to initiate marital interactions. We first used a structured procedure to help husbands and wives independently identify an incident in the month or two preceding the laboratory visit in which their partner did something that frustrated, disappointed, upset, or angered them. Participants were then asked to speak into a microphone to tape record for their partners a brief description of what their partner did that concerned them. The couple was then brought together to talk about the identified incidents. The order in which the incidents were discussed (husband's or wife's) was counterbalanced across couples. Couples were instructed as follows:

> You may have discussed these events before, but even if you have, we would like both of you to talk about your experience of the event, including your thoughts and feelings, and see if you can come to a better understanding of what happened. We'd like you to talk about this for 8 minutes. I will come back and knock on the door when the time is up.

The couple then played the tape recording of the spouse describing the first incident.

DESCRIPTION OF THE CODING SYSTEM

The items on the emotion questionnaire used during the HAMs were selected to represent at least two dimensions of negative affect that we have found useful in previous research on couple interactions: vulnerable emotions, such as sadness and fear, and more aggressive emotions, such as anger and contempt (Waldinger et al., in press). In addition, we selected items to capture a single positive emotional dimension indicative of pleasant engagement. Because we were particularly interested in the experience and regulation of negative emotions, 13 of the 16 specific emotions that we incorporated are negative emotions. Nine of the items from the Negative Affectivity scale of the Positive and Negative Affect Schedule (PANAS; Watson, Clark, & Tellegen, 1988) are represented directly or in modified form (e.g., we use "irritated" rather than "irritable"). Only "scared" was not incorporated because "afraid"—another item from the PANAS—captured highly similar content. To these nine items, we added three items found to be important in predicting marital quality and stability in past research—"disgusted," "critical," and "defensive" (Gottman, 1994). We also added "sadness," which is not included in the PANAS but which we felt was an important negative emotional experience to capture in the context of couple relationships. Finally, we incorporated three items to capture affectively salient positive aspects of couple relationships—"happy," "close to my partner," and "supported/validated."

CODER TRAINING

The only training required for the participants is instruction in the operation of the affect slide and how to complete the HAM emotion reports.

CODING PROCESS

Our video recall procedure consists of two phases. In the first phase, participants view the videotape of their interaction and use the affect slide to rate continuously their negativity–positivity during the interaction. In the second phase, the participants rate their and their partners' emotions during the six HAM segments. The recall procedure can be done with both partners simultaneously or independently with each partner. We have used the procedure effectively both ways, and the decision about what approach to use can be based largely on the particular demands of a study's overall protocol. If spouses do the recall procedure as a couple, researchers should take precautions to insure that spouses will not see each others' ratings and will not comment on the interactions during the recall session. We place a screen between the two partners when we have them do the recall simultaneously.

Video Recall Phase I: Affect Slide Ratings

The affect slide, which is equipped with a potentiometer, yields voltages that vary linearly with the position of the knob.[1] We used a basic psychophysiology system—the PowerLab from AD Instruments equipped with Chart software—to digitize this electrical signal and to make continuous recordings of the ratings synchronized with the time code on the videotape.

Participants are told that they will watch a videotape of their discussion and use the rating slide to indicate how they were feeling throughout the conversation. We tell participants that most people have a range of feelings during the discussion and that the purpose of the rating slide is to help us understand how their feelings changed over the course of their interactions. They are told that the center of the slide

[1]The exact voltage researchers utilize should only be influenced by the range of the equipment being used to convert the electrical signal into digital information. In our case, the voltages varied between –2 and +2 volts.

represents feeling neutral ("not feeling positive or negative"), the right side feeling positive, and the left side feeling negative. They are given examples of what we mean by positive and negative feelings and are told that moving the slide further away from the center indicates increasingly strong feelings. We show them that the slide naturally goes back to the neutral position if the knob is released and tell them that we would like them to hold the knob in the position that indicates the intensity of their feelings for as long as they have that intensity of feeling. Finally, they are encouraged to practice with the affect slide and to ask any questions about the procedure.

Video Recall Phase II: High Affect Moments (HAMs)

Based on participants' ratings from the first phase of the video recall procedure, we select six HAMs for each couple. For each spouse, we select, from each discussion, the 30-sec segment of interaction in which the spouse experiences the most negative feelings. This procedure yields a total of four negative HAMs (two rated as most negative by her and two by him) when we utilize a protocol with two discussions. We also select, for each spouse, the most positive 30-sec segment across all of the interactions, yielding two positive HAMs for the couple. The six HAMs are presented to the couple in the order of their occurrence on the tape.

Participants are told that we used their affect slide ratings to choose certain moments of their interactions for them to view again so we can ask them more about their and their partners' feelings and thoughts. (We also ask them about their thoughts during the HAMs using a second set of questions that inquire about intentions or attributions the participant may have had in the interaction. We comment briefly on this aspect of our video recall procedure in the final section of this chapter.) Participants are reminded that we are interested in their feelings and thoughts during the interaction rather than in the moment as they watch the videotape. They are given a self-report version of the HAM questionnaire and are encouraged to look at the items and ask any questions they might have. Participants are asked to rate how much they felt each emotion or emotionally charged state using a 7-point scale with 1 representing *not at all* and 7 representing *very much*. They then watch the first HAM segment and use the questionnaires to rate their feelings and thoughts. They are then handed a partner version of the HAM questionnaires and shown the same HAM segment again. This time they rate their partners' feelings and thoughts. This procedure is repeated for the remaining five HAM segments.

RELIABILITY

A principal components analysis with varimax rotation was conducted on the HAM self-report responses of 100 husbands and wives[2] (from 50 couples de-

[2]Although not all of the participants who contributed data to these analyses were married, we refer to the partners in all relationships as husbands and wives to facilitate fluency of writing.

scribed later in the Generalizability section). Four meaningful factors emerged. Factor 1, which we labeled *Hostile*, included the following aggressive negative emotion variables: anger, irritated, disgusted, upset, hurt, critical, and defensive. The vulnerable negative emotions fell into two separate factors, which we labeled *Sad* and *Anxious*. Factor 2, *Sad*, included sad, guilty and ashamed. The fourth factor, labeled *Anxious*, included afraid, nervous, and jittery. Factor 3, which we labeled *Happy*, included happy, close, and supported. Scale scores for the HAM factors were derived by taking the mean of all items on each factor . Alpha coefficients for the four scales ranged from .74 to .80, indicating good internal reliability.

The distinctions among the negative emotions identified in this study are similar to those obtained in a study of untrained judges' ratings of emotion in marital interactions (Waldinger et al., in press) and to those derived from a principal components analysis of similar self-reports of emotional experience in marital interactions (Gottman, 1994). In both studies, a negative factor characterized by hostile emotions and the active expression of criticism or irritation was distinguished from negative emotions that reflect more vulnerability such as fear and sadness. Participants in our studies of marital interactions distinguished between sad and anxious emotions within the larger category of vulnerable negative emotions. The Sad and Anxious scales correlated at .41, indicating an overlap of only 16.8% of their variance. Further study of these factors with larger samples will provide more information about the relative merits of making this finer distinction among negative vulnerable emotions. At this time, we suggest that researchers interested in more specific questions about anxiety and fear versus sadness and guilt (e.g., researchers studying couple violence where a partner's fear rather than overall distress is an important consideration) would be well served to use the four-factor solution. Others not interested in this distinction can collapse across these two negative vulnerable emotion factors. In the analyses we present in this chapter, we include findings only for the combined Sad-Anxious scale.

VALIDITY

In this section, we present evidence for the validity of the following: (a) the affect slide ratings of positivity–negativity, (b) the characterization of the 30-sec HAMs as emotionally salient positive and negative moments, and (c) the HAM emotion reports of specific emotions.

Affect Slide

Previous research has provided evidence that the feelings reported by participants using affect rating devices during a video recall correspond to feelings experienced during the interaction itself. Gottman and Levenson (1985) have shown that affect ratings from a video recall procedure were related to neutral observers' coding of participants' affect and that they discriminated high conflict from low conflict interactions. Moreover, they have provided evidence that suggests that participants' recall is enhanced partly because they "relive" their initial affective experiences while viewing their videotapes.

In our study, as in the Gottman and Levenson (1985) study, couples who engaged in a discussion of a problem area or negative event in their marriage reported feeling slightly negative on average during the discussion. In our study, there were also links between the mean affect slide ratings and couples' marital satisfaction as measured by the widely used Short Marital Adjustment Test (Locke & Wallace, 1959). Women who reported experiencing more positive feelings during their laboratory interactions were more satisfied with their marriages, $r = .29, p < .05$. Men had a similar positive relationship but this correlation was not statistically significant, $r = .18$, *ns*.[3]

High Affect Moments

The next question we address is whether it is appropriate to characterize the HAMs as emotionally significant segments of interaction. Fig. 16.2 shows the continuous affect slide ratings reported by one couple after viewing their 8-min discussion of a recent upsetting incident. The gray boxes represent the 30-sec HAMs in which the husband and the wife reported experiencing their most strongly positive and most strongly negative feelings. In our study, during the negative HAMs, husbands' and wives' affect slide ratings were about a standard deviation higher than their average ratings, indicating a substantially more negative experience during these epochs. In contrast, husbands and wives reported feeling more than a standard deviation more positive than their average ratings during their positive HAMs. These data strongly suggest that the HAMs were emotionally significant and also show that the difference in positivity–negativity between the positive and negative HAMs is of a sufficiently large magnitude (more than 2 standard deviations) to indicate that we have captured significantly different affective experiences.

HAM Emotion Scales

Participants' more differentiated reports of emotion using the HAM emotion scales were consistently linked to their ratings of overall negativity–positivity across the six HAMS. For women, there were moderate to strong correlations (r's ranged in magnitude from .42 to .66) between their mean affect slide ratings during the HAMs and their reports of hostility, sadness-anxiety, and happiness on the HAM emotion scales. For men, similar links were present although not as consistently

[3]Interestingly, in Gottman and Levenson's (1985) study, a similar gender pattern was evident. The affect slide ratings of the wives in their sample were consistently more strongly linked with marital satisfaction than the husbands' ratings.

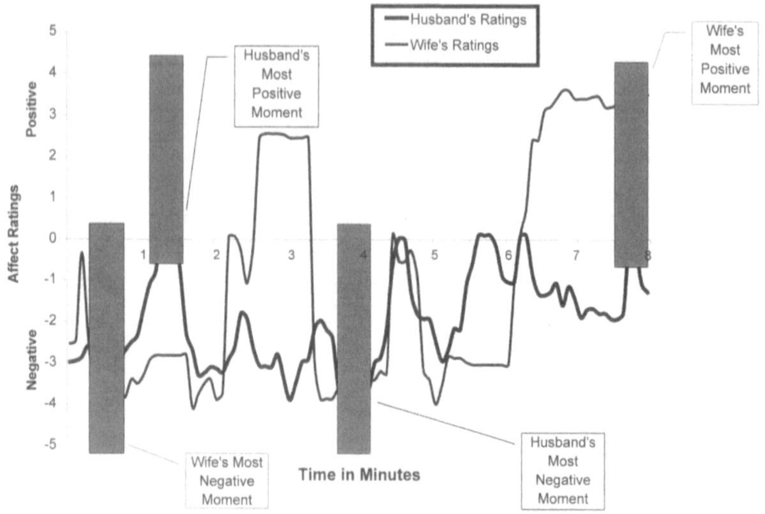

FIG. 16.2. Affect ratings and high affect moments (HAMs) for one couple.

strong. Men's affect slide ratings during the HAMs were significantly correlated with their reports of hostility and happiness (at a trend level), but not their reports of sadness-anxiety.

The consistency across reporters in ratings of participants' specific emotions during the HAMs provides additional support for their validity. Moderate to strong correlations between participants' self-reports of specific emotions during the HAMs and their partners' reports of the participants' specific emotions indicate an impressive degree of overlap across reporters (r's ranged from .40 to .66). The degree of overlap between reporters is particularly impressive when one considers that participants are rating their partners' emotions during the HAM periods when they themselves are likely to be experiencing strong emotions, which could impair their ability to infer accurately their partner's emotional experience.

External Indices of Validity

Additional evidence for the validity for the HAM emotion scales is provided by the pattern of links between participants' HAM emotion scales and measures of trait hostility, depressive symptomatology, and marital satisfaction (see Table 16.1). Men's and women's reports of their angry feelings, but not their happy feelings, during the HAMs were correlated with their total hostility scores on the Multidimensional Anger Inventory (MAI; Siegel, 1986). The HAM scales linked in

TABLE 16.1

Correlations Between High Affect Moments (HAM) Emotion Scales and Criterion Variables

	Wives			*Husbands*		
Criterion Variables	*Hostility*	*Sad-Anxious*	*Happy*	*Hostility*	*Sad-Anxious*	*Happy*
MAI Hostility	$.42^{**}$	$.24^{+}$	−.20	$.27^{+}$	$.26^{+}$	.10
Beck Depression	.18	.20	−.02	.29*	$.37^{**}$	.03
Couple Marital Satisfaction	−.53	$-.41^{**}$	$.36^{*}$	$-.53^{***}$	$-.25^{+}$	$.38^{**}$

$^{+}p < .1$. $^{*}p < .05$. $^{**}p < .01$. $^{***}p < .001$ (all two-tailed).
Note. HAM Emotion Scales were averaged for each participant across six HAMs.

expected ways with reports of depressive symptomatology as indexed by the Beck Depression Inventory (BDI; Beck & Steer, 1987). Sadness-anxiety and hostility were linked with depressive symptoms whereas happiness was not related to depression. All of the HAM emotion scales were linked, in the direction expected, with couples' reports of their marital satisfaction based on the widely used Short Marital Adjustment Test (Locke & Wallace, 1959).[4] Reports of anger during the HAMs, which accounted for 28% of the variance in marital satisfaction, were the most predictive for men and women.

GENERALIZABILITY

The analyses presented in this chapter were performed on data from the first 50 couples participating in a study of couple communication in the metropolitan Boston area. This community-based sample drew heavily from two groups at risk for emotionally volatile and unstable relationships—those with a recent history of domestic violence and those in which one or both partners had a history of abuse in childhood. The mean age for men and women was about 32 years. Nineteen couples (38%) were married and 31 (62%) were living together in a committed relationship for a minimum of 1 year. Among those living together but not married, couples had been living together an average of 2.7 years at the time of the study ($SD = 2.4$). The ethnic makeup of the sample was 72% White, 17% Black, 5% Hispanic, and 6% other. Sixty percent of participants had completed bachelor's or

[4]For ease of presentation, we present analyses using the average Short Marital Adjustment Test score of the husband and wife in each couple. Analyses using each partners' reports sedparately produced almost identical findings.

more advanced degrees, 11% had 2 or more years of college, and all but 4% of participants had finished high school. The mean family income for the couples was about $45,000. The men and women in the sample reported a range of marital satisfaction with a mean level of 107 ($SD = 25.7$) on the Short Marital Adjustment Test. We have successfully used the same procedures with a more stable, community-based sample of married couples in the Philadelphia metropolitan area. We recognize that there is likely to be variation in participants' personal understanding of the meaning of the affect slide ratings and the HAM emotion reports, and that this variation may be systematically linked to cultural or developmental differences.

An important strength of the video recall procedures we have presented is that they allow participants to tell experimenters what they were experiencing during couple interactions. We believe that these procedures can be effectively adapted to include children or other family members (see Powers & Welsh, 1999, for an excellent example with adolescents). In our experience, participants find the video recall tasks interesting but somewhat tiring. Researchers considering using these video recall techniques therefore need to consider the costs in terms of time and burden for the participants, as well as the financial expense of the specialized equipment required to implement the affect slide procedure.

CLINICAL UTILITY

The emotion recall procedures we have reviewed in this chapter provide an effective mechanism for communicating to others the internal subjective experience of individuals during interactions. This subjective experience can be difficult for any observer, including a clinician or a spouse, to access. The recall procedures could be adopted by a clinician to assess the dynamics of a couple's relationship and the individual experience of a particular partner (see Kagan, Krathwohl, & Miller, 1963, for an example). For most participants, the recall tasks offer an unprecedented opportunity to see how they and their partners appear when discussing conflicts, and this, in and of itself, may have therapeutic value. When used sensitively, the video recall procedures could be utilized to help partners communicate to each other what they are experiencing during important interactions and what they perceive their partners to be experiencing.

A particularly useful application may be to highlight differences for couples between how one member of the couple feels and how the other perceives the partner to feel. For example, a wife may not understand why her spouse is not responding more sympathetically to the sadness she is experiencing. Using a video recall procedure to highlight the wife's feelings and the husband's perceptions of her feelings may provide critical information for the couple. Similarly, these procedures would help clarify for a clinician whether he or she was accurately perceiving a client's internal experience in a relationship. These procedures could be used without the affect slide equipment by having participants informally indicate which moments in a videotaped interaction were emotionally most intense for them. Participants in our studies have told us that they found the video recall task to be the most interesting part of our protocol, and they often report having learned something new about themselves, their partners, or their relationship. It is important to note, however, that a small minority of the more distressed couples in our study are clearly disturbed by what they see when they watch their videotapes.

These procedures could also be used as part of a larger assessment strategy to examine the efficacy of a couples' intervention. The possible limitations of any of these clinical applications are similar to the time and financial costs identified earlier in research applications. It is also possible that some clinicians and some patients would find these tasks too intrusive or cumbersome for effective clinical work.

STUDIES USING THE CODING SYSTEM

The two emotion recall procedures we have described in this chapter are central pieces in two linked studies (one based in Boston and one in Bryn Mawr) that are focused primarily on identifying key emotion and emotion regulation processes in normal, distressed, and violent community-based couples. In both studies, we are employing an observational coding system, based on the variables in the SPAFF (Gottman, McCoy, et al., 1996), in which naïve raters use their intuitive judgments of emotion to code emotional expression (Waldinger et al., in press). The observations of emotional expression provided by this coding will allow us to provide additional information about the validity of our emotion recall procedures. Physiological data on heart rate, respiration, and electrodermal activity during the couple interactions are also being collected so that we can address important questions about coherence among the three principal channels of emotion—experience, expression, and physiology—that may shed light on important elements of emotion regulation and its links to couple functioning and satisfaction. For example, we have used our observational coding and affect slide ratings to identify moments in which participants appear to be suppressing their emotional experience—that is, expressing less emotion than they report experiencing (Andrew, 2001; Furterer, 2001). These "suppression moments" are linked to signs of increased physiological arousal (Zimmerman, Schulz, & Waldinger, 2003).

During the video recall of HAM moments, we ask participants to report on their goals, attributions, and appraisals in addition to their emotions. Personal goals (e.g., wanting to understand my partner) and appraisals (e.g., thinking that my partner was trying to make me angry) are critical elements of a cognitive mediational view of emotion (e.g., Lazarus, 1991; Schulz & Lazarus, in press) that has strongly shaped modern perspectives on emotion. We believe the video recall procedure we have outlined is particularly useful for obtaining accurate reports of individuals' goals and appraisals that shape the experience and regulation of emotions.

In a series of preliminary studies, we have used the HAM emotion scales to derive an index of empathic accuracy (e.g., Ickes et al., 1990; Thomas et al., 1997).

Empathic accuracy was operationalized as the accuracy of a partner's ratings of how intensely his or her partner felt specific emotions. Using a self-report measure of borderline personality traits (Inventory of Personality Organization; Lenzenweger, Clarkin, Kernberg, & Foelsch, 2001), we found that women who reported more signs of borderline personality traits were less accurate in rating their partners' emotions than women with lower levels of these traits (Waldinger, Moore, Chivers, Heaney, & Schulz, 2001). In another study, we found that women with a history of childhood sexual abuse were more likely to misread their partners' negative emotions than women without abuse histories (Heaney, Waldinger, Schulz, & Moore, 2000). We are also examining how the presence of intimate partner violence may influence empathic accuracy and how our observational measures of emotional expression are linked with our index of empathic accuracy.

ACKNOWLEDGMENTS

This work was supported by grants from the Solomon Asch Center for Ethnopolitical Conflict at the University of Pennsylvania and the Bryn Mawr College Faculty Research Fund to the first author and National Institute of Mental Health Grant K08 MH1555 to the second author. The authors gratefully acknowledge the technical assistance of Andrew Gerber and Rich Willard in the creation of the affect slide. We also thank Cindy Moore and Elizabeth Andrew for their roles in data collection and management of the data set.

IV

Information Processing

17

The Thematic Coding of Dyadic Interactions (TCDI): Observing the Context of Couple Conflict

Dina Vivian
State University of New York at Stony Brook

Jennifer Langhinrichsen–Rohling
University of South Alabama

Richard E. Heyman
State University of New York at Stony Brook

The Thematic Coding of Dyadic Interactions (TCDI–3rd, Vivian & Langhinrichsen–Rohling, 1995) is a global observational coding system designed to capture underlying dimensions of couple conflict, namely, the core individual needs displayed by each partner. It includes seven interpersonal content themes related to different aspects of emotional attachment and interpersonal power. It also includes four process themes associated with need negotiation in close relationships.

The TCDI was an outgrowth of our prior observational work with micro-analytical coding systems, such as the Rapid Marital Interactions Coding System (RMICS; Heyman & Vivian, 1993; Vivian, Heyman, & Langhinrichsen–Rohling, 1993; see also the chapter in this volume by Heyman) and the Kategoriensystem fur Partnershaftliche Interaktion (KPI; see Hahlweg in this volume, as well as Hahlweg, Reisner, et al., 1984; Vivian & O'Leary, 1987), as well as global coding systems such as the Specific Affect Measure (SAM; Smith, Vivian, & O'Leary, 1990; Smith, Vivian, & O'Leary, 1991). In addition, our clinical experience in treating discordant and partner abusive couples provided invaluable information about the complex nature and context of communication in close relationships. We concluded that a multilevel approach to coding couple communication was needed. This approach would combine overt behavioral coding with information about the content and context of the conflict. In sum, the TCDI was designed to complement existing coding strategies by providing a method for coding contextual and thematic information about the observed conflict.

THEORETICAL FOUNDATIONS

Observational studies of communication in intimate relationships during the past two decades have, for the most part, adopted topographical approaches to dyadic conflict (for a review, see Heyman, 2001). This work has repeatedly demonstrated that dyadic hostility and negative communication are trademarks of distressed relationships. However, sex differences in partners' communication during conflict have also been documented (for reviews, see Baucom, Notarius, Burnett, & Haefner, 1990; Heyman, 2001). For example, using overt behavioral coding systems, women have often been characterized as more critical and negative during conflictual marital interactions than have been men.

More recently, researchers have used these traditional behavioral coding systems to examine the characteristics of partner violent relationships. An understanding of conflict patterns in these couples is important for several reasons. First, two-thirds of discordant dyads seeking couples therapy are likely to report some physical aggression in the past year (O'Leary, Vivian, & Malone, 1992). Second, although both partners tend to report bidirectional use of physical aggression, women report greater negative impact from the violence than do men, suggesting a gendered aspect to dyadic violence that needs to be understood behaviorally (Cascardi, Langhinrichsen–Rohling, & Vivian, 1992; Vivian & Langhinrichsen–Rohling, 1994). Third, couple conflict has been identified as the most frequent antecedent of partner violence in clinic couples (Cascardi & Vivian, 1995), and as one of the strongest correlates of family violence in normative studies (Straus & Sweet, 1992).

Contrary to original expectations based on feminist theories of wife abuse (e.g., Dobash & Dobash, 1979; Yllo, 1993), observational communication studies have consistently shown that physically aggressive couples are characterized by reciprocal and contingent negativity (e.g., Burman, Margolin, & John, 1993; Cordova, Jacobson, Gottman, Rushe, & Cox, 1993; Jacobson et al., 1994; Margolin, John, & Gleberman, 1988). In addition, mutual, rather than unilateral, verbal hostility appears to be a stable conflict style of physically violent couples during their 1st year of marriage (Vivian, Mayer, Sandeen, & O'Leary, 1988).

However, the coding systems used to generate these findings have been topographical (i.e., based on the form of the overt behavior). Furthermore, codes have often been applied without concern for gender, despite the fact that gendered features of couples' conflict (e.g., context and function) are important to understanding the meaning of emitted behaviors. It is our contention that this likely leads to inaccurate and, perhaps, deleterious interpretations of data regarding the interpersonal dynamics of violent marriages. This concern is often echoed by feminist analyses of intimate relationships and woman abuse (e.g., Dobash & Dobash, 1979; White, Smith, Koss, & Figueredo, 2000). For example, although women may be as verbally hostile as, or even more hostile than, their partners during conflict, their hostility may occur because they are feeling helpless about changing the inequity in their relationships. We came to believe that skills-based models of close relationships used in isolation are at risk for depicting a gender "uninformed," or even a gender "insensitive," view of dyadic struggles. Thus, the TCDI was conceived as a tool to facilitate an analysis of the contextual and functional aspects of gender-specific communication between intimate partners in violent relationships. It was expected that the TCDI would add important contextual information that is not coded by traditional micro-analytic coding strategies.

The choice of interpersonal content areas to be included in the TCDI was determined by a review of the research on partner violent men. For example, Dutton (1988), using standardized videotaped situations, found that partner violent men, compared to nonviolent men, were more "sensitive" (i.e., reported that they would be likely to use a violent response) to themes of abandonment and engulfment. Holtzworth–Munroe and Anglin (1991), using similar standardized audiotaped stimuli, found that partner violent men, compared to nonviolent men, produced less competent responses to situations of challenge or humiliation, abandonment, and rejection. Finally, using questionnaires, researchers have found that partner violent men, compared to nonviolent men, are higher on partner dependence (e.g., Murphy, Meyer, & O'Leary, 1994), psychological abuse (e.g., coercive control, debasement, attacks to the partner's sense of self; Marshall, 1994), and narcissistic entitlement (e.g., Hamberger & Hastings, 1988).

The TCDI also extends work on "hidden agendas" by Gottman and colleagues (e.g., Gottman, 1979; Gottman, Notarius, Gonso, & Markman, 1976). Hidden agendas were operationalized as the unstated metamessages that often underlie couples' conflict. Krokoff (1990) reported that hidden agendas were more common in women who were fearful of being criticized or put down by their male partners and in men who were disgusted with a contemptuous partner whom they could not intimidate (Krokoff, 1990).

On the basis of our prior observational work, we were convinced that core interaction themes provided important clues to the context of couples' communication.

Further, we proposed that both dyadic distress and partner violence could be better understood by including thematic coding (see Epstein & Baucom, 2002, for a similar argument). In particular, integrating insights from cognitive–behavioral or psychological models of marital aggression (e.g., O'Leary & Vivian, 1990), sociopolitical analyses of wife abuse (e.g., Yllo, 1993), studies of power processes in intimate relationships (e.g., Gray–Little & Burks, 1983), and empirical work, we believed that "love," "respect," "interdependence," and "power/control" would be frequent core thematic issues associated with conflict in intimate relationships and with domestic violence.

Finally, by designing the TCDI to identify potential gender-specific issues in couples' communication, we believed that the TCDI could broaden the focus of couples' observation from overt behavior to the gendered context that may elicit particular overt behaviors. This could pay dividends for theory by allowing researchers to overlay feminist, sociopolitical explanations (e.g., Yllo, 1993), as measured by the coded core themes, on traditional topographical coding.

In the section to follow, we describe the various coding categories of the TCDI and the progression of efforts that shaped the final version of the system (TCDI–3rd, Vivian & Langhinrichsen–Rohling, 1995).

DEVELOPMENT OF THE CODING SYSTEM

Content and Process Themes

Pilot studies led to progressive refinements of an initial set of coding categories and criteria to increase the TCDI's conceptual clarity and reliability. The resulting system, the TCDI–3rd, includes several thematic issues underlying dyadic conflict, including individual and interpersonal "needs" related to (a) Love/Affection/Closeness; (b) Commitment/Fidelity; (c) Respect/Importance; (d) Empowerment/Equality; (e) Equity; (f) Partner's Role In Maintaining One's Public Image; and (g) Emotional/Behavioral Autonomy. Additionally, because dyadic conflicts often revolve around themes regarding interpersonal processes rather than (or in addition to) content areas, we targeted several process themes, as follows: (h) Resisting Change; (i) Prevailing or Controlling; (j) Invalidating/Pathologizing; and (k) Validating/Supporting.

Seeking a Change Versus Complaining About a Problem

It became important to be able to differentiate individuals who are seeking a change from their partners (e.g., asking for a greater level of togetherness) from those who are just complaining about a problem (e.g., dissatisfaction with amount of time apart). Therefore, each theme was coded according to two presenting forms, namely, (a) Seek A Change In X versus (b) Feel Unhappy About Or Complain About X.

One-Up Versus One-Down Distinction

An examination of recurrent coders' disagreements suggested that observers' inconsistencies were often associated with the degree to which observers viewed the partners' thematic communication during a conflict "in isolation" (i.e., specific to that conflict only) versus being reflective of dyadic power dynamics underlying the relationship and reflected in that specific area of discord (i.e., "in context"). Thus, we felt it was important that observers view interpersonal themes underlying dyadic conflict as embedded in (defined by and defining at the same time) the broader context of the relationship.

As a first step toward operationalizing this abstract concept and translating it into coding rules, in the TCDI–3rd we instructed the coders to observe the dyadic context of the conflict, namely, content, process, and function to identify (a) each partner's role during the conflict, and, if possible, infer (b) each partner's position of "power" in that specific problematic area of relationship before coding any of the themes as "present." Rules for the determination of One-Up or One-Down positions of each partner in the specific area of discord were informed by several lines of work, including investigations of power processes in relationships (Gray–Little & Burks, 1983) and interaction-based (family systems) approaches to the study of interpersonal relationships (e.g., the Relational Communication Control Coding System; Rogers & Farace, 1975). However, we found that, although this additional coding consideration moderately increased the reliability of about half of the TCDI codes, it did not increase coders' consensus regarding the themes Respect/Empowerment, and Prevail/Control. Thus, although this coding consideration has been retained in the TCDI–3rd, future research is needed to determine its importance.

TASK AND SETTING

The TCDI was initially designed to code laboratory-based, time-limited (10–15 min) videotaped or audiotaped conflictual interactions within intimate dyads. Our data were obtained in the following way. First, placed in an office-like setting, the partners were seated facing each other. The videotaping was conducted via two cameras (each centered on one partner), and occurred in the absence of the experimenter. Partners were asked to fill out the Dyadic Adjustment Scale (DAS; Spanier, 1976) prior to the interaction and, with the experimenter's assistance, they identified the top area of disagreement in their relationship by choosing among the first 15 items of the DAS (e.g., "We always disagree regarding money"). After choosing a topic, the partners were directed to discuss (and possibly resolve) the problem for 15 min "as they would in their typical discussions/conflicts at home." Although we made the a-priori assumption that any area of relationship disagreement was by definition a "dyadic" problem, each couple was free to focus on either partner's main gripe.

DESCRIPTION OF THE CODING SYSTEM

Content and Process Themes

As described earlier, the TCDI–3rd includes seven content themes (1–7) and four process themes (8–11). Definitions of the thematic codes, as well as examples of partners' statements that may reflect the presence of each theme, follows.

1. Love, Affection, and/or Closeness This theme includes requests for greater levels (or complains about inadequate levels) of love, physical affection, closeness or emotional sharing, time spent together, or sexual intimacy in the relationship. Examples of requests follow: "I want to spend more time with you;" "I feel unloved."

2. Commitment and/or Fidelity This theme pertains to whether the dyadic attachment, the relationship itself, or the expectation of sexual exclusivity in the relationship will continue and in what fashion. Issues of jealousy are also included here; for example, "I wish you would tell me that you really want to work at this relationship;" "I am jealous of your relationship with Allison. You seem to care more about her than me."

3. Respect and/or Importance This theme concerns the extent to which the target partner perceives his or her partner as failing to (a) contribute to his or her positive self-image and sense of importance, or failing to (b) support his or her self-esteem, self-worth, and personal achievements inside or outside the relationship. He or she may express feeling unimportant, disrespected, unappreciated, or not acknowledged in the relationship. Examples include, "You have to start respecting my needs and consider how I feel about things;" "You don't value my opinion;" "You are not interested in my accomplishments at work."

4. Empowerment and/or Equality Although conceptually similar to the Respect/ Importance theme, Empowerment/Equality includes issues specifically related to the power distribution in the relationship. The target partner perceives his or her partner as controlling and restricting his or her ability to make decisions, or limiting his or her activities or choices. The coder should infer that the target partner perceives himself or herself as being "one down" in this specific area of conflict or in the relationship. Examples follow: "You make all the decisions; it's always your way or no way. I never get things to be my way;" "It doesn't matter what I have to say, you always do what you want anyway, I have no say."

5. Equity Regarding Relationship Responsibilities This theme reflects discussions concerning the target partner's dissatisfaction with her or his part-

ner's degree of participation in relationship responsibilities or instrumental tasks (e.g., housework, financial responsibilities, child care, parenting, social functioning of the family, or labor). The target partner may appear overburdened with relationship or family responsibilities; for example, "You don't lift a finger when we have company, you just take a shower and show up;" "I have most of the housework to do and the children too. It's not fair and I can't stand it anymore."

6. Public Support This theme involves dissatisfaction with a partner's support of the target partner's public image. Discussions about the loss of self-image in front of others, or an overall sense of public embarrassment or humiliation due to one's partner's actions, are coded here. Examples include, "I wish you could, just once, stand up for me in front of your mother! You never support me around your family;" "You always disagree with me in front of others. I hate it."

7. Emotional and/or Behavioral Autonomy This theme concerns the target partner's dissatisfaction with the degree to which his or her partner (a) supports his or her individual needs outside of the relationship (e.g., to pursue individual hobbies, activities, or friendships), and (b) respects the target partner's emotional boundaries or the need for privacy and individuality. Examples follow: "I would like to register for an evening class [at the local college] and attend it alone. We do a lot together and I need to do this one thing just for myself;" "It seems as though you get upset when I make new friends. I feel like you always want me to be just with you, and it's too much for me."

8. Resist Change and/or Maintain the Status Quo This theme includes (a) refusing to negotiate a change during the discussion, (b) appearing to be unwilling to change, or (c) failing to take the partner's views into consideration. The target partner appears to be "one-up" in the specific area of disagreement (and, perhaps, in the relationship) and seeks to maintain this position during the conflict. This is a "passive" form of control, as the target partner is not actively trying to dominate the conflict or the decision making. Instead, she or he may counter-complain a lot, may give a myriad of reasons about why it is not possible for her or him to change, or may act defensively. Additionally, she or he may resist change by refocusing or shifting blame to her or his partner, or she or he may explicitly refuse to change; for example, "Give me a break, how could I have called you from the bar? I had no change, and thought I would be home soon. What is the big deal anyway?"

9. Prevail and/or Control The target partner acts as if she or he were the "queen or king of the castle." She or he may expect her or his partner to promptly anticipate and fully address her or his needs, wishes, and dreams

without regard for her or his partner's needs or wishes. The target partner may act as if she or he were entitled to have her or his views and standards govern the relationship. This is exemplified by active control strategies, both in the relationship and expressed during the interactions. Examples include, "If you love someone, you should always take their side, no matter what;" "I'm the one making the dough and I get to decide how we spend our money, let's not even talk about this."

10. Invalidate and/or Pathologize This theme is coded when the target partner displays a global negative view of her or his partner's personality, opinions, views or behavior. It includes negative conflict tactics such as "character-assassination," blaming the partner for the dyadic problems, dismissing the partner's needs, suggesting that the partner is stupid, mentally ill, or globally inept, or appearing to be totally unwilling to see things from her or his partner's point of view or to empathize with her or him. Examples include, "If it weren't for your problem with people, we wouldn't be discussing this now;" "You have no reason to feel that way;" "You're selfish just like your mother."

11. Validate and/or Support This theme involves expressing a positive view of the partner's personality, opinions, or behaviors. It also includes validating the partner by acknowledging the legitimacy of his or her needs, viewpoint, or empathizing with his or her feelings. Although not excluded, agreement with one's partner is not a prerequisite to validation and support or empathic responding; for example, "I see your point, and realize that I really hurt your feelings, I'm sorry about that;" "You're very good with the kids, you really do a lot with them."

12. No Theme and Other Target partner did not present any pervasive content or process theme. He or she may have hinted at issues, but did not present them clearly or frequently enough to warrant a rating throughout the conflict. In addition, thematic issues (content and process) not fitting the aforementioned categories are coded here.

Additional Coding Level. "Whose issue or gripe is it?" To further define the context of a dyadic conflict, we decided to extend the TCDI thematic coding by including a posthoc observer-based determination of which partner's gripe was primarily addressed during the conflict. The coder was asked to rate whether the gripe was (a) the man's, (b) the woman's, or (c) both partners' gripe.

CODER TRAINING

The first two authors developed this project during Jennifer Langhinrichsen–Rohling's postdoctoral training at the State University of New York at Stony

Brook. Several generations of coders, including graduate and undergraduate students at the Stony Brook Marital Therapy Clinic and at the University of Nebraska, underwent training and were certified as TCDI coders. Predictably, we found that coders who had prior experience with couples research and observational coding could be trained faster than could novices. Furthermore, graduate students were easier to train than undergraduate students. However, the most recent edition of the TCDI manual (TCDI–3rd, Vivian & Langhinrichsen–Rohling, 1995) includes enough detail and rule specificity to enable new coders to be trained with relative ease, under the supervision of criterion coders. At the Stony Brook Marital Therapy Clinic and the University of Nebraska, we found that advanced undergraduate coders with prior marital research experience reached acceptable levels of coding agreement within 12 to 14 weeks of training (based on about 9–10 hr of weekly involvement).

Training takes place by having coders watch a number of pilot tapes that have already been coded by the criterion coder(s). When intercoder and coder-criterion agreement improves, reliability is evaluated continuously through statistical approaches (e.g., Intraclass Correlations Coefficients and Kappa) until adequate levels across all TCDI codes are reached.

With regard to training materials, the TCDI–3rd manual can be obtained from the first or second author on request (dvivian@psych1.psy.sunysb.edu; jlr@usouthal.edu). However, we recommend that training be conducted under the supervision of certified TCDI coders.

CODING PROCESS

Coding Criteria

A coder initially observes the whole interaction without generating specific codes. While observing both partners concurrently, she or he is directed to keep in mind the following questions: "What is each partner trying to communicate, ask for, or complain about during this interaction? What is the main need that she or he is addressing during this interaction? What is the overall purpose, function, or goal of her or his communication?" Additionally, as described earlier, a number of coding considerations are included in this initial global observation (e.g., general gestalt of the conflict, content and processes, partners' power roles in the conflict and in that specific area of discord, whose gripe it is, function of each partner's communication during the conflict, etc.).

Next, the tape is divided into three equal segments (e.g., three 5 min segments for a 15-min discussion), and the two partners are concurrently observed again during each segment. At the end of each segment, each partner receives a rating of 0 (*theme is absent*) or 1 (*theme is present*) for each theme. In Table 17.1 we present an actual TCDI coding sheet.

TABLE 17.1

Thematic Coding of Dyadic Interactions (TCDI) Coding Sheet Coder #:__

Date Coded:______________________ Couple #:____________

CONTENT THEMES (Target partner is ***seeking a change*** [A] or ***complaining about ...*** [B]

Rating Scale:	0,1	0,1	0,1	0.3
Segment:	I	II	III	SUM
Partner:	H W	H W	H W	H W
1A. Seeking Love, Affection, and/or Closeness	__ __	__ __	__ __	__ __
1B. Feeling Unloved	__ __	__ __	__ __	__ __
2A. Seeking Commitment and/or Fidelity	__ __	__ __	__ __	__ __
2B. Feeling Insecure and Jealous	__ __	__ __	__ __	__ __
3A. Seeking Respect and/or Importance	__ __	__ __	__ __	__ __
3B. Feeling Unimportant and Disrespected	__ __	__ __	__ __	__ __
4A. Seeking Empowerment and/or Equality	__ __	__ __	__ __	__ __
4B. Feeling Controlled	__ __	__ __	__ __	__ __
5A. Seeking Equity regarding responsibilities	__ __	__ __	__ __	__ __
5B. Feeling unfairly burdened with responsibilities	__ __	__ __	__ __	__ __
6A. Seeking Public Support	__ __	__ __	__ __	__ __
6B. Feeling Publicly Humiliated and Unsupported	__ __	__ __	__ __	__ __
7A. Seeking Emotional and/or Behavioral Autonomy	__ __	__ __	__ __	__ __
7B. Feeling Engulfed and restricted	__ __	__ __	__ __	__ __
PROCESS THEMES				
8. Resisting Chanage and Maintaining Status Quo (appearing to be one up and maintaining this)	__ __	__ __	__ __	__ __
9. Seeking to Prevail or Actively Control	__ __	__ __	__ __	__ __
10. Invalidating and/or *Pathologizing* Partner	__ __	__ __	__ __	__ __
11. Validating and/or Supporting Partner	__ __	__ __	__ __	__ __
12. No theme	__ __	__ __	__ __	__ __
Whose issue was it? (Whose gripe was it overall?)			***H W***	***Both***

Note. Sum = Segments 1–111; H = Husband; W = Wife.

Final Global Rating: Combining Information About Frequency And Intensity

Two criteria are used in determining the ratings for each segment: frequency (i.e., estimated percentage time each partner spent talking about key issues during that segment of the interaction) and intensity (i.e., degree of both affective arousal and cognitive intensity expressed by the target partner while expressing the theme). Each criterion can be used separately, or combined to determine a final, global rating (0 or 1). Finally, the ratings for each segment are summed across the three segments, resulting in a 4-point index (0–3) for each TCDI theme, separately for each partner (see TCDI coding sheet in Table 17.1). However, the final 0 to 3 rating is allowed to reflect the coder's overall perception of the theme's frequency throughout the whole interaction combined with its emotional intensity or cognitive poignancy. Thus, the final global rating for each theme across the whole interaction represents a composite score.

RELIABILITY

Reliability evaluations of the TCDI codes were based on calculating several indices of interobserver agreement for each code. First, using the overall composite score (0–3), we calculated Intraclass Correlation Coefficients (ICC; Shrout & Fleiss, 1979). Second, after dichotomizing the overall composite score into theme absent (rating = 0) or present (ratings = 1–3), we calculated Kappa coefficients (κ; Cohen, 1960) and percentage agreements (%) for each theme, and for the additional coding of the category "Whose issue it is."

The evaluation of the TCDI–3rd reliability was based on the ratings of two masters-level coders, who coded the 15-min videotaped conflicts of 50 couples randomly chosen from those provided by couples participating in a larger study on partner abuse conducted by the first author and her colleagues. The overall population included discordant couples seeking marital therapy ($n = 205$) and a community control sample of happily married couples ($n = 51$); thus, reliability was evaluated in approximately 20% of the total sample. Reliability indices were as follows: (a) Love/Affection (ICC = .75; κ = .77; % = .95); (b) Commitment/Fidelity (ICC = .70; κ = .80; % = .99); (c) Respect/Importance (ICC = .57; κ = .53; % = .76); (d) Empowerment/Equality (ICC = .58; κ = .44; % = .87); (e) Equity (ICC = .78; κ = .88; % = .97); (f) Public Support (ICC = .72; κ = .39; % = .97); (g) Autonomy (ICC = .70; κ = .71; % = .97); (h) Resist Change (ICC = .84; κ = .69; % = .85); (i) Prevail/Control (ICC = .62; κ = .57; % = .86); (j) Invalidate/ Pathologize (ICC = .53; κ = .46; % = .73); (k) Validate/Support (ICC = .48; κ = .48; % = .75). Given the conceptual similarity between some codes, we also calculated reliability coefficients of the themes Respect/Importance and Empowerment/Equality, collapsed together (ICC = .72; κ = .57; % = .78), as well as Resist Change and Prevail/Control (ICC = .73; κ = .61; % = .80). Finally, interobservers' agreements for the TCDI–3rd category "Whose issue is it?" were as follows: male-focused (κ = .58; % = .86), female-focused (κ = .68; % = .84) and dyadic (κ = .31; % = .74). The overall pattern of agreements across the TCDI–3rd codes was satisfactory.

VALIDITY

As described earlier, the TCDI was initially designed to (a) evaluate the context of verbal dyadic conflicts associated with marital discord and partner violence, as well as, (b) to identify gender-specific issues associated with mutual verbal hostility in intimate relationships marked by discord and partner violence. It was also conceptualized as an instrument that would provide information at a level of analysis different from, and thus complementary to, that targeted by topographical and coding systems such as the RMICS. The extent to which the TCDI could indeed provide unique information about the context of couples' conflict was evaluated in a study comparing RMICS and TCDI–2nd coding of the same interactions. Results of this work, presented as part of a broader study by Vivian and Heyman (1994), are summarized next.

Two hundred and five couples seeking marital therapy and 51 community control (i.e., happily married) couples participated in this study. Based on both partners' reports about men's use of physical violence in the relationship, four groups of couples emerged, as follows: (a) Clinic Nonviolent (CNV), $n = 71$; (b) Clinic Moderately Violent (CMV), $n = 47$; (c) Clinic Severely Violent (CSV), $n = 87$; and (d) Community Controls (CC), $n = 51$. The TCDI–2nd codes included in this study were as follows: (a) Love/Affection, (b) Commitment/Fidelity, (c) Respect/Empowerment (in contrast to TCDI–3rd, in the TCDI–2nd the Respect/Importance and Empowerment/Equality were collapsed), (d) Equity, (e) Public Support, (f) Autonomy, (g) Resist Change, and (h) Prevail/Control. The TCDI–2nd code reliabilities were calculated using data from about 20% of the sample and ranged from ICC = .83 (Autonomy) to ICC = .58 (Commitment/Fidelity); the mean ICC across the eight codes was = .71. Micro-analytical coding was conducted with the RMICS (Heyman & Vivian, 1993; see Heyman's chapter in this volume for a description of RMICS).

The findings emerging from the Vivian and Heyman (1994) study suggest that the TCDI–2nd's discriminative validity for relationship discord and partner violence is moderate, as only three of the eight TCDI–2nd codes significantly differentiated the four groups with regard to discord status and, partially, partner violence. Specifically, the content theme Commitment/Fidelity was present more frequently in the conflicts of CNV partners ($M = .22$) than CC partners ($M = .01$). The themes Autonomy/Separateness and Resist Change characterized more strongly the CSV group ($M = .21$ and .75, respectively) than the CC group ($M = .01$ and .43). Whereas only a portion of the TCDI–2nd's codes were associated with marital discord and partner violence, most of the codes (five out of eight) yielded gender differences. Thus, the TCDI's discriminative validity for gendered aspects embedded in the conflicts of intimate partners is excellent. Specifically, women exhibited three content themes more strongly than did their partners: Affection/Togetherness (women = .37, men = .16), Equity Regarding Responsibilities (women = .37, men = .16), and Public Support (women = .41, men = .07). Conversely, men exhibited two process themes more often than did their partners. Resist Change (men = .98, women = .31) and Prevail/Control (men = .57, women = .39).

Interestingly, the theme Respect/Empowerment yielded a significant group by sex interaction, suggesting that this TCDI–2nd code may yield good discriminantive validity for both gender issues and relationship discord associated with dyadic conflict. Specifically, whereas men in the clinic groups and both partners in the community group did not differ on the frequency of the Respect/Empowerment theme (clinic nonviolent men = .48, moderately violent men = .67, severely violent men = .43, control men = .21, and CC women = .47), all groups of clinic women were more likely to complain about this area of dissatisfaction than were their partners (clinic nonviolent women = 1.3, moderately violent = 1.5, severely violent = 1.6), as well as more frequently than did control couples. All the results presented thus far did not change after controlling for participants' differences in relationship discord.

Thematic Coding Versus Topographical Coding

With regard to RMICS findings, all clinic couples expressed more frequent Partner Distress Maintaining Attributions and Hostility than did community couples. Further, both moderately and severely violent clinic groups had a higher frequency of Hostility than did the CNV group; conversely, community couples used Humor more frequently than did the clinic couples. Finally, partners in the CNV group emitted Self-Disclosures more often than CSV partners did. After controlling for levels of marital satisfaction, however, only the differences in Hostility and Self-Disclosure remained significant. With regard to gender differences, Hostility and Distress-Maintaining Attributions were more frequently emitted by women than by men. Women also emitted less frequent Acceptance than did their partners. These differences remained significant after controlling for levels of marital distress.

Overall, the findings from the Vivian and Heyman (1994) study underscore the fact that the two approaches to coding dyadic conflict provide useful and non redundant information about a number of important dimensions characterizing dyadic conflict. Of particular interest to us was the fact that the thematic content and process coding provided by the TCDI–2nd did yield a rich and gender-sensitive context for interpreting and understanding one of the most consistent findings in the observational marital literature; namely, the fact that women tend to be more verbally negative and hostile than their partners are during conflict, particularly women in discordant relationships. In fact, in considering conjointly the TCDI–2nd and RMICS findings, one could conclude that the verbal hostility during conflict expressed by women in a discordant couple relationship is likely to be associated with, and perhaps, born out of, their feelings of being disrespected and having low power in this relationship. However, pending further research, one cannot exclude other interpretations.

GENERALIZABILITY

Although, as described earlier, the TCDI's structure was shaped by task and setting specificity, we believe that the general nature of the interpersonal dimensions targeted by the system are likely to make it easily transportable to the observation and coding of other types of dyadic interactions, varying with regard to type of dyad (intimate vs. stranger), type of interpersonal event (disagreement vs. general need negotiation vs. positive discussion), and type of observational methodology (e.g., videotape, audiotape, or direct observation during therapy by a clinician). For example, some unpublished work from our group has shown that the TCDI–3rd can be reliably used to code partners' audiotaped descriptions of their relationship problems during an intake interview prior to entering couple therapy. We have also successfully used the TCDI to code 30-sec segments of couple conflicts and to code couples' discussions of their areas of agreement.

CLINICAL UTILITY

The TCDI provides information about couple interactions that can be easily translated into helpful assessment strategies and direct interventions. On the one hand, information based on a topographical level of analysis (e.g., RMICS-like observations) can help the clinician identify problematic communication skills presented by a couple. These skills can easily be targeted with communication-based training approaches. On the other hand, information about the function, relational context and gender specificity of communication skills displayed by partners during a conflict (i.e., TCDI-like observations) can help the clinician identify and address underlying dysfunctional attitudes or expectations held by partners, as well as inequitable relationship-marital contracts. For example, Vivian and Heyman (1996) described a clinical application of this multilevel observational approach to treating mild, bi-directional, partner violence in a conjoint therapy format.

STUDIES USING THE CODING SYSTEM

Langhinrichsen–Rohling, Heyman, Ehrensaft, and Seldar (1998) used a modification of the TCDI–2nd to code the conflictual and nonconflictual interactions of three types of early-married community couples (MaleViolent/Distressed, $n = 20$ couples; Nonviolent/Distressed, $n = 15$ couples, and Happy/Nonviolent, $n = 21$ couples). As the obtained results provide some additional information about the utility of the TCDI with different populations and tasks, this study is summarized next.

Data from both nonconflictual and conflictual communication tasks were analyzed with the RMICS and the TCDI. The only RMICS code to differentiate significantly among the three groups was Hostility. In both the positive and negative interaction tasks, men from the two distressed groups were more hostile than men in the Happy/Nonviolent group. Although this effect was also significant for women, there was a group by task interaction. In the negative task, women in the Male Violent/Distressed group were coded as most hostile, followed by women in the Nonviolent/Distressed group. Women in the Happy/Nonviolent group expressed the least hostility during conflict. In contrast, during the positive task, women in the Nonviolent/Distressed group were the most hostile, followed by women in the Male Violent/Distressed group. Women in happy and nonviolent relationships expressed virtually no hostility in the positive task.

Consistent with the Vivian and Heyman (1994) study, coding these same interactions with the TCDI yielded additional important information. The groups were significantly differentiated by the presence of particular negative themes in both the negative and positive interaction tasks. Partners in male violent relationships were significantly more likely to resist change than other partners. Partners in both types of distressed marriages were coded as feeling more disrespected than partners in happy relationships. Moreover, there was a significantly greater tendency for partners in distressed dyads to express a negative theme (i.e., feeling disrespected, seeking to prevail, resisting change) during the positive interaction task. These findings suggest the pervasiveness of these power-related interaction themes in unhappy relationships.

ACKNOWLEDGMENTS

Research presented in this chapter was supported by the National Institute of Mental Health (Grants R29MH44665 and T01MH19107). Preparation of this chapter was also supported by the National Center for Injury Prevention and Control, Centers for Disease Control and Prevention (Grant R49CCR218554–01).

The authors would like to express their deep appreciation to Christa Ayerle, a leading member of our research team at Stony Brook. During the course of 3 years, while working on her undergraduate Honor's Thesis and, subsequently, on her Master's Thesis, she spent countless hours observing and coding couple videotapes, training other coders, conducting reliability checks and assisting us in the development of the TCDI 1st, 2nd, and 3rd manuals. The TCDI–3rd uniquely reflects her contribution, particularly in the addition of the "one up" and "one down" coding consideration. Without her dedication, insightful feedback, endless enthusiasm, energy, and competent assistance, this project would not have been possible.

Last, we wish to also thank all the other coders who participated in the work described herein. Observational coding can be a challenging and taxing task for the observer. We are very grateful for all the patience, effort, and diligence that accompanied everyone's work.

18

The Relationship Schema Coding System: Coding the Behavioral Manifestations of Relationship Thinking

Laura J. Sullivan and Donald H. Baucom
University of North Carolina at Chapel Hill

The Relationship Schema Coding System assesses the behavioral manifestations of individuals' Relationship-Schematic Processing (i.e., the tendency to attend to and give relationship or emotional meaning to events that happen within and outside of an individual's romantic relationship). The coding system generally measures three dimensions of relationship processing: quantity, quality, and valence. The following example illustrates Relationship-Schematic Processing and highlights the utility of examining partners' processing styles:

> Judy feels neglected by her husband Stan because he does not talk to her when he gets home from work. Typically, he heads straight to the family room and turns on the television. Judy interprets Stan's behavior to mean that he does not value her enough to share the details of his day, and, subsequently, she feels neglected, foolish, and angry. Stan, on the other hand, is tired after work and does not want to talk about his day. He wants to leave his stress at the office and use home as his place to relax. At times, Judy attempts to coerce Stan into talking to her. He then becomes annoyed and frustrated that even his home is not relaxing. He does not understand why Judy cannot give him a few minutes alone to relax after work. He believes she blows the whole situation out of proportion.

In the aforementioned scenario, Stan and Judy process the same event (i.e., Stan coming home from work and turning on the television instead of talking to Judy) in different ways. Whereas Judy gives relationship meaning to the event (i.e., "He does not value me enough to share the details of his day."), Stan does not (i.e., he wants a few minutes alone to relax after work). Judy cannot believe that Stan does not see how his postwork routine impacts her and their relationship, whereas Stan is dismayed that Judy thinks his wanting to take a few minutes of quiet time has anything to do with their relationship. He just wants to relax, plain and simple.

The difference in information processing exhibited by Stan and Judy illustrates how partners can construe the same event quite distinctly. Although there is no single correct manner in which events should be cognitively processed, it likely is important for relationship success that partners recognize when events might have relationship meaning and when they seem unlikely to reflect on the relationship. Assuming, then, that reasonable relationship processing is associated with relationship satisfaction, it becomes important to investigate the frequency and quality of relationship processing engaged in by partners in a relationship. To this end, we developed the Relationship Schema Coding System, which assesses the behavioral manifestations of relationship processing and its component dimensions (e.g., quantity of relationship processing, quality of relationship processing, and valence of relationship processing).

THEORETICAL FOUNDATIONS

In recent years, there has been an increase in the amount of research linking social cognition to marital phenomenon. One such social cognitive variable that appears related to marital interactions is relationship processing (i.e., focusing attention on one's romantic relationship). Several studies suggest that women tend to engage in more relationship processing than do men. For example, Burnett (1987) studied gender differences in relationship "reflection," individuals' thoughts about their relationships, both when alone and when in interactions. Burnett found that women were more likely than men to make assessments of their relationships. They also "cared more about monitoring and evaluating intrinsic relationship events and experiences" than did men (Burnett, 1987, p. 89). Men, in contrast, were less interested, thoughtful, and communicative about relationships. They had more difficulty explaining relationships, and they were less likely to enjoy analyzing personal relationships than were women. Similarly, Acitelli (1992) investigated gender differences in "relationship awareness," defined as "a person's thinking about interaction patterns, comparisons, or contrasts between himself or herself and the other partner in the relationship" (p. 102). Acitelli found that wives were more relationship aware (i.e., they tended to talk more about their marital relationships) than were their husbands.

Given this apparent disparity between women's and men's relationship processing, it becomes important to investigate whether and how this gender difference impacts relationship functioning. Acitelli (1992) found that wives' marital satisfaction was positively associated with husbands' degree of relationship talk. In contrast, husbands' marital satisfaction was not related to either partner's relational talk. Fletcher, Fincham, Cramer, and Heron (1987) also demonstrated a link between relationship thinking and relationship satisfaction. However, these investigators did not test the correlation between relationship processing and relationship satisfaction separately for each gender. Fletcher and colleagues demonstrated that participants who described their relationships in interpersonal terms were happier with their relationships, more committed to their relationships, and more in love than those who described their relationships in individuals terms (i.e., commented on themselves or their partners as individuals rather than as a couple).

Whereas the aforementioned researchers each investigated a dimension of relationship processing, their operationalized definitions of these constructs differed (Acitelli, 1992; Burnett, 1997; Fletcher et al., 1987). For example, Acitelli (1992) deemed descriptions of interaction patterns between partners (e.g., I often get angry at him) to be indicative of relationship processing, whereas Fletcher et al. (1987) did not. However, both researchers concluded that relationship processing (i.e., relationship awareness, interpersonal descriptions) was associated with relationship satisfaction. Therefore, it appears that both Acitelli and Fletcher et al. analyzed important, albeit unique, components of relationship processing.

The Relationship Schema Coding System presents an integrated and expanded definition of relationship processing, which the present authors have titled Relationship-Schematic Processing. The term "schema" is used to denote a type of cognitive processing that guides and organizes an individual's perceptions. "Schematic information processing entails a readiness to sort and interpret information on the basis of some particular dimension [e.g., romantic relationship], despite the existence of other dimensions that could serve equally well in this regard" (Bem, 1984, p. 187). Individuals who engage in Relationship-Schematic Processing tend to organize the world into relationship categories. However, the degree to which individuals utilize Relationship-Schematic Processing exists along a continuum. Some individuals tend to give relationship meaning to a variety of events, whereas others make few connections between events that have occurred and their romantic relationships. Furthermore, some individuals frequently think about their relationships and interactions between the two partners, whereas other individuals give little thought to what is happening in the relationship.

Previous research highlights important findings regarding the quantity of relationship processing engaged in by participants (Acitelli, 1992; Burnett, 1997; Fletcher et al., 1987). However, little attention has been paid to the quality of relationship processing. We posit that, in addition to quantity, the quality of Relationship-Schematic Processing will be an important factor in understanding how

Relationship-Schematic Processing correlates with relationship satisfaction. For example, partners may exhibit varying aptitudes for how well they encode and integrate information. It is anticipated that if partners engage in a great deal of relationship processing but disregard important information, relationship satisfaction may be impacted differently than if partners engage in a great deal of relationship processing that incorporates all relevant information. Similarly, if partners include excessive and irrelevant information in their relationship processing, relationship happiness likely will be affected differently than if spouses engage in less relationship processing that incorporates only pertinent information. The present coding system incorporates both quantity and quality of Relationship-Schematic Processing.

Prior to the development of the current coding system, no studies had assessed the behavioral manifestations of relationship processing during couple interactions. Instead, participants were asked to provide retrospective reports about their lives and their relationships (Acitelli, 1992; Burnett, 1997; Fletcher et al., 1987). Unfortunately, there are limitations in using retrospective reports. For example, individuals may inadvertently or purposefully misreport their relationship thoughts. Furthermore, individuals who do not engage in a great deal of relationship processing in their daily lives may excel at providing retrospective reports of relationship phenomenon. The present authors utilize observational coding to assess how the presence or absence of Relationship-Schematic Processing in one or both partners manifests itself during interactions between partners.

Finally, no studies have assessed the valence of relationship-focused comments. Instead, previous research appears to assume that speaking in relationship terms is valuable, regardless of whether the comments are constructive or destructive. However, there may be an interaction between relationship processing and the valence of the comments used to communicate relationship processing. That is, individuals may report greater relationship satisfaction if their partners communicate their relationship thoughts constructively than they would if their partners communicated relationship thoughts destructively. As a result, the Relationship Schema Coding System incorporates ratings regarding the valence of relationship processing.

DEVELOPMENT OF THE CODING SYSTEM

The Relationship Schema Coding System was developed according to guidelines for developing new observational coding systems presented by Floyd, Baucom, Godfrey, and Palmer (1998). Floyd and colleagues suggested that three questions should be considered prior to constructing an observational coding system: (a) What behaviors do we want to observe? (b) What are our code categories? and (c) What is our unit of observation? Following is a discussion regarding how each of these questions was addressed during the construction of the Relationship Schema Coding System.

What Behaviors Do We Want to Observe?

The present observational coding system is intended to capture the behavioral manifestations (i.e., what partners say and do) of Relationship-Schematic Processing. (Actual cognitive processing cannot be observed, but the behavioral manifestations of that processing can be observed and coded.) Because clinical observations engendered the construct Relationship-Schematic Processing, the investigators first generated a list of behaviors believed to be associated with Relationship-Schematic Processing that they had observed in nondistressed and clinical couples. Next, a review of the relevant literature was conducted, and the list was expanded. Finally, the principal investigators reviewed numerous videotaped couple interactions. To obtain a diverse sample of Relationship-Schematic behaviors, videotapes of engaged couples completing a problem-solving interaction, distressed couples completing a problem-solving interaction, and community couples completing a task designed to elicit social support were reviewed. Again, the tentative list of Relationship-Schematic behaviors was expanded.

What Are Our Code Categories?

Floyd, Baucom, et al. (1998) suggested that codes be organized into groups that, if appropriate, fit into a hierarchical structure. With this guideline in mind, the principal investigators identified three fundamental dimensions of Relationship-Schematic Processing: (a) quantity of Relationship-Schematic Processing, (b) quality of Relationship-Schematic Processing, and (c) valence of Relationship-Schematic Processing. Each of these dimensions then was divided into meaningful categories and subcategories. For example, within the dimension "quantity of Relationship-Schematic Processing," two categories were defined: (a) content of Relationship-Schematic Processing, and (b) style of communicating Relationship-Schematic Processing. Next, within each of these categories, subcategories were designated. For example, within the "style of communicating Relationship-Schematic Processing" category, two subcategories were identified: (a) direct Relationship-Schematic comments, and (b) indirect Relationship-Schematic comments. After defining and classifying the coding categories, the investigators again surveyed the relevant literature and reviewed videotaped couple interactions. Subsequently, the coding system was refined by broadening some categories and tightening others to make finer distinctions between behaviors.

The components of information processing are thought to be dependent on one another. For example, coders rate overall how well (i.e., overall quality) participants engaged in Relationship-Schematic Processing. Then, coders rate how well individuals gathered and interpreted the information available to him or her. However, the code for gathering and interpreting information is limited by how well the individual engaged in Relationship-Schematic Processing overall. That is, if an individual does not utilize a Relationship Schema very well overall, he or she cannot gather and interpret information very well. Several coding rules were developed to help coders negotiate ambiguous decisions regarding dependent codes. These rules are elaborated in the coding manual.

What is Our Unit of Observation?

Coders watch the entire video of a couple's conversation and then make ratings of comments that reflected Relationship-Schematic Processing. This technique is called "event sampling," defined as "noting each occurrence of events during the entire observation period" (Floyd, Baucom, et al., 1998, p. 18). Based on this event sampling, each partner is rated on various quantity, quality, and valence dimensions for the entire conversation. That is, although specific instances of Relationship-Schematic comments are noted, partners are given a single code that sums their performance over the entire conversation. Therefore, the coding system can be viewed as a more global, macro-analytic coding system compared to coding systems that provide codes for smaller units, such as each talk turn or every 30 sec.

Event sampling becomes complicated in this coding system because individuals do not always express Relationship-Schematic Processing through the use of direct Relationship-Schematic comments. At times, they may use indirect Relationship-Schematic comments that, when taken in isolation, do not reflect the presence of a Relationship Schema. When these comments are considered across the whole conversation, however, it becomes apparent that the individual was processing in terms of the relationship. (For a more detailed description of the distinction between direct and indirect Relationship-Schematic comments, see the "Description of the Coding System" section.) As a result, it becomes more difficult to identify individual comments that reflect the use of a Relationship Schema. To manage this and similar difficulties, specific coding rules were developed. In this case, coders were instructed to base their ratings on direct Relationship-Schematic comments and then adjust their rating $\pm$ 1 point (within a 5-point rating system) based on indirect Relationship-Schematic comments. In other words, the unit of observation is a direct Relationship-Schematic comment. However, ratings given to this unit can be adjusted based on indirect Relationship-Schematic comments.

After codes were labeled, defined, and classified, a coding manual was written. The manual contains (a) a list of all codes, (b) a descriptive definition for each code, and (c) examples of behaviors that represent each code. Additionally, the coding manual includes a comprehensive introduction in which Relationship Schema is defined and specific rules designed to aid coders in resolving ambiguous decisions are outlined.

TASK AND SETTING

The Relationship Schema Coding System can be applied to a wide variety of couple interactions (e.g., problem-solving interactions, emotional expression interactions, social support interactions). However, the coding system requires coders to make very specific ratings regarding the quantity of the individual's total talk time and the quantity of the individual's Relationship-Schematic talk time. Consequently, the Relationship Schema Coding System is best applied to videotaped, rather than in vivo, interactions. Although the coding system can be applied to a variety of couple conversations, it is possible that Relationship-Schematic Processing is affected by the type of conversation. For example, partners engaged in social support conversations may utilize relationship processing differently than couples attempting to solve a problem. Consequently, it will be important for future research to investigate the ways in which the type of conversation influences Relationship-Schematic Processing for a couple.

DESCRIPTION OF THE CODING SYSTEM

The Relationship Schema Coding System consists of 15 codes, grouped into three categories: (a) quantity of Relationship-Schematic Processing, (b) quality of Relationship-Schematic Processing, and (c) valence of Relationship-Schematic Processing. Each code is rated on a 5-point Likert scale. Ratings are made after viewing the entire video, and each video is watched twice, once to observe each partner.

Prior to making ratings regarding quantity, quality, and valence of Relationship-Schematic Processing, coders make a global assessment of "Overall, how Relationship-Schematic was the individual?" This rating is intended to capture both how often (i.e., quantity) and how well (i.e., quality) individuals engage in Relationship-Schematic Processing. If individuals do not demonstrate relationship processing, coders rate only one additional question: "To what extent did stimuli in the videotaped interaction necessitate the individual's use of Relationship-Schematic Processing?" Coding is terminated at this point because it is not possible to rate various aspects of relationship processing if they did not occur. However, if the individual engages in relationship processing, coders rate that individual on all questions included in the Relationship Schema Coding System.

Quantity of Relationship-Schematic Processing

Quantity of Relationship-Schematic Processing is divided into three sections. First, coders rate the degree to which partners seemed to be using a Relationship Schema overall. To make this global rating, coders consider and rate distinct subcategories (i.e., internal–individual, internal–couple, external–individual, external–couple) and styles (i.e., direct and indirect) of Relationship-Schematic Processing. In all cases, for an event to be coded, the speaker must give emotional or relationship meaning to the event. These subcategories and styles are described below:

Internal-Individual. These comments reflect that the individual being rated thought about and imposed emotional or relationship meaning onto interactions between self and partner (e.g., "I loved it when you listened to me tell that whole, terrible story.") and aspects of the partner in relation to self (e.g., "We're never going to stay together if you continue to be such a slob! I know it's not a big deal to you, but it drives me crazy!").

Internal-Couple. These comments indicate that the individual monitored and evaluated relationship events (e.g., "That was fun to go out to dinner just the two of us.") or assessed the status and quality of the relationship (e.g., "The longer we're married, the better we get along.").

External-Individual. These comments suggest that the individual thought about and imposed emotional or relationship meaning onto interactions between the outside world and one partner in the couple (e.g., "I don't think you should say those things to our son—you treat him the same way you've always treated me, and I don't like it.").

External-Couple. These comments reflect that the individual thought about and imposed emotional or relationship meaning onto interactions between the outside world and the couple as a unit (e.g., "I swear your mother calls on Friday nights just to cause tension between us and ruin our weekend").

Direct Relationship-Schematic Comments. The individual might make comments that directly indicate that he or she is processing information in terms of the romantic relationship or giving relationship meaning to events. An example of a direct Relationship-Schematic comment is, "It made me happy when I got home from work late and you had made dinner for me." In this example, the individual directly communicated her use of a Relationship Schema by processing and commenting on the impact of her husband's behavior (i.e., he made dinner) on her (i.e., your making dinner made me happy).

Indirect Relationship-Schematic Comments. An individual who employs a Relationship Schema might make a series of comments that, when considered separately, do not reflect that the individual is engaged in Relationship-Schematic Processing. However, when the comments are considered together across the whole conversation, it appears that the person is processing information in terms of the relationship:

Husband: But, I come from a family where it was important to always have a clean house.

Wife: I still think it's a problem.

Husband: Well, you came from a family where it didn't really matter if you kept everything spotless.

Wife: So?

Husband: So I like things to be clean when company comes over..

Wife: So?

Husband: So, I think that's why we always fight before we have people over!

Although the husband's early comments, when considered in isolation, did not reflect the use of a Relationship Schema, it became evident over the course of the conversation that he was attempting to understand why the couple fights before company comes over by comparing his and his wife's different views on cleanliness.

Quality of Relationship-Schematic Processing

Quality of Relationship-Schematic Processing is divided into two sections. Coders first rate the overall quality of partners' Relationship-Schematic Processing. To make this global rating, coders consider and rate distinct components of information processing, including (a) attention to and interpretation of stimuli, (b) complexity of processing, and (c) appropriateness of processing. These dimensions are described next:

Attention to and Interpretation of Stimuli. An individual may attend to appropriate stimuli, or he or she may be overinclusive or underinclusive of some types of information. The following is an example of an individual who underattends to information: A husband does not call his wife to tell her that he will be home late. When he arrives home, she is upset, saying he does not love her. He becomes confused; how could she think that he does not love her? She reminds him that he is supposed to call her if he is going to be late. Despite his apologies, she insists that his actions reflect that he must not love her. Incredulous, he reminds her that he brought her flowers last week, he made breakfast two days ago, he kissed her and told her that he loved her before he left for work that morning, and so on. Still, she maintains that he did not call, so he must not love her. This wife used a Relationship Schema because she processed her reaction (i.e., feeling unloved) to his behavior (i.e., not calling). However, when Relationship-Schematic Processing, the wife was underinclusive of the available information. She only considered one incident to reach the conclusion that her husband does not love her, although he reminded her of several times in the past week when he had shown his love for her.

After the individual has attended to and gathered available information, he or she may integrate and interpret that information in a reasonable manner. However, some individuals assimilate information in a way that does not seem appropriate. For example, a couple is registered to take dance lessons. This was the husband's idea, and the wife reluctantly agreed. However, just before the first lesson, the wife fell off a ladder and broke her leg, so the couple had no choice but to cancel the lessons. The husband became furious; he knew his wife did not want to take the lessons, and now she broke her leg. He accused her of getting hurt just to avoid taking dancing. In this example, the husband gathered the appropriate information (i.e., his wife did not want to take dance lessons; his wife broke her leg), but he did not interpret the available information in a reasonable manner. His conclusion that she broke her leg just to avoid dance lessons seemed unlikely; her fall off the ladder was an accident that occurred when a dog ran by and hit the ladder.

Complexity of processing. Some individuals describe or comment on basic behavioral, cognitive, or affective relationship patterns or events (e.g., "You got so mad when I forgot to do laundry."), whereas others generate rich interpretations or conceptualizations of patterns and events (e.g., "Wow. I didn't realize you would get so mad when I forgot to do the laundry. I guess this gets us back into that whole issue of your not wanting me to just assume you'll do the housework. So, I understand that my forgetting to do the laundry made you feel disrespected and put you in a bind you didn't want to be in of whether you should just do the laundry or get mad at me.")

Appropriateness of Processing. Individuals might engage in Relationship-Schematic Processing at times when stimuli necessitate the use of relationship thinking. For example, a wife approaches her husband about why he seems distant every time she mentions having children. The wife's comments "pull for" Relationship-Schematic Processing from her husband; she wants him to discuss their interactions surrounding the topic of having children. In contrast, individuals may demonstrate relationship thinking in situations when it is inappropriate to discuss relationship phenomena. For example, a husband asks his wife if she either can take the children to school or drop off the dry cleaning because he was called for a sudden meeting. The husband wants his wife to engage in problem solving; it may not be appropriate for the wife to respond with comments about her feelings regarding how his work prevents the couple from spending time together.

Valence of Relationship-Schematic Processing

Valence of Relationship-Schematic Processing is assessed with four questions. First, coders assess the partner's emotional and behavioral reactions to the target individual's Relationship-Schematic comments. Then, coders rate the reaction a neutral third party likely would have to the target individual's Relationship-Schematic comments. Finally, coders evaluate the degree to which the target individual demonstrates healthy and constructive relationship thoughts or unhealthy and destructive Relationship-Schematic thoughts.

CODER TRAINING

Undergraduate and continuing education students have been trained to use the Relationship Schema Coding System. The authors informally screen potential student coders for their ability to understand Relationship-Schematic Processing. Those who appear to grasp the construct are then taught the coding system. That is, coders who do not engage in relationship processing likely will have trouble assessing it in others. Although the research described earlier indicates that as a group, women tend to think more in relationship terms than do males, there are many men who make fine coders. To avoid possible gender biases, particularly when coding quality and valence of relationship processing, we recommend, when possible, employing both genders as coders.

First, coders in training read the coding manual (which is available from the authors on request). Although the manual is intended to be comprehensive, the authors have found it helpful to engage in a training period with coders. Typically, the authors have met with coders for approximately 70 hr, over the course of several months, to view videotaped couple interactions. We recommend training coders on a subset of the videotaped interactions that are similar to those that will be included in the investigation under consideration; however, it is important to include couples with a wide range of functioning on the various variables. For example, distressed couples may engage in lower quality Relationship-Schematic Processing than nondistressed couples, so training on both types of couples can show raters anchor points for the full range of scores. After reviewing a videotape, the authors and coders employ the coding system to rate the couple's interaction. Then, the rationale each coder used to generate ratings is discussed, and coders receive feedback about the accuracy of their ratings. Additionally, the authors model various coding techniques and strategies for resolving ambiguous coding decisions. When coders' ratings consistently differ from those of the authors less than 10% of the time, coders begin coding independently. Weekly training meetings are scheduled with the coders to review their progress, resolve questions and concerns, and assess for coder drift.

Although individuals who construct coding systems attempt to be comprehensive when writing a coding manual, our experience is that there is no substitute for face-to-face training to develop an appropriate sense of anchor points for the various scales and for resolving idiosyncrasies of a specific couple not addressed in the manual. Therefore, we believe it would be beneficial for investigators who wish to utilize the Relationship Schema Coding System in their studies to engage in training with the present authors. Then, periodic consultation between the investigators and the present authors is recommended to help maintain the integrity of the coding system.

CODING PROCESS

To date, the Relationship Schema Coding System has been applied only to 7-min problem-solving interactions. It typically takes coders between 15 min and an hour to rate a 7-min interaction. The coding time depends on the sound quality of the videotape, the clarity with which the target individual speaks, the quantity of the target individual's total talk time, the quantity of the target individual's Relationship Schema talk time, and a variety of other variables. Prior to making ratings, coders watch the entire videotaped interaction one to three times, depending on the aforementioned variables. While watching the interaction, coders stop and start the videotape, as needed, to take notes regarding potential Relationship-Schematic comments. They tend to refer to their notes frequently when making ratings.

RELIABILITY

The authors have found that coders demonstrate adequate agreement when using the Relationship Schema Coding System (Sullivan & Baucom, 1999, 2001). Agreement has been assessed using the Rater Agreement Index (RAI; Burry–Stock, Shaw, Laurie, & Chissom, 1996). The RAI measures the degree to which coders agree on their ratings in reference to the possible range of ratings. The index ranges from 0 to 1 with 1 indicating perfect agreement. The basic formula for calculating the RAI is as follows: $RAI = 1 - (|R_1 - R_2| / (I-1))$. RAIs for the Relationship Schema Coding System ranged from .63 to 1. The average of the RAIs for all items of the coding system was .86, indicating that, on average, the two raters differed in their ratings by .56 points on a 5-point rating scale.

When two coders have rated a tape and their ratings are no more than 1 point apart, a consensus code is obtained by averaging the two raters' scores. If the raters are more than 1 point apart, then they meet and discuss their codes to arrive at an agreed-on score, with the trainers' assistance when coders cannot agree.

VALIDITY

The Relationship Schema Coding System is a relatively new coding system; therefore, the authors are in the early stages of establishing the convergent and discriminant validity of the system (Sullivan & Baucom, 1999, 2001).

Convergent Validity

As anticipated, Relationship-Schematic Processing is positively correlated with other prorelationship emotions. For example, relationship processing is significantly positively correlated with partners' feelings of intimacy, closeness, and trust toward their partner, as measured by the Interpersonal Relationship Scale (IRS; Guerney, 1977). Specifically, the authors found that the more wives engaged in Relationship-Schematic Processing and the better the quality of their processing, the more intimacy, closeness, and trust husbands reported feeling toward their wives. The higher the quality of men's relationship processing, the more feelings of intimacy, closeness, and trust wives reported feeling toward their husbands.

Note that these are across partner correlations; Relationship-Schematic Processing in one partner is related to feelings of closeness in the other partner.

Second, relationship processing is significantly negatively correlated with destructive relationship cognitions, as measured by the Relationship Beliefs Inventory (RBI; Epstein & Eidelson, 1981). The RBI is a self-report measure that consists of five subscales (i.e., Disagreement is Destructive, Mind Reading is Expected, Partners Cannot Change, Sexual Perfectionism, and the Sexes are Different) that are intended to reflect unrealistic relationship themes often observed in distressed couples. The findings indicate that, generally, one's partner's quantity of relationship processing is not correlated with his or her partner's RBI scores. However, it appears that partners' dysfunctional relationship cognitions tended to decrease when their partners demonstrated higher quality of Relationship-Schematic Processing. Specifically, husbands' quality of Relationship-Schematic Processing was negatively correlated with wives' scores on the Disagreement is Destructive subscale, the Mindreading is Expected subscale, the Partners Cannot Change subscale, and the Sexes are Different subscales. Wives' skill at Relationship-Schematic Processing was negatively correlated with husbands' scores on the Disagreement is Destructive subscale. Therefore, when individuals engage in higher quality Relationship-Schematic Processing, their partners generally have less negative cognitions about relationships. Given that these findings are correlational, cause–effect relationships cannot be determined. However, it is possible that living with someone who processes events in relationship terms in a reasonable manner (i.e., high quality Relationship-Schematic Processing) contributes to an atmosphere which allows the other partner to develop positive cognitions about how relationships function. For example, if a husband has high quality Relationship-Schematic Processing, then his wife might indeed find that having disagreements is not destructive because the couple is able to discuss issues productively.

Discriminant Validity

Finally, the authors have begun to assess the discriminant validity of the Relationship Schema Coding System. Previous dyadic interaction coding systems have assessed the valence of partners' communication (Weiss & Summers, 1983). For example, the Marital Interaction Coding System, Version III (MICS–III) includes positive verbal and nonverbal behavior codes (e.g., approve, comply, smile-laugh) and negative verbal and nonverbal behavior codes (e.g., complain, put down, turn off). In contrast, the quantity and quality components of the Relationship Schema Coding System are not intended to assess the valence of partners' comments. That is, both positive and negative remarks can be coded as Relationship-Schematic comments. To ensure that the Relationship Schema Coding System is not measuring in a new way constructs that have been measured previously, the authors compared the quantity of Relationship-Schematic Processing code and quality of Relationship-Schematic Processing code with the positive MICS and negative MICS scales (Sullivan & Baucom, 1999). The authors found that, in general, the quantity and quality codes of the Relationship Schema Coding System do not correlate with the MICS positive and MICS negative codes. Additionally, the quantity and quality codes of the Relationship Schema Coding System correlated with partner's relationship satisfaction, whereas the MICS positive and MICS negative codes did not.

GENERALIZABILITY

The Relationship Schema Coding System is applicable to various types of interactions completed by couples from various types of backgrounds. However, to date, the Relationship Schema Coding System only has been applied to brief problem-solving interactions completed by predominantly White, educated couples who had been married for approximately 10 years, had approximately two children, and who reported marital distress. Our expectation is that stable, individual differences in Relationship-Schematic Processing exist, such that some individuals generally think in relationship terms more often and with higher quality than other individuals. In addition, the different contexts in which couples find themselves are likely to influence the use of Relationship-Schematic Processing. Although it is expected that Relationship-Schematic Processing will play a role in most marriages, it is unclear whether applying the coding system to distinct types of couple interactions (e.g., emotional expression interactions, social support interactions) and diverse types of couples (e.g., Asian American couples, nondistressed couples) will elicit different patterns of Relationship Schema use.

CLINICAL UTILITY

In a clinical setting, strategies often are needed for assessing couples' communication and interaction. Although many clinicians tend to do so informally, a more systematic approach may be helpful and desirable. One such approach is for couple therapists to become familiar with observational coding systems, like the Relationship Schema Coding System. Once therapists have learned the coding system, they can either (a) formally use the actual coding, or (b) informally attend to the constructs underlying the coding system and some of the specific coding questions. Each approach has benefits and drawbacks. First, clinicians using both approaches are likely to gain valuable information regarding ways in which partners process events in their lives that are problematic or that are a particular strength for the couple. However, prior to formally using the Relationship Schema Coding System, clinicians would need to be trained. Additionally, they would need videotaping capabilities in their offices, time to code interactions, and an understanding of their findings in light of the current research regarding Relationship-Schematic Processing. For most clinicians, this investment in training and formal coding is unrealistic due to limitations in time and resources. However, if clinicians informally attend to the constructs underlying the coding system and some of the specific coding questions, it might provide them with a sense of whether one or both partners process information in relationship terms. For example, when a couple seeks therapy, and one partner complains that the other "just doesn't get it," this cues the clinician that the individual may not be engaging in Relationship-Schematic Processing.

Regardless of whether clinicians use the actual coding system or simply employ the ideas espoused by the coding system, they can integrate information regarding the couple's Relationship-Schematic Processing into a feedback session with couples. The authors have found it helpful to discuss Relationship-Schematic Processing directly with couples; in our experience, they have identified easily with the construct and its implications. Furthermore, the therapist might use information regarding the partners' relationship processing to adapt interventions to be maximally effective with a couple. For example, if neither partner engages in relationship processing, then the therapist must be careful not to describe their relationship to them in complex, interactional terms because neither partner is likely to comprehend the message. Treatment might also focus on making adjustments to one or both partners' relationship processing (e.g., helping one partner to avoid being overinclusive in giving relationship meaning to events). Epstein and Baucom (2002) discussed a variety of cognitive–behavioral interventions that can serve such purposes. Finally, the Relationship Schema Coding System can be used, either formally or informally, to assess treatment progress. Although we are in the early stages of testing our broad hypothesis, we believe that any efficacious form of couple therapy helps partners learn to process events in relationship terms with reasonable frequency and high quality.

STUDIES USING THE CODING SYSTEM

The authors applied the Relationship Schema Coding System to videotaped problem-solving interactions completed by 55 maritally-distressed couples who participated in Baucom, Sayers, and Sher's (1990) behavioral marital treatment outcome study (Sullivan & Baucom, 1999). Consistent with previous research, we found that prior to receiving treatment, wives engaged in significantly more frequent and higher quality relationship thinking than did husbands. We also found that husbands reported greater relationship satisfaction when wives engaged in more frequent and higher quality Relationship-Schematic Processing, and wives reported greater satisfaction when husbands engaged in higher quality relationship processing. Additionally, wives reported higher levels of relationship satisfaction the more similar the quality of their partners' Relationship-Schematic

Processing was to their own; that is, wives are less happy when they and their husbands process events in very different ways relative to the relationship.

In a later study, we (Sullivan & Baucom, 2001) applied the Relationship Schema Coding System to the posttreatment videotaped interactions completed by the same sample of couples who participated in the previous investigation. We found that after receiving marital therapy, wives did not display significant increases in relationship processing; they already were somewhat elevated in their scores prior to treatment. However, husbands' quantity and quality of Relationship-Schematic Processing did increase significantly in response to treatment. In fact, husbands' posttest scores were almost identical to wives' pretest scores. Additionally, these increases in husbands' Relationship-Schematic Processing were significantly positively associated with increases in wives' relationship satisfaction. That is, wives were happier at the end of treatment to the degree that their husbands had learned to think in relationship terms. However, changes in wives' quantity and quality of relationship processing did not correlate with changes in husbands' satisfaction. Instead, increases in men's satisfaction were correlated with increases in the positivity of wives' communication, as assessed using the MICS–III. These results suggest that if husbands become more relationship-focused over the course of treatment, wives become more satisfied with their marriage. However, if wives become more relationship-focused over the course of treatment, husbands do not achieve greater levels of relationship satisfaction. Rather, husbands report increased relationship happiness if, over the course of treatment, wives become more positive in how they communicate their relationship thoughts. All of these findings are based on the use of cognitive–behavioral couple therapy. Consistent with our hypothesis that a variety of approaches to couple therapy will influence Relationship-Schematic Processing, we currently are assessing whether participation in insight-oriented couple therapy (Snyder, 1989) also results in increases in Relationship-Schematic Processing. We plan to evaluate other therapies in the future.

ACKNOWLEDGMENTS

We thank Will Beasley, Chris Branson, Adriann Diers, Jeremy Heuts, Sarah King, Marisa Lipiello, Amber Messick, Katy Wilder, and Nicole Yoder for their assistance with coding videotaped interactions.

V

Social Support

19

The Social Support Behavior Code (SSBC)

Julie A. Suhr
Ohio University

Carolyn E. Cutrona
Iowa State University

Krista K. Krebs
Hastings Regional Center

Sandra L. Jensen
Roswell Park Cancer Institute

"In the coping process, it is the behavioral manifestation of support expressed by my close associates—its materialization in interpersonal transactions –that has greatest significance for the course and outcomes of my ordeal"

Gottlieb (1985, p. 361)

The Social Support Behavior Code (SSBC; Cutrona & Suhr, 1992, 1994; Suhr, 1990) was developed to assess social support behaviors in the context of help-intended dyadic interactions in which one member of the couple discloses a personal problem to the other. The SSBC yields a count of the number of times each of the following types of social support is provided by the listener to the discloser: (a) Emotional Support (communicating empathy or caring); (b) Esteem Support (communicating confidence in the other's worth, competence, or ability to solve the problem); (c) Information Support (providing information about the problem, how to appraise the problem, or how to cope with the problem); (d) Tangible Support (offering assistance or tangible resources to help solve the problem); and (e) Negative Behaviors (sarcasm, criticism, disagreement, interruption, complaint, refusals to help).

THEORETICAL FOUNDATIONS

The perception of one's partner as supportive is a consistent predictor of marital satisfaction, life satisfaction, and both physical and mental health (Brown & Harris, 1978; Gove, Hughes, & Style, 1983; Husaini, Neff, Newbrough, & Moore, 1982; Kiecolt–Glaser et al., 1987; Lieberman, 1982; Mermelstein, Lichtenstein, & McIntyre, 1983; Monroe, Bromet, Connell, & Steiner, 1986; Rogers, 1987; Waltz, 1986). However, we know relatively little about the specific behaviors that contribute to perceptions of the partner as supportive. The SSBC was developed as an observational measure of social support behaviors that would allow researchers to gain a better understanding of how couples communicate support to one another and the kinds of support communications that are most and least beneficial in specific contexts. Two perspectives guided the development of the SSBC: the behavioral perspective and a view of social support as a multidimensional construct.

The Behavioral Perspective

According to the behavioral perspective, perceptions of social support are based largely on actual supportive interactions exchanged between partners over time. Behavioral assessment of social support allows insight into the process through which support is communicated from one individual to another. By assessing the actual words and actions partners use to communicate support to each other, there is potential to evaluate which behavioral expressions of support are effective and which are ineffective, under specific circumstances.

The vast majority of studies of marital social support have relied on self-report measures. However, self-reports of partner behavior are prone to an array of biases (Christensen & Nies, 1980; Elwood & Jacobson, 1982; Jacobson & Moore, 1980; Sillars & Scott, 1983; Wills, Weiss, & Patterson, 1974). Self-report measures of spouse supportiveness may simply tap general marital satisfaction rather than actual frequency or quality of supportive behaviors performed by the partner. There is a need for observational studies of dyadic interactions to clarify which actual behaviors are perceived as supportive and to assess their relative contribution to overall perceptions of spousal supportiveness.

Multidimensional Model of Social Support

The SSBC was developed to reflect our belief that social support is a multidimensional construct. We originally drew from Weiss's (1974) model of the provisions of social relationships. Weiss outlined six different provisions or needs that are met by relationships with others: attachment, reassurance of worth, reliable alliance, guidance, social integration, and the opportunity to provide nurturance. We first developed a self-report measure to assess the extent to which key relationships supplied people with each provision, the Social Provisions Scale (Cutrona & Russell, 1987). We construed the Social Provisions Scale as a measure of perceived social support. We next sought to develop an observational measure of social support behaviors, based loosely on Weiss's conceptual framework. Thus, we expected that social support behaviors would fall into categories similar to those articulated by Weiss (1974). The need for attachment is addressed by behaviors that communicate emotional support; reassurance of worth is addressed by esteem support; reliable alliance by tangible support; guidance by information support; and social integration by social network support. Opportunity to provide nurturance refers to giving rather than receiving support and was not included in the code.

DEVELOPMENT OF THE CODING SYSTEM

Items for the SSBC were developed by surveying the existing literature for descriptions of social support that could provide ideas for the construction of items consistent with the multidimensional concept of social support (e.g., Barker & Lemle, 1984; Barrera, Sandler, & Ramsay, 1981; Cohen & Hoberman, 1983; Cohen & McKay, 1984; Cutrona, 1986; Gottlieb, 1978; Hinchliffe, Vaughan, Hooper, & Roberts, 1977, 1978a, 1978b; Procidano & Heller, 1983; Stone & Neale, 1984; Thoits, 1986). In addition to our search of the social support literature, we conducted two studies to generate items. In the first study, 32 married individuals (21–66 years old, married from 5 months to 41 years) read descriptions of four stressful life events and were asked to describe one actual stressful event from their own lives. Participants were then asked to identify what specific supportive behaviors they would like to receive from their partner in each of the five situations. In the second study, 40 undergraduate students (18–27 years old) were asked to react to the same four stressful situations plus a stressful situation from their own life. Half of the participants were asked to describe supportive behaviors they would like to receive from their best friend in those situations. The other half were told to describe supportive behaviors they would provide to their best friend if he or she were in the situation. The original code developed from this approach included 33 behaviors that fell into the five support categories of Information Sup-

TABLE 19.1

Social Support Behavior Code

Informational Support	
Suggestion and Advice (offer ideas, suggesting actions)	SA
Situation Appraisal (reassess the situation)	SI
Teaching (teach how to do something or teach facts)	TE
Emotional Support	
Relationship (express closeness and togetherness)	RL
Physical affection (hug, kiss, hand hold, touch)	PA
Confidentiality (proomise not to tell others)	CF
Sympathy (express sorrow and regret for situation)	SY
Understanding and empathy ("I understand," self-disclose)	UE
Prayer (pray with person)	PY
Expresses concern (inquires after well-being)	EC
Reassurance (nonspecific comfort)	R
Esteem Support	
Compliment (emphasize abilities, say positive things)	CM
Validation (agree with and take other's side)	VA
Relief of blame (say it's not other's fault)	RB
Tangible Aid	
Loan (offer money or material object)	LO
Direct task (offer to do something related to problem)	DT
Indirect task (offer to do something not related)	IT
Active participation (offer to join in reducing stress)	AP
Willingness (express sillingness to help any time)	WI
Complies with request (agrees to do something after stressed person requests it)	CR
Negative Behaviors	
Interrupt (changaes subject or interrupts other)	IP
Complain (talks about own problems)	CN
Criticism (negative comments about other or blaming)	CT
Isolation (will not help other, will not discuss it)	IS
Disagree or disapprove (does not agree with other)	DD

port, Tangible Support, Esteem Support, Emotional Support, and Social Network Support. A detailed definition, including examples, was written for each code. Social Network Support, which assessed reminders of connections with similar others, was later dropped from the coding system because it rarely occurred and was difficult to code reliably.

We piloted the original code with a sample of 32 female undergraduate students, who came into the laboratory in pairs. One member of the pair was asked to disclose a current problem in her life, and the other was instructed to react naturally and spontaneously. Conversations went for 10 min and were videotaped. Following the interaction, each participant completed a rating scale that assessed perceived supportiveness of the interaction. Two independent coders used the preliminary SSBC to code the behavior of the students and also rated their perceptions of the helper's supportiveness. The total number of supportive behaviors coded with the SSBC correlated significantly with both participant and observer ratings of interaction supportiveness. Preliminary inter-rater reliability was adequate, but some code definitions were judged to be vague. These were revised or eliminated. Differences between similar codes were clarified. A second major change was the addition of Negative Behavior codes to the SSBC. Studies have demonstrated that partner negative behaviors influence the perception of support within a close relationship (Barnett & Nietzel, 1979; Jacobson, Waldron, & Moore, 1980; Wills et al., 1974). Furthermore, negative spousal behaviors are predictive of depression among marital partners (Manne & Zautra, 1989), and often account for more variance than supportive behaviors in explaining depression following stress (Schuster, Kessler, & Aseltine, 1990; Vinokur & van Ryn, 1993). The revised SSBC consisted of 31 items divided into six subscales (the five types of support plus Negative Behaviors).

The revised SSBC was then tested in a sample of 30 married couples recruited from university family housing (19–47 years old, married from 1 to 11 years) at a large Midwestern university. Members of the couple were randomly assigned to play the role of discloser or listener. The discloser revealed a current personal problem, and the listener was instructed to react naturally and spontaneously. Couples then switched roles and repeated the self-disclosure task. The videotapes were coded using the SSBC. To assess reliability, a random sample of 25% of the videotapes was coded by a second independent rater. With the exception of Social Network Support, all subscales were reliably rated (intraclass correlations ranged from .73 to .86, $p < .001$). Social Network Support refers to shared interests and concerns with a valued social group. Although an individual can remind another person of his or her links to a group, we found that this rarely happened in interactions between marital partners. Given low inter-rater reliability and infrequent use of the code, the decision was made to remove Social Network Behavior from the SSBC, which left four support subscales (Emotional Support, Esteem Support, Information Support, and Tangible Support) plus the Negative Behavior subscale. A total of 25 behavior codes made up the final SSBC.

TASK AND SETTING

The SSBC was designed for use in a laboratory setting that allows unobtrusive videotape recording. However, it can be administered in other settings, such as in couples' homes. For in-home use, a portable video camera may be used. After starting the camera, study personnel should leave the room to allow the couple privacy during the interaction.

To set up the interaction, one member of the couple is designated as the discloser and the other as the listener. A flip of the coin or a random numbers table is used to assign roles. Each member of the couple is given his or her instructions separately. We deliver instructions separately to avoid the introduction of demand characteristics. The discloser is asked to think of a current personal problem of relatively high importance, for which the person does not blame his or her partner, and which has not been a topic of previous conflict with the partner. The discloser is told that he or she will discuss the problem with his or her partner while being videotaped. The person assigned to the listener role is told that his or her partner will be discussing a personally stressful situation, and that he or she should respond naturally and spontaneously. Participants are reminded that there are no right or wrong ways to behave, and to try to act naturally. The length of time for discussion is limited to 10 min. The interaction is videotaped for later coding. The video camera(s) should be situated to allow a clear view of both participants' faces and body language, to provide a context for coding. However, because SSBC codes focus only on the behavior of the listener, priority should be given to a clear view of the person playing the listener role.

DESCRIPTION OF THE CODING SYSTEM

The SSBC assesses the frequency of occurrence of 25 individual behaviors that fall into five categories: Informational Support, Tangible Aid, Emotional Support, Esteem Support, and Negative Behaviors (see Table 19.1). Five subscale scores are computed (four support scores and Negative Behaviors) plus an overall Total Support score. Each score reflects the total number of behaviors observed within that category. In our laboratory, we record scores in a way that reflects the minute in which the behavior occurred to allow within-interaction analyses of behaviors. Thus, we compute five subscale scores and a Total Support score for each minute of the interaction. All but one of the codes is verbal. The exception is Physical Affection, which is a code in the Emotional Support subscale. Because the content of verbal behavior is the basis for coding decisions for 24 of the 25 codes, audiotaping could be used rather than videotaping, although it is helpful to observe nonverbal behavior. All categories are mutually exclusive, with the exception of Physical Affection, which can be coded concurrently with any of the verbal codes.

The categories are not exhaustive, in that many of the behaviors emitted by members of the couple are not coded.

CODER TRAINING

Coders are trained using the SSBC manual and sample videotapes of couple interactions. Typical training requires approximately 20 hr of experience with the coding system. After an initial overview of the concept of social support, the subscales are introduced one by one. For example, if Emotional Support were taught first, the purpose and general characteristics of emotional support would be discussed, followed by introduction of the individual behavior codes that constitute Emotional Support. A training tape has been developed that demonstrates the behaviors that are coded for each of the four support subscales. In the first session devoted to Emotional Support, trainees view the demonstration tape and identify specific codes. Similarities and differences between codes are discussed. Before the next session, trainees are asked to memorize the definitions of all the behavior codes in the Emotional Support subscale. The following week, they are tested on these definitions. Tapes of actual couple interactions are used in the second session. The group spends the session identifying Emotional Support behavior codes and discussing their characteristics. Next, trainees code sample tapes that have previously been coded by experienced users of the SSBC. They receive feedback on the accuracy of their coding, and problem areas are identified and discussed with the instructor. When trainees have mastered the first subscale codes, the second subscale is introduced, and the process is repeated until all subscales and their behavior codes have been covered. Trainees spend about 2 weeks coding practice tapes after all behavior codes have been covered. In addition, they take written tests over code definitions. Inter-rater reliability is computed against experienced coders for these practice tapes. Once their reliability reaches acceptable levels on the individual tapes, they are ready to begin using the SSBC independently. Periodic reliability checks are conducted of randomly selected tapes to check for and correct observer drift. Weekly meetings are held throughout the coding process to allow coders to ask questions about problematic interaction segments.

The tapes that demonstrate each type of support and the coding manual are both available to researchers who wish to learn the coding system. Consultation on training is also available from Carolyn Cutrona, who should be contacted via email (ccutrona@iastate.edu).

CODING PROCESS

The first step in the coding process is to generate a verbatim transcript of the support provider's utterances. The transcript is marked with a slash to indicate the end of each talk turn. Before coding begins, the entire tape is viewed first without stopping to gain an overall sense of the interaction and to check for accuracy of the transcription. Next, with the transcript in front of the coder, the tape is viewed again, pausing and restarting as necessary to take time to code each separate behavior. Coding sheets are divided into 1-min segments. All behaviors that occur within a given minute are recorded in the appropriate box on the coding sheet. If a behavior begins during 1 min but continues into the next, it is only counted in the minute during which the behavior was initiated. Scoring is initiated each time there is a change from one of the 25 specific scoring categories to another or a change from one speaker to another (a shift in talk turn). Therefore, when consecutive verbal responses fall into the same category, they are coded as one occurrence of the behavior. However, if within one talk turn the support provider offers two different kinds of support behaviors, they are coded as two separate events. For example, "I understand what you are saying. I'm willing to help you in any way I can" is recorded as two separate codes, with the former coded as Understanding/Empathy and the latter as Willingness. Within one talk turn, if a support behavior (e.g., Understanding/Empathy) is followed by a different behavior (e.g., Suggestion/Advice), and then followed by a second instance of Understanding/Empathy, two instances of Understanding/Empathy and one instance of Suggestion/Advice would be recorded. If the support provider offers a support behavior (e.g., Understanding/Empathy), the partner speaks, then the provider continues to offer Understanding/Empathy again, two instances of Understanding/Empathy are recorded. After coding the tape, it is viewed one more time to double-check coding accuracy.

RELIABILITY

Two separate reliability studies have been conducted with the SSBC (Cutrona, Hessling, & Suhr, 1997; Suhr, 1990). In both studies, intraclass correlations were computed between pairs of independent raters. For the four support scales, intraclass correlations ranged from .73 for Esteem Support to .94 for Tangible Support (mean intraclass correlation = .85.) Total Support reliability averaged .89 and Negative Behavior reliability averaged .87 across the two studies. With proper training, all subscales can be coded with a high degree of reliability.

VALIDITY

If the SSBC taps behaviors that communicate support, then people in high quality supportive marriages should engage in these behaviors more frequently than do people in low quality nonsupportive marriages. We tested the extent to which individuals' ratings of their marriages predicted scores on the SSBC in a sample of 115 couples. The couples were recruited from married student housing at two different Midwestern universities (Cutrona et al., 1997; Suhr, 1990). Couples first completed questionnaires about their relationship. Marital adjustment was assessed with the Dyadic Adjustment Scale (DAS; Spanier, 1976) and perceived support from the partner was assessed with the Social Provisions Scale–Partner Version (SPS–S; Cutrona, 1989). After completing questionnaires, members of the couple took turns disclosing a current personal problem to their partner. Each member of the couple played the role of discloser (support recipient) and the role of listener (support provider). Marital adjustment (DAS) correlated positively with the number of Esteem Support and Total Support behaviors and correlated negatively with the number of Negative Behaviors received. Pre-interaction marital support ratings (SPS–S) correlated positively with SSBC Emotional Support, Esteem Support, Information Support, and Total Support, and negatively with Negative Behaviors. Thus, with the exception of Tangible Support, SSBC codes correlated as predicted with marital quality.

A second important validity criterion is the extent to which SSBC behavior codes predict support recipients' evaluations of the support they have received in specific interactions. In the sample described earlier, support recipients completed the Interaction Supportiveness Scale (ISS; Cutrona & Suhr, 1992) immediately following the interaction. The ISS asks for ratings of partner supportiveness during a specific interaction. It yields a total score and four subscales which correspond to the types of support tapped by SSBC subscales (Emotional, Esteem, Tangible, and Information Support). SSBC Total Support, as well as Emotional Support and Esteem Support, correlated positively with recipient ratings of interaction supportiveness. Negative Behaviors correlated negatively with recipient perceptions of interaction supportiveness. Neither Information nor Tangible Support correlated significantly with perceived interaction supportiveness. It appears that individuals base their overall views of interaction supportiveness on expressions of caring and confidence in their ability more than on efforts to help with problem solving. Individuals also base their views of interaction supportiveness on negative partner behaviors, which diminish perceived interaction supportiveness.

In a second set of validity analyses (Krebs, 2000), a subset of the videotapes was re-coded by an independent set of coders, using a global, macro-analytic coding system, the Iowa Family Interaction Rating Scales (IFIRS; Melby & Conger, 2001). Three codes from the IFIRS were used: Listener Responsiveness, Warmth, and Hostility. Coders use a 9-point scale to rate the degree to which each descriptor is characteristic of the interaction. Listener Responsiveness taps verbal and nonverbal behaviors that validate and indicate attentiveness to the speaker. Warmth measures positive emotional tone, including nonverbal and verbal expressions of affection and support. Hostility taps the degree to which a person displays angry, critical, or hostile behavior. Results showed that SSBC Emotional Support and

Esteem Support were the strongest predictors of Listener Responsiveness and Warmth. Tangible Support was also a significant predictor of Warmth, but not of Listener Responsiveness. SSBC Negative Behavior was significantly negatively correlated with Listener Responsiveness and positively correlated with Hostility. Thus, the overall emotional tenor of support interactions seems to be shaped by Esteem, Emotional, and Tangible Support, as well as Negative Behaviors. Information Support does not seem to trigger perceptions of support. As discussed in a later section, individuals sometimes react negatively to Information Support, especially if they feel qualified to solve their own problems (Cutrona & Suhr, 1992).

An important question is the extent to which SSBC codes discriminate among different kinds of support behavior. To examine this aspect of discriminant validity, we looked at the correlations between SSBC codes and corresponding postinteraction ratings of specific types of support received. Correlations between all four SSBC support codes and their corresponding postinteraction support subscales were significant. Comparisons between correlations for corresponding and noncorresponding support types reveal that Information Support and Tangible Support were measured with good disciminant validity. The correlations between corresponding behavioral and self-report measures were clearly higher than between noncorresponding support types. However, it appears that the Emotional and Esteem Support subscales measure closely related constructs. SSBC Emotional Support correlated as highly with perceived esteem support as with perceived emotional support. Similarly, SSBC Esteem Support correlated as highly with perceived emotional support as with perceived esteem support. Thus, it appears that the Information and Tangible Support subscales tap distinctive constructs, but that the Emotional and Esteem Support subscales are closely related. The combination of these two subscales into one Nurturant Support scale may be justified. At present, we have kept them separate because of our interest in potential differences in their associations with other constructs.

GENERALIZABILITY

To date, the SSBC has been validated only among relatively young, well-educated couples, almost all of whom were European American. Thus, no claims can be made at this time regarding its generalizability to older couples, less-educated couples, or couples from different ethnic or cultural groups. It is likely that the same behaviors can be reliably coded across a wide range of couples. However, an important question remains regarding the extent to which the behaviors have the same impact or play the same role for various groups. For example, we do not know if marital adjustment correlates with the same support behaviors across couples from different age, socioeconomic, and ethnic and racial groups. Different subgroups may have different standards for the types of support that are most reflective of commitment and caring.

CLINICAL UTILITY

Researchers have called for training on how to effectively communicate social support in preventive marital interventions (Bradbury, Rogge, & Lawrence, 2001; Cutrona, 1996a). Support communication training may also be a valuable component of interventions for maritally distressed couples and for couples who are confronting intensely stressful events, such as serious illness in a family member. SSBC codes may be useful as a starting place in teaching couples to broaden the range of support behaviors in their communication repertoire. The SSBC may be used as an assessment tool to highlight deficiencies in social support communication skills. It may also be used as a pre–post measure of intervention effectiveness. The SSBC is primarily useful in the context of research trials of clinical interventions because training for coders is time-consuming, as is the actual coding process.

STUDIES USING THE CODING SYSTEM

A variety of research questions have been addressed using the SSBC. Cutrona and Suhr (1992) used the SSBC to test predictions from the optimal matching model of social support (Cutrona, 1990; Cutrona & Russell, 1990). The model predicts that the controllability of problems is an important determinant of the type of social support that is optimally effective in dealing with the problem. For problems high in controllability, support that directly aids in problem solving, such as tangible and information support, should be most effective. For problems low in controllability, support that helps people deal with their feelings of loss and disappointment should be most effective. Cutrona and Suhr (1992) found partial support for the optimal matching model. The higher the controllability of the problem faced by the stressed individual, the more information support was provided by the partner. No other support type differed in frequency as a function of problem controllability. When predicting satisfaction with the support interaction, results differed depending on the degree of control over problem-solution held by each member of the couple. The more control held by the partner (support provider), the more positive the effect of his or her provision of information support (e.g., advice on problem-solving). By contrast, the more control held by the stressed individual, the more negative the effect of partner provision of information support. Information support is only welcome when the supporter has actual expertise or access to problem solutions. When the stressed person has expertise or access to problem solutions, information support is viewed negatively.

Predictions from equity theory were tested in another study (Cutrona, 1996b). In a sample of married couples, the effect of equity or lack of equity in the number of support behaviors given and received was examined. Number of support behaviors was assessed using SSBC Total Support scores. According to equity theory, the highest level of satisfaction should result when support received is equal to support given. Receiving more or less than one gives should lead to distress. However, results showed that the higher the level of support received, the more satisfied were the individuals. Receiving more than one gave was not a source of dissatisfaction. By contrast, violated expectations for the amount of support received did predict ratings of interaction supportiveness. When people received about the same level of support that they expected, they were most satisfied with the interaction. When they received either less or more support than they expected, their satisfaction was lower (Cutrona, 1996b).

Reciprocity in the provision of support behaviors was examined using the SSBC (Cutrona et al., 1997). When controlling for the personality characteristics of both partners, the number of support behaviors received from the partner in the previous 10-min interaction significantly predicted the number of support behaviors provided to the partner in a second 10-min interaction. Those who received high levels of support also provided high levels of support. Those who received low levels of support also provided low levels of support.

The extent to which personality characteristics predict the amount of social support given and received was examined by Cutrona and colleagues (Cutrona et al., 1997). Before engaging in a problem-disclosure interaction, both members of a sample of married couples completed measures of neuroticism and extraversion. The support provider's extraversion was a significant predictor of how much support (SSBC Total Support) he or she gave to his or her partner during the interaction. More extraverted individuals provided more support behaviors to their partners than did less extraverted individuals. Provider neuroticism did not predict amount of support given. Neither extraversion nor neuroticism on the part of the support recipient predicted the amount of support he or she received from the partner.

A recent study used the SSBC to validate a new observational measure of social support elicitation strategies (Jensen, 2001). Using time-series analysis, systematic relations were found between type of support elicitation strategy used by the problem-discloser and the amount and type of social support provided in the next 2 min by the support provider. Direct requests for support were most successful in eliciting Information Support and Tangible Support. However, across support types, the most successful elicitation strategy was positive feedback from the recipient regarding the provider's helpfulness and skill as a support provider. Consistent with reinforcement theory, when providers were praised for their support behaviors, they engaged in these behaviors more frequently.

20

The Social Support Interaction Coding System (SSICS)

Lauri A. Pasch, Keith W. Harris
University of California, San Francisco

Kieran T. Sullivan
Santa Clara University

Thomas N. Bradbury
University of California, Los Angeles

This chapter describes the interaction task we use to study the exchange of social support between intimate partners, the coding system we developed to quantify the nature of these interactions called the Social Support Interaction Coding System, and the research using the coding system to date.

Consider the following interactions in which one partner talks with the other about wanting to lose weight.

INTERACTION 1: JACK AND WENDY

Jack: Well, I gotta start really working on my diet and getting more exercise.

Wendy: Yes, you really do.

Jack: I already told you I need to join a gym again. I used to lift weights three times a week and it was great.

Wendy: Yeah, but that was only part of the class you were taking. I doubt you'd really go. You know we can't afford it. What you need to do is stop eating junk food after work.

Jack: What I need to do is join a gym. Your not letting me is the problem.

INTERACTION 2: THEO AND JULIE

Julie: I know you love me either way, but I think I would feel better about myself if I managed to lose some weight.

Theo: You've seemed stressed lately about it.

Julie: It's just that when I get home, I don't feel like exercising. I'm too tired and there's too much to do with the kids and all.

Theo: Do you think it would help if I took the kids for a half hour so you could focus on what you need to do for yourself?

Julie: Yeah, that would be great.

Theo: So you already know one thing we can do that might improve things. What else?

This chapter concerns how partners in committed relationships help each other contend with personal difficulties, and how they provide everyday support to one another. This might involve wanting to improve one's health or physical appearance, as in the aforementioned examples, or wanting to change careers, increase one's self-esteem, improve work or family relationships, and any number of issues or problems individuals face. These brief interactions provide a hint of the significance of these behaviors in couples' lives. First, these interactions seem like common everyday occurrences in couple relationships. Managing personal problems is a major part of the fabric of couples' lives, in happy as well as dissatisfied couples. The quality of these exchanges gives us a sense of the variability between couples in their ability to ask for and provide support in managing personal problems. In sharing her problem with Theo, Julie shared her feelings in a genuine way, acknowledging Theo as a source of strength. In sharing his problem with Wendy, Jack seemed to avoid responsibility and blame Wendy for not letting him join a gym. Similarly, Theo expressed concern and offered to assist Julie, whereas Wendy expressed pessimism about Jack's ability to change. Both of these interactions seem likely to affect each partner's satisfaction with the relationship. Whereas Julie is likely to come away from the discussion with Theo feeling loved and hopeful, leading her to feel more confident in the satisfying nature of her relationship, Jack is likely to come away feeling misunderstood and dejected, and he may even come to question whether Wendy is really the right person for him. In addition, these interactions seem to differ in the likelihood that positive personal change will occur. Julie seems more likely to make positive steps toward weight management than Jack. In short, understanding the nature of supportive interactions in committed couple relationships may help us to understand variation in individual and interpersonal functioning.

A basic premise of our research is that the manner in which partners help each other contend with personal, rather than relationship, difficulties is a largely unexplored but potentially important domain for understanding how relationships succeed and fail.

THEORETICAL FOUNDATIONS

The social learning model, on which most couples research is based, posits that relationship functioning is largely determined by couples' interaction patterns (e.g., Jacobson & Margolin, 1979). The rewarding or positive properties of partner behaviors are thought to enhance global evaluations of the relationship, whereas the punishing or negative properties are thought to detract from global evaluations of the relationship. Nothing in the social learning model restricts the domains of couple interaction that might affect judgments of relationship quality. In fact, early writings regarding the social learning model of marriage assigned an important role theoretically to support exchanged between spouses (Jacobson & Margolin, 1979; Weiss, 1980). Nevertheless, nearly all observational research on couple interaction has focused on the behaviors that partners exchange when attempting to resolve relationship conflicts (Heyman, 2001).

From a historical point of view, several factors contributed to the almost exclusive emphasis on conflict in research on couple relationships. First, conflict is very salient in distressed marriages, particularly in clinical populations, and was presumed to be a prime determinant of marital outcomes. Second, negative behaviors were found to discriminate more strongly than positive behaviors between distressed and nondistressed marriages (see Weiss & Heyman, 1990). Because social support was originally conceptualized as purely positive in nature, its potential significance in understanding relationship distress was downplayed. Thus the surprisingly small amount of observational research on social support in marriage probably owes to the presumed significance of conflict in marriage as the prime determinant of relationship outcomes and the mistaken view that social support necessarily involves only positive behavior.

In the last decade, there has been a surge of interest in understanding positive behaviors in committed relationships, particularly exchange of support (e.g., Carels & Baucom, 1999; Cutrona, 1996a; Dehle, Larsen, & Landers, 2001). Although data indicate that behavior in the context of resolving relationship conflicts is important for the ongoing functioning of couple relationships, the modest associations between such behaviors and changes in relationship satisfaction suggest that key interpersonal domains have yet to be studied (Karney & Bradbury, 1995). Because of this strong focus on conflict, the field has limited knowledge of other domains of couple interaction that might contribute to the longitudinal course of relationship functioning. Moreover, little is known about how skills in conflict management might interact with skills in other domains to determine relationship outcomes.

How partners solicit and provide support to each other is of particular interest in view of evidence from the larger social support literature, which shows that the spouse is a frequent and important source of social support (e.g., Beach, Martin, Blum, & Roman, 1993; Julien & Markman, 1991). A number of studies have shown that spouses who report higher levels of support from their partner are more maritally satisfied than those reporting lower levels of support (e.g., Acitelli & Antonucci, 1994; Julien & Markman, 1991) and that people often identify lack of spousal support as a major reason for relationship dissatisfaction and dissolution (e.g., Baxter, 1986). Although these findings suggest a link between spousal support and relationship quality, they are limited by their exclusive use of self-report methods to assess support behavior. Reliance on self-reports is open to question when addressing hypotheses about support behavior in relationships, because measures of support and satisfaction often share content and method variance (cf. Huston, McHale, & Crouter, 1986) and because partners can be shown to be unreliable reporters of events in their relationship (Christensen & Nies, 1980).

We developed the Social Support Interaction Coding System in 1992 to bridge the gap between social support and couples research. We hoped that it would help us understand how partners help each other to contend with life's dilemmas, and how this might impact both relationship and individual outcomes.

DEVELOPMENT OF THE CODING SYSTEM

The Social Support Interaction Coding System (SSICS) is based on a normative standard conceptualization of social support, or the idea that living in a particular culture leads all of us to develop norms concerning what types of behaviors are supportive and not, and that these can be generally agreed on by members of that culture (see Dunkel–Schetter, Blasband, Feinstein, & Herbert, 1992). We created a set of normative standards through group discussions and through a thorough review of social support research in which individuals had been queried regarding what behaviors they considered supportive and not in a variety of settings (e.g., Dunkel–Schetter et al., 1992; Lehman & Hemphill, 1990). This led to the development of definitions of positive and negative social support behaviors. Based on the prevailing view in the literature, for support providers, we included a distinction between positive instrumental support (i.e., offers specific suggestions or aid) and positive emotional support (i.e., provides reassurance).

We created a micro-analytic coding system because we thought that a global approach would increase the likelihood that coders would make decisions that were colored by general impressions of the individual and the relationship, as opposed to an in-depth examination of what actually transpired in the interaction.

Also, for some research questions, we were interested in studying behavioral interaction patterns such as negative reciprocity, which required a micro-analytic approach (e.g., Pasch, Bradbury, & Davila, 1997). Furthermore, the micro-analytic approach was adopted under the assumption that, if a longitudinal association between support behaviors and relationship outcomes was established, knowing the specific form of these behaviors would enable us to teach other couples these skills in intervention programs (see Rogge, Cobb, Johnson, Lawrence, & Bradbury, 2002).

TASK AND SETTING

To generate the sample of behavior to be examined with the SSICS, partners are asked to each identify something they would like to change about themselves. They are instructed specifically to talk about personal problems that are not relationship problems. Topics generated by newlywed participants are typically issues such as exercising more, getting a better job, or changing a bad habit. Partners are asked to discuss this topic with each other for 10 min. The other partner is told to respond in whatever way he or she wishes. These roles are then reversed so that, in two 10-min interactions, partners take turns as the support solicitor (what we call the *Helpee*) and the support provider (what we call the *Helper*). Following is the script we have used:

> "In each of these discussions, one of you will talk with the other about something you would like to change about yourself. This could be about almost anything, like your work habits, your career, something about your personality or your appearance, some problem you have, friendships or relationships within your family—and the important thing is that whatever you discuss is something you want to change about yourself, and that it is not really a problem in your marriage—it should be more of a personal thing that you want to change. Is that clear? Can each of you come up with something that you personally would like to work on or change?"

Ask each person to reveal the area they have identified and check to make sure that this area is not a problem within the marriage. Then proceed with:

> "We would like you to spend the next 10 minutes with [spouse 1] talking with [spouse 2] about [spouse 1's topic]. During this time [spouse 2] you can respond however you want to, but we do want you to be involved in some way in the discussion. When 10 minutes are up, we will come back and ask the two of you to switch roles, so that in the second 10 minutes, [spouse 2] will talk with [spouse 1] about [spouse 2's topic] with [spouse 1] responding to that."

Although these are the instructions that have been used by most researchers using the SSICS, it is also possible to define a slightly different task with the same goal of eliciting support seeking and provision. For example, Harris (2001) asked each person to identify a recent stressor in his or her life and to discuss that with his or her partner (similar to the task used in the work of Cutrona and colleagues; Cutrona, Hessling, & Suhr, 1997).

DESCRIPTION OF THE CODING SYSTEM

Table 20.1 provides a summary of the SSICS codes and sample statements. Interactions are divided into speaking turns, and each speaking turn is coded. Each Helper speaking turn is assigned one of six codes (Positive Instrumental, Positive Emotional, Positive Other, Negative, Neutral, or Off-Task), and each Helpee speaking turn is assigned one of four codes (Positive, Negative, Neutral, or Off-Task).

Among the Helper codes, Positive Instrumental includes behaviors such as making specific suggestions, giving helpful advice, and offering to assist in the development or enactment of a plan of action (e.g., "When you feel nervous like that, do you think it might help to rehearse in your mind what you're going to say?"); Positive Emotional includes behaviors such as reassuring, consoling, providing genuine encouragement, conveying that Helpee is loved, cared for, or esteemed, and encouraging expression or clarification of feelings, (e.g., "So that should make you feel good, that you've taken steps to improve things!"); Positive Other includes all positive behaviors that do not fall specifically into the first two categories, including general analysis of the problem, summarizing, and encouraging continued discussion (e.g., "Go on, talk more about how you would do that."); Negative includes behaviors such as criticizing or blaming the spouse, offering inconsiderate advice, and insisting that the Helpee employ his or her approach to the problem (e.g., "You really just need to figure this out and stop complaining about it."); Off-Task includes all behaviors involving matters not relevant to the problem under consideration (e.g., "What are we doing for dinner tonight?"); and Neutral includes all other behaviors relating to the problem under consideration or closely related issues (e.g., "What time will the new job start?"). Depending on the goals of the research, investigators can collapse the positive codes into a total positive, or retain the specific subtypes.

Among the Helpee codes, Positive includes behaviors such as offering a specific, clear analysis of the problem, expressing feelings related to the problem, and asking for help or stating needs in a useful way (e.g., "I know you love me either way, but I think my weight problem has been keeping me from feeling good about myself."); Negative includes behaviors such as making demands for help, criticizing or accusing the Helper, and whining or complaining (e.g., "You're not even trying to help me, you're just turning it around to what you want to do, you never even asked me what I want."). Helpee Off-Task and Neutral are defined in the same manner as for Helpers. In research we have conducted, because couples vary in the number of speech turns, the number of times each of the SSICS codes were given for each partner was divided by his or her total number of speech turns.

TABLE 20.1

Description of Codes from the Social Support Interaction Coding System

Actor	*Code Level*	*Description and Sample of Code*
Helper	Positive Emotional	Reassures, consoles, or provides genuine encouragement to spouse; conveys that Helpee is loved, cared for, or esteemed; acknowledges Helpee's beliefs, interpretations, and feelings; encourages expression or clarification of feelings. "So that should make you feel good, that you've taken steps to improve things."
Helper	Positive Instrumental	Makes specific suggestions, gives helpful advice or access to information regarding the problem, asks specific questions aimed at narrowing or defining the problem, offers to assist in the development or enactment of a plan of action regarding the problem; all reflect consideration of Helpee's needs and opinions. *"When you feel nervous like that, do you think it might help to rehearse in your mind what you're going to say?"*
Helper	Positive Other	All positive behaviors that do not fall specifically into the first two categories, including general analysis of the problem, summarizes, encourages continued discussion. *"Go on, talk more about how you would do that."*
Helper	Negative	Criticizes or blames the spouse; expresses negative affect at the spouse; insists that the Helpee employ his or her approach to the problem or recommendations; minimizes or maximizes the scope of the problem;expresses inappropriate pessimism or optimism; is inattentive or disengaged in the helping process; offers unhelpful or inconsiderate advice; discourages expression of feelings. *"You really just need to figure this out and stop complaining about it."*

TABLE 20.1 (cont.)

Actor	Code Level	Description and Sample of Code
Helper	Off-Task	All behaviors that involve matters not relevant to the problem under consideration.
Helper	Neutral	All other behaviors that relate to the problem under consideration or closely-related issues.
Helpee	Positive	Offers specific, clear analysis of the problem, expresses feelings related to the problem, asks for help or states needs in a useful way, responds positively to Helper questions or suggestions.
		"I know you love me either way, but I think my weight problem has been keeping me from feeling good about myself."
Helpee	Negative	Makes demands for help, criticizes, blames, or accuses Helper; expresses negative affect at the spouse; whines, or complains.
		"You're not even trying to help me, you're just turning it around to what you want to do, you never even asked me what I want."
Helpee	Off Task	All behaviors that involve matters not relevant to the problem under consideration.
Helpee	Neutral	All other behaviors that relate to the problem under consideration or closely-related issues.

Note. The Positive Emotional, Positive Instrumental, and Positive Other codes can be summed to form a Total Positive Code.

CODER TRAINING

The SSICS is a relatively simple coding system to learn. Undergraduate and graduate students have reached high levels of inter-rater reliability. Training consists of an introduction to the coding system and sample codes, presentation of the manual, group discussion of practice tapes, practice coding on sample interactions, and evaluation of each individual coder's reliability with master coded tapes. After training, coders independently code interactions using the SSICS. In our research, to prevent coder drift, meetings are held regularly during which coders practice coding new and previously coded tapes, discuss coding problems, and receive feedback on inter-rater agreement. For reliability purposes, a second coder codes a randomly selected subset of the interactions. Coder training can be accomplished over a period of 4 to 8 weeks depending on how often training meetings take place. For example, if training were to take place over a 6-week period, one might hold two introductory sessions of 4 hr each in the 1st week, followed by 5 weeks consisting of 5 hr per week of individual study and coding practice, and two 2-hr group sessions for group practice and review.

Investigators interested in using the SSICS in their own laboratories can contact the first author for materials and assistance. The materials include the coding manual, a training tape with sample excerpts and codes, and a master tape with four fully coded interactions to use as a reliability test for new coders. The first author provides consultation to individual laboratories in task design and implementation of the coding system. Interested individuals can also contact the first author for information on coding services, in which the investigator sends the interactions and the coding is completed and data returned to the investigator.

CODING PROCESS

To begin coding an interaction, coders should know the topic of the discussion and the role each spouse is assigned. Coders typically listen to the first few minutes of the interaction to get a sense for the topic and the speech patterns of the participants. Then coders return to the beginning and record codes for each speech turn, on paper or electronic coding sheets. Coders stop and start the tape as needed to review sections that are hard to understand or difficult to code. It is usually possible to code both partners' behavior in one review of the interaction. This is considered preferable to coding one partner and then going through the interaction again to code the other, because it is easier to keep track of speech turns, and one's impression of one partner is less likely to be colored by one's impression of the other. For complex interactions or interactions with many speech turns, it is often necessary to review the tape two or more times to be confident in the codes that are assigned. Coding a 10-min interaction takes approximately 45 to 90 min, depending on the skill and experience of the coder and the complexity of the interaction. During the process of coding, coders are encouraged to consider the context and tone of each statement. The same literal statement can have distinctly different meanings depending on the interactive context and the tone in which it is conveyed. Additionally, coders are instructed to consider alternative behaviors that the partner could have exhibited and to view each behavior as something the partner has chosen to do. By treating enacted behaviors as choices that participants make, we have found that we are able to understand a given behavior with reference to the entire behavioral repertoire that is possible; this in turn seems to facilitate reliable coding.

RELIABILITY

Inter-rater reliability has been assessed by having a randomly selected portion of the interactions (typically 20%–25% of the total number of interactions contained in the study) coded by a second observer. Pasch and Bradbury (1998) reported inter-rater reliability using intraclass correlations: for Helpers, positive = .88, negative = .84, neutral = .90, and off-task = .99; for Helpees, positive = .98, negative = .96, neutral = .90, and off-task = .98. Based on the same sample of couples, Pasch, Bradbury, and Davila (1997) reported inter-rater reliability using percentage agreement and Kappa—for Helpers, percentage agreement = 79%, Kappa = .71; for Helpees, percentage agreement = 87%, Kappa = .79.

Based on a different sample, Pasch, Bradbury, Davila, and Sullivan (1999) reported intraclass correlations: for Helpers, positive = .86, negative = .80; for Helpees, positive = .79, negative = .75. Cohan and Kleinbaum (2002) reported intraclass correlations: for Helpees, positive = .87, negative = .81; for Helpers, positive = .78, negative = .88 (see also Cohan, Booth, & Granger, 2003). Harris (2001) reported inter-rater reliability using Kappa: for Helpers, Kappa = .78; for Helpees, Kappa = .84. Holtzworth-Munroe, Stuart, Sandin, McLaughlin, and Smutzler (1997) also reported Kappa: for Helpees, Kappa = .66; for Helpers, Kappa = .70.

VALIDITY

To evaluate validity, we have examined the associations of SSICS codes with perceived support, marital satisfaction, relevant individual variables, and behavior in the conflict domain.

Associations With Perceived Support

We have argued that observed support behavior is related to, but not synonymous with, perceptions of support. To examine this relation, immediately following each support interaction, Helpees rated a set of support-related adjectives (supported, helped, valued, and respected) to describe how they were feeling in consideration of the discussion they had just completed on a scale from 1 (*not at all*) to 9 (*very much;* see Pasch, Bradbury, & Sullivan, 1997). Husbands tended to feel less supported when their wives were more negative as support providers ($r = -.26, p < .05$). Husbands' perceptions of support were not associated with wives' positive behavior. Wives tended to feel more supported after the discussion when their husbands were more positive ($r = .41, p < .01$) and less negative ($r = -.47, p < .001$) as support providers. Thus, what observers see in support interactions tends to have some association with perceived support, but the magnitude of the correlations suggests that these constructs are distinct.

Associations With Marital Satisfaction

Four studies using different samples have reported on the relation between SSICS codes and marital satisfaction (Cohan & Kleinbaum, 2002; Harris, 2001; Pasch & Bradbury, 1998; Pasch, Bradbury, Davila, & Sullivan, 1999). In all of these studies, marital satisfaction was concurrently associated with SSICS behavioral codes. The results vary between studies in the extent to which specific SSICS codes are related to marital satisfaction, perhaps due to differences between the samples in variability in marital satisfaction. In general, relatively satisfied spouses displayed more Positive behavior and less Negative behavior both as Helpers and Helpees. Relatively satisfied spouses had partners who displayed more Positive and less Negative behavior both as Helpers and Helpees.

Associations With Negative Affectivity and Depressive Symptoms

Pasch, Bradbury, and Davila (1997) examined the associations between indicators of negative affectivity (neuroticism and depressive symptoms; NA) and social support behavior. Husbands who were high in NA were less likely to provide specific, helpful suggestions when helping their wives than husbands who were low in NA. Wives who were high in NA were less positive and more negative when providing support, and more negative when soliciting support. Analyses of negative reciprocity sequences showed that, as Helpers, husbands were more likely to reciprocate negative behavior and to have their negative behavior reciprocated, to the extent that they were high in negative affectivity. We also examined the association between a spouse's behavior and the partner's level of NA. An interesting gender difference occurred. In response to a partner who was high in NA, husbands provided less positive support, whereas wives provided more positive support.

Davila, Bradbury, Cohan, and Tochluk (1997) found that wives with higher levels of depressive symptoms were more negative when soliciting and providing support and received more negative support than those with lower levels of depressive symptoms.

Associations Between Behavior in the Conflict and Support Domains

An important question in evaluating the validity of the SSICS is whether it is measuring a distinct sample of behaviors from those exhibited in interactions based on marital conflicts. This type of discriminant validity has been addressed in four different samples of couples, using four different measures of conflict behavior: the Specific Affect Coding System (Gottman, 1994), the Rapid Marital Interaction Coding System (Heyman & Vivian, 1993), the System for Coding Interactions in Dyads (Malik & Lindahl, 1997), and the Verbal Tactics Coding System (Sillars, 1982). These studies have shown that behaviors measured using the SSICS covary with behaviors in the conflict domain in expected ways (Cohan & Kleinbaum, 2002; Harris, 2001; Pasch & Bradbury, 1998, Pasch, Bradbury, Davila, & Sullivan, 1999). However, considerable variability in behaviors in each domain is not explained by the other. Correlations are not as high as one might expect if the support task were merely yielding additional behavior similar to the conflict task, and are generally not as high as when we coded the conflict task with two different coding systems (see Pasch & Bradbury, 1998). This suggests that the support task generates a relatively distinct sample of behaviors. However, these analyses represent only a partial test of discriminant validity. More detailed investigations using the same coding system for different tasks and different coding systems for the same task would address more completely the issue of discriminant validity.

GENERALIZABILITY

There is considerable demographic, geographic, and racial and ethnic diversity in the samples that have been used with the SSICS, particularly given the small number of studies. Several regions of the United States are represented. Regional differences have not appeared to affect the applicability of the coding system. However, based on the first author's involvement in coding efforts for all of these samples, there appear to be regional differences in the types of problems individuals present (e.g., exercise and appearance concerns are more common in California). Although the majority of the couples have indicated Caucasian or White for their racial or ethnic group (range 61%–98%), there has also been substantial representation of other groups, particularly African Americans, Asians, and Latinos. Although no studies have reported racial and ethnic differences in SSICS research, perhaps aggregating all of these samples might lead to relevant findings. To date, the coding system has only been applied to heterosexual, married couples, although there is no reason to expect that the system would not apply to any intimate adult relationship.

The SSICS has been used with three samples of relatively young couples in new marriages with high marital satisfaction and with two samples of relatively older couples in established marriages. One of the latter samples had relatively high marital satisfaction; the other was composed of four groups, two of which were relatively distressed, two of which were relatively nondistressed. The codes and code definitions for the SSICS were originally developed using a sample of newly-married couples. Although the coding system as a whole seems to apply well to other groups, some interesting anecdotal differences occurred. It appeared that more established couples as well as more distressed couples had difficulty identifying a topic for their discussion that fit the criteria of something they would like to change about themselves that was not currently a problem in the marriage. One memorable example was a husband whose topic was "controlling his temper." Although this may have been an excellent personal area for him to want to improve, it is highly likely that after years of marriage, it is also a source of significant marital problems.

CLINICAL UTILITY

Like most micro-analytic coding systems, the SSICS is probably not practical for use in everyday clinical settings, due to the length of time necessary for coding. It is certainly appropriate for use in treatment effectiveness research. Specifically, if support provision and solicitation skills were the primary focus of treatment, couples could participate in a support task pretreatment and posttreatment, and the SSICS could be used to code for improvements in these areas. In addition, familiarity with the coding system might provide clinicians with a guide for less structured application of it to listening to couple communication in this context and providing feedback to patients.

STUDIES USING THE CODING SYSTEM

Initial development and research using the SSICS was conducted in the laboratory of Thomas N. Bradbury at the University of California, Los Angeles, using two separate study samples of newlywed couples, one consisting of 60 couples, and one consisting of 172 couples. In both studies, couples participated in marital problem-solving interactions first (coded using the Verbal Tactics Coding System or the Specific Affect Coding System), followed by the social support task, coded using the SSICS.

With these samples, we demonstrated that support solicitation and provision behaviors can be reliably studied using observational methods similar to those used in standard marital conflict tasks. This is in contrast with the previously prevailing view that support was purely in the eyes of the beholder (see Dunkel–Schetter & Bennett, 1990). Also, in contrast to prevailing views, we have found few differences between men and women in the quality of their support solicitation and provision behaviors. We had originally hypothesized that women would display more positive behavior and less negative behavior when soliciting and providing support than would men. The one gender difference we did find is in contrast to these predictions: In three different samples, wives were more negative as Helpees than were husbands (Harris, 2001; Pasch, Bradbury, & Davila, 1997; Pasch et al., 1999). These findings are inconsistent with the evidence from nonobservational research favoring women's support skills over men's.

We have shown in two separate samples that behaviors spouses display when soliciting and providing support are not only associated concurrently with marital satisfaction, but also foreshadow the development of marital distress over time. As reported by Pasch and Bradbury (1998), wives in couples that were classified 2 years later as distressed were about half as likely to display positive behavior and twice as likely to display negative behavior when offering support, and twice as likely to display negative behaviors when soliciting support, when compared to wives who were either satisfied or very satisfied, after controlling for initial levels of marital satisfaction. Similarly, in the larger sample reported by Pasch et al. (1999), wives were less satisfied 4 years later if they and their husbands had exhibited poor support solicitation and provision skills at baseline, again controlling for initial levels of marital satisfaction. Interestingly, in this sample, husband's satisfaction was not dependent on support behavior. In both samples, it appeared that behavior in the support domain was as important, or even more important, than behavior in the conflict domain, for the maintenance of marital satisfaction.

Because behavioral deficits in both the conflict domain and the support domain foreshadow declines in marital satisfaction, we also asked whether those deficits are redundant with each other, that is, whether they account for the same variance in marital satisfaction, or whether behavioral skills in each domain make independent contributions. In both samples, we directly compared the contributions of conflict and support behavior to marital outcomes. We found that support behavior predicted marital outcomes over and above the effects of conflict behavior. In the first sample, we also examined whether behaviors in the two domains interact in predicting marital outcomes. We found that couples with relatively poor skills in both domains were at particularly high risk for marital deterioration.

In summary, our data suggest that the behavioral deficits that predict deterioration in marital functioning are not unique to conflict resolution skills, and conflict resolution skills are also not uniquely important. Not only do these findings have implications for understanding what makes marriages succeed and fail, they also have implications for intervention. Existing premarital programs have focused on marital problem solving. These results suggest that inclusion of support skills may increase the effectiveness of these programs (see Sullivan, Pasch, Eldridge, & Bradbury, 1998).

Since the initial research on the SSICS was published, several other samples and research articles have appeared using the coding system in a variety of different research areas. These are summarized next.

Endrocrine Functioning

Cohan, Booth, and Granger (2003) analyzed the association between testosterone levels and support behavior using the SSICS. They reasoned that because testosterone is related to dominance and aggression, low levels of testosterone should be associated with more supportive interactions. They found that husbands were more positive when they and their wives were low in testosterone, whereas wives were more positive when they were high and their husbands low in testosterone.

Autonomic Reactivity

In his doctoral dissertation, Harris (2001) measured autonomic reactivity during a social support task, hypothesizing that supportive transactions would be associated with reduced autonomic reactivity in the spouse seeking support (the Helpee). Using the SSICS, he found that positive support from husbands was associated with reductions in wives' systolic blood pressure. Furthermore, he found that positive support seeking was associated with reductions in heart rate for both husbands and wives.

Cohabitation

Cohan and Kleinbaum (2002) used the SSICS to compare the social support behavior of spouses who either did or did not cohabit before marriage. They found that, compared to those who lived together before marriage, those who did not exhibited more positive help seeking, less negative help seeking, and more positive helper behavior in the first 2 years of marriage.

Violence

Holtzworth–Munroe, Stuart, Sandin, Smutzler, and McLaughlin (1997) examined the support behaviors of husbands in four groups of 25 couples each: violent and distressed; violent and nondistressed; nonviolent and distressed; and nonviolent and nondistressed, hypothesizing that violent husbands would be more negative and less supportive than nonviolent husbands. They were unable to differentiate between the groups on the basis of support behavior as coded by the SSICS. They concluded that, because the SSICS was originally based on newlywed behavior, perhaps it "is not sensitive to behaviors that uniquely characterize violent couples" (p. 408).

Attachment Security

There is considerable conceptual overlap between attachment and social support, yet few studies assess these together. Cobb, Davila, and Bradbury (2001) measured perceptions of attachment security, social support behavior, and marital satisfaction. Spouses who had positive perceptions of attachment security (i.e., perceived their partner as being securely attached) were better support providers and receivers. Furthermore, they found support for a mediational model: positive perceptions of attachment security were associated with more positive support behavior, which was associated with husbands' concurrent marital satisfaction and wives' marital satisfaction 1 year later.

Marital Stress

Davila, Bradbury, Cohan, and Tochluk (1997) examined support behavior and perceptions as mediators in the relationship between depressive symptoms and the development of marital stress. They found that wives with higher levels of depressive symptoms were more negative when soliciting and providing support and received more negative support, and that such behavior was associated with increases in marital stress 1 year later. They also found that wives with higher levels of depressive symptoms expected their interactions with their husbands to be unsupportive, that these negative expectations were associated with more negative wife support behavior, and that this negative behavior was associated with increases in marital stress. These findings provided a mechanism whereby the generation of stress in depressed individuals may occur.

ACKNOWLEDGMENTS

This research was funded by National Institute of Mental Health Grant MH48674 to Thomas N. Bradbury. We thank Catherine L. Cohan, Joanne Davila, Matthew Johnson, Benjamin Karney, Erika Lawrence, and Lexi Rothman for their assistance with various aspects of this work.

References

Achenbach, T. M. (1991). *Manual for the Child Behavior Checklist and 1991 profile.* Burlington: University of Vermont, Department of Psychiatry.

Acitelli, L. K. (1992). Gender differences in relationship awareness and marital satisfaction among young married couples. *Personality and Social Psychology Bulletin, 18,* 102–110.

Acitelli, L. K., & Antonucci, T. C. (1994). Gender differences in the link between marital support and satisfaction in older couples. *Journal of Personality and Social Psychology, 67,* 688–698.

Acitelli, L. K., & Duck, S. (1987). Intimacy as the proverbial elephant. In D. Perlman & S. Duck (Eds.), *Intimate relationships: Development, dynamics, and deterioration* (pp. 297–307). Newbury Park, CA: Sage.

Alexander, J. (1973). Defensive and supportive communications in family systems. *Journal of Marriage and the Family, 35,* 613–617.

Allison, P. D., & Liker, J. K. (1982). Analyzing sequential categorical data on dyadic interaction: A comment on Gottman. *Psychological Bulletin, 91,* 393–403.

Anderson, E. R., & Greene, S. M. (1999). Children of stepparents and blended families. In W. K. Silverman & T. H. Ollendick (Eds.), *Developmental issues in the clinical treatment of children* (pp. 342–357). Needham Heights, MA: Allyn & Bacon.

Andrew, E. (2001). *Emotion suppression: New methodologies in the study of gender differences in emotion regulation.* Unpublished undergraduate thesis, Bryn Mawr College, Bryn Mawr, PA.

Aron, A., Norman, C., Aron, E., McKenna, C., & Heyman, R. E. (2000). Couples shared anticipation in novel and arousing activities and experienced relationship quality. *Journal of Personality and Social Psychology, 78,* 273–284.

Babcock, J. C., Waltz, J., Jacobson, N. S., & Gottman, J. M. (1993). Power and violence: The relation between communication patterns, power discrepancies, and domestic violence. *Journal of Consulting and Clinical Psychology, 61,* 40–50.

Bakeman, R. (2000). Behavioral observation and coding. In H. T. Reis and C. M. Judd (Eds.), *Handbook of research methods in social and personality psychology* (pp. 138–159). New York: Cambridge University Press.

Bakeman, R., & Adamson, L. B. (1984). Coordinating attention to people and objects in mother–infant and peer–infant interaction. *Child Development, 55,* 1278–1289.

Bakeman, R. Adamson, L. B., & Strisik, P. (1989). Lags and logs: Statistical approaches to interaction. In M. H. Bornstein & J. S. Bruner (Eds.), *Interaction in human development* (pp. 241–260). Hillsdale, NJ: Lawrence Erlbaum Associates, Inc.

Bakeman, R., & Brownlee, J. R. (1980). The strategic use of parallel play: A sequential analysis. *Child Development, 51,* 873–878.

Bakeman, R., & Gottman, J. (1986). *Observing interaction.* New York: Cambridge University Press.

Bakeman, R., & Gottman, J. M. (1997). *Observing interaction: An introduction to sequential analysis* (2nd ed.). New York: Cambridge University Press.

Bakeman, R., McArthur, D., & Quera, V. (1996). Detecting group differences in sequential association using sampled permutations: Log odds, kappa, and phi compared. *Behavior Research Methods, Instruments, and Computers, 28,* 446–457.

Bakeman, R., & Quera, V. (1995a). *Analyzing interaction: Sequential analysis with SDIS and GSEQ.* New York: Cambridge University Press.

Bakeman, R., & Quera, V. (1995b). Log–linear approaches to lag–sequential analysis when consecutive codes may and cannot repeat. *Psychological Bulletin, 118,* 272–284.

Bakeman, R., Quera, V., McArthur, D., & Robinson, B. F. (1997). Detecting sequential patterns and determining their reliability with fallible observers. *Psychological Methods, 2,* 357–370

Bakeman, R., & Robinson, B. F. (1994). *Understanding log–linear analysis with ILOG: An interactive approach.* Hillsdale, NJ: Lawrence Erlbaum Associates, Inc.

Bank, L., & Patterson, G. R. (1992). The use of structural equation modeling in combining data from different types of assessment. In J. Rosen & P. McReynolds (Eds.), *Recent advances in psychological assessment* (Vol. *8,* pp. 41–74). New York: Plenum.

Barker, C., & Lemle, R. (1984). The helping process in couples. *American Journal of Community Psychology, 12,* 321–336.

Barnett, L. R., & Nietzel, M. T. (1979). Relationship of instrumental and affectional behaviors and self–esteem to marital satisfaction in distressed and nondistressed couples. *Journal of Consulting and Clinical Psychology, 47,* 946–957.

Barrera, M., Sandler, I. N., & Ramsay, T. R. (1981). Preliminary development of a scale of social support: Studies on college students. *American Journal of Community Psychology, 9,* 435–447.

Baucom, D. H., & Epstein, N. (1990). *Cognitive–behavioral marital therapy.* New York: Brunner/Mazel.

Baucom, D. H., Hahlweg, K., & Kuschel, A. (2003). Are waiting list control groups needed in future marital therapy outcome research? *Behavior Therapy,* in press.

Baucom, D. H., Notarius, C. I., Burnett, C. K., & Haefner, P. (1990). Gender differences and sex–role identity in marriage. In F. D. Fincham & T. N. Bradbury (Eds.) *The psychology of marriage: Basic issues and applications.* New York: Guilford.

Baucom, D. H., Sayers, S. L., & Sher, T. G. (1990). Supplementing behavioral marital therapy with cognitive restructuring and emotional expressiveness training: An outcome investigation. *Journal of Consulting and Clinical Psychology, 58,* 636–645.

Baxter, L. A. (1986). Gender differences in the heterosexual relationship rules embedded in break–up accounts. *Journal of Social and Personal Relationships, 3,* 289–306.

Beach, S. R .H., Martin, J. K., Blum, T. C., & Roman, P. M. (1993). Effects of marital and co–worker relationships on negative affect: Testing the central role of marriage. *American Journal of Family Therapy, 21,* 312–322.

Beck, A. T., & Steer, R. A. (1987). *Manual for the revised Beck Depression Inventory.* San Antonio, TX: Psychological Corporation.

Beier, R. T., & Sternberg, D. P. (1977). Marital communication. *Journal of Communication, 27,,* 92–97.

Berlin, J. (1975). *Das offene Gespräch: Paare lernen Kommunikation* [Frankly speaking: Couples learn communication]. München, Germany: Pfeiffer.

Berns, S. B., Jacobson, N. S., & Gottman, J. M. (1999). Demand–withdraw interaction in couples with a violent husband. *Journal of Consulting and Clinical Psychology, 67,* 666–674.

Birchler, G. R., Clopton, J. R., & Adams, N. L. (1984). Marital conflict resolution: Factors influencing concordance between partners and trained coders. *American Journal of Family Therapy, 12,* 15–28.

Black, K. A. (2000). Gender differences in adolescents' behavior during conflict resolution tasks with friends. *Adolescence, 35,* 499–512.

Black, K. A., & McCartney, K. (1997). Adolescent females' security with parents predicts the quality of peer interactions. *Social Development, 6,* 91–110.

Blood, R. O., & Wolfe, D. M. (1960). *Husbands and wives: The dynamics of married living.* Glencoe, IL.: Free Press.

Bouthillier, D., Julien, D., Dubé, M., Moss, E., Lebeau, E., Bélanger, I., et al. (1998, July). Adult attachment mental models and regulation of negative affect in marital conflict interaction. In B. Pierrehumbert (Chair), *Links between adults' internal working models of attachment and couple relationships: Methods and concept.* Symposium conducted at the International Society for Social and Behavioral Development, Berne, Switzerland.

Bradbury, T. N., & Karney, B. R. (1993). Longitudinal study of marital interaction and dysfunction: Review and analysis. *Clinical Psychology Review, 13,* 15–27.

Bradbury, T. N., Rogge, R., & Lawrence, E. (2001). Reconsidering the role of conflict in marriage. In A. Booth, A. C. Crouter, & M. Clements (Eds.), *Couples in conflict* (pp. 59–81). Mahwah, NJ: Lawrence Erlbaum Associates, Inc.

Braukhaus, C., Hahlweg, K., Kroeger, C., Fehm–Wolfsdorf, G., & Groth, T. (2001). "Darf es ein wenig mehr sein?" Zur Wirksamkeit von Auffrischungssitzungen bei der Prävention von Beziehungsstörungen [The impact of adding booster sessions to a prevention training program for committed couples]. *Verhaltenstherapie, 11,* 55 62.

Braver, S. L., & Griffin, W. A. (2000). Engaging fathers in the post–divorce family. In E. Peters, G. Peterson, S. Steinmetz, & R. Day (Eds.), *Fatherhood: Research, intervention, and policies* (pp. 247–267). Binghamton, NY: Haworth.

Brennan R., & Prediger, D. (1981). Coefficient kappa: Some uses, misuses and alternatives. *Educational and Psychological Measurement, 41,* 687–699.

Brown, G. W., & Harris, T. (1978). *Social origins of depression.* London: Tavistock.

Buehlman, K. T., Gottman, J. M., & Katz, L. F. (1992). How a couple views their past predicts their future: Predicting divorce from an oral history interview. *Journal of Family Psychology, 5,* 295–318.

Burman, B., Margolin, G., & John, R. S. (1993). America's angriest home videos: Behavioral contingencies observed in home reenactments of marital conflict. *Journal of Consulting and Clinical Psychology, 61,* 28–39.

Burnett, R. (1987). Reflections in personal relationships. In R. Burnett, P. McGhee, & D. D. Clarke (Eds.), *Accounting for relationships: Explanation, representation and knowledge* (pp. 74–93). London: Methuen.

Burry-Stock, J. A., Shaw, D. G., & Laurie, C. (1996). Rater agreement indexes for performance assessment. *Educational & Psychological Measurement, 56,* 251-262.

Butler, M. H., & Wampler, K. S. (1999). A meta–analytical update of research on the couple communication program. , *27,* 223–237.

Butzlaff, R. L., & Hooley, J. M. (1998). Expressed emotion and psychiatric relapse: A meta–analysis. *Archives of General Psychiatry, 55,* 547–552.

Campos, J. J. (1982). *Human emotions: Their new importance and their role in social referencing* (Annual Report). Research and Clinical Center for Child Development, 1–7.

Cappelli, M., McGrath, P. J., Daniels, T., Manion, I., et al. (1994). Marital quality of parents of children with spina bifida: A case–comparison study. *Journal of Developmental and Behavioral Pediatrics, 15,* 320–326.

Carels, R. A., & Baucom, D. H. (1999). Support in marriage: Factors associated with on–line perceptions of support helpfulness. *Journal of Family Psychology, 13,* 131–144.

Carrère, S., Buehlman, K. T., Coan, J., Gottman, J. M., & Ruckstuhl, L. (2000). Predicting marital stability and divorce in newlywed couples. *Journal of Family Psychology, 14,* 42–58.

Cascadi, M., Langhinrichsen–Rohling, J., & Vivian, D. (1992). Marital aggression: Impact, injury and health correlates for husbands and wives. *Archives of Internal Medicine, 152,* 1178–1184.

Cascardi, M., & Vivian, D. (1995). Context for specific episodes of marital aggression. *Journal of Family Violence, 10,* 265–293.

Chambless, D. L., Bryan, A. D., Aiken, L. S., Steketee, G., & Hooley, J. M. (2001). Predicting expressed emotion: A study with families of obsessive–compulsive and agoraphobic outpatients. *Journal of Family Psychology, 15,* 225–240.

Chambless, D. L., Fauerbach, J. A., Floyd, F., Wilson, K., Remen, A., & Renneberg, B. (2002). Marital interaction of agoraphobic women: A controlled, behavioral observation study. *Journal of Abnormal Psychology, 111,* 502-512.

Chartrand, E., & Julien, D. (1994). Système d'Observation des Dimensions d'Interaction (SODI): Validation canadienne française du Interaction Dimension Coding System [Interaction Dimension Observation System: Validation of the Interaction Dimension Coding System with a French–Canadian population]. *Canadian Journal of Behavioral Sciences/Revue Canadienne des Sciences du Comportement, 26,* 121–130.

Chodorow, N. (1978). *The reproduction of mothering: Psychoanalysis and the sociology of gender.* Berkeley: University of California Press.

Christensen, A. (1987). Detection of conflict patterns in couples. In K. Halweg & M.J . Goldstein (Eds.), *Understanding major mental disorders: The contribution of family interaction research* (pp. 250–265). New York: Family Process Press.

Christensen, A. (1988). Dysfunctional interaction patterns in couples. In P. Noller & M. A. Fitzpatrick (Eds.), *Perspectives on marital interaction* (pp. 31–52). Philadelphia: Multilingual Matters.

Christensen, A., Atkins, D. S., Berns, S., Wheeler, J., Baucom, D. H., & Simpson, L. E. (2003). Traditional versus integrative behavioral couples therapy for significantly and chronically distressed married couples. *Journal of Consulting and Clinical Psychology,* in press.

Christensen, A., Eldridge, K. A., Grasshoff, A., Lim, V. R., & Santagata, R. (2003). Cross–cultural analysis of demand/withdraw interaction in couples. Manuscript in preparation.

Christensen, A., & Heavey, C. L. (1990). Gender and social structure in the demand/withdraw pattern of marital conflict. *Journal of Personality and Social Psychology, 59,* 73–81.

Christensen, A., & Heavey, C. L. (1993). Gender differences in marital conflict: The demand/withdraw interaction pattern. In S. Oskamp & M. Costanzo (Eds.), *Gender issues in contemporary society* (pp. 113–141). Newbury Park, CA: Sage.

Christensen, A., & Heavey, C. (1999). Interventions for couples. *Annual Review of Psychology, 50,* 165–190.

Christensen, A., & Nies, D. C. (1980). The Partner Observation Checklist: Empirical analysis and technique. *American Journal of Family Therapy, 8,* 69–79.

Christensen, A., & Shenk, J. L. (1991). Communication, conflict, and psychological distance in nondistressed, clinic, and divorcing couples. *Journal of Consulting and Clinical Psychology, 59,* 458–463.

Christensen, A., & Sullaway, M. (1984). *Communication patterns questionnaire.* Unpublished questionnaire, University of California, Los Angeles.

Claes, J. A., & Rosenthal, D. M. (1990). Men who batter: A study of interpersonal power. *Journal of Family Violence, 5,* 215–224.

Cohan, C. L., Booth, A., & Granger, D. A. (2003). Gender moderates the relationship between testosterone and marital interaction. *Journal of Family Psychology, 17,* 29-40.

Cohan, C. L., & Kleinbaum, S. (2002). Toward a greater understanding of the cohabitation effect: Premarital cohabitation and marital communication. *Journal of Marriage and Family, 64,* 180–193.

Cohen, J. (1960). A coefficient of agreement for nominal scales. *Educational and Psychological Measurement, 20,* 37–46.

Cohen, J., & Cohen, P. (1983). *Applied multiple regression/correlation analysis for the behavioral sciences* (2nd ed.). Hillsdale, NJ: Lawrence Erlbaum Associates, Inc.

Cohen, S., & Hoberman, H. M. (1983). Positive events and social supports as buffers of life change stress. *Journal of Applied Social Psychology, 13,* 99–125.

Cohen, S., & McKay, G. (1984). Social support, stress, and the buffering hypothesis: An theoretical analysis. In A. Baum, S. E. Taylor, & J. E. Singer (Eds.), *Handbook of psychology and health* (Vol, *4,* pp. 253–267). Hillsdale, NJ: Lawrence Erlbaum Associates, Inc.

Conger, R. D., Patterson, G. R., & Ge, X. (1995). A mediational model for the impact of parents' stress on adolescent adjustment. *Child Development, 66,* 80–97.

Cook, J., Tyson, R., White, J., Rush, R., Gottman, J., & Murray, J. (1995). Mathematics of marital conflict: Qualitative dynamic mathematical modeling of marital interaction. *Journal of Family Psychology, 9,* 110–130.

Cordova, A. D. (2000). *Teamwork and the transition to parenthood.* Unpublished doctoral dissertation, University of Denver, CO.

Cordova, J. V., Gee, C. B., Warren, L. Z., & McDonald, R. (2002). *Intimate safety: measuring the private experience of intimacy.* Manuscript submitted for publication.

Cordova, J. V., Jacobson, N. S., Gottman, J. M., Rush, R., & Cox, G. (1993). Negative reciprocity and communication in couples with a violent husband. *Journal of Abnormal Psychology, 102,* 559–564.

Cordova, J. V., & Scott, R. L. (2001). Intimacy: A behavioral interpretation. *The Behavior Analyst, 24,* 75–86.

Cordova, J. V., Warren, L. Z., & Gee, C. G. (2001). Motivational interviewing as an intervention for at–risk couples. *Journal of Marital and Family Therapy, 27,* 315–326..

Cormier, N., & Julien, D. (1996). Relation entre l'ajustement conjugal et des mesures subjectives et objectives de soutien social [Associations between marital adjustment, perceived support, and observed support in couples]. *Canadian Journal of Behavioral Sciences/Revue Canadienne des Sciences du Comportement, 28,* 302–309.

Cox, M. J., Paley, B., Burchinal, M., & Payne, C. C. (1999). Marital perceptions and interactions across the transition to parenthood. *Journal of Marriage and the Family, 61,* 611–625.

Cromwell, R. E., & Olson, D. H. (1975). *Power in families*. New York: Wiley.

Cronbach, L. (1972). *The dependability of behavioral measurements: Theory of generalizability for scores and profiles*. New York: Wiley.

Cutrona, C. E. (1986). Behavioral manifestations of social support: A microanalytic investigation. *Journal of Personality and Social Psychology, 51,* 201–208.

Cutrona, C. E. (1989). Ratings of social support by adolescents and adult informants: Degree of correspondence and prediction of depressive symptoms. *Journal of Personality and Social Psychology, 57,* 723–730.

Cutrona, C. E. (1990). Stress and social support – In search of optimal matching. *Journal of Social and Clinical Psychology, 9,* 3–14.

Cutrona, C. E. (1996a). *Social support in couples: Marriage a resource in times of stress.* Thousand Oaks, CA: Sage.

Cutrona, C. E. (1996b). Social support as a determinant of marital quality. In G. R. Pierce, B. R. Sarason, & I. G. Sarason (Eds.), *Handbook of social support and the family* (pp. 173–194). New York: Plenum.

Cutrona, C. E., & Russell, D. W. (1987). The provisions of social relationships and adaptation to stress. *Advances in Personal Relationships, 1,* 37–67.

Cutrona, C. E., & Russell, D. (1990). Type of social support and specific stress: Toward a theory of optimal matching. In I. G. Sarason, B. R. Sarason, & G. R. Pierce (Eds.), *Social support: An interactional view.*(pp. 319–366). New York: Wiley.

Cutrona, C., & Suhr, J. (1992). Controllability of stressful events and satisfaction with partner support behaviors. *Communication Research, 19,* 154–174.

Cutrona, C. E., & Suhr, J. A. (1994). Social support communication in the context of marriage: An analysis of couples' supportive interactions. In B. B. Burleson, T. L. Albrecht, & I. G. Sarason (Eds.), *Communication of social support: Messages, relationships, and community* (pp. 113–135). Thousand Oaks, CA: Sage.

Cutrona, C. E., Hessling, R. M., & Suhr, J. A. (1997). The influence of husband and wife personality on marital social support interactions. *Personal Relationships, 4,* 379–393.

Daugherty, M. K., Floyd, F. J., Zucker, R. A., Fitzgerald, H. E., & Bingham, C. R. (2001, November). *Dominance and power struggles in alcoholic marital interactions: Alcoholic subtype variations.* Paper presented at the meeting of the Association for Advancement of Behavior Therapy, Philadelphia.

Davila, J., Bradbury, T. N., Cohan, C. L., & Tochluk, S. (1997). Marital functioning and depressive symptoms: Evidence for a stress generation model. *Journal of Personality and Social Psychology, 73,* 849–861.

Dehle, C., Larsen, D., & Landers, J.E. (2001). Social support in marriage. *American Journal of Family Therapy, 29,* 307–324.

Dishion, T. J., Li, F., Spracklen, K. M., Brown, G., & Haas, E. (1998). The measurement of parenting practices in research on adolescent problem behavior: A multimethod and multitrait analysis. In R. S. Ashery, E. B. Robertson, & K. L. Kumpfer (Eds.), *Research on drug abuse prevention through family interventions* (National Institute on Drug Abuse Research Monograph No. *177*). Rockville, MD: National Institute on Drug Abuse.

Dobash, R. E., & Dobash, R. (1979). *Violence against wives*. New York: Free Press.

Dorian, M., & Cordova, J. V. (1999). *The Intimacy Coding System*. Unpublished coding manual, University of Illinois, Urbana–Champaign.

Dorian, M., & Cordova, J. V. (2001). Observing intimacy in the interactions of distressed and nondistressed couples. Unpublished manuscript, University of Illinois, Urbana–Champaign.

Driver, J. L., & Gottman, J. M. (2002). *Daily marital interactions during dinner time in an apartment laboratory and positive affect during marital conflict among newlywed couples.* Manuscript submitted for publication.

Driver, J. L., Tabares, A., Shapiro, A., Nahm, E. Y., & Gottman, J. M. (2003). Interactional patterns in marital success or failure: Gottman laboratory studies. In F. Walsh (Ed.), *Normal family processes: Growing diversity and complexity* (3rd ed.), pp. 493-513. New York: Guilford.

Dubé, M., Julien, D., Bouthillier, D., Lebeau, E., Bélanger, I., & Hamelin, M. (2001). La relation entre les conflits conjugaux, la satisfaction conjugale des mères et la qualité de la communication mère–adolescente. [Association between marital conflict, mothers' marital satisfaction and mother/adolescent daughters' communication]. *International Journal of Psychology/Revue Internationale de Psychologie, 36,* 329–339.

Dubé, M., Julien, D., Bouthillier, D., Lebeau, E., Bélanger, I, & Hamelin, M. (2003). Climat familial et réseau d'amis chez les adolescentes [Family relationships and adolescent daughters' social networks]. *Enfance,* in press.

Duda, R. O., Hart, P. E., & Stork, D. G. (2001). *Pattern classification* (2nd ed.). New York: Wiley.

Dufore, D. S. (2000). Marital similarity, marital interaction, and couples' shared view of their marriage. Dissertation Abstract.

Dumas, J. E., Lemay, P., & Dauwalder, J. P. (2001). Dynamic analyses of mother–child interactions in functional and dysfunctional dyads: A synergetic approach. *Journal of Abnormal Child Psychology, 29,* 317–329.

Dunkel–Schetter, C., & Bennett, T. L. (1990). Differentiating the cognitive and behavioral aspects of social support. In B. R. Sarason, I. G. Sarason, & G. R. Pierce (Eds.), *Social support: An interactional view* (pp. 267–296). New York: Wiley.

Dunkel–Schetter, C., Blasband, D. E., Feinstein, L. G., & Herbert, T. B. (1992). Elements of supportive interactions: When are attempts to help effective? In S. Spacapan & S. Oskamp (Eds.), *Helping and being helped in the real world* (pp. 83–114). Newbury Park, CA: Sage.

Dunn, G. (1989). *Design and analysis of reliability studies: The statistical evaluation of measurement errors*. New York: Wiley. (out of print)

Dutton, D. G. (1988). *The domestic assault of women*. Newton, MA: Allyn & Bacon.

Eddy, J. M., Dishion, T. J., & Stoolmiller, M. (1998). The analysis of intervention change in children and families: Methodological and conceptual issues embedded in intervention studies. *Journal of Abnormal Child Psychology, 26,* 53–69.

Eidelson, R. J. (1997). Complex adaptive systems in the behavioral and social sciences. *Review of General Psychology, 1,* 42–71.

Ekman, P., & Friesen, W. V. (1975). *Unmasking the face: A guide to recognizing emotions from facial clues*. Englewood Cliffs, NJ: Prentice Hall.

Ekman, P., Friesen, W. V. (1978). *Facial Action Coding System.* Palo Alto, CA: Consulting Psychologists Press, Inc.

Eldridge, K. A. (2000). *Demand–withdraw communication during marital conflict: Relationship satisfaction and gender role considerations.* Unpublished doctoral dissertation, University of California, Los Angeles.

Eldridge, K. A., & Christensen, A. (2002). Demand–withdraw communication during couple conflict: A review and analysis. In P. Noller & J. A. Feeney (Eds), *Understanding marriage: Developments in the study of couple interaction,* pp. 289-322. New York: Cambridge University Press.

Elwood, R., & Jacobson, N. (1982). Partners' agreement in reporting their behavioral interactions: A clinical replication. *Journal of Consulting and Clinical Psychology, 50,* 783–784.

Epstein, N., & Baucom, D. H. (2002). *Enhanced cognitive–behavioral therapy for couples: A contextual approach*. Washington, DC: American Psychological Association.

Epstein, N. B., & Baucom, D. H. (2002). *Enhanced cognitive–behavioral therapy for couples: A contextual approach.* Washington, D.C.: American Psychological Association.

Epstein, N., & Eidelson, R. J. (1981). Unrealistic beliefs of clinical couples: Their relationship to expectations, goals, and satisfaction. *American Journal of Family Therapy, 9,* 13–22.

Falloon, I. R. H., Hahlweg, K., & Tarrier, N. (1990). Family interventions in the community management of schizophrenia: Methods and results. In E. R. Straube & K. Hahlweg (Eds.), *Schizophrenia. Concepts, vulnerability, and intervention* (pp. 217–240). New York: Springer.

Feldman, L. (1995). Variations in the circumplex structure of mood. *Personality and Social Psychology Bulletin, 21,* 806–817.

Fincham, F. (1998). Child development and marital relations. *Child Development, 69,* 543–574.

Fletcher, G., Fincham, F. D., Cramer, L., & Heron, N. (1987). The role of attributions in the development of dating relationships. *Journal of Personality and Social Psychology, 53,* 481–489.

Floyd, F. J. (1988). Couples' cognitive/affective reactions to communication behaviors. *Journal of Marriage and the Family, 50,* 523–532.

Floyd, F. J. (1989). Segmenting interactions: Coding units for assessing marital and family behaviors. *Behavioral Assessment, 11,* 13–29.

Floyd, F. J., Baucom, D. B., Godfrey, J., & Palmer, C. (1998). Observational methods. In A. S. Bellack, M. Hersen, & N. R. Schooler (Eds.), *Comprehensive clinical psychology: Vol .3, research and methods* (pp. 1–21). Oxford, England: Elsevier Science Limited.

Floyd, F. J., Gilliom, L. A., & Costigan, C. L. (1998). Marriage and the parenting alliance: Longitudinal prediction of change in parenting perceptions and behaviors. *Child Development, 69,* 1461–1479.

Floyd, F. J., Harter, K., & VanWidenfelt, B. (2001, April). *Configurations of cooperative coparenting.* Paper presented at the Biennial Meeting of the Society for Research in Child Development, Minneapolis, MN.

Floyd, F. J., & Markman, H. J. (1983). Observational biases in spouse observation: Toward a cognitive/behavioral model of marriage. *Journal of Consulting and Clinical Psychology, 51,* 450–457.

Floyd, F. J., & Markman, H. J. (1984). An economical observational measure of couples' communication skill. *Journal of Consulting and Clinical Psychology, 52,* 97–103.

Floyd, F. J., O'Farrell, T. J., & Goldberg, M. (1987). Comparison of marital observational measures: The Marital Interaction Coding System and the Communication Skills Test. *Journal of Consulting and Clinical Psychology, 55,* 423–429.

Floyd, F. J., Weinand, J. W., & Cimmarusti, R. A. (1989). Clinical family assessment: Applying structured measurement procedures in treatment settings. *Journal of Marital and Family Therapy, 15,* 271–288.

Floyd, F. J., & Zmich, D. E. (1991). Marriage and the parenting partnership: Perceptions and interactions of parents with mentally retarded and typically developing children. *Child Development, 62,* 1434–1448.

Fogarty, T. F. (1976). Marital crisis. In P. J. Guerin (Ed.), *Family therapy: Theory and practice.* New York: Gardner.

Fogel, A., Lyra, M. C., & Valsiner, J. (1997). *Dynamics and indeterminism in developmental and social processes.* Mahwah, NJ: Lawrence Erlbaum Associates, Inc.

Fredrickson, B. (2001). The role of positive emotions in positive psychology. *American Psychologist, 56,* 218–226.

Furterer, J. (2001). *Experiencing and expressing emotion: Suppression of emotion in marital interactions.* Unpublished undergraduate thesis, Bryn Mawr College, Bryn Mawr, PA.

Gardner, W. (1995). On the reliability of sequential data: Measurement, meaning, and correction. In J. M Gottman (Ed.), *The analysis of change* (pp. 339–359). Hillsdale, NJ: Lawrence Erlbaum Associates, Inc.

Goldfried, M. R., & D'Zurilla, T. J. (1969). A behavioral–analytic model for assessing competence. In C. Speilberger (Ed.), *Current topics in clinical and community psychology* (Vol. *1,* pp. 151–196). New York: Academic Press.

Goldstein, M. J. (1985). Family factors that antedate the onset of schizophrenia and related disorders: The results of a fifteen year prospective longitudinal study. *Acta Psychiatrica Scandinavica, 71,* 7–18.

Goode, W. J. (1971). Force and violence in the family. *Journal of Marriage and the Family, 3,* 624–636.

Gottlieb, B. H. (1978). The development and application of a classification scheme of informal helping behavior. *Canadian Journal of Behavioral Science, 10,* 105–116.

Gottlieb, B. H. (1985). Social support and the study of personal relationships. *Journal of Social and Personal Relationships, 2,* 351–375.

Gottman, J. M. (1979). *Marital interaction: Experimental investigations.* New York: Academic.

Gottman, J. M. (1981). *Time–series analysis: A comprehensive introduction for social scientists.* New York: Cambridge University Press.

Gottman, J. M. (1993a). A theory of marital dissolution and stability. *Journal of Consulting and Clinical Psychology, 61,* 6–15.

Gottman, J. M. (1993b). The roles of conflict engagement, escalation, and avoidance in marital interaction: A longitudinal view of five types of couples. *Journal of Consulting and Clinical Psychology, 61,* 6–15.

Gottman, J. M. (1994). *What predicts divorce: The relationship between marital processes and marital outcomes*. Hillsdale, NJ: Lawrence Erlbaum Associates, Inc.

Gottman, J. M. (Ed.) (1996). *What predicts divorce? The measures*. Mahwah, NJ: Lawrence Erlbaum Associates, Inc.

Gottman, J. M. (1999). *The marriage clinic: A scientifically based marital therapy*. New York: Norton.

Gottman, J. M., & Bakeman, R. (1979). The sequential analysis of observational data. In M. E. Lamb, S. J. Suomi, & G. R. Stephenson (Eds.), *Social interaction analysis*. Madison: University of Wisconsin Press.

Gottman, J. M., Coan, J., & McCoy, K. (1996). *The Specific Affect Coding System*. Hillsdale, NJ: Lawrence Erlbaum Associates, Inc.

Gottman, J. M., Coan, J., Carrére, S., & Swanson, C., (1998). Predicting marital happiness and stability from newlywed interactions. *Journal of Marriage and the Family, 60,* 5–22.

Gottman, J. M., & Levenson, R. W., (1983). Marital interaction: physiological linkage and affective exchange. *Journal of Personality and Social Psychology, 45,* 587–597.

Gottman, J. M., & Levenson, R. W. (1985). A valid procedure for obtaining self–report of affect in marital interaction. *Journal of Consulting and Clinical Psychology, 53,* 151–160.

Gottman, J. M., & Levenson, R. W. (1986). Assessing the role of emotion in marriage. *Behavioral Assessment, 8,* 31–48.

Gottman, J. M., & Levenson, R. W. (1988). The social psychophysiology of marriage. In P. Noller and M. A. Fitzpatrick (Eds.), *Perspectives on marital interaction* (pp. 182–200). Philadelphia: Multilingual Matters.

Gottman. J. M., & Levenson, R. W. (1992). Marital processes predictive of later dissolution: Behavior, physiology, and health. *Journal of Personality and Social Psychology, 63,* 221–233.

Gottman J. M., & Levenson, R. W. (1997). The role of positive affect in long term marital stability. Unpublished manuscript, University of Washington at Seattle.

Gottman J. M., & Levenson, R. W. (1999). Rebound from marital conflict and divorce prediction. *Family Process, 38,* 287–292.

Gottman, J. M., & Levenson, R. W. (2000). The timing of divorce: Predicting when a couple will divorce over a 14–year period. *Journal of Marriage and the Family, 62,* 737–745.

Gottman, J. M., & Levenson, R. W. (2002). A two–factor model for predicting when a couple will divorce: Exploratory analyses using 14–year longitudinal data. *Family Process, 41,* 83–96.

Gottman, J. M., Levenson, R. W., Swanson, C., Swanson, K., Tyson, R. & Yoshimoto, D. (2003). Observing gay, lesbian and heterosexual couples' relationships: Mathematical modeling of conflict interaction. *Journal of Homosexuality, 45,* 65-91.

Gottman, J. M., Markman, H., & Notarius, C. (1977). The topography of marital conflict: A sequential analysis of verbal and nonverbal behavior. *Journal of Marriage and the Family, 39,* 461–476.

Gottman, J. M., McCoy, K., Coan, J., and Collier, H. (1996). The Specific Affect Coding System (SPAFF) for observing emotional communication in marital and family interaction. In J. M. Gottman (Ed.), *What predicts divorce? The measures*. Mahwah, NJ: Lawrence Erlbaum Associates, Inc.

Gottman, J. M., Murray, J. D., Swanson, C. C., Tyson, R., & Swanson, K. R. (2002). *The mathematics of marriage: Dynamic nonlinear models.* Cambridge, MA: MIT Press.

Gottman, J. M., & Notarius, C. I. (2002). Marital research in the 20th century and a research agenda for the 21st century. *Family Process, 41,* 159–197.

Gottman, J. M., Notarius, C. I., Gonso, J., & Markman, H. J. (1976). *A couple's guide to communication.* Champaign, IL: Research Press.

Gottman, J. M., Notarius, C. I., Markman, H. J., Bank, S., Yoppi, B., & Rubin, M. E. (1976). Behavior exchange theory and marital decision making. *Journal of Personality and Social Psychology, 34,* 14–23.

Gottman, J. M., Swanson, C., & Murray, J. (1999). The mathematics of marital conflict: Dynamic mathematical nonlinear modeling of newlywed marital interaction. *Journal of Family Psychology, 13,* 3–19.

Gove, W. R., Hughes, M., & Style, C. B. (1983). Does marriage have positive effects on the psychological well–being of the individual? *Journal of Health and Social Behavior, 24,* 122–131.

Granic, I., & Hollenstein, T. (2003). Dynamic systems methods for models of developmental psychopathology. *Development and Psychopathology, 15,* 641-669.

Gray–Little, B., Baucom, D. H., & Hamby, S. L. (1996). Marital power, marital adjustment, and therapy outcome. *Journal of Family Psychology, 10,* 292–303.

Gray–Little, B., & Burks, N. (1983). Power and satisfaction in marriage: A review and critique. *Psychological Bulletin, 93,* 518–538.

Greene, S., & Griffin, W. A. (1998). The influence of marital satisfaction on symptom expression in Parkinson's disease. *Psychiatry, 61,* 35–45.

Griffin, W. A. (1993a). Transitions from negative affect during marital interaction: Husband and wife differences. *Journal of Family Psychology, 6, 3,* 230–244.

Griffin, W. A. (1993b). *Family therapy: Fundamentals of theory and practice.* New York: Brunner/Mazel.

Griffin, W. A. (2000). A conceptual and graphical method for converging multi–subject behavioral observational data into a single process indicator. *Behavior Research Methods, Instruments, and Computers, 32,* 120–133.

Griffin, W. A. (2002). Affect pattern recognition: Using discrete hidden Markov models to discriminate distressed from nondistressed couples. *Marriage and Family Review, 34,* 139-163.

Griffin, W. A., & Greene, S. M. (1994). Social interaction and symptom sequences: A case study of orofacial bradykinesia exacerbation in Parkinson's disease during negative marital interaction. *Psychiatry, 54,* 269–274.

Griffin, W. A., & Greene, S. M. (1999). *Models of family therapy: The essential guide.* New York: Brunner/Mazel.

Griffin, W., Krainz, S., & Northey, S. (1994). The *Family Interaction Tactics (FIT) Coding System.* (Tech. Rep. No 94-01). Marital Interaction Laboratory, Dept. of Family and Human Development, Arizona State University, Tempe.

Griffin, W. A., Parrella, J., Krainz, S., & Northey, S. (2002). Behavioral differences in families with and without a male asthmatic: Beyond the psychosomatic family model. *Journal of Social and Clinical Psychology, 21,* 223–252.

Gross, J. J. (1998). Antecedent– and response–focused emotion regulation: Divergent consequences for experience, expression, and physiology. *Journal of Personality and Social Psychology, 74,* 224–237.

Guerney, B. G. (1977). *Relationship enhancement.* San Francisco: Jossey–Bass.

Gunnell, G. (2002). *Correspondence between speaker affect and nonverbal behavior among married couples: Differences by marital quality and gender.* Unpublished masters thesis, Arizona State University, Tempe.

Hahlweg, K. & Conrad, M. (1983) *Interactional Coding System (ICS).* Unpublished manuscript, University of California, Los Angeles.

Hahlweg, K., Kaiser, A., Christensen, A., Fehm–Wolfsdorf, G., & Groth, T. (2000). Self–report and observational assessment of couples conflict: The concordance between the Communication Patterns Questionnaire and the KPI observation system. *Journal of Marriage and the Family, 62,* 61–67.

Hahlweg, K., Markman, H., Thurmaier, F., Engl, J., & Eckert, V. (1998). Prevention of marital distress: Results of a German prospective–longitudinal study. *Journal of Family Psychology, 12,* 1–14.

Hahlweg, K., Reisner, L., Kohli, G., Vollmer, M., Schindler, L., & Revenstorf, D. (1984). Development and validity of a new system to analyse interpersonal communication. KPI: Kategoriensystem für partnerschaftliche Interaction. In K. Hahlweg, & N. S. Jacobson (Eds.), *Marital interaction: Analysis and modification* (pp. 182–198). New York: Guilford.

Hahlweg, K., Revenstorf, D., & Schindler, L. (1984). The effects of behavioral marital therapy on couples' communication and problem solving skills. *Journal of Consulting and Clinical Psychology, 52,* 553–566.

Hahlweg, K., Schindler, L., Revenstorf, D., & Brengelmann, J. C. (1984). The Munich marital therapy study. In K. Hahlweg & N. S. Jacobson (Eds.), *Marital interaction: Analysis and modification* (pp. 3–26). New York: Guilford.

Halford, W. K. (2001). *Brief therapy for couples: Helping partners help themselves.* New York: Guilford.

Halford, W. K., Hahlweg, K. & Dunne, M. (1990). The cross-cultural consistency of marital communication associated with marital distress. *Journal of Marriage and the Family, 52,* 487-500.

Hamberger, L. K., & Hastings, J. E. (1986). Personality correlates of men who abuse their partners: A cross–validation study. *Journal of Family Violence, 1,* 323–341.

Harris, K. W. (2001). *The psychophysiology of marital interaction: Differential effects of support and conflict.* Unpublished doctoral dissertation, University of Oregon, Eugene.

Haynes, S. N. (2001). Clinical applications of analogue behavioral observation: Dimensions of psychometric evaluation. *Psychological Assessment, 13,* 73–85.

Haynes, S. N., & O'Brien, W. H. (2000). *Principles and practice of behavioral assessment.* New York: Kluwer.

Haynes, S. N., Richard, D. C. S., & Kubany, E. S. (1995). Content validity in psychological assessment: A functional approach to concepts and methods. *Psychological Assessment, 7,* 238–247.

Hazan, C., & Shaver, P. (1987). Romantic love conceptualized as an attachment process. *Journal of Personality and Social Psychology, 52,* 511–524.

Heaney, A., Waldinger, R. J., Schulz, M. S., & Moore, C. (*2000, November). You just don't understand: Child abuse and empathic accuracy in adult couples.* Poster session presented at the annual meeting of the International Society for Traumatic Stress Studies, San Antonio, TX.

Heavey, C. L., Christensen, A., & Malamuth, N. M. (1995). The longitudinal impact of demand and withdrawal during marital conflict. *Journal of Consulting and Clinical Psychology, 63,* 797–801.

Heavey, C. L., Gill, D. S., & Christensen, A. (1996). *The Couples Interaction Rating System.* Unpublished manuscript. University of California, Los Angeles.

Heavey, C. L., Layne, C., & Christensen, A. (1993). Gender and conflict structure in marital interaction: A replication and extension. *Journal of Consulting and Clinical Psychology, 61,* 16–27.

Hermanns, J., Florin, I., Dietrich, M., Rieger, C., & Hahlweg, K. (1989). Maternal criticism, mother–child interaction, and Bronchial asthma. *Journal of Psychosomatic Research, 33,* 469–476.

Hetherington, E. M., & Martin, B. (1972). Family interaction and psychopathology in children. In C. Quay & J. S. Werry (Eds.), *Psychopathological disorders of childhood* (pp. 247–302). New York: Wiley.

Heyman, R. E. (1988). *Withdrawal in close relationships.* Unpublished master's thesis, University of Oregon, Eugene.

Heyman, R. E. (2001). Observation of couple conflicts: Clinical assessment applications, stubborn truths, and shaky foundations. *Psychological Assessment, 13,* 5–35.

Heyman, R. E., Brown, P. D., Feldbau, S. R., & O'Leary, K. D. (1999). Couples' communication variables as predictors of dropout and treatment response in wife abuse treatment programs. *Behavior Therapy, 30,* 165–190.

Heyman, R. E., Chaudhry, B. R., Treboux, D. T., Crowell, J., Lord, C., Vivian, D., et al. (2001). How much observational data is enough? An empirical test using marital interaction coding. *Behavior Therapy, 32,* 107–122.

Heyman, R. E., Eddy, J. M., Weiss, R. L., & Vivian, D. (1995). Factor analysis of the Marital Interaction Coding System. *Journal of Family Psychology, 9,* 209–215

Heyman, R. E., Feldbau-Kohn, S. R., Ehrensaft, M. K., Langhinrichsen–Rohling, J., & O'Leary, K.D. (2001) Can questionnaire reports correctly classify relationship distress and partner physical abuse? *Journal of Family Psychology, 15,* 334–346.

Heyman, R. E., Sayers, S. L., & Bellack, A. S. (1994). Global marital satisfaction vs. Marital adjustment: construct validity and psychometric properties of three measures. *Journal of Family Psychology, 8,* 432–446.

Heyman, R. E., & Slep, A. M. S. (2003). Analogue behavioral observation. In M. Hersen (Ed.) & E. M. Heiby & S. N. Haynes (Vol. Eds.), *Comprehensive handbook of psychological assessment: Vol. 3. Behavioral assessment* (pp. 162-180). New York: Wiley.

Heyman, R. E., & Vivian, D. (1993). *Rapid Marital Interaction Coding System Coding Manual.* Retrieved at www.psy.sunysb.edu/marital.

Heyman, R. E. Vivian, D., Weiss, R. L., Hubbard, K., & Ayerle, C. (1993, November). *Coding marital interaction at three levels of abstraction.* Paper presented at the 27th Annual Meeting of the Association for Advancement of Behavioral Therapy, Atlanta, GA.

Heyman, R. E., Weiss, R. L., & Eddy, J. M. (1995). Marital Interaction Coding System: Revision and empirical evaluation. *Behavioural Research and Therapy, 33,* 737–746.

Hinchliffe, M. G., Vaughan, P. W., Hooper, D., & Roberts, F. J. (1977). The melancholy marriage: An inquiry into the interaction of depression II. Expressiveness. *British Journal of Medical Psychology, 50,* 125–142.

Hinchliffe, M. K., Vaughan, P. W., Hooper, D., & Roberts, F. J. (1978a). The melancholy marriage: An inquiry into the interaction of depression III. Responsiveness. *British Journal of Medical Psychology, 51,* 1-13.

Hinchliffe, M. K., Vaughan, P. W., Hooper, D., & Roberts, F. J. (1978b). The melancholy marriage: An inquiry into the interaction of depression IV. Disruptions. *British Journal of Medical Psychology, 51,* 15-24.

Ho, C. K. (1990). An analysis of domestic violence in Asian American communities: A multicultural approach to counseling. In L. Brown & M. Root (Eds.), *Diversity and complexity in feminist therapy* (pp. 129–150). New York, NY: Haworth.

Holtzworth–Munroe, A., & Anglin, K. (1991). The competency of responses given by maritally violent versus nonviolent men to problematic marital situations. *Violence and Victims, 6,* 257–269.

Holtzworth–Munroe, A., & Jacobson, N. S. (1988). Toward a methodology for coding spontaneous causal attributions: Preliminary results with married couples. *Journal of Social and Clinical Psychology, 7,* 101–112

Holtzworth–Munroe, A., Smutzler, N., & Stuart, G. L. (1998). Demand and withdraw communication among couples experiencing husband violence. *Journal of Consulting and Clinical Psychology, 66,* 731–743.

Holtzworth–Munroe, A., Stuart, G. L., Sandin, E., Smutzler, N., & McLaughlin, W. (1997). Comparing the social support behaviors of violent and nonviolent husbands during discussions of wife personal problems. *Personal Relationships, 4,* 395–412.

Hooley, J. (1986). Expressed emotion and depression: Interactions between patients and high– versus low expressed emotion spouses. *Journal of Abnormal Psychology, 95,* 237–246.

Hooven, C., Gottman, J. M., & Katz, L. F. (1995). Parental meta–emotion structure predicts family and child outcomes. *Cognition and Emotion, 9, 229–264.*

Hooley, J. M., & Hahlweg, K. (1986). The marriages and interaction patterns of depressed patients and their spouses: Comparison of high and low EE dyads. In M. J. Goldstein, I. Hand, & K. Hahlweg (Eds.), *Treatment of schizophrenia: Family assessment and intervention* (pp. 85–96). New York: Springer

Hooley, J. M., & Hahlweg, K. (1989). Marital satisfaction and marital communication in German and English couples. *Behavioral Assessment, 11,* 119–133.

Hooven, C., Rush, R., & Gottman, J. M. (1996). The play-by-play interview. In J. M. Gottman (Ed.), *What predicts divorce? The measures*. Mahwah, NJ: Lawrence Erlbaum Associates, Inc.

Hops, H., Wills, T. A., Weiss, R. L., & Patterson, G. R. (1972). *Marital Interaction Coding System (MICS)*. Eugene: University of Oregon, Oregon Research Institute.

Husaini, B. A., Neff, J. A., Newbrough, J. R., & Moore, M. C. (1982). The stress–buffering role of social support and personal competence among the rural married. *Journal of Community Psychology, 10,* 409–423.

Huston, T. L. (1983). Power. In *Close relationships* (pp. 169–219). New York: Freeman.

Huston, T. L., McHale, S. M., & Crouter, A. C. (1986). When the honeymoon's over: Changes in the marriage relationship over the first year. In R. Gilmour & S. Duck (Eds.), *The emerging field of personal relationships* (pp.109–132). Hillsdale, NJ: Lawrence Erlbaum Associates, Inc.

Ickes, W., Stinson, L., Bissonnette, V., & Garcia, S. (1990). Naturalistic social cognition: Empathic accuracy in mixed–sex dyads. *Journal of Personality and Social Psychology, 59,* 730–742.

Jacob, T. (1975). Family interaction in disturbed and normal families: A methodological and substantive review. *Psychological Bulletin, 82,* 33–65.

Jacob, T., Tennenbaum, D. L., & Krahn, G. (1987). Factors influencing the reliability and validity of observation data. In T Jacob (Ed.), *Family interaction and psychopathology* (pp. 297-328). New York: Plenum.

Jacobson, N. S. (1977). Problem solving and contingency contracting in the treatment of marital discord. *Journal of Consulting and Clinical Psychology, 45,* 92–100.

Jacobson, N. S. (1978). Specific and nonspecific factors in the effectiveness of a behavioral approach to the treatment of marital discord. *Journal of Consulting and Clinical Psychology, 46,* 442–452.

Jacobson, N. S., & Addis, M. E. (1993). Research on couples and couple therapy: what do we know? Where are we going? *Journal of Consulting and Clinical Psychology, 61,* 85–93.

Jacobson, N. S., & Christensen, A. (1996). *Integrative couple therapy: Promoting acceptance and change.* New York: W.W. Norton.

Jacobson, N. S., Gottman, J. M., Gortner, E., Berns, S., & Shortt, J. W. (1996). Psychological factors in the longitudinal course of battering: When do the couples split up? When does the abuse decrease? *Violence & Victims, 11,* 371-392.

Jacobson, N. S., & Margolin, G. (1979). *Marital therapy: Strategies based on social learning and behavioral exchange principles.* New York: Brunner/Mazel.

Jacobson, N. S., & Moore, D. (1980). Partners as observers of the events in their relationship. *Journal of Consulting and Clinical Psychology, 49,* 269–277.

Jacobson, N. S., Waldron, H., & Moore, D. (1980). Toward a behavioral profile of marital distress. *Journal of Counseling and Clinical Psychology, 48,* 696–703.

Jensen, S. L. (2001). *Development of a scale to code the elicitation of social support.* Unpublished doctoral dissertation, Iowa State University, Ames.

Jourard, S. M., & Lasakow, P. (1958). Some factors in self–disclosure. *Journal of Abnormal and Social Psychology, 56,* 91–98.

Julien, D., Chartrand, E., Simard, M. C., Bouthillier, D., & Bégin, J. (2003). Conflict, social support, and conjugal adjustment: An observational study of heterosexual, gay, and lesbian couples' communication. *Journal of Family Psychology, 17.*

Julien, D., & Markman, H. J. (1991). Social support and social networks as determinants of individual and marital outcomes. *Journal of Social and Personal Relationships, 8,* 549–568.

Julien, D., Markman, H. J., & Lindahl, K. M. (1989). A comparison of global and microanalytic coding systems: Implications for future trends in studying interactions. *Behavioral Assessment, 11,* 81–100.

Kagan, N, Krathwohl, D. R., & Miller. R, (1963). Stimulated recall in therapy using video tape: A case study. *Journal of Counseling Psychology, 10,* 237.

Kaiser, A., Hahlweg, K., Fehm–Wolfsdorf, G., & Groth, T. (1999). Indizierte Prävention bei Beziehungsstörungen. Evaluation eines psychoedukativen Kompaktprogrammes für Paare [The efficacy of a compact psychoeducational group training program for married couples]. *Verhaltenstherapie, 9,* 76–85.

Karney, B. R., & Bradbury, T. N. (1995). The longitudinal course of marital quality and stability: A review of theory, method, and research. *Psychological Bulletin, 118,* 3–34.

Kerig, P. K., & Lindahl, K. M. (Eds.) (2001). *Family observational coding systems: Resources for systemic research.* Mahwah, NJ: Lawrence Erlbaum Associates, Inc.

Kiecolt–Glaser, J. K., & Newton, T. L. (2001). Marriage and health: His and hers. *Psychological Bulletin, 127,* 472–503.

Kiecolt–Glaser, J. K., Fisher, L. D., Ogrocki, P., Stout, J. C., Speicher, C. E., & Glaser, R. (1987). Marital quality, marital disruption, and immune function. *Psychosomatic Medicine, 49,* 12–34.

Kline, G. H., Low, S., & Stanley, S. M. (2002, November). *Duration of cohabitation and the synchronicity of self–report and objectively–coded interaction skills.* Paper presented at the meeting of the Association for the Advancement of Behavior Therapy, Reno, NV.

Kline, G. H., Stanley, S. M., Markman, H. J., Olmos-Gallo, P. A., St. Peters, M., Whitton, S. W., & Prado, L. M. (2003). Timing is everything: Pre-engagement cohabitation and increased risk for poor marital outcomes. *Journal of Family Psychology,* in press.

Knox, D. (1971). *Marriage happiness.* Champaign, IL: Research Press.

Komarovsky, M. (1967). *Blue–collar marriage.* New York: Vintage.

Krebs, K. (2000). Comparison of macro and micro observational methods for measuring marital social support. . Unpublished doctoral dissertation, Iowa State University, Ames.

Kroeger, C., Hahlweg, K., Braukhaus, C., Fehm–Wolfsdorf, G., & Groth, T. (2000). Fragebogen zur Erfassung partnerschaftlicher Kommunikationsmuster (FPK): Reliabilität und validität [Communication Pattern Questionnaire: Reliability and validity of the German version]. *Diagnostica, 46,* 189–198.

Krohne, H.W., Pieper, M., Knoll, N., & Breimer, N. (2002). The cognitive regulation of emotions: The role of success versus failure experience and coping dispositions. *Cognition and Emotion, 16,* 217–243.

Krokoff, L. (1987). Anatomy of negative affect in working class marriages. *Dissertation Abstracts International, 45,* 7A. (University Microfilms No. 84–22 109).

Krokoff, L. (1990). Hidden agendas in marriage. *Communication Research, 17,* 483–499.

Krokoff, L. J., Gottman, J. M., & Hass, S. D. (1989). Validation of a global Rapid Couples Interaction Scoring System. *Behavioral Assessment, 11,* 65–79.

Kuhn, T. S. (1970). *The structure of scientific revolutions (2nd ed.).* Chicago: The University of Chicago Press.

L'Abate, L. (1977). Intimacy is sharing hurt feelings: A reply to David Mace. *Journal of Marriage and Family Counseling, 4,* 13–16.

Langhinrichsen-Rohling, J., Heyman, R. E., Ehrensaft, M., & Sedlar, G. (1998, November). *Communication in husband–to–wife aggressive, nonaggressive/distressed and nonaggressive/nondistressed couples: Differences across task and level of coding analysis.* Poster session presented at the annual meeting of the Association for Advancement of Behavior Therapy, Washington, DC.

Lazarus, R. S. (1991). *Emotion and adaption.* New York: Oxford University Press.

Lehman, D. R., & Hemphill, K. J. (1990). Recipients' perceptions of support attempts and attributions for support attempts that fail. *Journal of Social and Personal Relationships, 7,* 563–574.

Lenzenweger, M. F., Clarkin, J. F., Kernberg, O. F., & Foelsch, P. A. (2001). The Inventory of Personality Organization: Psychometric properties, factorial composition, and criterion relations with affect, aggressive dyscontrol, psychosis proneness, and self–domains in a nonclinical sample. *Psychological Assessment, 13,* 577–591.

Levenson, R. W., Carstensen, L. L., & Gottman, J. M. (1994). Influence of age and gender on affect, physiology, and their interrelations: A study of long–term marriages. *Journal of Personality and Social Psychology, 67,* 56–68.

Levenson, R. W., & Gottman, J. M. (1983). Marital interaction: Physiological linkage and affective exchange. *Journal of Personality and Social Psychology, 49,* 85–94.

Levenson, R. W., & Gottman, J. M. (1985). Physiological and affective predictors of change in relationship satisfaction. *Journal of Personality and Social Psychology, 49,* 85–94.

Levenson, R. W., & Ruef, A. M. (1992). Empathy: A physiological substrate. *Journal of Personality and Social Psychology, 63,* 234–246.

Lewis, M. D., Lamey, A. V., & Douglas, L. (1999). A new dynamic systems method for the analysis of early socioemotional development. *Developmental Science, 2,* 457–475.

Lieberman, M. A. (1982). The effects of social support on responses to stress. In L. Golberger & S. Bretznitz (Eds.), *Handbook of stress: Theoretical and clinical aspects* (pp. 764–784). New York: Academic.

Lindahl, K. M. (1996). System for Coding Interactions in Parent–Child Dyads (SCIPD). Unpublished manual, University of Miami, Coral Gables, FL.

Lindahl, K. M., Clements, M., & Markman, H. (1997). Predicting marital and parent functioning in dyads and triads: A longitudinal investigation of marital process. *Journal of Family Psychology, 11,* 139–151.

Lindahl, K. M., & Malik, N. (1999). Observations of marital conflict and power: Relations with parenting in the triad. *Journal of Marriage and the Family, 61,* 320–330.

Lindahl, K. M., & Malik, N. M. (2001). The System for Coding Interactions and Family Functioning. In P. K. Kerig & K. M. Lindahl (Eds.), *Family observational coding systems: Resources for systemic research* (pp. 77–91). Mahwah, NJ: Lawrence Erlbaum Associates, Inc.

Locke, H., & Wallace, K. (1959). Short marital adjustment test and prediction tests: Their reliability and validity. *Marriage and Family Living, 21,* 251–255.

Mahoney, A., Coffield, A., Lewis, T., & Lashley, S. L. (2001). Meso–analytic behavioral rating system for family interactions: Observing play and forced–compliance tasks with young children. In P. K. Kerig and K. M. Lindahl (Eds.), *Family observational coding systems: Resources for systemic research* (pp. 225–242). Mahwah, NJ: Lawrence Erlbaum Associates, Inc.

Malik, N. M. (1998, November). *Specifying the roles of cultural, dyadic, and individual factors and domestic violence.* Paper presented at the 32nd annual convention of the Association for the Advancement of Behavior, Washington, DC.

Malik, N. M., & Lindahl, K. M. (1998). Aggression and dominance: The roles of power and culture in domestic violence. *Clinical Psychology: Science and Practice, 5,* 409–423.

Malik, N. M., & Lindahl, K. M. (1997). *System for Coding Interactions in Dyads SCID).* Unpublished manual, University of Miami, Coral Gables, FL.

Malik, N. M., & Lindahl, K. M. (2000). *System for Coding Interactions in Dyads (SCID).* Unpublished manual, University of Miami, Coral Gables, FL.

Malik, N. M., & Lindahl, K. M. (2001, August). *Relations among family subsystems: Marital power, family processes, and ethnicity.* Paper presented at the meeting of the American Psychological Association, San Francisco.

Manne, S., Ostroff, J., Sherman, M., Heyman, R. E., & Ross, S. (2002). *Couples' support–related communication and distress in women with early stage breast cancer.* Manuscript submitted for publication.

Manne, S. L., & Zautra, A. J. (1989). Partner criticism and support: Their association with coping and psychological adjustment among women with rheumatoid arthritis. *Journal of Personality and Social Psychology, 56,* 608–617.

Margolin, G. (1984, August). *Interpersonal and intrapersonal factors associated with marital violence.* Paper presented at the Second National Conference for Family Violence Researchers, Durham, NH.

Margolin, G., John, R. S., & Gleberman, L. (1988). Affective responses to conflictual discussions in violent and nonviolent couples. *Journal of Consulting and Clinical Psychology, 56,* 24–33.

Margolin, G., Oliver, P. H., & Gordis, E. B. (1998). The nuts and bolts of behavioral observation of marital and family interaction. Clinical *Child & Family Psychology Review, 1,* 195-213.

Margolin, G., & Wampold, B. (1981). Sequential analysis of conflict and accord in distressed and nondistressed marital partners. *Journal of Consulting and Clinical Psychology, 47,* 554–567.

Marín, G., & Marín, B. V. (1991). *Research with Hispanic populations*. Newbury Park, CA: Sage Publications.

Markman, H. J. (1992). Marital and family psychology: Burning issues. *Journal of Family Psychology, 5,* 264–275.

Markman, H. J., Floyd, F. J., Stanley, S. M., & Storaasli, R. D. (1988). Prevention of marital distress: A longitudinal investigation. *Journal of Consulting and Clinical Psychology, 56,* 210–217.

Markman, H. J., & Notarius, C. I. (1987). Coding marital and family interaction: Current status. In T. Jacob (Ed.), *Family interaction and psychopathology: Theories, methods, and findings* (pp. 329–390). New York: Plenum Press.

Markman, H. J., Renick, M. J., Floyd, F., Stanley, S. M., & Clements, M. (1993). Preventing marital distress through communication and conflict management training: A four and five year follow–up. *Journal of Consulting and Clinical Psychology, 61,* 70–77.

Markman, H. J., Stanley, S. M., & Blumberg, S. L. (2001). *Fighting for your marriage (new and revised).* San Francisco: Jossey–Bass.

Marshall, L. L. (1994). Physical and psychological abuse. In W. R. Cupach & B. H. Spitzberg (Eds.), *The dark side of interpersonal communication* (pp. 281 – 311). Hillsdale, NJ.: Lawrence Erlbaum Associates, Inc.

Mash, E. J., & Foster, S. L. (2001). Exporting analogue behavioral observation from research to clinical practice: Useful or cost–defective? *Psychological Assessment, 13,* 86–98.

McDonald, G. W. (1980). Family power: The assessment of a decade of theory and research, 1970–1979. *Journal of Marriage and the Family, 42,* 841–854.

McGoldrick, M. & Rohrbaugh, M. (1987). Researching ethnic family stereotypes. *Family Process, 26*, 89-99.

Melby, J. N., & Conger, R. D. (2001). The Iowa Family Interaction Rating Scales: Instrument summary. In P. K. Kerig & K. M. Lindahl (Eds.), *Family observational coding sys-*

tems: Resources for systematic research (pp 33–57). Mahwah, NJ: Lawrence Erlbaum Associates, Inc.

Mermelstein, R., Lichtenstein, E., & McIntyre, K. (1983). Partner support and relapse in smoking–cessation programs. *Journal of Consulting and Clinical Psychology, 51,* 465–466.

Mitchell, S. (1979). Interobserver agreement, reliability, and generalizability of data collected in observational studies. *Psychological Bulletin, 86,* 376–390.

Monroe, S. M., Bromet, E. J., Connell, M. M., & Steiner, S. C. (1986). Social support, life events, and depressive symptoms: A 1–year prospective study. *Journal of Consulting and Clinical Psychology, 54,* 424–431.

Müller, U., Hahlweg, K., Feinstein, E., Hank, G., Wiedemann, G., & Dose, M. (1992). Familienklima und interaktionsprozesse in familien mit einem schizophrenen mitglied [Expressed emotion and patient–relative interaction in families of schizophrenics]. *Zeitschrift für Klinische Psychologie, 21,* 332–351.

Murphy, C. M., & Meyer, S. (1991). Gender, power, and violence in marriage. *The Behavior Therapist, 14,* 95–100.

Murphy, C. M., Meyer, S. L., & O'Leary, K. D. (1994). Dependency characteristics of partner assaultive men. *Journal of Abnormal Psychology, 103,* 729–735.

Napier, A. Y. (1978). The rejection–intrusion pattern: A central family dynamic. *Journal of Marriage and Family Counseling, 4*: 5–12.

Newell, K. M., & Molenaar, P. C. (1998). *Applications of nonlinear dynamics to developmental process modeling.* Mahwah, NJ: Lawrence Erlbaum Associates, Inc.

Nisbett, R. E., & Wilson, T. D. (1977). Telling more than we can know: Verbal reports on mental processes. *Psychological Review, 84,* 231–259.

Noldus, L. (1991). The Observer: A software system for collection and analysis of observational data. *Behavior Research Methods, Instruments, and Computers, 23,* 415–429.

Noller, P. (1984). *Nonverbal communication and marital interaction* (Vol. 9). Oxford, England: Pergamon Press.

Noller, P. (1993). Gender and emotional communication in marriage: Different cultures or differential social power? *Journal of Language and Social Psychology, 12,* 132–152.

Northey, S., Griffin, W. A., & Krainz, S. I. (1998). A partial test of the psychosomatic family model: marital interaction patterns in asthma and non–asthma families. *Journal of Family Psychology, 12,* 220–233.

Norton, R. (1983). Measuring marital quality: A critical look at the dependent variable. *Journal of Marriage and the Family, 45,* 141 151.

Notarius, C. I., Benson, P. R., Sloane, D., & Vanzetti, N. A. (1989). Exploring the interface between perception and behavior: An analysis of marital interaction in distressed and nondistressed couples. Special issue: Coding marital interaction. *Behavioral Assessment, 11,* 39–64.

Notarius, C. I., & Markman, H. J. (1981). The couples interaction scoring system. In E. E. Filsinger & R. A. Lewis (Eds.), *Assessing marriage. New behavioral approaches* (pp. 112–127). Beverly Hills, CA: Sage.

Notarius, C. I., & Markman, H. J. (1989). Coding marital interaction: A sampling and discussion of current issues. *Behavioral Assessment, 11,* 1–11.

Notarius, C. I., & Markman, H. J. (1993). We *can work it out: Making sense of marital conflict.* New York: Putnam.

Notarius, C. I., & Vanzetti, N. (1983). The Marital Agendas Protocol. In E. Filsinger (Ed.), *Marital and family assessment* (pp. 209–227). Beverly Hills, CA: Sage.

O'Leary, K. D., Heyman, R. E., & Jongsma, A. E. (1998). *The couples therapy treatment planner.* New York: Wiley.

O'Leary, K. D., & Vivian, D. (1990). Physical aggression in marriage. In F. D. Fincham & T. N. Bradbury (Ed.) *The psychology of marriage: Basic issues and applications.* New York: Guilford.

O'Leary, K. D., Vivian, D., & Malone, J. (1992). Assessment of physical aggression against women in marriage: The need for multimodal assessment. *Behavioral Assessment, 14,* 5–14.

Olson, D. H., & Ryder, R. G. (1975). *Marital and Family Interaction Coding System (MFICS).* Unpublished manuscript, University of Minnesota, Minneapolis.

Oregon Marital Studies Program. (1990). *Marital Interaction Coding System (MICS–IV): Coding manual.* Department of Psychology, Oregon Marital Studies Program, Eugene.

Paley, B., Cox, M. J., Burchinal, M. R., & Payne, C. C. (1999). Attachment and marital functioning: Comparison of spouses with continuous–secure, earned–secure, dismissing, and preoccupied attachment stances. *Journal of Family Psychology, 13,* 580–597.

Pasch, L. A., & Bradbury, T. N. (1998). Social support, conflict, and the development of marital dysfunction. *Journal of Consulting and Clinical Psychology, 66,* 219–230.

Pasch, L. A., Bradbury, T. N., & Davila, J. (1997). Gender, negative affectivity, and observed social support behavior in marital interaction. *Personal Relationships, 4,* 361–378.

Pasch, L. A., Bradbury, T. N., Davila, J., & Sullivan, K. T. (1999, November). Social support communication and the development of marital dysfunction: Extension of previous findings. In K.W. Harris (Chair), *Beyond marital conflict: Social support and the search for unexplained variance.* Symposium conducted at the annual meeting of the Association for Advancement of Behavior Therapy, Toronto, Ontario, Canada.

Pasch, L. A., Bradbury, T. N., & Sullivan, K. T. (1997). Social support in marriage: An analysis of intraindividual and interpersonal components. In G. Pierce, B. Lakey, I. Sarason, & B. Sarason (Eds.), *Sourcebook on social support and personality.* (pp. 229–256). New York: Plenum.

Patterson, G. R. (1982). *Coercive family process.* Eugene, OR: Castalia.

Patterson, G. R. (1993). Orderly change in a stable world: The antisocial trait as a chimera. *Journal of Consulting and Clinical Psychology, 61,* 911–919.

Patterson, G. R., Reid, J. B., & Dishion, T. J. (1992). *Antisocial boys.* Eugene, OR: Castalia.

Paykel, E. S., Emms, E. M., Fletcher, J., & Rassaby, E. S. (1980). Life–events and social support in puerperal depression. *British Journal of Psychiatry, 136,* 334–346.

Peplau, L. A., & Gordon, S. (1985). Women and men in love: Gender differences in close heterosexual relationships. In V. E. O'Leary, R. K. Unger, and B. S. Wallston (Eds.), *Women, gender, and social psychology,* Hillsdale, NJ: Lawrence Lawrence Erlbaum Associates, Inc.

Poling, A., Methot, L. L., & LeSage, M. G. (1995). *Fundamentals of behavior analytic research.* New York: Plenum.

Powers, S. I., & Welsh, D. P. (1999). Mother–daughter interactions and adolescent girl's depression. In M. J. Cox & J. Brooks–Gunn (Eds.), *Conflict and cohesion in families:*

Causes and consequences. (pp. 243–281), Mahwah, NJ: Lawrence Erlbaum Associates, Inc.

Prado, L. M., & Markman, H. J. (1999). Unearthing the seeds of marital distress: What we have learned from married and remarried couples. In M. J. Cox & J. Brooks–Gunn (Eds.), *Conflict and cohesion in families: Causes and consequences.* (pp. 51–85). Mahwah, NJ: Lawrence Erlbaum Associates, Inc.

Prager, K. (1995). *The psychology of intimacy.* New York: Guilford.

Procidano, M. E., & Heller, K. (1983). Measures of perceived social support from friends and from family: Three validation studies. *American Journal of Community Psychology, 11,* 1–24.

Raush, H. L., Barry, W. A., Hertel, R. K., & Swain, M. A. (1974). *Communication, conflict, and marriage.* San Francisco: Jossey–Bass.

Reid, J. B. (Ed.) (1978). *A social learning approach to family intervention: Vol. 2. Observation in home settings.* Eugene, OR: Castalia.

Reid, J. B., Patterson, G. R., & Snyder, J. (Eds.). (2002). *Antisocial behavior in children and adolescents: A developmental analysis and model for intervention.* Washington, DC: American Psychological Association.

Reis, H. T., & Shaver, P. (1998). Intimacy as an interpersonal process. In S. Duck (Ed.) *Handbook of personal relationships: Theory, relationships, and intervention* (pp. 367–389). Chichester, England: Wiley.

Revenstorf, D., Hahlweg, K., Schindler, L., & Vogel, B. (1984). Interaction analysis of marital conflict. In K. Hahlweg & N. S. Jacobson (Eds.), *Marital Interaction: Analysis and modification* (pp. 159–181). New York: Guilford.

Revenstorf, D., Vogel, B., Wegener, C., Hahlweg, K., & Schindler, L. (1980). Escalation phenomena in interaction sequences: An empirical comparison of distressed and nondistressed couples. *Behavior Analysis and Modification, 2,* 97–116.

Rieg, C., Müller, U., Hahlweg, K., Wiedemann, G., Hank, G., & Feinstein, E. (1991). Psychoedukative rückfallprophylaxe bei schizophrenen patienten: Ändern sich die familiären Kommunikationsmuster? [(Behavioral family management in schizophrenia: Do we change the communication patterns?] *Verhaltenstherapie, 1,* 283–292.

Rogers, K. R. (1987). Nature of spousal supportive behaviors that influence heart transplant patient compliance. *Journal of Heart Transplant, 6,* 90–95.

Rogers, L. E., & Farace, R. V. (1975). Analysis of relational communication in dyads: New measurement procedures. *Family Process, 1,* 222–239.

Rogge, R. D., Cobb, R., Johnson, M., Lawrence, E., & Bradbury, T. N. (2002). The Care Program: A preventive approach to marital intervention. In N. S. Jacobson and A. S. Gurman (Eds.), *Clinical handbook of couple therapy* (3rd ed). New York: Guilford.

Rosenberg, E. L., & Ekman, P. (1997). Coherence between expressive and experiential systems in emotion. In P. Ekman & E. L. Rosenberg (Eds.), *What the face reveals: Basic and applied studies of spontaneous expression using the facial action coding system* (pp. 63–88). New York: Oxford University Press.

Rugel, R. P. (1997). *Handbook-focused marital therapy: An approach to dealing with marital distress.* Springfield, IL: Thomas.

Russell, J., & Mehrabian, A. (1977). Evidence for a three–factor theory of emotions. *Journal of Research on Personality, 11,* 273–294.

Ryan, K. D., Gottman, J. M., Murray, J. D., Carrére, S., & Swanson, C. (2000). Theoretical and mathematical modeling of marriage. In M. D. Lewis and I. Granic (Eds.), *Emotion, Development, and Self Organization: Dynamic Systems Approaches to Emotional Development* (pp.).

Sackett, G. P. (1979). The lag sequential analysis of contingency and cyclicity in behavioral interaction research. In J. Osofsky (Ed.), *Handbook of infant development* (pp. 623–649). New York: Wiley.

Saiz, C. C. (2001). *Teaching couples communication and problem solving skills: A self–directed videotape version of the Prevention Relationship Enhancement Program (PREP).* Unpublished doctoral dissertation, University of Denver, CO.

Sandler, I. N., Ayers, T. S., Wolchik, S. A., Tein, J., Kwok, O., Haine, R., et al. (2003). The family bereavement program: Efficacy evaluation of a theory–based prevention program for parentally bereaved children and adolescents. *Journal of Consulting and Clinical Psychology,* in press.

SAS Institute, Inc. (1992). *SAS/ETS software: Applications guide. Time series modeling and forecasting, financial reporting, and loan analysis.* Version 6, 1st ed. Cary, NC: SAS Institute, Inc.

Sayers, S. L., Baucom, D. H., Sher, T. G., Weiss, R. L., & Heyman, R. E. (1991). Constructive engagement, behavioral marital therapy, and changes in marital satisfaction. *Behavioral Assessment, 13,* 25–49.

Schaefer, M. T., & Olson, D. H. (1981). Assessing intimacy: The PAIR inventory. *Journal of Marital and Family Therapy, 7,* 47–60.

Schapp, C. (1984). A comparison of the interaction of distressed and nondistressed married couples in a laboratory situation: Literature survey, methodological issues, and an empirical investigation. In K. Hahlweg & N. S. Jacobson (Eds.), *Marital interaction: Analysis and modification* (pp. 133-158). New York: Guilford Press.

Schilling, E. A., Baucom, D. H., Brunett, C. K., Allen, E. S., & Ragland, L. (2003). Altering the course of marriage: The effect of premarital communication skills acquisition on couples' risk of becoming maritally distressed. *Journal of Family Psychology, 17,* 41-53.

Schröder, B., Hahlweg, K., Fiedler, P., & Mundt, Ch. (1996). Marital interaction in couples with a depressed or schizophrenic patient. In C. Mundt, M. J. Goldstein, K. Hahlweg, & P. Fiedler (Eds.), *Interpersonal factors in the origin and course of affective disorders* (pp. 257–276). London: Gaskell.

Schulz, M. S., & Lazarus, R. S. (2003). Emotion regulation during adolescence: A cognitive–mediational conceptualization. In A. M. Cauce & S. T. Hauser (Eds.), *Adolescence and beyond: Family interactions and transitions to adulthood.* Mahwah, NJ: Lawrence Erlbaum Associates, Inc., in press.

Schuster, T. L., Kessler, R. C., & Aseltine, R. H., Jr. (1990). Supportive interactions, negative interactions, and depressed mood. *American Journal of Community Psychology, 18,* 423–438.

Seligman, M., & Czikszentmihalyi, M. (2000). Positive psychology. An introduction. *American Psychologist, 55,* 5–14

Shapiro, A. F., Gottman, J., M., & Carrére, S. (2000). The baby and the marriage: Identifying factors that buffer against decline in marital satisfaction after the first baby arrives. *Journal of Family Psychology.*

Shaw, E. (1970). Schooling in fishes: Critique and review. In L. Aronson, E. Tobach, D. Leherman, & J. Rosenbatt (Eds.),. *Development and evolution of behavior* (pp. 452–480). San Francisco: Freeman.

Sher, T. G., & Weiss, R. L. (Eds.) (1991). Negativity in marital communication: A misnomer? [Special issue]. *Behavioral Assessment*, 13.

Shoham, V., Rohrbaugh, M. J, Stickle, T. R., & Jacob, T. (1998). Demand–withdraw couple interaction moderates retention in cognitive–behavioral versus family–systems treatments for alcoholism. *Journal of Family Psychology, 12,* 557–577.

Shortt, J. W., & Gottman, J. M. (1997). Closeness in young adult sibling relationships: Affective and physiological processes. *Social Development, 6,* 142-164.

Shrout, P. E., & Fleiss, J. L. (1979). Intraclass correlations: Uses in assessing rater reliability. *Psychological Bulletin, 86,* 420–428.

Siegel, J. M. (1986). The multidimensional anger inventory. *Journal of Personality and Social Psychology, 51,* 191–200.

Sillars, A. L. (1982). *Verbal Tactics Coding Scheme: Coding manual.* Unpublished manual, Ohio State University, Columbus.

Sillars, A., & Scott, M. (1983). Interpersonal perception between intimates: An integrative review. *Human Communication Research, 10,* 153–176.

Simard, M. C., Julien, D., Bouthillier, D., & Dubé, M. (2003, April). *Longitudinal study of the links between mother-adolescent communication and the representational model of attachment in adulthood.* Paper presented at the Biennial Meeting of the Society for Research in Child Development, Tampa, FL.

Skinner, B. F. (1953). *Science and human behavior.* New York: Free Press.

Smith, D. A., Vivian, D., & O'Leary, K.D. (1990). The longitudinal prediction of marital discord from premarital expression of affect. *Journal of Consulting and Clinical Psychology, 58*, 790–798.

Smith, D. A., Vivian, D., & O'Leary, K. D. (1991). The misnomer proposition: A critical reappraisal of the longitudinal status of "negativity" in marital communication. *Behavioral Assessment, 13,* 7–24.

Snyder, D. K. (1979). Multidimensional assessment of marital satisfaction. *Journal of Marriage and the Family, 41,* 813–823.

Snyder, D. K., & Wills, R. M. (1989). Behavioral versus insight-oriented marital therapy: Effects on individual and interspousal functioning. *Journal of Consulting and Clinical Psychology, 57,* 39-46.

Snyder, D. K., Wills, R. M., & Keiser–Thomas, W. (1981). Empirical validation of the marital satisfaction inventory: An actuarial approach. *Journal of Consulting and Clinical Psychology, 49,* 262–268.

Spanier, G. B. (1976). Measuring dyadic adjustment: New scales for assessing the quality of marriage and similar dyads. *Journal of Marriage and the Family, 38,* 15–28.

Spanier, G. B., & Thompson, L. (1984). *Parting: The aftermath of divorce and separation.* Beverly Hills, CA: Sage.

Spitznagel, E. L., & Helzer, J. E. (1985) A proposed solution to the base rate problem in the kappa statistic. *Archives of General Psychiatry, 42,* 725–728.

SPSS, Inc. (2003). *SPSS for windows trends, rel. 12.0*, Chicago: SPSS, Inc.

Stanley, S. M., Blumberg, S. L., & Markman, H. J. (1999). Helping couples fight for their marriages: The PREP approach. In R. Berger & M. T. Hannah (Eds.), *Preventive approaches in couples therapy*. Philadelphia: Brunner/Mazel.

Stanley, S. M., & Markman, H. J. (1992). Assessing commitment in personal relationships. *Journal of Marriage and the Family, 54,* 595–608.

Stanley, S. M., Markman, H. J., Prado, L. M., Olmos–Gallo, A., Tonelli, L., St. Peters, M., et al. (2001). Community based premarital prevention: Clergy and lay leaders on the front lines. *Family Relations, 50,* 67–76.

Sternberg, R. J. (1988). Triangulating love. In R. J. Sternberg & M. L. Barnes (Eds.), *The psychology of love (pp. 119-138).* New Haven, CT: Yale University Press.

Stone, A. A. (1997). Measurement of affective response. In S. Cohen, R.C. Kessler, & L.U. Gordon (Eds.). *Measuring stress: A guide for health and social scientists* (pp. 148–171). New York: Oxford University Press.

Stone, A. A., & Neale, J. M. (1984). New measure of daily coping: Development and preliminary results. *Journal of Personality and Social Psychology, 46,* 892–906.

Straus, M. A. (1979). Measuring intra–family conflict and violence: The Conflict Tactics Scale. *Journal of Marriage and the Family, 41,* 75–88.

Straus, M. A., & Sweet, S. (1992). Verbal/symbolic aggression in couples: Incidence rates and relationship to personal characteristics. *Journal of Marriage and the Family, 54,* 346–357.

Suhr, J. A. (1990). *The development of the Social Support Behavior Code*. Unpublished master's thesis. University of Iowa, Iowa City.

Sullivan, K. T., Pasch, L. A., Eldridge, K. A., & Bradbury, T. N. (1998). Social support in marriage: Translating research into practical applications for clinicians. *The Family Journal: Counseling and Therapy for Couples and Families, 6,* 263–271.

Sullivan, L. J. (1999, November). *Observational measurement of relationship schemas.* Paper presented at the meeting of the Association for Advancement of Behavior Therapy, Toronto, Canada.

Summers, K. J. (1983). Marital Interaction Coding System–III. In E. E. Filsinger (Ed.), *A sourcebook of marriage and family assessment* (pp. 85–115). Beverly Hills, CA: Sage.

Thoits, P. A. (1986). Social support as coping assistance. *Journal of Consulting and Clinical Psychology, 54,* 416–423.

Thomas, D. L., & Diener, E. (1990). Memory accuracy in the recall of emotions. *Journal of Personality and Social Psychology, 59,* 291–297.

Thomas, G., Fletcher, G. J. O., & Lange, C. (1997). On–line empathic accuracy in marital interaction. *Journal of Personality and Social Psychology, 72,* 839–850.

Thurmaier, F., Engl, J., & Hahlweg, K. (1999). Eheglück auf dauer? Methodik, inhalte und effektivität eines präventiven paarkommunikationstrainings. Ergebnisse nach 5 jahren [Marital happiness forever? Methods, content, and efficacy of a premarital prevention program: 5 year results.] *Zeitschrift für Klinische Psychologie, 28,* 64–62.

Tronick, E. Z., & Gianino, A., (1986) Interactive mismatch and repair: Challenges to the coping infant. *Zero–to–Three, 6,* 1–6.

VanWidenfelt, B., Harter, K., & Floyd, F. J. (1996, November). Effects of child illness and disability on marriage and the parenting partnership: Comparison of four groups. Paper presented at the meeting of the Association for the Advancement of Behavior Therapy, New York.

Vega, W. A. (1990). Hispanic families in the 1980's: A decade of research. *Journal of Marriage and the Family, 52,* 1015–1024.

Verman, S. (2001). *Microsocial indicators of relationship quality for noncustodial fathers and their children.* Unpublished masters thesis, Arizona State University, Tempe.

Vincent, J. P., Friedman, L. C., Nugent, J., & Messerly, L. (1979). Demand characteristics in observations of marital interaction. *Journal of Consulting and Clinical Psychology, 47,* 557–566.

Vinokur, A. D., & van Ryn, M. (1993). Social support and undermining in close relationships: Their independent effects on the mental health of unemployed persons. *Journal of Personality and Social Psychology, 65,* 350–359.

Vissing, Y. M., Straus, M. A., Gelles, R. J., & Harrop, J. W. (1991). Verbal aggression by parents and psychosocial problems of children. *Child Abuse and Neglect, 15,* 223–238

Vivian, D., & Heyman, R. E. (1994, November). *Aggression against wives: Mutual verbal combat "in context."* Paper presented at the 28th annual convention of the Association for Advancement of Behavior Therapy, San Diego, CA.

Vivian, D., & Heyman, R. E. (1996). Is there a place for conjoint treatment of couple violence? *In session: Psychotherapy in practice, 25,* 25–48.

Vivian, D., Heyman, R. E., & Langhinrichsen–Rohling, J. (1993, November). *A multi–faceted approach to coding aggressive couples' conflictual communication.* Paper presented at the 27th annual convention of the Association for the Advancement of Behavior Therapy, Atlanta, GA.

Vivian, D., & Langhinrichsen–Rohling, J. (1994). Are bi–directionally violent couples mutually victimized? A gender sensitive comparison. *Violence and Victims, 9,* 107–124.

Vivian, D., & Langhinrichsen–Rohling, J. (1995). *The Thematic Coding of Dyadic Interactions (TCDI) 3rd* . Unpublished manual. SUNY, Department of Psychology, Stony Brook, NY.

Vivian, D., Mayer, F., Sandeen, E., & O'Leary, K. D. (1988). *Longitudinal assessment of the role of communication skills in interpersonal aggression.* Symposium conducted at the meeting of the World Congress in Behavior Therapy, Edinburgh, Scotland.

Vivian, D., & O'Leary, K. D. (1987, July). *Communication patterns in physically aggressive engaged couples.* Paper presented at the Third National Family Violence Research Conference, University of New Hampshire, Durham, NH

Wagner, W., Kirchler, E., Clack, F., Tekarslan, E., & Verma, J. (1990). Male dominance, role segregation, and spouses' interdependence in conflict. *Journal of Cross–Cultural Psychology, 21,* 48–70.

Walczynski, P. T. (1997). *Power, personality, and conflictual interaction: An exploration of demand/withdraw interaction in same–sex and cross–sex couples.* Unpublished doctoral dissertation, University of California, Los Angeles.

Walczynski, P. T., Schmidt, G. W., Christensen, A., & Sweeney, L. (1991, August). *Demand/withdraw interaction in dating couples.* Paper presented at the annual meeting of the American Psychological Association, San Francisco.

Waldinger, R. J., Moore, C., Chivers, L., Heaney, A., & Schulz, M. S. (2001, December). *Mountains out of molehills?: How borderline individuals read their partners' emotions.* Poster session presented at the annual meeting of the American Psychoanalytic Association, New York.

Waldinger, R.J., Schulz, M.S., Hauser, S.T., Allen, J.P., & Crowell, J.A. (in press). Reading others' emotions: The role of intuitive judgments in predicting marital satisfaction, quality and stability. *Journal of Family Psychology.*

Walsh, V. L., Baucom, D. H., Tyler, S., & Sayers, S. L. (1993). The impact of message valence, focus, expressive style and gender on communication patterns among maritally distressed couples. *Journal of Family Psychology, 7,* 163–175.

Waltz, M. (1986). Marital context and post–infarction quality of life: Is it social support or something more? *Social Science and Medicine, 22,* 791–805.

Wampold, B. E. (1989). Kappa as a measure of pattern in sequential data. *Quality & Quantity, 23,* 171–187.

Wampold, B. E., & Holloway, E. L. (1983). A note on interobserver reliability for sequential data. *Journal of Behavioral Assessment, 5,* 217–255.

Waters, E. B. (1978). The reliability and stability of individual differences in infant–mother attachment. *Child Development, 49,* 483–494.

Watson, D., Clark, L. A., & Tellegen, A. (1988). Development and validation of brief measures of positive and negative affect: The PANAS scales. *Journal of Personality and Social Psychology, 54,* 1063–1070.

Watzlawick, P., Beavin, J. H., & Jackson, J. (1967). *Pragmatics of human communication.* New York: Norton.

Wegener, C., Revenstorf, D., Hahlweg, K., & Schindler, L. (1979). Empirical analysis of communication in distressed and non–distressed couples. *European Journal of Behaviour Analysis and Modification, 3,* 178–188

Weiss, R. L. (1968). Operant conditioning techniques in psychological assessment. In P. W. McReynolds (Ed.), *Advances in psychological assessment* (pp.169-190). Palo Alto: Science and Behavior Books.

Weiss, R. L. (1974). The provisions of social relationships. In Z. Rubin (Ed.), *Doing unto others* (pp. 17–26). Englewood Cliffs, NJ: Prentice–Hall.

Weiss, R. L. (1980). Strategic behavioral marital therapy: toward a model for assessment and intervention. In J. P. Vincent (Ed.), *Advances in family intervention, assessment, and theory* (Vol. 1, pp. 229–271). Greenwich, CT: JAI.

Weiss, R. L. (1992). *Marital Interaction Coding System, Version IV.* Unpublished manual. University of Oregon, Eugene.

Weiss, R. L., & Cerreto, M. C. (1980). The Marital Status Inventory: Development of a measure of dissolution potential. *The American Journal of Family Therapy, 8,* 80–86.

Weiss, R. L., & Heyman, R. E. (1990). Marital distress. In A. S. Bellack & A. E. Kazdin (Eds.), *International handbook of behavior modification and therapy* (pp. 475–501). New York: Plenum.

Weiss, R. L., & Heyman, R. E. (1997). Couple interaction. In W. K. Halford & H. J. Markman (Eds.), *Clinical handbook of marriage and couple intervention* (pp. 13–41). New York: Wiley.

Weiss, R. L., Hops, H., & Patterson, G. R. (1973). A framework for conceptualizing marital conflict: A technology for altering it, some data for evaluating it. In L. D. Handy & E. L. Mash (Eds.), *Behavior change: Methodology concepts and practice* (pp. 309–342). Champaign, IL: Research Press.

Weiss, R. L., & Summers, K. J. (1983). Marital Interaction Coding System–III. In E. E. Filsinger (Ed.), *Marriage and family assessment: A sourcebook for family therapy* (pp. 85–115). Beverly Hills, CA: Sage.

Weiss, R. L., & Tolman, A. O. (1990). Validity of the Marital Interaction Coding System–Global (MICS–G): A global companion to the MICS. *Behavioral Assessment, 12,* 271– 294.

Wenninger, K., Ehlers, A. & Gieler, U. (1991). Kommunikation von Neurodermitis-Patienten mit ihren Bezugspersonen: Eine empirische Analyse [Communication behavior of neurodermatitis patients and their relatives: An empirical analysis]. *Zeitschrift für Klinische Psychologie, 20,* 251-264.

White, J., Smith, P. H., Koss, M. P., & Figueredo, A. J. (2000). Intimate partner aggression: What have we learned? Comment on Archer (2000). *Psychological Bulletin, 126,* 690–696.

Wickens, T. D. (1989). *Multiway contingency tables analysis for the social sciences.* Hillsdale, NJ: Lawrence Erlbaum Associates, Inc.

Wickens, T. D. (1993). Analysis of contingency tables with between subjects variability. *Psychological Bulletin, 113,* 191–204.

Wiggins, J. (1977). *Personality and prediction.* Reading, MA: Addison–Wesley.

Wile, D. B. (1981). *Couples therapy: A non–traditional approach.* New York: Wiley.

Wile, D. B. (1988). *After the honeymoon: How conflict can improve your relationship.* New York: Wiley.

Williams, E., & Gottman, J. (1981). *A user's guide to the Gottman–Williams time-series programs.* New York: Cambridge University Press.

Wills, T. A., Weiss, R. L., & Patterson, G. R. (1974). A bchavioral analysis of the determinants of marital satisfaction. *Journal of Consulting and Clinical Psychology, 42,* 802–811.

Wolchik, S. A., West, S. G., Sandler, I. N., Tein, J., Coatesworth, D., Lengua, L., et al. (2000). An experimental evaluation of theory–based mother and mother–child programs for childrcn of divorce. *Journal of Consulting and Clinical Psychology, 68,* 843–856.

Yaffee, R. A. (2000). *Introduction to time series analysis and forecasting.* San Diego, CA: Academic.

Yik, M., Russell, J., & Barrctt, L. (1999). Structure of self–reported current affect: Integration and beyond. *Journal of Personality and Social Psychology, 77,* 600–619.

Yllö, K. A. (1993). Through a feminist lens: Gender, power & violence. In: R. J. Gelles & D. R. Loseke (Eds.) *Current controversies on family violence.* Newbury Park: Sage.

Yoder, P. J., & Feuer, I. D. (2000). Quantifying the magnitude of sequential association between events or behaviors. In T. Thompson, D. Felce, and F. J. Symons (Eds.), *Behavioral observation: Technology and applications in developmental disabilities* (pp. 317–348). Baltimore, MD: Brookes.

Yoder, P. J., & Tapp, J. T. (1990). SATS: Sequential analysis of transcripts system. *Behavior Research Methods, Instruments, and Computers, 22,* 339–343.

Zahn–Waxler, C., Radke–Yarrow, M., Wagner, E., & Chapman, M. (1992). Development of concern for others. *Developmental Psychology, 28,* 126–136.

Zimmerman, V.D., Schulz, M.S., & Waldinger, R.J. (2003, November). *The Measurement and Consequences of Emotion Suppression in Marital Interactions: Does Hiding Your Emotions Require Physiological Work?* Poster presented at the annual meetings of the Association for the Advancement of Behavior Therapy, Boston, MA.

Author Index

Subject Index